VĀKĀṬAKAS
Sources and History

GREAT AGES OF INDIAN HISTORY

VĀKĀṬAKAS
Sources and History

Ajay Mitra Shastri

Aryan Books International
New Delhi

VĀKĀṬAKAS
Sources and History

ISBN: 978-81-7305-123-4

First Published: 1997

Reprinted: 2022

Published by:

Aryan Books International
Pooja Apartments, 4B, Ansari Road, New Delhi-110 002 (India)
Tel.: 23287589, 23255799; Fax: 91-11-23270385
E-mail: aryanbooks@gmail.com
www.aryanbooks.com

Printed in India

Books That Live!

Aryan Books International was established in 1992. Though it began as a commercial venture, business was only a part of the whole. The primary aim was to bridge the gap between the history taught and the real history of our country, and also to present its lesser known and sometimes deliberately neglected facets. In academia, the legacy of our art, culture and ethos was being undermined to perpetuate a narrative which left us looking weak, soft and lagging behind the so-called progressive West.

It was this narrative that we sought to contest. The journey over the last thirty years has not been an easy one. However, it gives us a sense of satisfaction to have possibly made a small difference by publishing over 750 titles written by the most acclaimed authors in the field. We have specialized in publishing ingenious and outstanding scholarship, both established as also fresh. While we focus on our long forgotten history, we also bring to the fore certain extremely important aspects of Indian art, culture and traditions.

Apart from pioneering content, we also ensure that our production quality remains the best in the business, as we continue with the mission to publish books that **Live Forever**!

We are also aware that this is just the beginning of a long journey. A long road lies ahead. A lot more needs to be said. A lot more needs to be explored. We assure you that we're on it with renewed commitment!

To

the sacred memory of

My Esteemed Friend and Great

Late Dr. Ram Shankar Bhatta

who by his example inspired me t

Contents

Contents

Preface

THE Vākāṭakas as they are styled in their inscriptions and known to modern historians or Vindhyakas as they are called in the Purāṇas geographically, supplanted the Andhra-Sātavāhanas in the Vidarbha region about the end of the third century AD and later spread their wings far and wide. The original centre of their power was the Vindhyan region of Madhya Pradesh from where they moved southward and domiciled themselves in the Deccanese trans-Narmadā region, thus furnishing one of the rare examples of Indian history. The period of their rule in the Deccan covering some two centuries constitutes a glorious epoch in the political and cultural annals of this region. Though confined politically to the Deccan, they had close relations with the Imperial Guptas and nearer home with the Nāgas of Padmāvatī the Kadambas of Karnataka and the Vishṇukuṇḍins of Andhra Pradesh. They were great patrons of art, and the Mahāyāna phase at Ajantā is purely their creation. Some of the Vākāṭaka monarchs were great Prakrit poets with their works highly eulogised by later literary critics. But though their greatness is quite well-known, several aspects of their history still continue to baffle their annallists partly due to preconceived notions and partly lack of requisite evidence. The present monograph aims at solving the problems as best as warranted by the available evidence including that brought to light in recent years with the discovery and publication of a major portion of which the author was closely connected.

The work falls into two parts. The Part I takes a stock of the epigraphic and numismatic source-material bearing on the subject. The inaugural chapter of this section summarises the contents and highlights some of the baffling issues concerning them. Here are dealt with the epigraphs incorporated by the late Professor V.V. Mirashi in his *Inscriptions of the Vākāṭakas* published in 1963 as Volume V of the celebrated *Corpus Inscriptionum Indicarum* series. A perusal of this section would suffice to show that it is much more than a mere abstract and in most cases fresh interpretations have been offered. The three appendices attached to this chapter deal at length with the problem of the attribution of the Nachnā-kī-Talāi and Ganj inscriptions of the time of Pṛithivī Sheṇa who has been identified with the first monarch bearing this name. Appendix II sheds new light on the contents of the unissued Bālāghāṭ charter of the last known member of the Nandivarhana branch of the Vākāṭakas, Pṛithivī Sheṇa II, especially in the perspective of the recent discoveries of his complete charters at Māhurjharī and Māṇḍhal and tries to remove some unwarranted notions. The date of the Bamhanī and Mallār charters of Śūrabala Udīrṇavaira, earlier supposed to have been a vassal of the Vākāṭaka king Narendra Sena, forms the theme of the third Appendix where, besides discussing summarily the problem of the ascription of the former grant, it has been demonstrated that a gap of over a century separated the two monarchs and that even otherwise the charters do not warrant such a notion.

Chapter II takes stock of the recent discoveries of Vākāṭaka charters which constitute more than 50% of the total volume of Vākāṭaka epigraphy known earlier and with a major portion of whose discovery the present writer was intimately associated. A perusal would leave no doubt that it is substantial not only in volume but extremely rich in contents and has helped remove some erroneous notions going round till recently. Epoch-making discoveries of Vākāṭaka coins presently in the cabinets of some known collectors including Shri Prashant Kulkarni and Shri Raghunath Sanghi of Nagpur which were first published by the present writer form the subject-matter of the closing chapter of this part. These finds have helped remove certain deeply entrenched wrong notions prevailing hitherto.

Literary sources, which are constituted exclusively by Purāṇic references, have not been dealt with in this part as they are discussed at length in the following one.

Having familiarised the readers with the source-material, we have taken up a detailed critical presentation of the historical outline. Both the known offshoots of the dynasty have been dwelt upon in fairly good affordable detail. The critical assessment of the evidence has led the author to certain drastic conclusions some of which may be referred to here *en passim*. It has been shown that the original territory of the Vākāṭakas lay in the Vindhyan region of Central India which continued under them up to at least the time of Pṛithivī Sheṇa I as indicated by a critical analysis of the Purāṇic data and the Nachnā-kī-Talāi and Ganj inscriptions of his time. They shifted to the Vidarbha region under Pravara Sena I who dislodged the remnants of Sātavāhana power around 300 AD. Kāñchanakā, identifiable with modern Nachnā in the Pannā District of Madhya Pradesh, was their only capital when their authority was confined to the Vindhyan region, and Purikā is not mentioned at all in the Purāṇas in connection with Pravara Sena I as it is commonly assumed irrationally. Padmapura, somewhere in the Nāgpur-Wardhā region and not yet located correctly, appears to have become their first capital in the Vidarbha region. During the closing years of Pravara Sena I's reign the Vākāṭaka territory was partitioned among his four sons as averred in the Purāṇic texts; out of these only two branches are known at present, one ruling successively from Nandivardhana and Pravarapura and the other from Vatsagulma identified with modern Wāshim in the Akolā District of Vidarbha. It is difficult to decide as to which of these offshoots can be called 'Main' or 'Senior', and in our opinion it would be better to steer clear of this unnecessary controversy and name them after their respective capitals as Padmapura-Nandivardhana-Pravarapura and Vatsagulma branches. As for the former branch, we think that the Vindhyan region continued under its rule through a vassal line for a few generations up to some time in Pṛithivī Sheṇa I's reign whereafter they had to abandon it owing to the pressure of the Imperial Guptas. As of now there is absolutely nothing tangible to show any real impact of the Imperial Guptas during the regency of Prabhāvatī Guptā, lasting at least thirteen years, during the minority of her eldest son Divakara Sena who passed away as the crown prince. Recently discovered evidence has helped in resolving the uncalled for controversy regarding the post-Divākara Sena Vākāṭaka history. Even the evidence of the Riddhapur grant of Prabhāvatī Guptā by itself was enough to show that the period of her regency was followed by her sons Dāmodara Sena and Pravara Sena II who came to the throne successively. However, some scholars believed that they were not two distinct personages but one as Dāmodara Sena assumed Pravara Sena as his coronation name after his accession. The issue has been finally clinched by the discovery of a hitherto unpublished copperplate charter of Prabhāvatī Guptā which in the text of the inscription contains her description in terms identical with that of the Riddhapur grant but the legend on the seal attached to it, which is fortunately preserved and must have been similar to that of Riddhapur charter, clearly avers that she was the mother of two valiant sons who were evidently Damodara Sena and Pravara Sena II, thus setting the unwarranted debate to rest finally. Next came the latter's son born of his queen Ājñākabhaṭṭarikā, Narendra Sena by name, who had a disputed succession in which he was initially successful but was later deprived of the throne by his own relations, perhaps cousins of the Vatsagulma line. He had nothing to do with the Pāṇḍavas of Mekalā, either Bharatabala or his son and successor Śūrabala, who were far removed from him in point of time. The next and the last known king of this branch was Narendra Sena's son by his queen Ajjhitabhaṭṭarikā, most probably hailing from the Kadamba house of Vanavāsī, Pṛithivī Sheṇa II, who recovered the ancestral throne from his cousins and also kept the tide of the aggressive Nalas of Bastar under check though only for a while.

The Vatsagulma branch founded by Sarva Sena was looking for greener pastures further south from the very start as seen from his son Vindhya Sena's claim to have conquered Kuntala which was then under the Kadambas. It bore fruit in the time of the latter's grandson Sarva Sena II who intervened in the internal affairs of the Kadambas and installed Siṁhavarman on the throne, as averred by the latter's recently discovered Mudigere grant. Sarva Sena II's son and successor, Deva Sena, was much more ambitious and followed an utterly aggressive policy which proved immensely rewarding. In the south he controlled all the territory lying in between his ancestral kingdom and the Bīdar region of Karnataka and also tried to aggrandise at the cost of his cousins at Pravarapura, and the troubles faced by Narendra Sena appear to have been his creation. Hari Sheṇa, the last known monarch of this line, was indeed a great military commander and adopted the policy of raiding far-flung areas and probably exacting booty from the humbled chiefs, though it did not add much to his kingdom.

Nothing is known of the Vākāṭakas after Pṛithivī Sheṇa II and Hari Sheṇa. It is impossible at present to ascertain the factors which led to an abrupt end of this great political power. The belief that Daṇḍin's *Daśa-kumāra-charita* contains a running commentary on the fall of the Vākāṭakas following the demise of Hari Sheṇa has nothing to commend itself. It were the aggressive designs of the Vishṇukuṇḍins, Kadambas, Nalas, Muṇḍa-putras, Kalachuris of Māhishmatī, early Rāshṭrakūṭas and Kumbhakarṇas who were earlier their allies or subordinates or had felt the brunt of their intruding arms that hastened the fall of the once stupendous might that had launched itself on the path of decline because of loss of vigour and imperial ambitions due to the natural ageing process. Thus ended the mighty power about the beginning of the sixth century AD.

Almost from the very start, at least from the time of the ambitious Pravara Sena I, the Vākāṭakas had adopted Sena as the family surname. We have examples of its members adopting Sena-ending names on their coronation. Thus Pṛithivīrāja and Narindarāja ascended the throne under the names Pṛithivī Sheṇa and Narendra Sena respectively. We have therefore spelt the names as consisting of two parts, each beginning with a capital letter. It is done for the first time in the present work.

It is our pleasant duty to express our indebtedness to people who have been helpful in the completion of the present work. First and foremost, we have immensely benefited from the writings of such eminent epigraphists and historians as F. Kielhorn, J.F. Fleet, Hira Lal, K.P. Jayaswal, K.B. Pathak, A.S. Altekar, D.C. Sircar, K.N. Dikshit, V.V. Mirashi, D.R. Bhandarkar, H.C. Raychaudhuri and a host of others, but for whose painstaking efforts our knowledge of early Indian history in general and of the Vākāṭaka phase in particular would have been much poorer than what it is today and we owe a great debt to these *pūrvasūris.* Special mention must be made of the late Professor V.V. Mirashi who edited a number of Vākāṭaka records very meticulously and compiled all the epigraphs of the dynasty known till 1963 in his *Inscriptions of the Vākāṭakas* (*CII,* V) and rendered a yoeman's service to Vākāṭaka studies. The readers will find that we have often differed from his views and interpretations; but this honest divergence would not have been possible had we not had his work supplemented by subsequent discoveries which often occasioned the correction and modification of his as well as other savants' views. This is indeed a tribute to their great work. We have also derived benefit from the works of a number of other living scholars who have been duly acknowledged at proper places and in the bibliography. To all of them we are highly indebted and greateful.

Some of our colleagues and friends have obliged us by offering their spontaneous help in various ways. Dr. I.K. Sarma, Director, Salarjung Museum, Hyderabad, and Dr. G. Kamalakar, Director, Birla Archaeological and Cultural Research Institute, Hyderabad, deserve thanks for providing photographic illustration of the iron replica of the Bīdar charter of Deva Sena. Dr. Chandrashekhar Gupta, our former student and Head of the Department of Ancient Indian History, Culture and Archaeology, Nagpur University, who has collaborated with us in editing a number of recently discovered Vākāṭaka records, has been of great help in the preparation and arrangement of illustrative material. Shri C.N. Saharkar, Draughtsman of the same department of the Nagpur University, has redrawn the map showing the distribution of Vākāṭaka epigraphs and coins. Dr. Malati Mahajan, our former student and colleague, has contributed materially to the indentification of some of the locatities named in recently discovered Vākāṭaka records. We are obliged to all of them.

The present work is dedicated as a mark of our high esteem for Dr. Ram Shankar Bhattacharya, Chief Editor, *Purāṇam*, All-India Kashiraja Trust, and Librarian, Theosophical Society, Varanasi, whose illustrious example inspired us to undertake the research activities in general. We express our indebedness to him.

Shri Vikas Arya, the Proprietor of the Aryan Books International, deserves our sincere thanks and appreciation for undertaking the present publication and bringing it out in such a short time in a neat good form which is solely due to his keen interest and promptness.

'Prachi'
23, Vidya Vihar,
Rana Pratap Nagar,
Nagpur 440 022.

Ajay Mitra Shastri

List of Illustrations

MAP

Distribution of Vākāṭaka Inscriptions and Coins

PLATES

Abbreviations

ABORI	:	*Annals of the Bhandarkar Oriental Research Institution*
AIU	:	*The Age of Imperial Unity* edited by R.C Majumdar and A.D. Pusalkar
ASWI	:	*Archaeological Survey of Western India*
AV	:	*The Age of the Vākāṭakas* edited by Ajay Mitra Shastri
BSOA5	:	*Bulletin of the School of Oriental and African Studies*
CHI	:	*A Comprehensive History of India*
CII	:	*Corpus Inscriptionum Indicarum*
DKA	:	*The Purāṇa Text of the Dynasties of the Kali Age* by F.E. Pagiter
EHD	:	*Early History of the Deccan* by R.G. Bhandarkar
EHDPP	:	*Early History of the Deccan : Problems and Perspectives* by Ajay Mitra Shastri
EHDY	:	*Early History of the Deccan* edited by Ghulam Yazdani
EI	:	*Epigraphia Indica*
HCIP	:	*The History and Culture of the Indian People*
HISWK	:	*The History and Inscriptions of the Sātavāhanas and the Western Kshatrapas* by V.V. Mirashi
IA	:	*Indian Antiquary*
IC	:	*Indian Culture*
IH	:	*Indian Historical Quarterly*
INC	:	*Indian Numismatic Chronicle*
JAIH	:	*Journal of Ancient Indian History*
JASB	:	*Journal of the Asiatic Society of Bengal*
JBBRAS	:	*Journal of the Bombay Branch of the Royal Asiatic Society*
JBORS	:	*Journal of the Bihar and Orissa Research Society*
JESI	:	*Journal of the Epigraphical Society of India*

JIH	:	*Journal of Indian History*
JNSI	:	*Journal of the Numismatic Society of India*
JRAS	:	*Journal of the Royal Asiatic Society*
JRASB	:	*Journal of the Royal Asiatic Society of Bengal*
MSGH	:	*Maharashtra State Gazetteer, History*
NIA	:	*New Indian Antiquary*
ND	:	*Numismatic Digest*
NS	:	New Series
PHAI	:	*Political History of Ancient India* by H.C. Raychaudhuri
PIHC	:	*Proceedings of Indian History Congress*
PAIOC	:	*Proceedings of All-India Oriental Conference*
SIPN	:	*Studies in Indian Place Names*
VSMV	:	*Vidarbha Saṁśodhana Maṇḍaḷa Vārshika*

Part I
ARCHAEOLOGICAL SOURCES

I

Known Vākāṭaka Inscriptions

This chapter summarises and discusses briefly the contents of Vākāṭaka inscriptions included in V.V. Mirashi's *Inscriptions of the Vākāṭakas* published as volume 5 of the well-known *Corpus Inscriptionum Indecarum* series. Serial numbers of inscriptions in this volume are indicated at the beginning in round brackets with 'M' standing for 'Mirashi'. Contents of chatters with multiple plates are abstracted in a tabular form, while others are discussed in a brief essay form.

PADMAPURA-NANDIVARDHANA-PRAVARAPURA BRANCH

1 (M 1)
DEOṬEK INSCRIPTION OF RUDRA SENA (I OR II)
(Pls. I-II)

This inscription is engraved on a large rectangular stone-slab, 9 ft. long, and 3½ and 2.10 ft. broad at the two ends, one side being broader than the other, found at the village of Deoṭek in the Chandrapur district, some 50 miles south-east of Nagpur, Māhārashtra. The slab was located by G.D. Beglar, an assistant of General A. Cunningham, who visited the place in 1873-74 and described it and the temple situated nearby in Cunningham's *Archaeological Survey Report,* VII, pp. 123-25. Later, the site was visited by V.V. Mirashi in October 1935 or 1936,[1] and it was he who brought out the true character of the record.[2] The slab bears actually two records: one engraved lengthwise in four lines composed in Prakrit and inscribed in Mauryan Brāhmī characters and most probably put up by an officer of the Maurya emperor Aśoka, it being comparable in contents to his Rock Edict V restricting the destruction of the animals, and the other belonging to Rudra Sena, most probably of the Vākāṭaka dynasty, engraved in box-headed characters used generally in Vākāṭaka inscriptions and composed in Sanśkrit. Both the records are damaged, the first one by the engraver of the second epigraph and the second because of being peeled off due to exposure and use as seat by shepherds tending cattle.

The Vākāṭaka inscription, which is engraved breadthwise commencing from the narrow end of the slab, refers to king Rudra Sena whom, following Cunningham, Mirashi equates with the first Vākāṭaka monarch of this name. There is, however, absolutely nothing to vindicate or negate this identification and it can as well belong to his homonymous grandson and grand successor. The point cannot be decided with certitude at present.

To explain the damage to the earlier inscription, Mirashi argues that it was due to Rudra Sena's callous disregard for non-violence which reverberated through the Aśokan edict as he was himself a follower of Vedic sacrificial religion and had no scruples in chiselling out the earlier inscription to make room for his own record supposedly intended to register the construction of a Śaiva shrine. It is worth remembering in this context that it was not the king himself who incised a record but it was almost invariably left to artisans to choose a stone to record such deeds, the role of the patron, especially royal one, being confined to order the recording of the meritorious act. And as an older block of stone was already available it came handy and was used by the mason to register his patron's meritorious act, no matter if it involved chiselling a portion of the earlier record which and whose purpose was not intelligible to him. Thus, it was not the king himself who decided, that too deliberately, to efface a part of the Aśokan edict whose contents he was most probably not aware of, but the engraver himself erased it unintentionally to make room for the new record that he was asked to incise. Had it been a deliberate decision on the monarch's part, he would have chiselled out the whole record and not just a portion.

Then what was the object of the inscription? Mirashi has rightly read the word *dharma-sthāna* at the end of the fifth line before which, however, he has added on his own the expression *sva*, 'his own', and taken the expression as a whole to mean 'a special place of religious worship'. According to him, it may have been a Śiva temple. However, the expression *dharma-sthāna* was never used in ancient times in the sense of a temple or place of worship. As against this, it is clearly employed to denote a court of justice (*dharma* = justice; *sthāna* = place). *Śaṅkha-Likhita* as cited in the *Smṛiti-chandrikā* lays down that *dharma-sthāna* should be built in the eastern quarter of a town and should be endowed with fire and water. According to the *Sarasvatī-vilāsa, dharma-sthāna* is the place where the judges decide the cases according to the Dharmaśāstra. It is equivalent to *Dharmādhikarana* and *Dharmāsana.*[3] Thus, it was the construction of the 'court of justice' that was recorded in the inscription. Some of the Vākāṭaka charters record that they were granted by the kings at *vaijayika dharma-sthāna.*[4] Here *vaijayika*, 'victorious', has to be taken as an honorific without much significance, and the fact that grants are said to have been made here would indicate that the court-buildings were also used for the purpose of declaring land-grants.[5] They were located not only at the royal capitals but also at some other places of importance in the kingdom as indicated by the mention of places like Rāmagiri-sthāna,[6] Bemṇātaṭasthāna[7] and Pṛithivī-samudra or Pṛithivī-pura[8] in the charters of Pṛithivī Sheṇa II. One such *dharma-sthāna* was also located and most probably erected by one of the two Rudra Senas of the Padmapura-Nandivardhana-Pravarapura branch of the Vākāṭaka dynasty.

Both the records call the locality where the inscriptions were put up as Chikumburi (Aśokan edict)[9] or Chikkamburi (Rudra Sena's inscription) which was obviously the name of the greater administrative centre wherein the present Deoṭek was situated. It is evidently identical with the adjoining village known as Chikmārā as pointed out by Hiralal.[10] It was definitely a flourishing town right from at least the Maurya period to the age of the Vākāṭakas, roughly for at least seven centuries. Its importance is clearly indicated by the facts that Aśoka's officers, probably the Dharma-mahāmātra stationed in the region, felt it desirable to have an edict restricting injury to faunal life incised here and the Vākāṭaka king Rudra Sena (I or II) had built a structure for housing a *dharma-sthāna* (court of justice) here. How long thereafter it continued to enjoy the importance is not possible to ascertain for want of subsequent epigraphic evidence and due to the lack of interest among archaeologists who have preferred to ignore it despite clear epigraphic references, which are extremely rare, indicating the location of this great administrative centre in Vidarbha.

2-4 (M 20-21)
NACHNĀ-KĪ-TALĀI AND GANJ STONE INSCRIPTIONS OF THE TIME OF PṚITHIVĪ SHEṆA I
(Pls. III-V)

These records of Vyāghradeva, a feudatory or officer under the Vākāṭaka monarch Pṛithivī Sheṇa, at the places called Nachnā-kī-Talāi and Ganj in the Pannā district of Madhya Pradesh, are commonly ascribed to the time of the second king of this name in the Padmapura-Nandivarhana-Pravarapura branch of the dynasty and regarded as an evidence of the northward expansion of the dynastic power during his reign. However, a perusal of Appendix I of this part should leave absolutely no doubt that these must be assigned to the time of his homonymous predecessor and indicate only the continuation of the hold of the dynasty over this region of Central India.

For a detailed discussion of the contents of these short but highly important lithic records, *vide* Appendix I.

5 (M 17)
AN UNFINISHED MOHALLĀ PLATE OF PṚITHIVĪ SHEṆA I (?)
(Pl. VI)

This single plate of copper was found at the village called Mohallā in the Durg district of the Chhattīsgaḍh (ancient Kosalā or South Kosalā) region of Madhya Pradesh. Incised in the box-headed variety of the southern Brāhmī and composed in Sanskrit prose, it formed the first plate of a multi-plate charter of a Vākāṭaka monarch of the Padmapura-Nandivardhana-Pravarapura branch. Being the initial plate, it bears writing only on one side. It was intended to be issued from Padmapura as indicated by the initial word *Padmapurāt*, 'from Padmapura'. The absence of any suffix like *vāsaka*, 'camp or temporary residence, or *skandhāvāra*, 'military camp', would show that it served as the dynastic capital at the time of the issuance of the intended charter. That it was left incomplete is vouched for by the fact that space enough for a few letters is left blank at the end of the last (fifth) line of the plate if not by the absence of the word *dṛishṭam*, 'seen', which was something like authorisation of the charter and is seen in most of the Vākāṭaka grants,[11] at the beginning of the record even though space for three letters has been left blank deliberately. The absence of the word *dṛishṭam* by itself would not have mattered much as we have certain exceptions where this word is absent, but what is interesting is that despite the space for it having been left blank it has not been engraved. The charter was thus left unfinished for reasons unascertainable at present. The fact that the word *Gautamīputrasya*, for which there is enough space left blank at the end of the fifth and last line, has not been engraved would show that the incising of the charter was abandoned quite abruptly.

The extant portion, besides specifying the place of issue, contains only the conventional description of Pravara Sena I and his son's son (Gautamīputra whose name has been left uninscribed) and the Bhāraśiva king Bhavanāga already known from several characters of the Vākāṭakas and adds nothing to our knowledge.

It is highly difficult to determine precisely the issuer of the intended charter in the absence of his name which would have come on the second or third plate had the record been completed. According to Mirashi, the record belongs to the post-Pravara Sena II period palaeographically and he is inclined to attribute it to his son Narendra Sena for whom we have no record and for information about whom we are dependent only on his son Pṛithivī Sheṇa II's charters. But after Mirashi wrote several new records of the Vākāṭakas have come to light and have nullified his palaeographical observations. And we feel that the same and other palaeographical and other considerations should force us to date it much earlier and assign it to an earlier king.[12]

The key to its attribution is supplied by the fact that it was intended to be given from the issuer's capital Padmapura. Mirashi proposes to identify this Padmapura with the modern village of Padampur, two miles from Āmgāon in the Bhaṇḍārā district where some old images and fragments of some old architectural members have been found. According to him, Narendra Sena might have shifted his capital from Pravarapura to this Padampur in the east due to the menace of the Nala invasion against which he hoped for support from 'his loyal feudatories' in Mekalā and Kosalā. First, there is at present nothing to show that the rulers of Kosalā (Chhattīsgaḍh region) and Mekalā (Amarkaṇṭak region) of present Madhya Pradesh were Vākāṭaka vassals, both being purely imaginary notions. As for Mekalā, the notion was based on the assumption that the word *narendra* occurring in verse 11 of the Bamhanī plates supposedly issued by the Pāṇḍava king Bharatabala[13] alluded to the Vākāṭaka king Narendra Sena besides its ordinary dictionary meaning 'king'. It was accordingly held that the Pāṇḍava monarch of Mekalā, Bharatabala, was a vassal of Narendra Sena. When these plates were originally discovered such a notion was perhaps possible though quite gratuitous. But the subsequent discovery of the Mallār plates of Śūrabala *alias* Udīrṇavaira shows that the Bamhanī plates were also issued by the same king, and not by his father Bharatabala *alias* Indra as it was felt by scholars due to the inadvertent omission of the prose portion introducing Śūrabala after the description of Bharatabala was over by the scribe in the latter charter. So the word *narendra* referred to only Śūrabala as 'king' and did in no way allude, even casually, to the Vākāṭaka king Narendra Sena.[14] Moreover, Śūrabala Udīrṇavaira and Narendra Sena were separated chronologically by such a long period that it is ludicrous to establish any relationship between the two.[15]

Then, this Padmapura would have been more open to the menacing invasion of the Nalas from the east than Pravarapura, and any sane person could not think of shifting his capital to such a place. And then there is absolutely nothing to prove that this was the Padmapura wherefrom the charter in question was intended to have been issued in preference to nearly half a dozen other places in the Chandrapur and Bhaṇḍārā districts. But we have positive evidence to show that none of these Padmapuras was meant in the instant case. We find one Padmapura mentioned in a couple of Vākāṭaka records discovered in recent years, one belonging to Rudra Sena II and the other to his son Pravara Sena II. The Māṇḍhaḷ plates issued by Rudra Sena II in his fifth regnal year register his grant of some villages located in the eastern administrative division (*mārga*) of Padmapura,[16] while the Māsoda plates of Pravara Sena II aim at granting some land in the village Matsyadraha in its western division (*apara-mārga*).[17] Both these records show the great importance enjoyed by this Padmapura during the Vākāṭaka age. The location of the villages mentioned in these grants[19] leaves absolutely no doubt that this Padmapura was situated somewhere in the Nāgpur-Wardhā region, a conclusion reinforced by the provenance of the two records. Obviously it is the same Padmapura as the one mentioned as the place of issue of the unfinished grant in question. Strangely enough, it is no longer traceable in the region at present. Although found at Mohallā[20] in the Durg district, it must have originally belonged to some person in this region and reached its find-spot with him like the Puṇe plates of Prabhāvatī Guptā and the Indore plates of Pravara Sena II to be discussed below.

In all likelihood the capital was shifted to Padmapura during the reign of Pṛithivī Sheṇa I whose hold on the Vindhyan region to the north of the Narmadā was slackening due to the imperial designs of the Gupta emperor Samudra Gupta and who was compelled to leave it to the care of his vassal Vyāghradeva whose records have been spotted at the localities called Nachnā-kī-Talāi and Ganj in the Pannā district of Madhya Pradesh[18] and to look for a new capital in Vidarbha instead of Chanakā or Nachna in Bundelkhaṇḍ and his choice fell on Padmapura. It was from here that he intended to issue his Mohallā charter as well as, maybe, a few other grants that may be discovered in future. Accordingly the inscription in question probably belongs to Pṛithivī Sheṇa I or his son and successor Rudra Sena II. The mention of the western administrative subdivision of Padmapura in a later record proves that at least up to the reign of Pravara

Sena II the city continued to enjoy some importance despite the dynastic capital being shifted from it at first to Nandivardhana and then to Pravarapura.

6 (M 2)
PUNE PLATES OF PRABHĀVATĪ GUPTĀ, YEAR 13
(Pls. X-XI)

PROVENANCE : Puṇe, from a copper-smith who originally hailed from Ahmadnagar, Māhārāshṭra.

PUBLICATION : K.B. Pathak, *IA*, XLI, pp. 214-15: K.B. Pathak and K.N. Dikshit, "Poona Plates of the Vākāṭaka Queen Prabhāvatī guptā, The 13th Year", *EI*, XV, pp. 39-45; V.V. Mirashi, *CII*, V, pp. 5-9.

PLACE OF ISSUE : Nā(Na)ndivardhana, identified with modern Nandardhan or Nāgardhan, near Rāmṭek, Nagpur district, Vākāṭaka capital.

DONATRIX : Queen Prabhāvatī Guptā, daughter of *Mahārājādhirāja* Chandra Gupta (II) and his queen (*Mahādevī*) Kuberanāgā of Nāga-kula, chief queen (*agra-mahishī*) of the Vākāṭaka king Rudra Sena II and regent for her son Divākara Sena, the *Yuvārāja*. She is described as *atyanta-bhagavad-bhaktā* (staunch devotee of Bhagavat, i.e. Vishṇu).

DONEE : Chanālasvāmin, described as *bhagavad-bhakta* (devotee of Bhagavat, i.e. Vishṇu) and *āchārya* (spiritual teacher in this case).

GIFT DETAILS : Da(or I)ṅguṇa-grāma included in the Supratishṭhāhāra, situated to the east of Vilavaṇaka, south of Śirsha-grāma, west of Kadāpiñjana and north of Sidivivaraka. The donated village has been identified with modern town of Hingaṇghāt, the headquarters of the *tahsīl* of the same name in Wardhā district, Māhārāshṭra. Some other bordering villages also have been located in the same *tahsīl*.

DATE : Kārttika-śukla dvādaśī (12th of the bright half of Kārttika), 13th year of the regency of Prabhāvatī Guptā.

SCRIPT & LANGUAGE : Nail-headed variety of Brāhmī with a little admixture of box-headed variety. Sanskrit, in prose except only an imprecatory stanza at the end.

ENGRAVER : Chakkradāsa.

OBSERVATIONS

Although the plates were found at Puṇe, the mention of the donated village as situated in Supratishṭhāhāra which has almost satisfactorily been located in the Hingaṇghāṭ *tahsīl* of the Wardhā district as well as the location of a few bordering villages, clearly indicates that the grant originally belonged to this region and must have travelled to its provenance along with its owner or the person whom it may have been given for some reason.

The *tithi* when the grant was made by the regent queen mother for her own merit is quite significant for religious history. The preceding *tithi* (eleventh of the bright fortnight of the month of Kārttika) is especially sacred for the Vaishṇavas who believe that on this date god Vishṇu wakes up from his four-month long sleep and the date is therefore appropriately called Prabodhinī ekādasī. The grant is said to have been first presented at the feet of Bhagavat, perhaps at nearby Rāmagiri (Rāmṭek), and then made over to the donee who, like the donatrix, was a devotee of Bhagavat, viz. god Vishṇu, and the record begins with the well-known Vaishṇava formula *jitam bhagavatā*, 'god Vishṇu is victorious'. It is, thus, evident that among the Vaishṇavas already the *tithi* in question had attained a great sanctity and the grant was definitely made deliberately on the sacred occasion of breaking the fast (*pāraṇā*) observed on the preceding *tithi.*

The great historical value of the charter lies in the fact that it has enabled historians to (i) settle on firm grounds the general Vākāṭaka chronology showing that the Vākāṭakas were contemporaries of the Imperial Guptas and (ii) brought to notice, for the first time, the critical phase in Vākāṭaka history when the dowager queen mother Prabhāvatī Guptā had to look after the kingdom as regent during the minority of *Yuvarāja* Divākara Sena[21] following the demise of her husband Rudra Sena II, facts still remaining unknown otherwise.

The charter shows conclusively that at least in the Vākāṭaka context Supratishṭhāhāra connoted roughly the Hingaṇghāt *tahsīl* of the present Wardhā district of Māhārāshṭra as Da(or I)ṅguṇa-grāma, the donated village, has been identified fairly satisfactorily with the town of Hingaṇghāt itself and some of the bordering villages have also been located in the same *tahsīl.* There could, of course, have been other areas of the same name in other regions in the same or different periods.

The inscription gives the genealogy of the Imperial Guptas from Ghaṭotkacha to her father Chandra Gupta II which is somewhat defective and not in accordance with that met with in the Gupta inscriptions. Then, the record is engraved predominantly in nail-headed variety of Brāhmī instead of the common box-headed variety.[22] These facts have led historians to infer that there was tremendous Gupta influence and interference in the Vākāṭaka affairs following the demise of Rudra Sena II and his father-in-law is supposed to have despatched several officers to assist his daughter in the administration of the kingdom. However, these facts are easily explicable without resorting to this totally unfounded guesswork. The employment of the variety of script was not dictated by the queen[23] whose other known records are in box-headed characters.[24] The choice of the type of script depended entirely on the scribes, the ruling patrons being only interested in getting their deed and other details properly recorded. Had the Gupta officers been responsible for the draft of the charter, the gross deviations in genealogy met with would not have occurred. And Prabhāvatī Guptā was naturally keen to describe her parentage and her relationship with Rudra Sena and Divākara Sena on whose behalf she was acting as regent administrator of the kingdom. And that is what she did. All, or most of, the queens when they are known to have described themselves, referred to their parentage, especially when they hailed from great ruling families, with justifiable pride. And therefore there is nothing surprising if Prabhāvatī Guptā did so. The reverse would have been more astonishing. The Vākāṭakas, too, were proud of their relationship with the Guptas till the end as indicated undoubtedly by the reference to this matrimonial relationship in all their official charters.

The charter was issued from Nandivardhana which was obviously the capital at the time of the issue of the charter. The capital had obviously been shifted to this place from Padmapura during the later years of Rudra Sena II or by Prabhāvatī Guptā for some reasons which cannot be determined at present.[25]

7 (M 3)
JĀMB PLATES OF PRAVARA SENA II, YEAR 2
(Pls. XII-XIV)

PROVENANCE : Jāmb, seven miles north-east from Hinganghāt, Wardhā district, Māhārāshṭra.

REFERENCE : V.V. Mirashi, "Kothuraka Grant of Pravārasena II", *EI*, XXVI, pp. 155-61; *CII*, V, pp. 10-15.

PLACE OF ISSUE : Nandivardhana.

DONOR : Pravara Sena II. Styled *parama-Māheśvāra* (staunch devotee

		of god Māheśvāra) and as one who had brought about Kṛita-yuga by the favour of god Śambhu.
DONEE	:	Brahmachārin (celibate) Kālakuṭṭa, *gaṇa-yājin* (performer of *gaṇa-yāga*) and belonging to Kauṇḍinya *gotra* and the Taittirīya *śākhā* (recension) of *Kṛishṇa* (Black) *Yajurveda.*
GIFT DETAILS	:	Village Kothuraka included in the Supratishṭhāhāra and situated west of the river Umā, north of the village Chiñchāpallī, east of the village Bonthikavāṭaka, and south of the village Maṇḍuki. The grant was made at the victorious (*vaijayika*) *dharmasthāna.*
DATE	:	Twelfth day (*dvādasī*) of the bright half of the month of Āśvayuja in the second year of the donor's reign. The grant was probably made on the occasion of *pāraṇā* or breaking the fast observed on the preceding *ekādasī* which is even now observed as fast day by the devout Śaivas.
SCRIPT	:	Box-headed variety of Brāhmī of the southern class.
OFFICER	:	Chakradeva acted as the *Dūtaka.* Was engraved by Nāgavarman.

OBSERVATIONS

The charter is the earliest one belonging to the Vākāṭaka king Pravara Sena II, a son of Rudra Sena II born of Prabhāvatī Guptā, daughter of *Mahārājādhirāja* Deva Gupta (i.e. the Gupta Emperor Chandra Gupta II). The official Vākāṭaka genealogy is already seen in a fully developed form in the Māṇḍhaḷ charter of his father Rudra Sena II[26] and may have been finalised even earlier if our ascription of the unfinished Mohallā plate to Pṛithivī Sheṇa I is acceptable. To this draft was added only the portion describing succeeding rulers in later period, and this is what we find in the present charter which adds the account of Pravara Sena II to the genealogical draft met with in the only known grant of his father Rudra Sena II.

Nandivardhana, which had become the capital of this branch of the Vākāṭakas during the later years of Rudra Sena II or the regency of Prabhāvatī Guptā, continued to occupy this position up to at least the eleventh year of Pravara Sena II as shown by his Belorā plates to be noted presently.

The beneficiary of the grant is described as a *gaṇa-yājin,* ''performer of *gaṇa-*

yāga'', which has no fixed connotation and has been explained differently by our authorities. It could mean a sacrifice performed for a *gaṇa* or guild and in that case it may be equated to *śreṇi-yāga*. The performers of such sacrifices were abhored by ancient writers who prohibited them from being invited to a *śrāddha*. Moreover, as the donor was an individual, i.e. Pravara Sena II, the meaning is totally inapplicable in the instant case. The intention appears to have been to refer to him as a performer of a *gaṇa-homa* described in the *Baudhāyana-dharma-sūtra*. It was a very difficult rite involving observance of certain restraints, offering boiled rice and clarified butter into fire with the recitation of certain *mantras* in the morning, noon and evening for one full week followed by the entertainment of Brāhmaṇas by food and gift of cattle, land, sesamum and gold. In exceptional cases one could employ a priest for the performance of this rite to free himself from sin, but the priest will be tainted by guilt. The performers of a *gaṇa-homa* for others for a consideration were therefore extremely rare. Kālakuṭṭa, the donee, was evidently one such, and was befittingly rewarded with the grant of a village by the Vākāṭaka king.[27]

We see no justification for calling the plates as 'Kothuraka Grant' as Mirashi has done in his paper in *EI* except only that the charter registers the grant of the village Kothuraka which cannot be identified.[28] It has to be called 'Jāmb' charter after its provenance following the normal convention in such cases.[29]

8 (M 4 & 5)
BELORĀ CHARTER OF PRAVARA SENA II, YEAR *11*
(Pls. XV-XVII, XVIII)

PROVENANCE : Belorā, Arwī *tahsīl*, 6 miles south-east of Morshī, Wardhā district, Māhārāshṭra.

REFERENCES : V.V. Mirashi, ''Two Incomplete Grants of Pravara Sena II'', *EI*, XXIV (1937-38), pp. 260-67; N.P. Chakravarti, editorial note no. 6, *ibid*., p. 262; V.V. Mirashi, *CII*, V, pp. 16-21.

PLACE OF ISSUE : Nā(Na)ndivardhana.

DONOR : Pravara Sena II.

DONEE : Sūryasvāmin, a resident of Pravareśvāra-shaḍvimśati-vāṭaka and belonging to the Taittirīya *śākhā* of the Black *Yajurveda* and Kāśyapa *gotra*.

GIFT DETAILS : Village Mahallalāṭa included in the Asi-*bhukti* of the *mārga* (subdivision) of Śailapura.

The grant was made at the victorious (*vaijayika*) *dharmasthāna*.

DATE : Thirteenth day (*trayodaśi*) of the bright half (*śukla-paksha*) of the month of Kārttika in the eleventh year of the donor's reign. The grant had probably something to do with the *pāraṇā* on the preceding day, though it is difficult to be sure on this point.

SCRIPT : Box-headed variety of Brāhmī of southern class.

OFFICER : *Senāpati* (army commander) Chitravarman drafted the charter.

OBSERVATIONS

The plates bearing this charter were discovered in a rather strange situation which has led to some confusion among scholars. There were in all four plates, one of them inscribed only on one side and the rest on both sides. The plate bearing writing only on one side is the first plate of the complete charter which consisted of three plates. Mirashi, who edited them, felt that they fell into two sets of charters called Set A and Set B. According to him, the last (third) plate of Set A and the first one of Set B have been lost, both the charters being thus incomplete.[30] As pointed out by him, the plates of the Set called A are somewhat larger and heavier as compared to those of Set B.

Set A, issued from Nandivardhana, aims at recording the grant of the village Mahalla-Lāṭa in the Asi-*bhukti* forming part of the subdivision called Śailapura-*mārga*. The place of issue of Set B, according to him, is unknown in the absence of the first plate. The charter, however, records the grant of the village Dīrghadraha included in the *rāshṭra* or administrative division called Pākkaṇa together with the village granted through the other charter (Set A) but here called Mahalla-Lāṭa. The beneficiary in both the cases was the same, viz. Sūryaśvāmin belonging to the Taittirīya *śākhā* of the *Kṛishṇa Yajurveda* and the Kāśyapa *gotra* and a resident of the headquarters of the administrative division Pravaresvāra-shaḍviṁśati-vāṭaka. The date of Set B is given at the end of the record as the thirteenth day of the bright half of Kārttika in the eleventh regnal year and the *Senāpati* responsible for drafting (*likhita*) it was Chitravarman, while these details remain unknown in the case of Set A due to the loss of its last plate. That the Set B is later is clearly indicated by the fact that it records not only the grant of Mahalla-

Lāṭa of Set A (under a slightly different form, viz. Mahallama-Lāṭa) but also of the other village named Dīrghadraha.

On a careful examination the charters appear to be palimpsests as they were engraved after beating in the earlier writing on the plates; but from such traces as can be made out of the earlier charter, it becomes quite clear that the writing was also in the same characters, leaving no doubt that the earlier charter, too, was issued by a Vākāṭaka king. This together with the mention of the same donated village in the two sets in addition to another in the second set raises some doubt about its genuineness. This is also strengthened by the fact that the writing on the second plate of both the sets commences and concludes with identical words, showing that the second plate of Set B could have been easily substituted for that of Set A. However, after all this discussion Mirashi concludes that the second set is also genuine and that the mention of Mahallama-Lāṭa granted already through Set A in it again was probably due to the donee's request to give him a consolidated charter.

However, the circumstances are transparent enough to raise serious suspicion regarding the genuineness of the so-called second set. As pointed out by N.P. Chakravarti in his editorial note on Mirashi's paper in *EI*, there was really only one set, and plates I and II of Set A and plate III of Set B were intended to form the complete charter of Pravara Sena II. Probably the grant of two villages in plate II of Set B was found to be wrong on examination and this plate was meant to be substituted by plate II of Set A which was engraved later. This explanation finds some support from the ornamental mark noticed following the word *atisṛishṭaḥ* at the end of plate II of Set A which marked the conclusion and was evidently incised to prevent further addition about the gift. But Chakravarti did not try to explain as to why the original plate was not removed and only indicated the possibility that the charter along with the original second plate did not leave the secretariat.

We feel very strongly, however, that it was a case of clear-out forgery with official connivance and, may be, even collusion. The avaricious donee appears to have been a very influential person and got the grant of two villages instead of the one actually given by the king inscribed on the second plate of the so-called Set B and even after the mischief was detected and corrected on another plate he was allowed to retain the original wrongly inscribed plate with official connivance. It is also likely alternatively that the one regarded as corrected by Chakravarti was actually the original one and the fraudulent donee got the second plate of the alleged Set B (Pl. XVIII) inscribed later and had it attached to the original charter and preserved both of them. While forgeries of land-grants by greedy donees often with the connivance and even active role of the officials at the royal secretariat are referred to and highly condemned in Dharmaśāstra texts and epigraphic records,[31] the present one is perhaps the unique, or at least one of the ubiquitous, cases where both the original and faked charter have been found together. In fact, in the normal case such fraudulent persons would have been punished severely, but in the instant case they not only managed to move scotfree but even to retain the charter.

Pravareśvara-shaḍviṁśati-vāṭaka was evidently a cluster of twenty-six villages around a temple of god Śiva originally built by Pravara Sena I and named after himself. The cluster of villages grown around it had come to be called by this name and turned into an administrative subdivision by the time of Pravara Sena II.

9 (M 6)
CHAMMAK PLATES OF PRAVARA SENA II, YEAR 18
(Pls. XXIII-XXIX)

PROVENANCE : Chammak, a village about 4 miles north-west of Achalpur, Amarāwatī district, Māhārāshṭra.

REFERENCES : Bhagwanlal Indraji, *Notes on the Bauddha Rock-Temples of Ajantā*, Pamphlet No. 9 of the Archaeological Survey of Western India, 1879, pp. 54ff.; G. Bühler, *Archaeological Survey of Western India*, IV, 1883, pp. 116ff.; *IA*, XII, pp. 239 ff.; J.F. Fleet, *Inscriptions of the Early Gupta Kings and their Successors, CII*, III, 1888, pp. 235-43; Mirashi V.V., *CII*, V, pp. 23-27; D. C. Sircar, *Select Inscriptions*, I, pp. 442-49.

PLACE OF ISSUE : Pravarapura, identified with some probability with modern Pavnār, Wardhā district, Māhārāshṭra.

DONOR : Pravara Sena II. Grant made at the request of Koṇḍarāja, son of Śatrughnarāja.

DONEES : 1,000 Brāhmaṇas of various *gotras* and Vedic *charaṇas*. Only forty-nine of them are named at the end.*

GIFT DETAILS : The village Charmāṅka (modern Chammak, find spot of the charter), on the bank of Madhunadī (now called Chandrabhāgā), measuring 8,000 (*nivartanas*) by royal measurement (*rājamānika*), situated in the *rājya* (province) of Bhojakaṭa.

DATE : Thirteenth day (*trayodaśī*) of the bright half of the month of Jyeshṭha in the eighteenth year of the donor's reign.

SCRIPT : Box-headed variety of Brāhmī of the southern class.

OFFICER : Written when Chitravarman was *Senāpati*.

*The donees mentioned by name are as follows:-

NAME		*GOTRA*
Gạñarya		Śāṭyāyana
Devārya		Vātsya
Guhaśarman		Pārāśarya
Devārya		Kāśyapa
Māheśvarārya	*gotra* not named, but probably	
Mātrārya	of the preceding (Kāśyapa) *gotra*[31a]	
Rudrārya		Kauṇḍinya
Somārya	Perhaps	do
Hariśarmārya		do
Kumāraśarmārya	Perhaps	Bharadvāja
Mātriśarmārya	"	Kauṇḍinya
Vārasarman	"	do.
Goṇḍaśarman	"	do.
Nāgaśarman	"	do.
Śāntiśarman		Bhāradvāja
Rudraśarman	Perhaps	do.
Bhojakadevārya		Vātsya
Maghaśarman	Perhaps	do.
Devaśarman	"	do.
Mokshaśarman		Bhāradvāja
Nāgaśarman	Perhaps	do.
Revatiśarman	"	do.
Dharmārya	"	do.
Śarmārya		Bhāradvāja
Nandanārya	Perhaps	Bhāradvāja
Mūlaśarmārya	"	do.
Īśvāraśarman	"	do.
Vāraśarman	"	do.
Skandārya		Vātsya

Bappārya		Bhāradvāja
Dharmārya	Perhaps	do.
Skandārya		Ātreya
Somaśarmārya		Gautama
Bhartrisarman	Perhaps	do.
Rudraśarmārya	"	do.
Maghārya	"	do.
Mātṛiśarman	"	do.
Īśvāraśarmārya	"	do.
Mātṛiśarmārya		Gautama
Devaśarmārya		Kauṇḍinya
Vāraśarmārya	Perhaps	do.
Rohārya	"	do.
Svāmidevārya		Gautama
Revatīśarmārya	Perhaps	do.
Jyeshṭhaśarmārya	"	do.
Kumāraśarmārya		Śāṇḍilya
Svātiśarmārya	Perhaps	do.
Kāṇḍarya		Śāṭyāyana

That these were not the only donees is clearly indicated by the employment of the word-form *prabhṛitayaḥ* after the above enumeration. They, however, appear to have represented the other donees as shown by the expression *vāraniyuktāḥ* preceding the above names. It is quite possible that the number may not have been exactly 1,000, but may be taken to indicate an exceptionally large number.

OBSERVATIONS

Till recently this was the earliest charter mentioning Pravarapura as the place of issue and capital of the Padmapura-Nandivardhana-Pravarapura branch of the Vākāṭakas and it was therefore commonly held that the capital was shifted from Nandivardhana to Pravarapura sometime between the eleventh (the date of the Belorā plates) and eighteenth years of Pravara Sena II's reign. But the recent discovery of his Māṇḍhaḷ charter[32] has established finally that this act had taken place sometime in or prior to his sixteenth regnal year.

This happens to be the only charter not only of this branch of the dynasty but of the Vākāṭakas to register a grant to such a large number of beneficiaries and perhaps one of the exceptionally few in the entire Indian subcontinent in this respect. In case the number of donees was actually 1,000, each of them would have received as his share only eight *nivartanas*[33] which is somewhat lower than most other grants.

Although the measurement of the donated village is not specified and it is said to have comprised only 8,000 *bhūmis* according to royal measure (*rāja-mānika-bhūmi-sahasrair=ashṭābhiḥ* 8,000), it should most probably have been *nivartana* which is mentioned in so many Vākāṭaka[34] and preceding Sātavāhana[35] records and appears to have been the most common land-measurement in the Deccan during the early centuries AD. It appears to have differed from locality to locality[36] and, maybe, even different connotations prevailed in the same region and locality. Therefore it was felt necessary to standardise it, and this (standard *nivartana*) is meant by the term *rāja-mānika* in this as well as in some other records of Pravara Sena II's reign.[37]

10 (M 7)
SIWANĪ PLATES OF PRAVARA SENA II, YEAR 18
(Pls. XXX-XXXIV)

PROVENANCE : Not known definitely. But the charter is called after Siwanī in Madhya Pradesh as it was in the possession of a zamīndār named Hazari Gond Malguzar living at the village of Piṇḍarāi in the Siwanī district, Madhya Pradesh. However, from the localities mentioned in the charter, it appears to have originally belonged to the Gondiā region of Māhārāshṭra.

REFERENCES : James Prinsep, *JASB*, V, pp. 726ff.; J.F. Fleet, *CII*, pp. 243-49; V.V. Mirashi, *CII*, V, pp. 28-32.

DONOR : Pravara Sena II.

DONEE : Devaśarmāchārya, an *Adhvaryu* belonging to the Maudgalya *gotra* and the Taittirīya recension (*śākhā*) of the Black *Yajurveda*. The adjective *adhvaryu* applied to the donee perhaps indicates that the grant was made probably on the occasion of a sacrifice and perhaps as his sacrificial fee (*dakshiṇā*) for officiating at the sacrifice.

GIFT DETAILS : The village named Brahmapūraka situated in the *bhoga* (district) known as Beṇṇākārpara (the Waingaṅgā region), to the north of Vaṭapūraka, west of Kiṇihikheṭaka, south of Pravarajjavāṭaka (Skt. Pravarāryavāṭaka) and east of Kollapūra.

All these localities have been identified in the Goṇdia region of the Bhaṇḍārā district, Māhārāshṭra.

DATE : Twelfth day (*dvādaśī*) of the white half of the month of Phālguna in the eighteenth year of the donor's reign.

SCRIPT : Box-headed variety of Brāhmī of the southern class.

OFFICER : Written by Āchārya when Bāppadeva held the office of *Senāpati*.

OBSERVATIONS

The mention of Bāppadeva as *Senāpati* is quite important. We have already seen that Chitravarman held this office till the thirteenth of the bright half of the month of Jyeshṭha in Pravara Sena II's eighteenth year as seen from his Chammak grant. From this record we learn that after this date and sometime prior to the date of the issue of the present grant Chitravarman was replaced in this office by Bāppadeva.

The charter is quite reticent regarding the place wherefrom it was issued. But Mirashi thinks that it was probably issued from the royal capital Pravarapura as the grant is said to have been made at the 'victorious place of religious worship' (*vaijayika dharma-sthāna*). However, this is quite untenable in the light of our observations on the meaning of the word *dharma-sthāna* while dealing with inscription No. i (Deoṭek inscription of Rudra Sena, I or II) and the fact that the expression in question appears not only in the charters issued from the royal capital but in connection with the grants made at other places as well. It is therefore not possible to be certain about this point.

11 (M 8)
ṚIDDHAPUR PLATES OF PRABHĀVATĪ GUPTĀ, YEAR 19 OF PRAVARA SENA II
(Pls XXXV-XXXVII)

PROVENANCE : Ṛiddhapur, Morshī *tahsīl*, Amarāwatī district, Māhārāshṭra; in possession of *Mahanta* Dattarāja of the Mahānubhāva sect.

REFERENCES : Y.R. Gupte, *Bhārata Itihāsa Saṁśodhaka Maṇḍaḷa Traimāsika* (Quarterly Journal of the Bhārata Itihāsa Saṁśodhaka Maṇḍaḷa, Puṇe), III, Parts 2-4, pp. 89ff. (Marathi); "Ṛiddhapur plates of the Vākāṭaka Queen Prabhāvatī-guptā of the 19th year", *JASB*, New Series, XX, pp. 53-62; V.V. Mirashi, *CII*, V, pp. 33-37; Jagannath Agrawal, *PIHC*, IV Session, p. 59; *Researches in Indian Epigraphy and Numismatics*, pp. 27-28; R.C.

Majumdar, "Note on Geneology and Chronology of the Vākāṭakas", *JRASB*, XII, pp. 1-5; *ibid.*, XX, pp. 101-05; D.C. Sircar, "A Note on the Vākāṭakas", *ibid.*, XII, pp. 71-73, XIII, pp. 75-78; *Select Inscriptions*, I, pp. 439-42; *HCIP*, III: *CA*, pp. 180-81; Ajay Mitra Shastri, "The Vākāṭaka Kings Dāmodara Sena and Pravara Sena II", *JESI*, XIV, pp. 38-40.

PLACE OF ISSUE : The foot-prints of the Lord of Rāmagiri (*Rāmagiri-svāminaḥ pāda-mūlāt*), i.e. Rāmṭek near Nagpur.

DONATRIX : Prabhāvatī Guptā, described as chief queen of Vākāṭaka king Rudra Sena II and mother of the Vākāṭaka kings Damodara Sena and Pravara Sena II and devoted to the feet of Bhagavat (*Bhagavat-pād-ānuuddhyātā*).

DONEES : Brāhmaṇas belonging to the Taittirīya *śākhā* of the Black *Yajurveda* and Parāśara *gotra* with or without sons.

GIFT DETAILS : A field meant only for enjoyment (*bhuktak-ābhoga-kshetram*) together with a farm-house (*abhyantara-niveśana*) and four residences of ploughmen (*karshaka-niveśana*) situated in the Aśvattha-nagara included in the administrative division (*mārga*) of Kośika.

DATE : Twelfth day (*dvādaśī*) of the bright fortnight of the month of Kārttika during the nineteenth year of the reign of the Vākāṭaka king Pravara Sena II.

SCRIPT : Box-headed variety of the southern class of Brāhmī.

OFFICERS : Devanandasvāmin acted as the conveyor of the grant (*dūtaka*), while the charter was written by Prabhusiṁha.

OBSERVATIONS

This charter, though issued by Prabhāvatī Guptā, is incised in box-headed variety of the southern class of Brāhmī script, showing thereby that the choice of the particular variety of alphabet depended entirely on the scribe and the rulers had nothing to do with it. This is also indicated by the fact that the Rāmṭek inscription commemorating the demise of Prabhāvatī Guptā which was put up most probably by her son Pravara Sena II and his sister of unknown name was inscribed in nail-headed variety when there was nothing to compel its employment. Both these records were evidently incised by the official scribes of Pravara Sena II.

The charter, like the Puṇe plates, introduces Prabhāvatī Guptā not only as the chief queen of Vākāṭaka Rudra Sena II but also as the mother of the (two) Vākāṭaka kings Damodara Sena and Pravara Sena II,[38] and as the daughter of the Gupta emperor (*Mahārājādhirāja*) Chandra Gupta II and in that context the Gupta genealogy up to his time is given. As the charter was dated in Pravara Sena II's reign and was evidently issued with his consent, it must have been drafted in his records office and with his consent; had he disliked the idea of giving Gupta genealogy, there was nothing to prevent him from omitting it and replacing it by Vākāṭaka genealogy. But he deliberately retained Gupta genealogy because he prided in his descent on mother's side from the Guptas and had high respects for his mother even though she had ceased to act as regent about twenty-nine years before as we shall soon see. Obviously she had played a crucial role in securing the throne of this branch of the Vākāṭakas against all odds including perhaps danger from the other branch and therefore carved a powerful niche for herself in the Vākāṭaka court which held her in high esteem.

The Gupta genealogy met with in the charter, like that in the Puṇe plates, is highly defective. Thus Ghaṭotkacha is said quite explicitly to have been the first king of the Guptas (*Guptānām=ādirāja*);[39] both Chandra Gupta I and Samudra Gupta are styled only *Mahārāja* (against the superior title *Mahārājādhirāja* actually borne by and applied to them in most of the official Gupta records) and only her father Chandra Gupta II is given the imperial title *Mahārājādhirāja*, and several epithets usually applied to his father Samudra Gupta are erroneously used for Chandra Gupta II. Obviously the person responsible for drafting this genealogical account was not well acquainted with actual facts.

What is interesting historically is that Prabhāvatī Guptā is said to have been the mother of the Vākāṭaka *Mahārājas* Dāmodara Sena and Pravara Sena (II).[40] This expression has given rise to some unwarranted controversy with a great bearing on Vākāṭaka history. Most of the historians of the Vākāṭakas following K.P. Jayaswal[41] held that Dāmodara Sena and Pravara Sena were the same, the former being the original name and the latter the name adopted by him at the time of coronation. This view was prompted by, *inter alia*, the use of the regal title *Mahārāja* only before the former name and its omission prior to the latter name. The same may be said regarding the honorific *śrī*. Some other scholars including R.C. Majumdar[42] and D.C. Sircar[43] held that the two names represented different kings who followed one after the other on the Vākāṭaka throne. It is surprising that great Sanskritists[44] could not realise that the use of the title and honorific in a compound applied to all the names that followed and their repetition before all the names is not at all required. Thus, even with the expression as it is the separate existence of the two kings was self-evident.[45] As if in order to put the controversy to rest, the seal of the rather recently discovered Miregāon (Sākolī) plates issued by the queen a little over a year later (20th year) refers to her as the 'mother of two valorous Vākāṭaka kings',[46] who could have been only Damodara Sena and Pravara Sena II as there is absolutely no evidence that their elder brother Divākara Sena ever came to throne. As against it, we have definite evidence that he died as crown prince (*Yuvarāja*).[47]

Prabhāvatī Guptā is also described as *s-āgra-varsha-śata-jīva-putra-pautrā,*[48] which has given rise to a protracted controversy among historians. Some split the expression into two parts viz. (i) *s-āgra-varsha-śata* which they correct to *s-āgra-varsha-śatā* and take to refer to the queen as living upwards of a hundred years, and (ii) *jīva-putra-pautrā*, 'whose sons and grandsons are alive'.[49] However, as pointed out by Jagannath Agarwal,[50] the entire expression is to be taken as a single compound with *s-āgra-varsha-śata-jīva* referring to *putra-pautra* and indicating the desire that her sons and grandsons who were alive may live for upwards of hundred years; such expressions are found in connection with women in ancient Indian literature and inscriptions.[51] Thus, Prabhāvatī-guptā was not over a hundred years of age at the time of making this as well as her grant recorded in the Miregāon plates a year later.

Mirashi takes the expression *bhuktātaka-ābhoga-kshetram* to mean that the field donated by this charter was 'enjoyed (*so far*) by Bhuktaka',[52] thus taking Bhuktaka to be a personal name of the original owner. It is not explained as to why the field was withdrawn from him before being granted to the Brāhmaṇa beneficiaries. And Bhuktaka is a rather strange name for a person to bear. We are inclined to take it as a revenue term meaning 'field meant only for enjoyment', thereby prohibiting its alienation or sale or transfer otherwise. D.C. Sircar takes it to mean that the donees were already enjoying the field.[53]

12 (M 9)
INDORE PLATES OF PRAVARA SENA II, YEAR 23[54]
(Pls. XLIII-XLV)

PROVENANCE : Not known exactly, but in the possession of Pandit Vamanshastri Islampurkar of Indore, Madhya Pradesh. Probably collected

		by him from somewhere else; but the localities mentioned in the charter show that it most probably belonged to the Bālāghāṭ district, Madhya Pradesh.
REFERENCES	:	Sushil K. Bose, "Indore Plates of Pravārasena II", *EI*, XXIV, pp. 52-56; V.V. Mirashi, *CII*, V, pp. 38-42.
PLACE OF ISSUE	:	Temporary Residence at Tripurī (*Tripurī-vāsakāt*) as known from plate I of the charter discovered later. *Vide* No. V of the next chapter.
DONOR	:	Pravara Sena II and the Merchant Chandra.
DONEES	:	Viśākhārya's son Goṇḍārya and the latter's sons Manorathārya, Govārya, Devārya, Bāppārya, Kumārārya and Droṇārya who were residents of the village Ārāmaka and belonged to the Vājikausika *gotra*.
GIFT DETAILS	:	A village whose name is given as Viśākhārya-vāṭaka situated to the north of Āramāka, east of Kovidārikā, south of Kośambaka and west of Añjanavāṭaka.
DATE	:	Fifth day (pañchamī) of the bright half of the month of Vaiśākha in the twenty-third year of the reign of Pravara Sena II.
SCRIPT	:	Box-headed variety of Brāhmī of the southern class.
OFFICERS	:	Koṭṭadeva, who held the office of Rājuka, drafted it, while the order about the gift (or its formalisation) was ordered by the king himself.

OBSERVATIONS

This is one of the most interesting charters of Pravara Sena II and certain points deserve to be noticed especially. It was engraved very carelessly with several words of the original draft having been left out originally from the draft and engraved afresh at wrong places. In most of the places correct placements have been restored by V.V. Mirashi.

The charter was intended only to formalise an earlier grant by the issue of a charter and not to record a new grant. It is clear from the sentence *pūrvvadattā iti kṛitvā yato=smābhiḥ śāsana-nibandhaḥ kṛitaḥ* in lines 17-18. However, the following expression *a-pūrvvadattyā*, which refers to a fresh grant, and some other expressions occur only as a conventional matter without much real significance. Such a phenomenon is noticed in a few other grants of other ruling families as well.[55] Who was the original benefactor is difficult to determine. Half of the village (*vāṭaka*) was probably purchased by the trader Chandra (from whom we are not told) for gifting away to the Brāhmaṇas and the remaining half may have been added by the unknown original Vākāṭaka donor who also might have been responsible for conferring the immunities and privileges normally attached to such grants.

Mirashi feels that the engraver by oversight left out the actual name of the donated village and instead mentioned the name of Viśākhārya who was in fact the father of Brāhmaṇa Goṇḍārya and grandfather of other donees. But we are inclined to believe that Viśākhārya was the original donee after whom the originally granted village came to be popularly known. Thus, the scribe in this case did not commit any mistake. The original donor might have been one of the royal predecessors of Pravara Sena II, maybe Rudra Sena II or Prabhāvatī Guptā as regent for *Yuvārāja* Divākara Sena. The latter suggestion finds support from the specification that the grant was made at the footprints of the Bhagavat[56] (Vishṇu) which is also averred in the latter's Puṇe plates. What Pravara Sena therefore did was only to formalise the grant by issuing a formal charter.

Koṭṭadeva, the drafter of the grant, is styled *Rajuka* which is obviously the same as *Rajjuka* of the *Arthaśāstra* of Kauṭilya and *Rajju-grāhaka amātya* of the Jātakas who was a revenue officer in charge of assessing land-revenue by measuring with the help of a rope. In Aśoka's edicts we find him placed in charge of hundreds of thousands of people and entrusted with wider duties, very much like the present collector who was originally only a revenue officer but put in charge of a much wider gambit of activities. The present inscription perhaps contains the latest reference to this ancient institution and thereby reveals the continuation of ancient Mauryan and pre-Mauryan administrative traditions during the Vākāṭaka period in Vidarbha, though we cannot be sure regarding his official functions.

13 (M 10)
DUDIĀ PLATES OF PRAVARA SENA II, YEAR 23
(Pls. XLVI-XLVIII)

PROVENANCE : Found in possession of some Goṇḍs at the village of Dudiā, Aser *pargaṇā*, Chhindwārā district, Madhya Pradesh.

REFERENCES : F. Kielhorn, "Dudia Plates of Pravara Sena II", *EI*, III, pp. 258-62; V.V. Mirashi, *CII*, V, pp. 43-47.

PLACE OF ISSUE	:	Pravārapura.
DONOR	:	Pravara Sena II.
DONEES	:	Brāhmaṇas Yakshārya of Kauśika *gotra* and Kāliśarman of Kauṇḍinya *gotra*.
GIFT DETAILS	:	Twenty-five *bhūmis (nivartanas)* in the village Darbbhamalaka in Chandrapura-saṅgamikā to Yakshārya and sixty *bhūmis* (*nivartanas*) of land in the village Karmakāra-grāma included in the district (*bhoga*) of Hiraṇyapura to Kāliśarman; both the localities and administrative divisions formed a part of the higher division called Ārammirājya.
DATE	:	Tenth day of the fourth fortnight of the rainy season (*varshā-paksha*) in the twenty-third year of the donor's reign.
SCRIPT	:	Box-headed variety of Brāhmī of the southern class.
OFFICERS	:	Written by Goladāsa while Navamidāsa held the office of *Senāpati*.

OBSERVATIONS

There was a lot of controversy regarding the location of the Ārammi-*rājya* wherein both Hiraṇyapura-*bhoga* and Chndrapura-*saṅgamikā* and obviously the donated pieces of land in the villages Darbhamalaka and Karmakāra-grāma were situated. Hiralal felt that Ārammi, the headquarters of the *rājya* named after it is identical with the present town of Ārvī in the Wardhā district.[57] However, Ārammi-*rājya* is also mentioned in the Pāṇḍhurṇā plates of the same king[58] as well as in the recently discovered Māhurjharī grant of his grandson Pṛithivī Sheṇa II, in the latter in the form Ārambi.[59] Now, as all the grants have been found in the Chhindwārā district of Madhya Pradesh and the Nāgpur district of Māhārāshṭra and the localities named therein have been located in this region, it is evident that Āramm(b)i-*rājya* must have included these adjoining areas[60] and its headquarters should be looked for here. Mirashi's equation of Ārammi with Āmlā, some 40 miles north by west of Pāṇḍhurṇā in the Chhindwārā district is in keeping with this consideration, though it is quite unlikely in view of the great phonetic difference between the two names. As against this, there is still a village named Ārambhi near Kāṭol in the Kāṭo*l tahsīl* of the Nāgpur district which most probably represents ancient Ārammi or Ārambi.[61]

The date of the record is given according to seasons, in the instant case *varshā* or rainy season. According to this system of dating, each of the three main seasons (*grīshma* or summer, *varshā* or rainy season, and *hemanta* or winter) was divided into eight fortnights of fifteen days each which were numbered serially. Most of the Deccanese inscriptions of the early centuries AD are dated according to this system. In later times with the employment of months becoming more popular its vogue became much less common though it lingered on for a few centuries more. When this record was found very few Vākāṭaka epigraphs were known to have been dated following this system. But in recent years several records bearing such dates have come to light and have shown the continuation, though naturally on a reduced scale, of such practice of dating up to about the sixth century AD.[62]

13 (M 11)
TIROḌĪ PLATES OF PRAVARA SENA II, YEAR 23
(Pls. XLIX-LI)

PROVENANCE : Manganese mines at Tirodī, eight miles south-east of Kaṭaṅgī, Bālāghāṭ district, Madhya Pradesh.

REFERENCES : V.V. Mirashi, "Tiroḍī Plates of Pravarasena II", *EI*, XXII, pp. 167-76; *CII*, V, pp. 48-52.

PLACE OF ISSUE : Narattaṅgavāristhāna, doubtfully equated with Narnālā, still regarded as a scared spot, in the Ākoṭ *tahsīl* of the Akolā district, and Wāri, also known as Bhairavagaḍh, now a deserted place on the river Bāṇ or Wāṇ, in the extreme south-west of the same *tahsīl*. The name is treated as a joint name like Nāgapura-Nandivardhana occurring in a Rāshṭrakūṭa record.

DONOR : Pravara Sena II.

DONEE : Varuṇārya, a resident of Chāndrapura, belonging to the *Atharvaveda* and the Harkari *gotra* and a master of the three Vedas (*Triveda*).

GIFT DETAILS : The village Kosambakhaṇḍa, to the west of Jamali, north of Vardhamānaka, east of Mṛigasīma and west of Mallakapedhaka included in the western division (*apara-paṭṭa*) of Bennākaṭa, a district comprising the territory with its headquarters being represented, perhaps, by the village Beṇī, thirty-five miles

		east of Kosamba in the Gondiā *tahsīl* of the Bhaṇḍārā district, Māhārāshṭra.
DATE	:	Twelfth day of the dark half of the month of Māgha (*Māgha-bahula-pakshe*) during the twenty-third year of the donor's reign.
SCRIPT	:	Box-headed variety of Brāhmī of the southern class.
OFFICER	:	Written by the state officer (*rājyādhikṛita*) named Navamidāsa.

OBSERVATIONS

Narattangavāri-sthāna was a holy spot as indicated by the word *sthāna* suffixed to the name.[63] The word *vāri* shows that it was in the proximity of a water-source like river or lake. It is unfortunate, however, that the place cannot be identified satisfactorily. Its location proposed by Mirashi in the Ākoṭ *tahsīl* of the Akolā district is quite doubtful and efforts should be made to locate it somewhere near the locality Beṇī which is named after the river Beṇā or Veṇā, modern Waingaṅgā.

Mirashi argues that the expression *vaijayike dharmasthāne* does not occur in this charter as it was issued from Narattaṅgavāri-sthāna, and not from the capital, where the chief temple (*vaijayika dharmasthāna*) was situated. As pointed out above in connection with the Deoṭek inscription, the word *dharma-sthāna* was never employed for temple, and the expression in question occurs not only in the charters issued from the metropolis but also from other places. Not to cite later instances, Pravara Sena II's own Indore plates issued from Tripurī-vāsaka and Waḍgāon charter issued from Hiraṇyānadī-vāsaka which were certainly not capitals, also contain the expression *vaijayike dharma-sthāne;* it had become a part of the conventionalised draft of the charters, and its absence in any charter is to be explained as due to oversight on the part of the officer entrusted with its drafting and not deliberate.

The grant was made not only for the donor's religious merit, long life and happiness in this and the other world but also for the increase of religious merit of his mother which is interesting. She had made a grant just three years back as shown by the recently discovered but yet unpublished Miregāon (Sākolī) plates, and here we find the son holding her in esteem and anxious for her earning religious merit. That he had a high respect for her is known also from the recently discovered Rāmṭek inscription put up during his reign to commemorate her death by the construction of a temple and excavation of a water-reservoir called Sudarśana. Being very elderly and widowed, she just wanted to add to her merit and naturally did not hanker for longevity any more.

The grant was obviously made after bathing at the Narattaṅgavāri *tīrtha* before breaking the fast observed on the previous day, viz. Māgha kṛishṇa ekādasī, which was regarded as quite holy. It was called Shaṭ-tilā ekādaśī and is highly eulogised in the Purāṇas. The ceremonial ablution in the month of Māgha is even now regarded as especially sacred not to speak of ancient times. It is evident that this was a *fait accompli* by the Vākāṭaka period.

Mirashi reads the name of the writer as Chamidāsa; but even a casual glance at the accompanying facsimile (last line) would bear out the suggestion of N.P. Chakravarti that the correct reading is Navamidāsa; this is undoubtedly the full form of the name (Namidāsa) of the *Senāpati* responsible for the draft of the Dudiā plates of the same year.

Navamidāsa, the drafter of the charter, is styled *rājy-ādhikṛita* which is translated by Mirashi as 'the Chief Minister'. However, it actually means a 'state officer' which Navamidāsa was. If he be identical with Namidāsa,[64] as is quite likely, he was *Senāpati* who was a very senior state officer.

14 (M 12)
WAḌGĀON PLATES OF PRAVARA SENA II, YEAR 25
(Pls. LII-LIV)

PROVENANCE : Waḍgāon in the Warorā *tahsīl* of the Chandrapur district, Māhārāshṭra.

REFERENCES : V.V. Mirashi, "Waḍgāon Plates of Vākāṭaka Pravarasena II", *EI*, XXVII, pp. 74-79; *CII*, V, pp. 53-56.

PLACE OF ISSUE : Temporary residence or camp (*vāsaka*), on the river Hiraṇyā.

DONOR : Pravara Sena II.

DONEE : Brāhmaṇa Rudrārya, resident of Ekārjuna, reciter of *vishuva*, belonging to Vāji-Lohitya *gotra*[65] and a master of two Vedas (*dviveda*).

GIFT DETAILS : Four hundred *nivartanas* by royal measurement of land in the village of Velusuka included in the district (*āhāra*) of Supratishṭha and situated to the east of Gṛidhragrāma, south of Kadambasaraka, west of Nīlīgrāma and north of Kokilāra.

DATE : Tenth day of the bright half of the month of Jyeshṭha in the twenty-fifth year of the donor's reign.

SCRIPT : Box-headed variety of the southern class of Brāhmī.

OFFICER : Written while Bāppadeva was the *Senāpati*.

OBSERVATIONS

The donee is styled *vishuva vāchanaka* (reciter of *vishuva*) and from this Mirashi infers that the grant was actually made by way of *dakshiṇā* for reciting the *vishuva* on the immediately preceding *vishuva* or Mesha *saṅkrānti* falling in Chaitra. But as pointed out by the editors in their editorial note,[67] it may have been only the donee's epithet without any reference to an actual recital. It would, however, indicate that the ceremony involving the recital on the occasion of the equinox had already become popular in the Deccan by the fifth century AD.

The grant was actually made in the twentieth regnal year by the king but got recorded only in the twenty-fifth year, there being thus a gap of about five years between the actual date of donation and that of its recording. This is certainly an unusually long gap but is not quite impossible.[68] This is perhaps the only family charter next only to the Māṇḍhaḷ charter of the same king dating a few years earlier (to be exact, eight)[69] where the regnal year is mentioned twice: once in connection with the grant and the other in the context of its recording, for which obviously the need of specification and explanation was felt.[70]

Bāppadeva, the *Senāpati* under whom the grant was recorded, is also known to have held this office in the donor's eighteenth year when the Siwanī plates were issued. Obviously, he had ceased to be the *Senāpati* concerned with the land-grants during the interval between the two grants being entrusted with some other unascertainable responsibilities as we find mention of other *Senāpatis* (Chitravarman and Navamidāsa) in the charters issued during this period. Alternatively he may have been kept off from normal duties in the gap. It is also possible that there were more than one *Senāpati* at the same time.

The charter ended with an auspicious expression like *śubham=astu* of which only the last two *aksharas* have been engraved, the remainder having been left out by oversight. In *EI*, XXVII, p. 79, fn. 9, Mirashi suggested this reading[71] but in *CII* indicated alternatively the possibility of the intended expression being *sidham=astu*.[72] Both these are auspicious formulae and could definitely be employed as a *maṅgal-ācharaṇa*, with an almost identical connotation. It is noteworthy that among the Vākāṭaka records this happens to be the only one as of now to employ such an expression at its end.

15(M 13)
PAṬṬAN PLATES OF PRAVARA SENA II, YEAR 27
(Pls. LVII-LXI)

PROVENANCE : Paṭṭan, a village in Multāi *tahsīl*, Betūl district, Madhya Pradesh. Found while ploughing a field.

REFERENCES : V.V. Mirashi, "Paṭṭan Plates of Pravarasena II"; *EI*, XXIII, pp. 81-88; *CII*, V, pp. 57-62.

PLACE OF ISSUE : Pravarapura.

DONOR : Pravara Sena II. At the request of Nārāyaṇarāja.

DONEE : A *sattra* (free feeding house) at the footprints of Mahāpurusha (Vishṇu).

GIFT DETAILS : Four hundred *nivartanas*, according to royal measure, of land at the village of Aśvatthakheṭaka in the administrative division (*mārga*) of Varadākheṭa in the district (*bhoga*) of Lohanagara. The village led by the Brāhmaṇas was the addressee.

DATE : Seventh day of the dark half of the month of Kārttika in the twenty-seventh year of the donor's reign.

SCRIPT : Box-headed variety of the southern class of Brāhmī.

OFFICERS : Drafted by one Kālidāsa when Kātyāyana was *Senāpati*; engraved (*khāta*) by the goldsmith Īśvaradatta, attached to Kauṇḍarāja (*Kauṇḍarāja-santaka*); the charter was caused to be prepared by Pitāmaha and Nanda.

OBSERVATIONS

This happens to be a unique charter not only of the reign of Pravara Sena II but of the Vākāṭakas as a whole in that it records a grant for the maintenance of a free feeding house as against all other official records which aim at registering land-grants for individual Brāhmaṇas or their groups. Although Pravara Sena II himself was a devout Śaiva, he granted this piece of land to a *sattra* of Mahāpurusha or Vishnu, evidently attached to a temple of the god, obviously because Nārāyaṇarāja, at whose behest the grant was made, was, as indicated by his name, a Vaishṇava.

Nārāyaṇarāja and, perhaps, Kauṇḍarāja were members of the royal family, as indicated by the name-ending *rāja* and the fact that they were important enough to make the king grant land and to get the charter prepared. That *rāja*-ending names were borne by the princes of the family is shown by the name Prithivirāja used for Prithivī Sheṇa in the Tigāon Plates of Pravara Shena in II whose account will presently follow. When a Vākāṭaka prince ascended the throne, *sena* was added to his name; it served like a surname and in the case of the Vākāṭakas it may be taken to indicate the status of a king or crown-prince.

As admitted by Mirashi after a lot of discussion, the Kālidāsa responsible for drafting this charter cannot be identical with the homonymous celebrated Sanskrit poet-playwright. But its occurrence should leave no doubt about the popularity of this name which is clearly indicative of the passage of a long period that must have elapsed between the poet of the name and Pravara Sena II.

16 (M 14)
TĪGĀON PLATES OF PRAVARA SENA II, YEAR 29
(Pls. LXII-LXIV)

PROVENANCE	:	Tīgāon,[73] a village six miles south-west of Pāṇḍhurṇā, Chhindwārā district, Madhya Pradesh.
REFERENCE	:	V.V. Mirashi, *CII*, V, pp. 63-68.
PLACE OF ISSUE	:	Temple of Pravareśvara (*Pravareśvara-devakula-sthānāt*).
DONOR	:	Pravara Sena II.
DONEES	:	Brāhmaṇas of various *gotras* and *charaṇas* of whom prominent ones (*pramukha*) were Yajñārya, Bhojārya, Somārya and Dharmārya belonging to the Vājasaneyī *saṁhita* of the *Yajurveda* and Kauṇḍinya *gotra*. Somārya was a resident of the village Kāllāra and received an additional grant for performing *tilavāchanaka* (viz. *śrāddha*).
GIFT DETAILS	:	Two thousand *nivartanas* of land by the royal measure in the village Dhu(Dhru)vavāṭaka included in the Vāruchcha-*rājya* lying in the low ground by the western boundary of the village Brāhmaṇavāṭaka, north of the way to the village Ajakarṇa, east of the village Badarī and west of the village called Darbhapatha or the way leading to the village Darbha. An

additional twenty-five *nivartanas* of land by royal measure together with an additional *nivartana* of land for residence in the village called Lekhapallikā and another twenty-five and one *nivartanas* for the same purpose in the village called Saṅgamikā, both included in the Ārammi-*rājya*, were given to Somārya.

The first grant was in exchange (*prativastu*) for the earlier gift of the village Vijayavallī-vāṭaka made by Prithivīrāja (viz. Prithivī Shena I).

DATES : Dates are given in two contexts, viz. (i) making the grants and (ii) registering them. The former are (i) seventh day of the fifth fortnight of rainy season in the donor's twenty-ninth regnal year, (ii) ninth day of the seventh fortnight of the rainy season in the twenty-ninth year and (iii) fifth day of the seventh fortnight of the rainy season, perhaps of the same regnal year. The latter is the tenth day of the dark fortnight of the month of Vaiśākha in the twenty-ninth year of the donor's reign.

SCRIPT : Box-headed variety of the southern class of Brāhmī script.

OFFICERS : Written by Āyārya (Skt. Āchārya) attached to Mādhappa during the period when the latter was holding the office of *Senāpati*.

OBSERVATIONS

First as regards nomenclature. Mirashi calls it "Pāṇḍhurṇā plates" as if they were found at Pāṇḍhurṇā itself, whereas he himself states in the very beginning of his account that these were found 'when the old house of one Kadu Patil was being demolished at Tīgāon', which is also a well-known locality. In keeping with the common practice of naming a charter after its provenance we have captioned it as 'Tīgāon plates'.

The grant was made from the temple (*devakula-sthāna*) known as Pravareśvara, evidently after the founder who must have been the benefactor's homonymous ancestor, viz. Pravara Sena I. As we have seen in connection with the Belorā plates of Pravara Sena II, in course of time the village (*pravareśvara-vāṭaka*) where it was situated became the chief village of a group of twenty-six villages (*shaḍviṁśati*). While it is difficult to decide the location of the temple and the village which might have been situated in the Wardhā district close to modern Paunār or elsewhere in the Vākāṭaka kingdom, what is interesting to note is that the grant, though not issued from the capital, does refer to *vaijayika dharmasthāna* as the place where the grant was made. This along with a few other instances makes it clear enough that the expression *vaijayika dharmasthāna* should not be taken to mean the chief temple at the capital as Mirashi has done.

The present grant is said to have been made in exchange for an earlier gift made by Pravara Sena II's grandfather Pṛithivīrāja who has been rightly equated with Pṛithivī Sheṇa I. This is very important, for it shows that the latter also had issued some charter/charters which have, however, yet to be discovered and located and may come to light in future. It is therefore not impossible if the Mohallā charter issued from Padmapura actually belongs to him as suggested earlier.

The original donees who received the original charter from Prithivī Shena I probably lived some seventy odd years earlier that must have elapsed between this grant and its substitution by his grandson Pravara Sena II. The beneficiaries of the exchange must therefore have been their descendants in the second or third generation and must have requested the latter for the change which was complied with by him.

Mirashi is right in pointing out that the third plate (Pl. LXV) recording the additional grant for one of the four donees specified, viz. Somārya, is suspect regarding its nature. But the grounds he has adduced for such an important suggestion, viz. careless inscribing involving imperfect formation of letters often running into one another, faulty language and the employment of Prakrit words and suffixes, are not only not conclusive but are actually in keeping with the draft on the preceding and following plates. In fact, though the charters of this branch of the Vākāṭakas are drafted entirely in Sanskrit it is often defective in most of the charters and shows that the persons responsible for drafting them were not well up in Sanskrit. They often exhibit Prakritism, especially in the date portion, and often exhibit trends of Māhārashtri Prakrit and the beginnings of proto-Marathi. Therefore these are no grounds at all for regarding the plate as spurious and inserted later into the charter. There is, however, *another clear-cut proof for treating the plate, especially the portion recording additional grant to Somārya, as spurious and forged which has somehow eluded Mirashi's keen vision.* There are more than one dates mentioned in the record: one at the end as that of registration of the grant and two dates as those of the twin donations. While the first date (at the end) is of the usual day-fortnight-month-year type as in most of the Vākāṭaka charters, the other two are season dates and what is interesting is that all these are in the twenty-ninth year of Pravara Sena II. The month named at the end is Vaisakha while the season in the middle two dates is *varshā* or rains. How could the rainy season come in or before Vaiśākha? It is obvious that this point escaped the notice of the otherwise shrewd forger as well as of Mirashi. And this comes very handy to a detecting eye. The cunning Somārya not only forged the plate but also succeeded in substituting it for the original, thus showing his one-upmanship. Obviously he must have occupied and must have been enjoying the land in question unauthorisedly with the connivance of the state officials concerned and had it recorded in the plate that he got substituted in the place of the original genuine plate.

Āchārya, who wrote the charter in question, was evidently identical with the homonymous writer of the Siwanī plates of the same monarch. He was apparently attached to the office of the *Senāpati* and continued at least from the eighteenth to at least the twenty-ninth year of Pravara Sena II's reign. That he did not write some grants only shows that he was entrusted at that time with some other duties.

17 (M 15)
BĀLĀGHĀṬ PLATE OF PRAVARA SENA II
(Pl. LXVI)

PROVENANCE : Found while digging the foundation for the bungalow or one of its outhouses of the District Superintendent of Police at Bālāghāṭ, Madhya Pradesh.

REFERENCES : A.S. Altekar, *JBORS,* XIV, pp. 465ff.; K.P. Jayaswal, *History of India, 150 A.D. to 350 A.D.*, p. 74; Hiralal, *Inscriptions in the Central Provinces and Berar*, p. 5; V.V. Mirashi, *Journal of Nagpur University*, No. II, pp. 48ff.; *CII*, V, pp. 69-72.

DONOR : Pravara Sena II.

DONEES : There were three beneficiaries as under: Gaṅgārya, son of Vedārya of Bhāradvāja *gotra*, Vasurārya (Skt. Vasvārya) of Kauṇḍinya *gotra* and Rudrārya of Kauṇḍinya *gotra* and Taittiriya *saṁhitā* of the Black *Yajurveda*.

GIFT DETAILS : The village Śrīparṇakā in the administrative division (*mārga*) of Sundhāti to the east of the village Brahmapūraka, west of Millukadraha, north of Madhukajjharī and south of Darbhaviraka. The grant was made in exchange for an earlier one (*pūrvva-parigraha-prativastu*) of the village Māṇapallikā situated in the administrative division (*mārga*) of Yaśapura.

SCRIPT : Box-headed variety of the southern class of Brāhmī.

OBSERVATIONS

There was considerable uncertainty regarding the provenance of this plate. A.S. Altekar, who first published it, observed that it was found 'somewhere in the Central Provinces', while K.P. Jayaswal regarded it as hailing from Jabalpur and Hiralal felt that it belonged to a set of three or four plates found near Rāmṭek. By his persevering efforts Mirashi ascertained that it was actually found at Bālāghāṭ as stated above. *What is surprising is that even though the plate was known to have been found at Bālāghāṭ definitely, he captioned it as "Patna Museum Plate" after the place of its deposition as it is now preserved in the Patna Museum. We are inclined to call it Bālāghāṭ plate.*

Unfortunately this, the third one, happens to be the only plate of the charter now known and therefore details like the place of issue, the date and the writer, scribe and the officer under whom it was prepared and, maybe, some other details are unascertainable at present.

It was an exchange gift in lieu of an earlier grant made evidently by the same benefactor, the reasons for the exchange remaining unspecified. Had it been made by some other ruler, it must have been clearly stated as in the previous charter.

The description of Pravara Sena II is accommodated partially; but it contains a *unique statement* about him, viz. 'he wielded a spear by the grace of Śambhu' (*Śambhoḥ prasāde-dhṛita-śūlāyudhasya*) which is not met with anywhere else though he was known to have been a devout worshipper of god Maheśvara and the description that he brought Kṛitayuga by the favour of Śambhu is found in many a record of his.

Like the earlier Tiroḍī charter, the present grant was made only for the augmentation of the religious merit of his honourable mother (*māṭṛi-bhaṭṭārikāṇāṁ puṇy-opachaye*) and her well-being in this and the other world. It is obvious that the reigning king's mother Prabhāvatī Guptā was alive and held in high esteem[74] at the time of the issue of the charter of which the present plate formed a part. Unfortunately its date is not known: whether it was issued prior to or after the Tiroḍī plates which were given in the king's twenty-third year.

18 (M 16)
MANSAR PLATE OF PRAVARA SENA (?)
(Pl. LXVIII)

As averred by Mirashi, the plate was discovered while digging for manganese at Mansar in the Nāgpur district very close to Rāmṭek. But he calls the plate "*Ramtek Plate*" *which is a misnomer*. We prefer to call it after its actual find-spot.

This happens to be the fourth plate of a five-plate charter and mentions only the royal command regarding the privileges and immunities attached to the grant which must have been specified on the previous plate which is now missing. As the first three and the fifth plates are missing, we get no information regarding the place of issue, the family genealogy including the name of the donor, the details about the grant, date and the officials connected with the grant. However, Mirashi attributes it to Pravara Sena II because of the general similarity in palaeographic formations between this and the other plates, including the preceding one. However, such similarity may be noticed even with Rudra Sena II's and Pṛithivī Shena II's records, and as such the attribution cannot be treated as certain.

The charter was briefly noticed by Hiralal[75] and then published by V.V. Mirashi, first in a periodical[76] and thereafter in the *Corpus Inscriptionum Indicarum* volume on the Vākāṭaka inscriptions.

19 (M 18)
UNFINISHED BĀLĀGHAṬ PLATES OF PṚITHIVĪ SHEṆA II
(Pls. LXXXI-LXXXII)

These plates were published originally by F. Kielhorn and thereafter by V.V. Mirashi. We have discussed the contents of this unfinished charter and its historical implications in detail in Appendix II of this part.

VATSAGULMA BRANCH

1 (M 23)
WĀSHIM PLATES OF VINDHYAŚAKTI II, YEAR 37
(Pls. LXXXIII-LXXXV)

PROVENANCE : Wāshim, Wāshim *tahsīl*, Akolā district, Māhārāshṭra.

REFERENCES : Y.K. Deshpande and D.B. Mahajan, *PIHC*, III, pp. 359ff; V.V. Mirashi and D.B. Mahajan, ''Bāsim Plates of Vākāṭaka-Vindhyaśakti II'', *EI*, XXVI, pp. 137-55; D.C. Sircar, ''The Vatsagulma Copper-Plate Grant of Vākāṭaka Vindhyasakti regnal Year 37'', *IHQ*, XVI, pp. 182-86; ''The Vatsagulma Copper-Plate Grant of King Vindhyaśakti II,'' *ibid.*, XVII, pp. 110-16, XVI, pp. 182ff; XVII,pp. 110ff.; *Select Inscriptions,* I, pp. 431-35; V.V. Mirashi, *CII*, V, pp. 93-100.

PLACE OF ISSUE : Vatsagulma, modern Wāshim, Akolā district, Māhārāshṭra.

DONOR : Vindhyaśakti II.

DONEES : Fourteen Brāhmaṇas belonging to Ātharvaṇika *charana* (*Atharvaveda*) of various *gotras* as under. The donated village was divided into four parts of which three were given to the thirteen Brāhmaṇas in various proportions as specified below:

Donee's Name	*Gotra*	*Share*
Jivujja (Jīvārya)	Bhālandāyana	½
Ruddajja (Rudrārya)	Kapiñjala	½
Bhaṭṭidejja (Bhartṛidevārya)	Śrāvishthāyana	½
Deaja (Devārya)	Kauśika	½
Veṇhujja (Vishṇvārya)	do.	½
Vidhijja (Vidhyārya)	do.	½
Pituja (Pitrārya)	Paippalāda	½
Chāndaja (Chandrārya)	Bhālandāyana	½
Jeṭṭhajja (Jyeshthārya)	Kauśika	½
Buddhajja (Buddhārya)	Bhālandāyana	2
Bhāddilajja (Bhadrilārya)	Kauśika	2
Sivajja (Śivārya)	do.	2
Hariṇaja (Hariṇārya)	do.	2
The remaining fourth ($^1/_4$) of the village was given to Revatija (Revatyārya)	do.	

GIFT DETAILS : The village A¯kāsapadda (A¯kāśapadra) close to Tākālakkhoppaka situated in the northern division (*mārga*) of Nāndīkaḍa (Nāndikaṭa). To be divided into four parts as stated in the preceding entry.

DATE : Fourth day of the first fortnight of the winter (hemanta) season falling in the thirty-seventh year of the donor's reign.

SCRIPT : Box-headed variety of the southern class of Brāhmī.

OFFICER : Drafted by *Senāpati* Vaṇhu (Vishṇu).

OBSERVATIONS

From the point of the dynastic history of the Vākāṭakas this charter enjoys the position of a unique source inasmuch as it confirms at least partially the Purāṇic statement that Pravara Sena I, the second member of the undivided family, had at least four sons all of whom became kings. Till the discovery of this record historians were suspicious about the veracity of this averment. This charter for the first time established the existence of another branch of the dynasty ruling from Vatsagulma, the same as modern Wāshim, provenance of the epigraph under reference. The founder of this branch, Sarva Sena (I), was a son of Pravara Sena I with the result that we now know the names of two of the four sons of the latter, the other being Gautamīputra[77] whose son Rudra Sena I was already known to have come to the throne of the other branch of the dynasty.

Although all the members of the Vatsagulma branch were mentioned in the inscription in Cave XVI at Ajantā, its greatly mutilated and fragmentary state made it difficult, nay impossible, to read them with the consequence that there was a lot of confusion and uncertainty among the scholars on its interpretation. The discovery of the present charter made it possible to restore most of the names to their proper place in this branch of the dynasty. With the help of some subsequent discoveries to be noted in the next chapter we are now in a much better position to restore the genealogy and chronology of this branch.

Another important point is that it is composed partly in Prakrit and partly in Sanskrit: the genealogical portion with which the common people had not much to do was composed in Sanskrit while the rest which was in the form of address to the common people of the village in question is drafted in Prakrit showing thereby that the latter was commonly spoken while the former was understood only by the educated people. What is of special interest from a linguistic point of view is that the Prakrit employed in it contains elements of not only what is known to grammarians as Māhārashṭrī but also of other dialects of Prakrit. It shows that the dialects were yet to get localised in the areas after which they got christened later.

From this (viz. linguistic) point it is comparable to the Hirahaḍagallī charter of the early Pallava king Śivaskandavarman which is also drafted partly in Sanskrit and partly in Prakrit.[78] Both these epigraphs reveal a stage when Sanskrit was gradually replacing Prakrit as an epigraphical language.

The charter registers grant of a village to a group of Brāhmaṇas as detailed above. However, Mirashi has misunderstood the grant portion. He observed, "The land or the revenue of the village was divided into four parts, of which three were assigned to eight Brāhmaṇas and the remaining one to one Brāhmaṇa. The shares of the former, again, were not equal; four of them received only half a share and the remaining four, two shares each."[79] As we have seen above, there are many more Brāhmaṇas named as beneficiaries. The correct position is as stated above.

Further, the grant shows that the rule of this branch was not confined to the region of Vidarbha earlier known as Berār but included some more area to its south. If the identification of Nāndīkaḍa with Nañdeḍ, the chief town of the district of that name, is correct, we may conclude that at least during the reign of the second member of this branch, Vindhyaśakti (or Vindhya Sena) II at least a part of the adjoining Marāṭhwāḍā region also formed a part of its domain. Later it paved the way for southward expansion of the kingdom right up to northern Karnataka as will be seen in the sequel.

This happens to be one of the very few Vākāṭaka inscriptions to conclude with an auspicious formula, viz. *siddhir=astu*, 'let there be success'. Another charter, this time belonging to the other branch of the dynasty, that concluded with a similar formula is Waḍgāon plates of the twenty-fifth year of the reign of Pravara Sena II; this grant, however, ended with the expression *śubham=astu*, 'let there be auspicious things'.

The above details about the villages follow V.V. Mirashi as in most of the cases hitherto. However, we feel that D.C. Sircar's interpretaion is preferable. According to it, A¯kāśapadra is here indicative of the village-group denoted by it. So we may render A¯*kāsapaddesu* (Skt. A¯kāśapàdreshu) by 'in the village-group called A¯kāsapadda'. Likewise, Bhākālakkhoppaka may have reference to three villages instead of being the name of just a village; the villages intended may have been known as Bhākā, Lākshā and Uprakā.

Then, Mirashi's and Mahajan's rendering of *Nāndīkaḍasa uttaramagge* by 'on the road going to the North from Nāndīkada'[80] is defective. In fact, in the Vākāṭaka inscriptions *mārga* is frequently employed for a small administrative division like modern *tahsīl* or *tālukā*. It is, of course, true that originally the word must have been used in the sense of a 'path' or 'road'; but like Uttarāpatha and Dakshiṇāpatha, which too originally connoted roads to north and south and later came to be used in the sense of the regions the routes traversed through, its connotation also came to be expanded to cover the area through which it passed. Mirashi seems to have realised it later and in his later edition in the *CII* he corrected the original rendering substituting it by 'in the northern division of Nāndīkaḍa'.[81]

2 (M 24)
INDIA OFFICE PLATE OF DEVA SENA
(Pl. LXXXIX)

How and from where this single plate of a charter of Deva Sena reached the India Office at London is not known. This is the first plate of a multiplate plate-grant and was published by H.N. Randle in the *New Indian Antiquary*, II, pp. 177-80,[82] and a note on it was published in *ibid.*, pp. 721-23[83] by V.V. Mirashi who edited it later in the *Corpus Inscriptionum Indicarum*, V, pp. 101-02. Unfortunately the remaining plates of the charter are not forthcoming.

As the plate does not commence with the word *dṛishṭam*, 'seen', does not give the genealogical account in the beginning and contains several grammatical errors, Randle felt that the Vākāṭaka official concerned rejected the plate before the charter could be completed.[84] However, these arguments are not convincing. The word *dṛishṭam*, though met with in most of the charters, is not found in the Ṛiddhapur plates of Prabhāvatī Guptā about whose genuineness there can be no doubt. Almost all the Vākāṭaka copper-plate charters are replete with numerous grammatical errors, and this obviously cannot be taken as a ground for their spuriousness. Then, the recent discovery of the Bīdar charter of Deva Sena[85] and the Thāḷner plates of Hari Sheṇa[86] shows that the members of the Vatsagulma branch of the dynasty were keen on introducing novelty and made some experiments with the genealogical account, and it is quite possible that the plate in question represents an early stage in this venture.

The charter was issued from Vatsagulma, and begins straightaway with the mention of the Vākāṭaka *Mahārāja* Deva Sena's order regarding the grant. The addresses include the touring royal officers (*kula-putras*) like *bhaṭas* (policemen), *bhojakas* (district officers), and *daṇḍa-nāyakas* (military or judicial officers) in the northern division (*uttara-mārga*) of Nāṅgara-kāṭaka wherein probably the donated village was situated, its name being perhaps Yappajja. The donees were the Brāhmaṇas Dharmasvāmin and Bhavasvāmin of the Śāṇḍilya *gotra*. None of these localities can be identified definitely, though they might have been situated in the Akolā district or nearby.

3 (M 25)
AJANTĀ CAVE (XVI) INSCRIPTION OF VARĀHADEVA, MINISTER OF HARI SHEṆA
(Pl. XCIII)

This large lithic inscription of the time of the last known member of the Vatsagulma branch of the Vākāṭakas has been known now for over a century and a quarter[87] and has been noticed and edited by a number of well-known epigraphists since 1862 when it was first noticed by Bhau Daji.[88] Thereafter it was edited with an introductory note and an English rendering by Pandit Bhagvanlal Indraji in 1881 and it marked a great improvement over Bhau Daji's edition. It was next published in 1883 by George Bühler[90] and in 1941 by V.V. Mirashi[91] who also included it in his work on the inscriptions of the Vākāṭakas published in 1963.[92] D.C. Sircar has re-published it with some improvements[93] and some other scholars also wrote on and discussed its historical contents.[94]

The inscription is very badly damaged owing to the inclemencies of weather for over a millennium and a half and chipping, perhaps deliberate, of some parts of the stone which have led to a lot of confusion and glaring differences of readings and interpretations. When this inscription was first noticed little was known about the Vākāṭakas and absolutely nothing regarding their Vatsagulma branch. With the subsequent discovery of the Wāshim grant of Vindhyasakti II historians came to know of the existence of an offshoot of the dynasty ruling from Vatsagulma and it became clear that the Ajantā lithic inscription belonged to the minister Varāhadeva of the last known member of this branch, viz. Hari Sheṇa.

The large inscription aims at recording the excavation and decoration with paintings and sculptures of the caye (XVI) at Ajantā, the provenance of the epigraph, and its donation to the Buddhist Order of monks (*bhikshu-saṅgha*) by Varāhadeva, a minister of the Vākāṭaka king Hari Shena. And, what is more important historically, it gives an account of the genealogy and some account of the Vatsagulma branch of the dynasty beginning from Vindhyaśakti I, the founder, and his son and successor Pravara Sena I, whose sons and grandsons established different branches of the family. One of his sons was Sarva Sena (I) who founded the Vatsagulma branch.

Vindhyaśakti is called a *dvija* (Brāhmaṇa in this case), and his successes over his unspecified enemies are lauded in hyperbolic terms (verses 2-5). Though no regal title is used for him in the preserved portion of this highly damaged record, it need not be stretched too much in view of the fact that the record is composed in verses and the poet had to cope up with metrical exigencies. The following stanza (6) is devoted to his son and successor Pravara Sena I whose feet are said to have been embraced by the crowned heads of his enemy kings. The poet next naturally switches over to the Vatsagulma branch whose founder Sarva Sena was Pravara Sena I's son and is described as the overlord of kings (*pārthiv-endra*) and as one who conquered all the armies (*jita-sarva-sena*).[95] His son and successor Vindhya Sena, evidently identical with Vindhyaśakti (II) of the Wāshim plates and Vindhya Sena of the Bīdar grant of his descendent Deva Sena,[96] is eulogised in verse 8 which materially adds to our knowledge by crediting him with a victory over the Kuntala (southern part of Māhārāshṭra and the adjoining region of Karnataka including the Kadamba capital Vanavāsī in the Uttara [North] Kannada district) king who must have belonged to the Kadamba dynasty. He was followed by his son named Pravara Sena (II) after his illustrious homonymous great-grandfather (verse 9), and the latter by his eight-year-old son (verse 10) whose name is lost in the record under reference but is known to be Sarva Sena (II) from the Thālner charter of his descendent Hari Shena.[97] The next king was his son and successor Deva Sena (verse 11) whose minister Hastibhoja is described eulogistically in as many as five stanzas (12-16). About his son and successor Hari Shena (verses 17-18), the last known member of this branch, we get the unique information[98] that he did something (perhaps defeated) to (the kings of) Kuntala, Avanti, Kaliṅga, Kosala(ā), Trikūṭa, Lāṭa and Andhra and perhaps Aparānta[99] (verse 18). The description is, of course, to be taken as hyperbolic and indicating not actually victories but only as hurried raids without any permanent outcome. His minister was Hastibhoja's son Varāhadeva,[100] the hero of the inscription, whose qualities of head and heart claim as many as three stanzas (19-21). Next we are told that realising the transient character of life, riches and worldly pleasures and for the religious merit of his mother and father he got a residence (*veśma*), evidently the cave in which the record is incised, for the enjoyment (viz. residence) of the best of ascetics (*yatīndra-sevya*), executed on the mountain. It was endowed with the painted galleries, windows, doors, ledges, female figures, beautiful columns, staircases, and *chaitya-mandira* inside (viz. at the rear-end) as well as a Nāga shrine and a reservoir of water. It was made over to the *saṅgha* by Varāhadeva together with his relations and dedicated to the three jewels (*ratna-traya*). It was nicknamed by the people as ...viśāla[101] out of love, joy and gratification. At the end a wish for its permanence is expressed (verses 22-32) as usual in all such cases.

One very important point that has escaped the notice of all the scholars who have written on this record is that there is a clear indication in the inscription itself that there must have elapsed some time between the execution of this exquisite rock monument, which is one of the best at Ajantā, and the incision of this epigraph. Verse 29 states that the people gave it a *viśāla*-ending name out of love, joy and satisfaction. If the name were given by the benefactor himself, it was possibly simultaneously or before or immediately after its excavation. But the record clearly ascribes this name to the people, and therefore it is obvious that there must have elapsed a few years, say ten, after the execution of the cave and causing the inscription to be incised, both, of course, during the reign of the Vākāṭaka king Hari Shena.

4 (M 26)
GHAṬOTKACHA CAVE INSCRIPTION OF VARĀHADEVA, MINISTER OF HARI SHEṆA
(Pls. XCIV-XCV)

This completely versified inscription in eighteen lines and like number of verses in a variety of metres composed in Sanskrit and incised in the box-headed characters of the southern variety of Brāhmī, like the previous one, belongs to Hari Sheṇa's minister Varahādeva but is much more damaged and several verses, especially towards the end are almost lost with only some words decipherable now. It is engraved on the left end of the back wall of the verandah of the cave called Ghaṭotkacha at the place known as Gulwāḍā, eleven miles west of Ajantā. It was first edited by Pandit Bhagvanlal Indraji in 1881[102] and a couple of years later by George Bühler.[103] Finally it was edited by V.V. Mirashi with the help of better impressions available to him which marked several improvements in the readings and made more dependable interpretations possible.[104]

While the previous epigraph gives a fairly dependable geneaological account of the Vatsagulma branch of the Vākāṭakas and of the undivided dynasty for two earlier generations, the present inscription refers only to the last two members of the Vatsagulma branch only incidentally in the context of their ministers Hastibhoja and Varāhadeva while at the same time giving a detailed account of the ministerial line from the very start. Thus, the two records are complementary to each other in their contents.

The inscription is sectarian and relates to Buddhism. The first two stanzas are devoted to the praise of the Buddha, Dharma and Gaṇa or Saṅgha, the three jewels of Buddhism. From the next stanza starts the account of the family of Varāhadeva, a minister (*sachiva*) of the last known member of the Vatsagulma branch of the Vākāṭakas, and we are introduced to the famous Brāhmaṇa family of the south called Vallūra, so-called perhaps after the place Velūr in the Karīmnagar district of Andhra Pradesh (verse 3). The first member of this line was Yajñapati who is compared to the well-known sages Bhrigu, Atri, Garga and Angiras, but had no political importance (verse 4). His son Deva was evidently more important and is said to have been endowed with polity and action and the whole kingdom (*rāshṭra*) together with its king is described as performing its pious duties on account of him (5). His son Soma took Brāhmaṇa and Kshatriya wives and from the latter had a handsome son named Ravi marked with regal signs who established his authority over the whole province (*vishaya*). The sons born of Brāhmaṇa wives became excellent Vedic scholars and were still well-known as Vallūra in the southern direction, viz. south India (6-8). Ravi's son was Pravara, Pravara's son was Śrī-Rāma, the latter's son was Kīrti and Kīrti's son was Hastibhoja (9) who rose to an important position under the Vākāṭaka king Deva Sena who is also called Devarāja (10-12).[105] Hastibhoja's son Varāhadeva became the minister under Devarāja's son Hari Shena. It appears that Hastibhoja had several sons of whom Varāhadeva was very dear to him and endowed with hundreds of virtues (13-18).[105]

The object of the inscription, which must have been recorded in one of the concluding stanzas which are sadly mutilated, was evidently to register the excavation of the Vihāra cave presently known as Ghaṭotkacha and its dedication to the local Budhist *saṅgha*. But unfortunately its details cannot be made out now because of the highly fragmentary condition of the epigraph in this portion.

Mirashi, to whom we owe the best possible edition of the inscription, has tried to show that all the members of the Vallūra Brāhmaṇa line from Deva to Varāhadeva were ministers of the Vākāṭakas from the time of the founder Vindhyaśakti (I) through Pravara Sena (I) to the last member of the Vatsagulma branch and has given the likely order of succession of the two families.[106] This inscription, according to him, constitutes one of the evidences for the alleged southern original home of the Vākāṭakas. But the reconstruction is purely gratuitous and based on an unproved hypothesis. There is absolutely nothing to show that the two lines were connected with each other from the very start. The second member of the Vallūra Brāhmaṇa line, Deva, is no doubt described as associated with some kingdom, but it is not specified and might have been some South Indian ruling family, perhaps in Andhra Pradesh. The first member clearly associated with the Vākāṭakas was its penultimate progeny Hastibhoja who was a minister (*sachiva*) under the Vākāṭaka king Deva Sena of the Vatsagulma branch to be followed by Varāhadeva who inherited this office from his father Hastibhoja under the next king Hari Sheṇa, the son and successor of Devarāja *alias* Deva Sena. As is well-known, the ministerial families are known to have hailed from distant localities, and it is not at all surprising if some of the members of the Vatsagulma branch of the Vākāṭakas took their ministers (or some of them, for Hastibhoja and Varahadeva only are called *sachivas*) from the neighbouring Andhra country. It may be pointed out that the last two members of this branch of the Vākāṭakas had very close contacts with some of the South Indian ruling families like the Vishṇukuṇḍins and the Kadambas and exerted a lot of influence on the latter. It would have therefore been in keeping with the guidelines laid for the victors by ancient Indian political thinkers to appoint some ministers from the newly conquered or annexed territory. Therefore the inscription has nothing to do with the theory of South Indian origin of the Vākāṭakas: neither positive nor negative.

5 (M 27)
AJANTĀ CAVE XVII INSCRIPTION OF RAVISĀMBA, VASSAL OF HARI SHEṆA
(Pl. XCVI)

The inscription is incised on a side-wall outside the verandah in cave XVII at Ajantā in box-headed variety of the southern class of Brāhmī in twenty-nine Sanskrit stanzas in a variety of metres. It was edited first by Bhau Daji in 1863[107] though it had been noticed several times earlier.[108] Next it was edited by Bhagvanlal Indraji[109] and George Bühler[110] and finally by V.V. Mirashi.[111]

The inscription is very badly damaged owing to exposure to the inclemencies of weather for over fifteen centuries and a considerable part of each of the twenty-nine lines has been lost irretrievably owing to the trickling of rain-water over it in addition to a few letters at places becoming faint and illegible. Resultantly, it has become almost impossible to determine its contents correctly and with certainty. As will be seen, some of the names are lost and the mutual relationships of some of the personages, which were specified in the epigraph, cannot be ascertained.

The record was put up by the penultimate member of a ruling family brought to light by it only. It or at least its last chief was a vassal of the Vākāṭaka king Hari Shena. It opens with an adoration of the Buddha followed by an account of the family of the donor of the *vihāra* (*vihāra-kartṛi*), which may be given in a tabular form as under:-

Name lost
1
Dhṛitarāshṭra
1
(son ?)
Harisāmba
1
Śaurisāmba
1
(son ?)
Upendragupta
1
(younger son)
Kācha I
1
(son ?)
Bhikshudāsa
1
Nīladāsa
1
(son ?)
Kācha II
1
Kṛishṇadāsa married Atichandrā
1
Dharādhipa Ravisāmba

The interrogation marks after 'son' within parentheses indicate the absence, within the preserved portion, of any indication of the mutual relationship of the personages concerned, though it may be assumed, with great probability, that they were related to one another as father and son. Mirashi observes that the name of the elder brother of Ravisāmba, the last known member of the family, has not been preserved though 'he bore the title of a king'.[112] However, the expression *Dharādhip-ākhyam* employed in connection with the first prince (*kumāra*) appears to denote 'one bearing the name Dharādhipa' even as *Ravisāmba-saṁjñam* used for the second son and rightly taken to mean bearing 'the appellation Ravisāmba'.[113] The name Dharādhipa, 'lord of the earth', need not be regarded as unusual as names like Narendra, 'lord of men', and Bhūpati or Avanīndra, 'lord of the earth', are known to have been borne by individuals.

Utterly grieved at the untimely decease of Ravisāmba, his elder brother Dharādhipa developed an utter distaste for worldly pleasures and riches and pursued a pious life dedicated to Buddhism. He covered his kingdom with *stūpas* and *vihāras* and made charities to the suppliants. Finally, and that is the object of the epigraph, a monolithic hall (Cave XVII) with a *chaitya* of the Munirāja (viz. Buddha) and near it a large water-cistern and a grand *gandha-kuṭi* Chaitya (Cave XIX) to its west was created at a huge cost and donated to the local Buddhist *saṅgha*. And the record ends with a wish for the longevity and permanence of these monuments.

Mirashi feels that the ruling family represented by the above genealogy was ruling over the Khāndesh region of Māhārāshṭra anciently known as Ṛishīka, which he further equates with Asika of the Nāsik inscription of the nineteenth year of the reign of the Sātavāhana monarch Vāsishṭhīputra Puḷumāvi.[114] However, it is not warranted by the evidence at our disposal. We have already seen that the last two inscriptions of the reign of Hari Sheṇa register the execution of caves at Ajantā and nearby Gulwāḍā by his minister Varāhadeva, and the absence of any allusion to the local ruling family clearly shows that the region was governed directly by the Vākāṭakas. As against this, we know from the Thāḷner grant of Bhānusheṇa that his ancestors of the Kumbhakarṇa line were ruling, perhaps as feudatories of the Vākāṭakas, over the nearby Dhule region,[115] and if at all the Ajantā region was administered by any feudatory family it should have been that called Kumbhakarṇa. Then, there is clear literary evidence to show that Asika was not the Prakrit form of Ṛishīka as commonly supposed by historians, and both these are known as two distinct people and regions to ancient Indian geographical tradition.[116]

We are inclined to support Bhagvanlal Indraji's view that the ruling family belonged to the Aśmaka country, which in our opinion included the southern part of the Marāṭhwādā region to the south of the river Godāvarī together with some part of the Telaṅgānā region of Andhra Pradesh. In verse 10 of the record in question containing the name Aśmaka etc. (*Aśmak-ādi*), Mirashi read before it the four letters as *nīyochchhrita* which, according to him, referred to the subjugation of the prosperous countries like Aśmaka by the last two members of the ruling family.[117] However, even if his reading were to be accepted,[118] it would not support the suggested meaning. For referring to victory *jitvā* would have been the most efficient expression and *jitv=ochchhritam=Aśmak-ādikam* would not have affected the metre also. Holy places in ancient India were nobody's monopoly and any one could visit them and do pious acts there unhindered by the ruling family of the region. However, when an outsider, particularly a member of the ruling family, did such things, he felt it desirable to introduce himself, and this explains why we are faced with the genealogical account of the ruling family which had under its rule Aśmaka and other regions which are said to have prospered under the two royal brothers.

Verse 21 contains the conventional coaxing description of the family's overlord: we are told that the earth was then protected by Hari Sheṇa, the moon among the kings with his face resembling the lotus and the moon and engaged in doing good to his subjects.[119] We thus learn from this inscription that Aśmaka was one of the dependencies of the Vatsagulma branch of the Vākāṭakas during at least the reign of its last known member, if not earlier. Thus the rule of this branch of the family extended at least up to the Telangānā region of Andhra Pradesh in the south. And herein lies the great historical value of the epigraph.

Notes and References

1. The year is printed differently in *Studies in Indology*, I, 2nd ed., p. 126 (1936) and in the *Inscriptions of the Vākāṭakas*, *CII*, V, p. 1 (1935).
2. *Proceedings and Transactions of the All-India Oriental Conference*, 8th session, pp. 613 ff.; *Studies in Indology*, I, 1960, pp. 109-17; 2nd ed., pp. 125-34; *CII*, V, pp. 1-4.
3. For original citations, *vide* P.V. Kane, *History of Dharmaśāstra*, III, p. 243, fn. 326; Laxmanshastri Joshi, *Dharmakośa*, Vyavahāra-kāṇḍa, I, p. 26.
4. Jāmb (*CII*, V, p. 12, line 23), Belorā (Set A, *ibid.*, p. 19, line 17; Set B, *ibid.*, p. 20, I. 18), Siwanī (*ibid.*, p. 30, line 26), Tirodī (*ibid.*, p. 40, line 12) and Indore (*ibid.*, p. 40, line 12) plates of Pravāra Sena II and Wāshim plates of Vindhyaśakti II of the Vatsagulma branch of the dynasty contain this expression which has been taken by Mirashi to refer to the chief temple at the capital which is not only quite unwarranted but in fact negated by some other charters not only of Pravara Sena II but of some other rulers of the dynasty given from places other than their capital.
5. During the earlier Sātavāhana-Kshatrapa period the grants were announced in the town assembly (*nigama-sabhā*) and the deeds of grants (*paṭikā* or *phalaka*) preserved in the records office (*phalaka-vāra*) according to the prevailing custom (*charitra*) as we learn from a Nāsik inscription of Nahapāna (*HISWK*, p. 99, lines 4 and 6), who had temporarily occupied western Maharashtra (Nāsik-Puṇe region) about mid-first century AD.
6. Māṇḍhaḷ Pls. of Pṛithivī Sheṇa II, Year 2, *EI*, XLI, p. 167, line 20.
7. Māṇḍhaḷ Pls. of Pṛithivī Sheṇa II, Year 10, *ibid.*, p. 178, line 30.
8. Māhurjharī Pls. of Pṛithivī Sheṇa II, Year 17, *ABORI*, LIII, pp. 193-94, lines 31-32.

9. Mirashi reads Chikambari in the Aśokan edict, but there is a faint trace of the medial sign for *u* at the right bottom of the letter *b*.
10. *Inscriptions in the Central Provinces and Berar*, p. 15.
11. There are a few exceptions like the Ṛiddhapur plates of Prabhāvatī Guptā (*CII*, V, No. 8) and the India Office Plate of Deva Sena (*ibid.*, No. 24).
12. V.B. Kolte ("Mahurzari Plates of Pṛithivīṣeṇa II", *ABORI*, LIII, 1972, pp. 183-94) is also of the view that palaeographically the plate belongs to pre-Pravara Sena II period.
13. B. Ch. Chhabra, "Bamhanī Plates of Pāṇḍava King Bharatabala, Year 2", *EI*, XXVII, pp. 132-45; V.V. Mirashi, *CII*, V, pp. 83-84.
14. Ajay Mitra Shastri, *Inscriptions of the Śarabhapurīyas, Paṇḍuvaṁśins and Somavaṁśins*, Part II, pp. 80-85.
15. For discussion of the problem, see *ibid.*, Part I, pp. 122-27; "The Date of the Bamhanī and Mallār Plates of Śūrabala Udīrṇavaira", *Bhāratī-Bhānam* (Dr. K.V. Sarma Felicitation Volume), pp. 439-43.
16. Ajay Mitra Shastri and Chandrashekhar Gupta, "Dvitīya Rudrasenāchā Māṇḍhaḷa Tāmrapaṭa", *Saṁśodhanāchī Kshitije* (Marathi), pp. 222-32.
17. Ajay Mitra Shastri and Chandrashekhar Gupta, "Māsoda Copper-Plate Charter of Pravāra Sena II, Year 19", *JESI*, X, p. 113, line 19. For its date, *vide ibid.*, XI, p. 114.
18. For discussion, *vide* Appendix I of this part.
19. Identified localities are situated in the Nāgpur-Wardhā area.
20. Still designated after 'Durg', the district wherein it is located, by Mirashi.
21. The inordinately long regency of Prabhāvatī Guptā when Divākara Sena must have become fairly aged to assume the charge of the kingdom might have as well been dictated by some other considerations like illness.
22. The scribe tried to inscribe a few letters in box-headed variety but later adopted the nail-headed variety with which he was more familiar.
23. And for that matter, kings generally did not interfere in the scribes' work.
24. Recently discovered but yet to be published Miregāon and Ṛiddhapur charters.
25. For a discussion, see Appendix II of Part II.
26. *Vide* No. 1 of Chapter II for details.
27. For discussion, see *EI*, XXVI, pp. 157-58.
28. *Vide ibid.*, p. 155, caption.
29. Probably Mirashi realised it later and accordingly captioned his writing on it in the *CII* volume as 'Jāmb Plates'.
30. Vide caption in *EI*, XXIV, p. 260.
31. *Vide* P.V. Kane, *History of Dharmaśāstra*, II, 867; D.C. Sircar, *Indian Epigraphy*, p. 435; J.F. Fleet, *IA*, XXX, pp. 201ff; L.S. Joshi (ed.), *Dharmakośa*, vol. I, Part III, p. 1609.
31a. In all cases where the *gotra* is not named, the preceding one is to be understood.
32. *Vide* no. 2 of Chapter II of this Part.
33. According to A.S. Altekar (*MSGH*, I, p. 178), 'it was about four acres in extent'; however, no authority is cited in support.

34. *CII*, V, pp. 45, 55, 69; *EI*, XXXVIII, p. 55. Another grant of Pravāra Sena II from Māsoda (*JESI*, X, p. 113, line 20) also, like the present charter, mentions 300 lands and should refer to 300 *nivartanas.*

35. *ASWI*, IV, pp. 96-97, nos. 20, 24-29; Lüders List, nos. 1158, 1162, 1163, 1164, 1166, 1167. The gifted pieces of land measured 26, 20, 15, 12, 8, 4, 3 and 2 *nivartanas. Vide* also V.V. Mirashi, *HISWK*, pp. 26-27, 34.

36. Ancient texts like the *Charaka-saṁhitā* refer to two sets of weights and measures prevailing in Magadha and Kaliṅga; the former was generally adopted in extensive areas under the Mauryas and became more popular in course of time. Likewise, some other systems might have obtained in some other areas.

37. *Vide CII*, V, p. 55, line 20 (Waḍgāon); *JESI*, X, p. 113, line 20 (Māsoda); *EI*, XXXVIII, p. 55, lines 20-21 (Pauni).

38. For their separateness, see below.

39. The Puṇe plates have in this place the expression *Gupt-ādirāja* which might admit of a stretched interpretation, viz. 'who was preceded by Gupta'.

40. The actual expression is *Vākāṭakānām Mahārāja-śrī-Dāmodarasena-Pravārasena-jananī*, line 19.

41. *History of India 150-350 A.D.*, p. 63.

42. *JRASB*, XII, pp. 1ff.; XX, pp. 101-05.

43. *Ibid.*, XII, pp. 71ff.; XIII, pp. 75-78; *Select Inscriptions*, I, p. 440, fn. 2.

44. Like V.V. Mirashi, *CII*, V, pp. 35 (discussion) and 37 (translation).

45. *Vide* Ajay Mitra Shastri in *JESI*, XIV, pp. 38-40.

46. *Vide* Chapter II, No. IV, of this Part for the stanza and discussion.

47. A stanza of his is cited by Śrīdharadāsa in his anthology *Saduktikarṇāmṛita* (II. 31.4) where he is mentioned only as *Yuvarāja*.

48. Y.R. Gupte read *di* instead of (*jī*) and the whole expression accordingly was taken by him to read as *s-āgra-varsha-śata-diva-putra-pautrā*. He proposed to render it as (i) who has sons and grandsons, a life of full hundred years and will (in the end) live in heaven, or (ii) who has renowned sons and grandsons and who has lived a life of full hundred years. *Vide JASB*, NS, XX, pp. 56 and 60. As pointed out by Jagannath Agarwal (*PIHC*, IVth Session, Lahore, 1940, pp. 58f.; *Researches in Indian Epigraphy and Numismatics*, pp. 27-28), the scribe by oversight omitted the top horizontal stroke here as well as in *jitam* at the beginning of the record and that the correct reading is *jiva* (*jīva*).

49. This is the view of R.C. Majumdar and D.C. Sircar.

50. *Op.cit.* A widow would hardly take pride in living a life of over 100 years in ancient India. She had to lead a very simple and frugal life as seen from the Nāṇeghāṭ sacrificial inscription and the Nāsik inscription of the nineteenth year of Vāsishṭhīputra Puḷumāvi and from the prescriptions in the Dharmaśāstra texts.

51. For other parallels, *vide* Jagannath Agarwal, *op.cit.; CII*, V, pp. viii, fn. 2, 34, fn. 4.

52. *Ibid.*, p. 37, translation.

53. D.C. Sircar (*Select Inscriptions*, I, p. 441, fn. 1) takes the expression to mean 'field that

they already enjoy' which may also be correct.

54. *Vide* also No. V of the next chapter for the first plate of the charter.

55. D.C. Sircar, *Indian Epigraphy*, pp. 111-13.

56. The word is misplaced: *bhagavat-pāda* in line 20 and *mūla* in line 13.

57. *Inscriptions in the Central Provinces and Berar*, No. 168, p. 93.

58. *CII*, V, p. 66, lines 26 and 29.

59. V.B. Kolte (*ABORI*, LIII, p. 193, line 27) read it as *Surambī-rājye*, but we (*ibid.*, LXXVI, pp. 36-37; *AV*, p. 246) corrected it to *Arambī-rājye* which is admitted by Kolte (*vide* his *Mahārāshṭrātīla kāhī Tāmrapata va Śilālekha* [Marathi], p. 52) also.

60. It included parts of the Nāgpur, Sāoner and Kāṭol *tehsīls* of the Nāgpur district and the adjoining areas of the Chhindwārā district.

61. *Vide ABORI*, LXXVI, p. 37.

62. The latest such record is the Malhārā charter of the Muṇḍaputra king Ādityarāja of the post-Vākāṭaka period. *Vide* our paper in *JESI*, IV, pp. 30-41.

63. *Cf. Rāmagiri-sthāna* and *Bennatata-sthana* mentioned as issuing places in the two Māṇḍhaḷ charters of Pṛithivī Sheṇa II.

64. Namidāsa even otherwise appears to be rather a strange name as Chamidāsa undoubtedly is.

65. It is also possible that in this as well as in another record (No. 27) *Vaji* actually refers to the Vājasaneyī *śākhā* of the White *Yajurveda* to which the donees belonged while the next component might have been the *gotra*-name.

66. This is one of the few explicit mentions of the land-measure *nivartana* as such whereas in other cases it is indicated either only by the figures or figures preceded by the word *bhūmi*, *nivartana* being left only to inference.

67. *EI*, XXVII, p. 76, fn. 1. As B. Ch. Chhabra and N. Lakshminarayana Rao are both named editors on the title page, it is difficult to decide the name of the editor of this paper.

68. While editing the record in *EI*, XXVII, pp. 74-79, Mirashi ignored the reference to the twentieth year (*viśatima saṁvatsare*) in lines 20-21 altogether and felt that it was perhaps a mistake for *pañchaviṁśatitame* (*vide* p. 77, fn. 12) and described the *akshara ñcha* in line 42 as superfluous (p. 79, fn. 9). But in *CII*, V, p. 54, fn. 1, he makes a reference to it and observes that it is a mistake and perhaps *pañcha* is omitted before *viśatima* in line 20 and that the syllable *ñcha* in the last line may have been a part of *pañcha* inserted in the wrong place. He finds it difficult to explain the phenomenon of the grant remaining unregistered for five years.

69. Ajay Mitra Shastri, "Mandhal Copper-Plate Charter of Pravāra Sena II, Year 16", *EI*, pp. 74 and 76 and lines 19 and 44 respectively.

70. If the grant and its recording were made in the same year, the additional mention of the regnal year will have to be explained.

71. This was the only reading suggested there.

72. *CII*, V, p. 56, fn. 13.

73. Mirashi spells the initial letter as cerebral (Ṭ), but it should be dental.

74. Note the use of the suffix *bhaṭṭārikā*.

75. *Inscriptions in the Central Provinces and Berar*, pp. 4-5.
76. *Nagpur University Journal*, III, pp. 20-21.
77. It is only a matronymic, the personal name of this prince still remaining unknown.
78. D.C. Sircar, *Select Inscriptions*, I, pp. 461-66. The short inscription on the seal and line 52 (last line) giving respectively the donor's name and containing an auspicious formula only are in Sanskrit and the rest in Prakrit.
79. *EI*, XXVI, p. 139; *CII*, V, pp. 94-95.
80. *EI*, XXVI, p. 140.
81. *CII*, pp. 94, 98.
82. Under the title "An Unpublished India Office Plate of the Vākāṭaka Maharaja Davasena".
83. The note is captioned "A Note on the India Office Plate of Devasena".
84. *NIA*, II, p. 182.
85. See No. XII of the next chapter.
86. *Ibid.*, No. XIII.
87. It was first noticed in 1862.
88. *JBBRAS*, VII, 1862, pp. 73-74.
89. *Inscriptions in the Cave-Temples of Western India*, pp. 69-73.
90. *ASWI*, IV, pp. 124-28.
91. *Hyderabad Archaeological Series*, No. XIV, 1941.
92. *CII*, V, pp. 103-11. He also discussed its contents in *EI*, XXVI, pp. 142-48 where he first brought out the real significance of the inscription in the light of the Wāshim plates of Vindhyaśakti II.
93. *Select Inscriptions*, I, pp. 449-55. He also referred to its contents in *CA*, pp. 185ff.
94. A.C. Biswas, "A Note on the Ajanta Inscription of the Vākāṭakas", *IC*, VII, pp. 372-75, etc.
95. It is obviously inspired by the desire of the composer to have a Yamaka based on the name Sarva Sena and not much value can be attached to this statement.
96. For Bīdar grant, see next chapter, No. XII. Some earlier scholars read *Pṛithivī Sheṇa* and D.C. Sircar (*Select Inscriptions*, I, p. 451, fn. 3; *CA*, p. 185) feels that if this reading be correct, Pṛithivī Sheṇa may have been a brother of Vindhya Sena. The name Vindhya Sena, which is found not only in this record but also in the Bīdar charter of Deva Sena, was obviously felt to be in line with the name-ending or surname Sena which is added to the names of all the members not only of this but also of the only other branch of the dynasty known hitherto.
97. For this charter, see No. XIII of the next chapter.
98. Such information is not recorded in any official charter of any of the two hitherto known branches of the dynasty which contain highly conventionalised draft. And it is only in this inscription that we meet with such information about Vindhya Sena and the last known king Hari Sheṇa. It is possible that similar information regarding a few other members of the branch was also recorded but is now lost.
99. *Vide* Shobhana Gokhale, "Epigraphical Evidence on Harisheṇa's Conquest from Kānherī", *AV*, pp. 277-78.

100. Like several other records, it shows the hereditary nature of the various offices in ancient India including the Deccan.
101. Unfortunately the first part of the name is lost irretrievably.
102. *Inscriptions in the Cave-Temples of Western India*, pp. 88ff.
103. *ASWI*, IV, pp. 138ff.
104. *CII*, V, pp. 112-19.
105. The long description in these stanzas is unfortunately almost completely lost with only some names preserved; it is likely that this portion contained some important historical information regarding the closing phase of the Vatsagulma line; but it cannot be retrieved.
106. *Ibid.*, p. 114.
107. *JBBRAS*, VII, pp. 53ff.
108. *JASB*, V, p. 554; *JBBRAS*, VII, pp. 55f.
109. *Inscriptions from the Cave-Temples of Western India*, 1881, pp. 73ff.
110. *ASWI*, IV, pp. 128ff.
111. *Hyderabad Archaeological Series*, No. 15; *CII*, V, pp. 120-29.
112. *Ibid.*, V, p. 122.
113. *Ibid.*, V, p. 128 (Engl. translation of verse 9).
114. *Ibid.*, V, pp. 123-24. For reference to Asika, *vide HISWK*, p. 45, line 2.
115. For the charters, see Moreshwar G. Dikshit, "Two Charters of Bhānusheṇa,. Year 30", *EI*, XXXVIII, pp. 69-75; for discussion, see Ajay Mitra Shastri, "A Note on the Thālner Plates of Bhānu Sheṇa", *JESI*, XII, 1985, pp. 53-58.
116. See Ajay Mitra Shastri, *Varāhamihira's India*, pp. 67 and 90.
117. *CII*, V, pp. 123, 128 (translation of verse 10).
118. On checking the facsimile accompanying his edition of the text, we find that while the reading-*chchhrita* is quite certain, the reading of the two preceding *aksharas* is highly doubtful.
119. The wording of the preserved portion of the stanza is *vadan-āravinda-chandre paripālayati kshitīśa-chandre Harisheṇe hita-kāriṇi prajānām.* It reminds us of similar descriptions of the Gupta overlords in some of the epigraphs of their feudatories.

APPENDIX I

Nachnā-kī-talāi and Ganj Inscriptions of the Time of Vākāṭaka Pṛithivī Sheṇa: The Problem of Attribution

(Pls. III-V)

Sir Alexander Cunningham located in 1883-84 a couple of inscriptions in a small village called Nachnā-kī-talāī (literally, 'tank of Nachnā') on two faces of a loose lithic slab found lying in the ground outside the fort of Kuṭhārā or Kuṭhārgaḍh in the Jaso State now included in the Pannā district of Madhya Pradesh. Of these, one inscription is only partially engraved and the scribe after engraving the first few words comprising sixteen letters realised that the face was too rough and then inscribed the entire record again on another face completely. Cunningham gave his reading of the text of the complete inscription together with the lithographs of both of them in the *Reports of the Archaeological Survey of India*, Vol. XXI (1885), pp. 97f. Later, both the inscriptions together with illustrations were incorporated by J.F. Fleet in his *Inscriptions of the Early Gupta Kings and their Successors.*[1] A few decades later in 1919 Rakhaladas Banerji found another identical inscription engraved on a detached slab lying at the bottom of a *ḍongā* close to a ruined structure, perhaps a dam to hold the waters of the stream passing along the said *ḍongā,* at the village of Ganj, not very far from the provenance of the aforesaid records then included in the Ajaygaḍh State of the Bundelhaṇḍ Agency now forming part of the Pannā district. It was published by V.S. Sukthankar.[2] V.V. Mirashi included all these three records in his *Inscriptions of the Vākāṭakas.*[3]

If we ignore the incomplete inscription,[4] the two inscriptions are identical literally in text and script which respectively are in Sanskrit and box-headed variety of the southern Brāhmī. They refer to some pious acts of a personage called Vyāghradeva and described as meditating upon the feet of Pṛithvī Sheṇa, the *Mahārāja* of the Vākāṭakas, for the religious merit of his parents.[5] What these pious acts were is nowhere specified. The only word used is *kṛitam* which is an error for *kṛitavān* meaning 'did' or 'made'. Obviously the slabs in question in both the cases formed part of the structure erected by Vyāghradeva which could have been anything. But it appears most likely on circumstantial evidence that the Ganj inscription refers to the construction of the aforesaid dam. Similar might have been the case with the Nachnā-kī-talāi inscription though the possibility of an allusion to some temple or image cannot be ruled out altogether.

Vyāghradeva is said to have been meditating on the feet of the Vākāṭaka king named Pṛithvī Sheṇa, and even though he is not clearly described so, scholars have generally taken him to be a vassal of the said Vākāṭaka monarch. And as till the publication of the Bālāghāṭ plates in 1907-08 only one king of this name in the Vākāṭaka dynasty was known, he was naturally identified with the homonymous overlord of Vyāghradeva. However, after the discovery of these Bālāghāṭ plates,[6] which brought to light another later king of this name who was the great-great-grandson of the Pṛithvī Sheṇa known till then, it became known that there were two, not one, kings of this name in the Vākāṭaka dynasty who came to be designated as Pṛithvī Sheṇa I and II, and it became a problem to identify the homonymous king mentioned in the Nachnā-kī-talāī and Ganj inscriptions. Kielhorn himself, who edited the Bālāghāṭ plates, did not express any opinion on the issue. But Sukthankar attributed the Ganj inscription to Pṛithvī Sheṇa I.[7] But after this the opinion on this question got divided, with some scholars continuing to identify him with the first king of this name[8] and others favouring the second king.[9] However, as this question is of paramount importance to the students of Vākāṭaka history in particular and of early Indian history in general, it is of vital interest to arrive at a definite conclusion on this issue taking into account all the possible evidence which could have a direct/indirect bearing on this question.

There was an interval of a little less than a century between the reigns of the two Pṛithivī Sheṇas: Pṛithivī Sheṇa I, according to our chronology,[10] ruled from *c*. 355 to 385 AD, while the second ruler of this name flourished between *c*. 480-500/505 AD. And as the Vākāṭaka records are not dated in any known reckoning but only in the years of the individual reigns, we have to determine the chronology of the dynasty on other considerations, and synchronisms with other dynasties of known dates have gone a long way in fixing the general chronology.

Palaeography is sometimes used as a means of fixing the dates of individual records and correspondingly those of the rulers referred to in them. But as indicated by a comparison of the palaeographical arguments of D.C. Sircar[11] and V.V. Mirashi,[12] on palaeographical considerations the inscriptions in question cannot be assigned definitely to any of the two kings. We have therefore to be guided by some other evidences in deciding one of the two kings in question.

V.V. Mirashi takes these inscriptions as the evidence of the expansion of the Vākāṭaka kingdom into the Bundelhaṇḍ region during the time of Pṛithvī Sheṇa II. And he finds support for his ascription of these records to the reign of this king in the mention of his vassal Vyāghradeva whom he proposes to identify with the Uchchakalpa *Mahārāja* Vyāghra, father of *Mahārāja* Jayanātha, mentioned in some of the records of the family, who seems to have ruled almost contemporaneously with Pṛithivī Sheṇa II : as Jayanātha is known to have been ruling in the Gupta years 174 and 177,[13] his reign may be taken to have extended from 490 AD onwards and that of his father Vyāghradeva may be taken to have ruled immediately prior to it.[14]

This view, however, is based entirely on the identity of the two names and as such cannot be taken seriously. As we have just seen, there is no palaeographical compulsion to date these records in the latter half of the fifth century AD. Secondly, and this is most important, the inscriptions under review give the name of the supposed vassal of the Vākāṭaka Mahārāja Pṛithivī Sheṇa as just Vyāghradeva without any regal title, whereas the Uchchakalpa charters in question refer to him as Vyāghra, not Vyāghradeva, and his name is preceded by the feudal title *Mahārāja* which is conspicuous by its absence in the Nachnā-kī-talāī and Ganj inscriptions. Moreover, the Uchchakalpa records nowhere indicate that Mahārāja Vyāghra was a Vākāṭaka feudatory, and the employment of the Gupta era for dating by his son Jayanātha would, following Mirashi's argument, indicate that he acknowledged the suzerainty of the Imperial Guptas in a general way[15] though was free to act completely independently in the internal matters as would follow from his inscriptions which record land-grants made by him and his successors without allusion to the Gupta overlords. Moreover, it is also possible that the Vyāghradeva mentioned in the Nachnā and Ganj inscriptions was, going by their wording, an important/ordinary state official, and not a vassal of Pṛithivī Sheṇa, as generally assumed by scholars. In view of these facts the identity of Vyāghradeva mentioned in the Nachnā and Ganj inscriptions with the Uchchakalpa *Mahārāja* Vyāghra based as it is squarely on that of the two names is extremely doubtful and cannot form the basis of such an important theory as the expansion of the Vākāṭaka kingdom in the Baghelkhaṇḍ-Bundelkhaṇḍ region during the reign of Pṛithivī Sheṇa II. Moreover, as observed by H.C. Raychaudhuri,[16] the Bundelhaṇḍ-Baghelkhaṇḍ region including Nachnā and Ganj was under the Gupta, not Vākāṭaka, suzerainty for quite some time (to be precise, at least up to 528 AD) since the days of the mighty Gupta emperor Samudra Gupta. His Eraṇ (Sāgar district, Madhya Pradesh) inscription[17] shows that he had extended his direct rule at least up to Sāgar in the south. Moreover, as the Parivrājaka *Mahārājas* ruling to the west of the Uchchakalpa kingdom explicitly acknowledged the suzerainty of the Imperial Guptas,[18] their Uchchakalpa neighbours must have also owned, as a matter of geopolitical, if not anything else, compulsion, the Gupta suzerainty, even though their records are reticent on this point. Moreover, the recently discovered Shankarpur (Sidhi district, Madhya Pradesh) charter of *Mahārāja* Harivarman, dated in the Gupta year 168 leaves no doubt whatever that the Baghelkhaṇḍ-Bundelhaṇḍ region, where Nachnā and Ganj were situated, was ruled by Harivarman as a feudatory of the Gupta emperor Budha Gupta in 487-88 AD.[19] The inscription refers to a couple of generations preceding Harivarman which would indicate that the area in question formed part of the Gupta empire since a much earlier date. This should conclusively establish that the Nachnā and Ganj inscriptions cannot be attributed to the time of Pṛithivī Sheṇa II.[20]

Let us now examine a few other arguments adduced in support of the theory identifying the Vākāṭaka king Pṛithivī Sheṇa of these inscriptions with the second king of this name. It is argued that the Vākāṭaka expansion to the north of the Narmadā had begun as early as the reign of his grandfather Pravara Sena II, maternal grandson of Chandra Gupta II, himself. While other plates of his Indore grant were known much earlier,[21] the first missing plate was found recently and the text on it began with the expression *Tripurī-vāsakāt*, 'from a temporary abode at Tripurī', showing that the charter was issued from his (Pravara Sena II's) camp at Tripurī, modern Tewar, in the Jabalpur district of Madhya Pradesh.[22] Mirashi took it to indicate that Pravara Sena II carried his victorious arms north of the river Narmadā into Ḍāhala or Baghelkhaṇḍ region of Madhya Pradesh and was in occupation of the city of Tripurī in the twenty-third year of his reign roughly equal to 443 AD.[23] He invites our attention to verse 4 of Skanda Gupta's Bhītarī pillar inscription[24] which is generally taken to refer to the invasion of the Gupta empire by the Pushyamitras towards the close of the reign of Kumāra Gupta I in which the Guptas were reduced to such a hopeless situation that Skanda Gupta, who led the defensive operations, had to spend a night on bare ground. And as the reading *Pushyamitrāṁs=cha* is not beyond doubt, he accepts the alternative reading *yudhyamitrāṃś=cha* suggested by H.R. Divekar[25] and conceded by some other epigraphists,[26] and holds that the enemies said to have been routed by Skanda Gupta during the closing years of his father, Kumāra Gupta, included the Vākāṭaka king Pravara Sena II who went all out to expand his kingdom north of the Narmadā at the cost of his maternal uncle Kumāra Gupta I.[27] And identifying as he does the Vākāṭaka monarch Pṛithivī Sheṇa spoken of as Vyāghradeva's sovereign in the latter's records in question with the second Vākāṭaka ruler of that name, he holds that the Baghelkhaṇḍ region, which was annexed by Pravara Sena II, continued under the Vākāṭakas till the close of Pṛithivī Sheṇa II's reign in c. 490 AD, i.e. up to the time of the Gupta emperor Budha Gupta.[28]

This line of argument is, however, beset with many a difficulty. First, the term *vāsaka* does not connote only a military camp but refers simply to camp or temporary residence.[29] Taking the case of the Vākāṭakas themselves, the Waḍgāon plates of Pravara Sena II himself were granted from the king's *vāsaka* on the bank of the river Hiraṇyā[30] which was included very much within the Vākāṭaka territory and there could absolutely be no question of any military camp there. Moreover, if the intention were to refer to a military camp set up in course of an invasion of an enemy territory, an expression with an unambiguous connotation like *skandhāvāra* or *jaya-skandhāvāra* which is known to Indian epigraphy,[31] would have been employed. It is therefore not at all necessary to assume that Pravara Sena II had gone to Tripurī only for military purposes. His relations with the Guptas being very close, he could have gone to and stayed at Tripurī (and, for that matter, any place in the Gupta empire) for any purpose including holidaying or pilgrimage, for Tripurī appears to have been treated as a holy place.[32] There would perhaps have been some justification for Mirashi's assumption had the villages named in the epigraph in connection with the grant recorded in this inscription been situated in the Tripurī region which, as admitted by him, is not the case.[33] Moreover, had the Gupta-Vākāṭaka relations become that hostile during Pravara Sena II's reign as Mirashi would have us believe, the reference to the matrimonial alliance, which is definitely indicative of friendly and cordial relations, would have been dropped in later records of the dynasty. However, the phrase expressing this relationship continues to find a proud place not only in the subsequent records of Pravara Sena II himself, but to the very end of this branch of the dynasty.[34] Not only this, the recently discovered Rāmṭek inscription put up to commemorate the death of Pravara Sena II's mother Prabhāvatī Guptā extols not only his maternal grandfather Chandra Gupta II but a few of his successors including Ghaṭotkacha Gupta, and this inscription, it is important to remember, was put up after the twenty-third year of his reign.[35] Thus the Indore plates have absolutely no bearing on the problem under review.

It is sometimes felt that Narendra Sena at least had established his authority over a substantial part of the territories included earlier in the Gupta empire. This naive assumption is based on the uncritical acceptance of the claim made on his behalf in three of the copper-plate charters of his son Pṛithivī Sheṇa II that his father's behests were obeyed by the lords of Kosalā (Chhattīsgaḍh region), Mekalā (Amarkaṇṭak region) and Mālava (Mālwā) in the present State of Madhya Pradesh.[36] We have to view these boastful claims in the perspective of the calamitous situation faced by Narendra Sena at the beginning as well as in the later part of his reign. An expression found in these charters with reference to Narendra Sena was read by earlier epigraphists as *pūrvv-ādhigata-guṇa-viśvāsād=-apahṛita-vaṁśa-śriyaḥ.*[37] It has now been proved to be erroneous by the recent discovery of the Māṇḍhal plates of Pṛithivī Sheṇa II's tenth year and checking with its help the proposed reading in other charters. The correct reading now is *pūrvv-ādhigata-guṇavad=dāyād-āpahṛita-vaṁśa-śriyaḥ*[38] which should refer to two important phases of his life and is pregnant with enormous historical significance. It would mean that his family fortune which was earlier acquired by him (Narendra Sena) was (later) carried away (or forcibly seized) by (his) minor relations.[39] Thus the demise of his father Pravara Sena II appears to have been followed by a struggle for succession wherein, to begin with, Narendra Sena succeeded only to lose later to his minor relations, most probably of the Vatsagulma branch. The claim that he (Narendra Sena) 'held in check the enemies bowed down by his valour' *(pratāpa-praṇat-āri-śāsanasya)* most probably refers to his success against the enemies that had obstructed his succession, and not to any fresh conquests. During the later part of his reign the whole or a major chunk of his kingdom was under enemy occupation, and the enemy in question was most probably Deva Sena of the Vatsagulma branch of the dynasty. In view of these recently known facts the claim about his successes against Kosalā, Mekalā and Mālava has to be taken with a pinch of salt and as highly exaggerated. In any case at present we have no independent evidence to sustain this claim. Neither any record of the Vākāṭakas has been reported from these regions nor do the records of other ruling families of these regions provide any hint of Vākāṭaka occupation. The claim in regard to Mekalā was till recently sought to be supported on the assumption that the Bamhanī plates made a veiled allusion to Narendra Sena and that Bharatabala, the Pāṇḍava chief of Mekalā and the supposed issuer of this charter, was a vassal of Narendra Sena.[40] However, this unfounded assumption, which derived its inspiration from the claim in respect of Narendra Sena's authority over Mekalā in his son and successor Pṛithivī Sheṇa's charters,[41] has now been proved to be erroneous by the rather recently published Mallār plates of Śūrabala Udīrṇavaira. These plates have a prose sentence introducing Bharatabala's son and successor, Śūrabala Udīrṇavaira, which has been left out by inadvertence in the Bamhanī plates which are otherwise generally identical and leave absolutely no doubt that these plates also, like the Mallār charter, belong to Śūrabala Udīrṇavaira.[42] Furthermore, as we have shown elsewhere,[43] Bharatabala and his son Śūrabala were separated from Narendra Sena by a long period of time and consequently there is no question of any one of them owing allegiance to him. In view of these facts it is difficult to appreciate the exact significance of these claims. It is not impossible that in view of the family's friendly relations with the Imperial Guptas he participated in some campaigns for restoring Gupta authority in these regions during the reigns of Skanda Gupta and Budha Gupta and might have claimed success against these rulers as his own. Alternatively it may be surmised that he took advantage of the precarious situation in which his Gupta cousin was placed to carry out hurried raids in these territories. Moreover, it was just impossible for him to entertain any idea of a campaign of victory in view of the difficulties at home. To sum up, it leads us nowhere in the matter of the identification of Vākāṭaka Pṛithivī Sheṇa of the two records in question with the second king of that name. And by the rule of elimination the only Vākāṭaka king of this name that is available for identification is Pṛithivī Sheṇa I.

That the Vākāṭaka king Pṛithivī Sheṇa of the Nachnā and Ganj epigraphs could be only Pṛithivī Sheṇa I is established by a few other considerations as well. The original home of the Vākāṭakas has long been a matter of controversy, and the only guiding evidence is that furnished by the rather brief Purāṇic statement about the first two kings of the dynasty, viz. Vindhyaśakti and his son Pravīra (i.e. Pravara Sena I). The Purāṇas mention Vindhyaśakti and his son Pravīra at the end of a list of the kings of various regions or countries *(deśika)*.[44] They inform us that Pravīra had four sons all of whom became rulers, viz. the kingdom was split into four parts under four sons.[45] These same kings are in another context called Vindhyaka, viz. 'belonging to the Vindhyan region'.[46] The founder's or first king's name Vindhyaśakti, 'one whose strength is Vindhya', also points in the same direction.[47] In ancient times, the Vindhya was regarded as one of the seven major mountain chains *(kula-parvatas)*. It is interesting to note that the Purāṇas name the Sātavāhanas also as Andhra or Andhra-jātīya[48] after their original habitat as they do also in the case of the Imperial Guptas whose original home lay in and is mentioned in the Purāṇas as Prayāga on the Gaṅgā, Sāketa and Magadha even though they were compiled during the reign of, at the earliest, Samudra Gupta,[49] who had extended the empire far and wide. So the stress almost always was on the original territory even after the expansion of a given kingdom. So the Vākāṭakas, too, had their original home or kingdom in the Vindhyan region. However, there exists a considerable uncertainty regarding the location of the Vindhya *vis-a-vis* the adjacent Ṛikshavat range both in ancient tradition and among modern geographers. But generally speaking, when used in a wider sense the name Vindhya denotes the whole mountain range roughly from Mirzapur in Uttar Pradesh to the Arabian Sea in Gujarat and covers both these mountain ranges which are regarded as *kula-parvatas.* But when an attempt is made to distinguish these, the only point of agreement is that the Narmadā divides the two. But as regards the respective connotations, there is great controversy: some scholars applying both these names to the mountain ranges on the two sides of the river Narmadā. But there are some considerations that finally establish that the names Vindhya and Ṛikshavat denoted the ranges to the north and south respectively of the Narmadā. At present the ranges to its south are called Sātpuḍā of which the first component, viz. Sāt, is definitely a derivative of Ṛikshavat. In the Nāsik inscription of the nineteenth year of Vāsishṭhīputra Puḷumāvi his father Gautamīputra Sātakarṇi is described as the lord of a number of mountains including Ṛikshavat which is mentioned in its Prakrit form Chhavata.[50] Sāta is clearly a derivative from Chhavata which would naturally change into Chhāta by the substitution of *va* by *a* which was assimilated with the preceding a which, as per the normal process, got lengthened into *ā*. Then in the southern Prakrit sibilants and *ch* and *chh* were interchangeable as we know from inscriptions, coins and literary evidence. Thus *Chhimuka*[51] became *Simuka,*[52] *Śānta* became *Chāta* or Chāṁta,[53] Sātakarṇi[54] became *Chātakaṇi,*[55] and *Vāsithī*[56] turned into

Vāchiṭṭi.[57] Conversely, *Chhāta* could well turn into *Sāta.* And the terminal *puḍā* got suffixed to it to indicate the layers. Secondly, the reference in the *Harsha-charita* (VII and VIII) to the Vindhya mountain and forest *(Vindhyāṭavi)* in connection with Ṛājyaśrī's rescue by her brother Harsha, the description of Vindhya as a pleasure-mound *(krīḍā-giri)* of the Chandella king Vākpati[58] and the allusion to the occupation of the slopes of the Vindhya (*Vaindhya-taṭa)* by the Kalacuri king Kokkalla[59] evidently cannot refer to the mountain chain to the south of the Narmadā. Then, there are several places named after the Vindhya (e.g. Vindhyāchal, Vindhyavāsinī, etc.) in the north while such names are conspicuously absent to the south of the Narmadā. The issue is finally clinched by the *Śākaṭāyana-Vyākaraṇa* which observes that the Pāriyātra is situated to the north of the Vindhya *(Uttaro Vindhyāt Pāriyātraḥ,* II, 2.75),[60] which would have been meaningless if the two were intervened by the Ṛikshavat. The available evidence therefore leaves no doubt that Vindhya was the name of the mountain ranges situated to the north of the river Narmadā.

The original home of the Vākāṭakas thus lay in the Vindhyan region (Bundelkhaṇḍ-Baghelkhaṇḍ), and the Purāṇas further inform us that Pravīra-Pravara Sena I ruled over the city of Kāñchanaka[61] which must be looked for in that region. And fortunately for us there is the village of Nachnā or Nachnā-Kuṭhārā which satisfies all the considerations. It has a couple of early Vākāṭaka records in question and an early Gupta-Vākāṭaka temple.[62] It appears that both the initial and concluding *kā*-s have disappeared in course of some seventeen centuries and the remainder—*ñchana* —has been corrupted into Nachnā. Even though Pravara Sena I had expanded his kingdom southward so as to include the Vidarbha and other adjoining regions, he continued to have his capital at Kāñchanakā or Nachnā and so did his grandson Rudra Sena I who succeeded him and his son and successor Pṛithivī Sheṇa I for at least the earlier part of his reign.

The Purāṇic evidence, if interpreted in the perspective of the light offered by the epigraphic data, leads one to the unmistakable conclusion that the Vākāṭakas till at least the time of Rudra Sena I, father of Pṛithivī Sheṇa I, continued to hold the Vindhyan (Bundelkhaṇḍ) region. The Purāṇas tell us that Pravira or Pravara Sena I had four sons all of whom became kings. But we have to remember in this connection that the numerous charters of the Padmapura-Nandivardhana-Pravarapura branch of the dynasty are clear that one of the sons of Pravara Sena I, viz. Gautamiputra,[63] did not ascend the throne and in this branch Pravara Sena

I was succeeded by his grandson Rudra Sena I. The Wāshīm grant of Vināḍhyaśakti-II[64] brought to light the only other known branch of the dynasty, viz. Vatsagulma, which was founded by another son of Pravara Sena I, viz. Sarva Sena (I). We know at present no other branch of the dynasty, and it is only future discoveries that may enable us to locate the other two branches. Therefore it is quite likely that Pravara Sena I divided his kingdom into four parts during his own lifetime, and as his son Gautamīputra was a minor he kept the northern portion of the kingdom with him waiting for his attaining majority. But as the things would have it, he passed away without becoming major and Pravara Sena I had to bequeath the throne in due course to his grandson Rudra Sena I. Thus in this case we have to take the Purāṇic statement in a modified sense referring to his grandson, not son. Rudra Sena I continued to hold the Vindhyan region along with his part of the kingdom in Vidarbha together with the intervening area of Central India. From, him the whole of this region was inherited by his son Pṛithivī Sheṇa I. His hold over the Vindhyan region, which had already slackened due to the shifting of the focus further south in Vidarbha as well as because of the decline of the Bhāraśiva Nāga power[65] in Central India, however, continued during at least a portion of his reign as indicated by the Nachnā and Ganj inscriptions of Vyāghradeva, perhaps a Vākāṭaka vassal,[66] only to be put to an end by the mighty Gupta emperor Samudra Gupta. If Vyāghradeva was a feudatory, it is likely that his rule was brought to an end and he was included among the rulers of Āryāvarta extirpated by him and alluded to among the numerous other *(ādi)* kings besides those named specifically in Samudra Gupta's Allahabad pillar inscription.[67] It is equally likely that he is identical with Vyāghrarāja of Mahākāntāra referred to as one of the kings of Dakshiṇāpatha (Deccan and South) vanquished and reinstated by Samudra Gupta. The objection that Vyāghrarāja is spoken of as a Deccanese ruler whereas Vyāghradeva was ruling over the Vindhyan region of northern India can be easily met as ancient Indian writers on geography like Varāhamihira include even Chitrakūṭa hill in the Bāndā district of Uttar Pradesh, sixty-five miles west-south-west of Allāhābād in the southern division.[68] Mahākāntāra may in that case refer to the Aṭavi or forest region stretching from Jabalpur in Madhya Pradesh to Mirzāpur in Uttar Pradesh. It comprised eighteen kingdoms as stated in the Betūl plates of the Parivarājaka Mahārāja Saṅkshobha.[69] And even if he, like other kings of the South, was reinstated by Samudra Gupta, his fief, like those of the Mālavas, Yaudheyas, etc., ceased to exist under the unbearable Gupta pressure. Thus, the Vākāṭaka hold over the Vindhyan region, which had persisted right from the beginning of the family about mid-third century AD for over a century disappeared during the reign of Pṛithivī Sheṇa I sometime in the period *c.* 351-375 AD.

To sum up, there is absolutely no doubt that the Nachnā and Ganj records of Vyāghradeva belong to the reign of the Vākāṭaka king Pṛithivī Sheṇa I of the Padmapura-Nandivardhana-Pravarapura branch.

We learn from the purāṇas that sons of Pravīra (Pravra Sena I) became kings. Only two of these branches, *viz.* (1) Padmapura-Nandivardhana-Pravarapura and (2) Vatsagulma-are known to us from their epigraphical records. It is not impossible that Pṛithivī Sheṇa known from the inscription under reference represented a different branch.[70]

Notes and References

1. *CII*, III, Nos. 53-54, pp. 233-35.
2. *EI*, XVII (1923-24), pp. 12-14.
3. *CII*, V, Nos. 20-22, pp. 89-91 (Nachnā-kī-talāī) and 92 (Ganj).
4. The engraved portion is literally identical with the initial portion of the complete inscriptions.
5. The complete corrected text of both these inscriptions engraved in four (Nachnā-kī-talāī) and three (Ganj) lines respectively runs as follows :- *Vākāṭakāṇā(nāṃ) mahārāja-sri-(śri)-Prithivi(vī) shena-pād-ānuddhyāto Vyāghradevo mātā-pitro[h*] punyā(ṇyā)rtthe kṛitaṁ (kṛitavān)=iti*
6. F. Kielhorn, "Bālāghāṭ Plates of Pṛithivīsheṇa II", *EI*, IX, 1907-08, pp. 267-71.
7. "Vākāṭaka Inscription from Ganj", *ibid.*, XVII, p. 13.
8. K.P. Jayaswal, *History of India: 150 A.D. to 350 A.D.*, p. 73; H.C. Raychaudhuri, *Political History of Ancient India,* 6th ed., pp. 541-42; A.S. Altekar, *A New History of the Indian People,* VI: *The Vākāṭaka-Gupta Age,* pp. 109-10; *Early History of the Deccan,* ed. G. Yazdani, p. 173; D.C. Sircar, *History and Culture of the Indian People,* III: *The Classical Age,* p. 179, etc. Later, as will be seen in the sequel, Sircar's views on the subject underwent great change.
9. J. Dubreuil, *IA*, LV, pp. 103ff.; R.C. Majumdar, *JRASB*, XII, pp. 1ff.; K.N. Dikshit, *EI*, XVII, p. 362; V.V. Mirashi, *CII*, V, pp. xxvii-xxviii, 91-92; *A Comprehensive History of India,* III, Part I, p. 141. D.C. Sircar who, as we have seen above, was earlier inclined in favour of his identification with Pṛithivīsheṇa I, later gave this position up and favoured his equation with the second king of this name (*Select Inscriptions,* 1, 2nd ed., p. 456 and note 1) and felt that the Vākāṭakas ousted the Gupta rule from Bundelkhaṇḍ about the close of the fifth century AD, though he now assigned the characters of the Ganj inscription to the box-headed variety of the late Brāhmī of the southern class of the sixth century AD.

10. With major adjustments necessitated by the recently discovered evidence, our chronological scheme is generally the same as that of most of the historians of the Vākāṭakas.
11. *The Classical Age,* p. 179, fn. 1; *Select Inscriptions,* I, p. 456 and note 1.
12. *CII,* V, pp. 89-90.
13. J.F. Fleet, *CII,* III, pp. 117 and 121. Mirashi agrees that the dates of the Uchchakalpa inscriptions are assignable to the Gupta era. *Vide EI,* XXIII, pp. 171ff.
14. *CII,* V, pp. xxvii-xxviii, 91.
15. Of course, we do not believe in the theory that a vassal invariably dated his records in the same era as his overlord though in a way it is likely. We have instances of vassals continuing employing an era traditionally despite accepting the suzerainty of a dynasty which had its own era. Mirashi is dead against it.
16. *Political History of Ancient India,* pp. 541-42.
17. D.C. Sircar, *Select Inscriptions,* I, pp. 268-70, which describes the city of Erakiṇa (modern Eraṇ) as his *svabhoganagara.*
18. The Parivrājaka records commence with the expression *Gupta-nṛipa-rājya-bhuktau.*
19. B.C. Jain, "Shankarpur Plate of Budhagupta and Harivarman, Year 166", *JESI,* IV, pp. 62-66. That the date of the charter actually is 168, not 166, was pointed out by K.V. Ramesh (*ibid.,* p. 64, fn. 1 and p. 66, fn. 17). The supposed connection of Harivarman with the Maukharis can at best be regarded as a brilliant conjecture in the absence of any dependable evidence on the point.
20. After the discovery of the above plate Sircar feels that there is not much time available for the rule of Pṛithivī Sheṇa II which he regarded then as an unproved guess and floats the conjecture that his vassal Vyāghradeva might have gone to Nachnā and Ganj in course of a pilgrimage. *Vide* his "Vākāṭaka Occupation of Baghelkhand-Bundelhaṇḍ Region", *AV,* pp. 47-49.
21. *EI,* XXIV, pp. 52ff.; *CII,* V, pp. 38ff.
22. See *Indological Research Papers,* I, p. 72, line 1. For a detailed study of the history of this ancient town, see our Hindi work *Tripurī.*
23. *Indological Research Papers,* I, p. 69.
24. J.F. Fleet, *CII,* III, pp. 53-54.
25. *ABORI,* I, p. 103.
26. D.R. Bhandarkar, *Inscriptions of the Early Gupta Kings, CII,* III, p. 315; B.Ch. Chhabra in *Dr. Mirashi Felicitation Volume,* p. 367.
27. *Indological Research Papers,* I, p. 70.
28. *Ibid.,* p. 71.
29. Like *vāsa, vāsaka* also connotes an abode, dwelling or habitation. See Monier Monier-Williams, *A Sanskrit-English Dictionary,* s.v. *vāsaka.* But in inscriptions, when mentioned as the place of the issue of a charter, it is generally employed in the sense of a temporary residence.
30. *CII,* V, p. 54, line 1. The river Hiraṇyā has been identified with the modern Erāī flowing from north to south in the Wardhā tehsīl and ultimately joining the Wardhā.

31. *Cf.* the Nāsik inscription of the eighteenth year of Gautamīputra Sātakarṇi (D.C. Sircar, *Select Inscriptions,* I, p. 198, line 1), which is in the nature of a copper-plate charter, was issued from the *vijaya-skandhāvāra* at Govardhana.

32. For references, see our *Tripurī,* pp. 167-68.

33. Some of the villages mentioned in this charter have been located in the Bālāghāṭ district. *Vide CII,* V, p. 40.

34. It is found in all the copperplate charters of Pṛithivī Sheṇa II.

35. For a discussion of its contents, see *infra,* pp. 125-35.

36. *Kosalā-Mekalā-Mālav-ādhipatibhir=abhyarchchita-śāsanasya* is the expression met with in the Māṇḍhal (tenth year), Māhurjharī and Bālāghāṭ charters of Pṛithivī Sheṇa II.

37. This was the reading of F. Kielhorn, V.V. Mirashi and V.B. Kolte. It was not clear in the Bālāghāṭ plates and therefore Kielhorn doubtfully suggested this reading with an interrogation mark. But the Māhurjharī plates have the reading suggested by us even clearer than on the Māṇḍhaḷ plates; but Kolte merely followed the reading surmised by Kielhorn, only dropping the question mark.

38. See Ajay Mitra Shastri, "Māṇḍhaḷ Plates of Pṛithivī Sheṇa II, years 2 and 10," *EI,* XLI, pp. 172-74 (for discussion) and 177, line 17 (text).

39. *Guṇavad* cannot be taken in the instant case to mean 'virtuous' and must stand for *gauṇa* 'minor'. For a discussion on this point as well as the meaning of *dāyāda, vide ibid.,* pp. 172-74.

40. B.Ch. Chhabra (*ibid.,* XXVII, pp. 137-38) followed by V.V. Mirashi (*CII,* V, pp. 83-84). This view was based on the unwarranted assumption that the word *narendra* in the Bamhanī plates (verse 11) alludes to Vākāṭaka Narendra Sena.

41. This claim is found in all his charters except only the Māṇḍhaḷ plates of the second year which just mention him (Narendra Sena) without any description of his achievements.

42. For the Mallār plates of Śūrabala Udīrṇavaira, *vide* Ajay Mitra Shastri, *Inscriptions of the Śarabhapurīyas, Pāṇḍuvaṁśins and Somavaṁśins,* Part II, pp. 83-85.

43. "The Date of the Bamhanī and Mallār Plates or Śūrabala Udīrṇavaira", *Bhāratī-Bhānam : Dr. K.V. Sarma Felicitation Volume,* pp. 439-43; impra, pp. 80-84.

44. The expression *Nṛipān vai deśikān* used in the Purāṇas while introducing some rulers including the first three generations of the Vākāṭakas has been generally split as *Nṛipān Vaideśikān* and taken to refer to the rulers of Vidiśā (see F.E. Pargiter, *DKA,* pp. 42-43 [text] and 72 [Engl. tr.]. But as some rulers who had apparently nothing to do with Vidiśa are also included in the list, it would be better to split the expression into *vai desikan* and take it to mean 'rulers of various countries or regions'. See also K.V. Ramesh, "*On the Vākāṭakas and their Inscriptions*", AV, p. 29.

45. *Tasya putrās=tu chatvāro bhavishyanti narādhipāḥ, DKA,* p. 50.

46. *Vindhyakānāṁ kulasy-ānte, ibid.,* p. 50, line 1 under 'Dynasties of the Third Century A.D.' after describing the four sons of Pravīra.

47. Vindhyaśakti, also called Vindhya Sena, the second ruler of the Vatsagulma branch of the dynasty, had nothing to do with the Vindhyan region and was merely nāmed after the founder of the dynasty without any intrinsic significance.

48. *Ibid.*, pp. 37 and 45 (Andhra) and 38 (Andhra-jātīya). We have discussed at length the question of the original home and nomenclature of the Sātavāhanas in our *Sātavāhanas and the Western Kshatrapas: A Historical Framework.*

49. This is evident from the use of plural in the expression *Gupta-vamsajāḥ*.

50. V.V. Mirashi, *HISWK,* p. 45, line 2.

51. This is the form of the name found on his coins.

52. This is the form met with in one of the Nāṇeghāṭ label inscriptions which, in our opinion, was put up by Chhimuka-Simuka's brother Kṛishṇa.

53. *Chāṁtasa* for *Śāntasya* on a copper-pot containing 5,534 silver punch-marked coins found at Chik Sandogi in the Dhārwāḍ district of Karnataka (Ajay Mitra Shastri, "Presidential Address", *PIHC,* 1978, p. 969), and *Chātamūla* for *Śāntamūla* met with in the Ikshvāku inscriptions.

54. This is the form of the name met with in the inscriptions and in the obverse Prakrit legends on coins.

55. This is the correct reading of the name in the reverse legend of the Sātavāhana silver coins.

56. This is the form of the first component of the metronymic met with in the inscriptions and obverse coin legend of kings bearing the metronymic Vāsiṭhīputa.

57. In our opinion this is the correct reading of the first part of the metronymic in the legend on the reverse of the silver portrait coins of the Sātavāhana monarchs who were Vāsithīputas.

58. Khajurāho Stone Inscription of Yaśovarman, Vikrama year 1011, *EI,* I, verse 13, pp. 125-26.

59. Bilhārī Stone Inscription of the Chedis, *ibid.*, I, verse 16, p. 256.

60. *Vide* V.S. Agrawala, *Matsya-purāṇa—A Study,* p. 194.

61. The relevant passage of the text as reconstructed by Pargiter runs as follows : *bhokshyate cha samāḥ shashṭiṁ puriṁ Kāñchanakāṁ cha vai. Vide DKA,* p. 50. Jayaswal (*op.cit.*, p. 16, fn. 3 and p. 70) followed by Mirashi (*CII,* V, introduction, p. xii) held that the expression *puriṁ Kāñchanakāṁ cha* should be modified and split into *Purikāṁ Chanakāṁ cha* and that there is actually mention of two capitals here, viz. Purikā and Chanakā, as otherwise it would be difficult to explain the particle *cha,* 'and'. It must be noted in this context that not a single manuscript consulted by Pargiter (*DKA,* p. 50, fn. 33) contained this reading and that the use of particles *cha, hi, tu* and *vai* is more often than not due to metrical exigencies only and in the present portion also there are two such particles, viz. *cha* after *bhokshyate* and *vai* at the end. And if one were to look for the meaning everywhere one shall be landing oneself into an unenviable situation. We are therefore of the firm view that the reference here is only to the city of Kāñchanakā, and not to Purikā and Chanakā. The identification of Chanakā with Nachnā was suggested long back by Jayaswal who also felt that it and Kāñchanakā were probably alternative names. It was possibly founded by Vindhyaśakti though as of now we have no evidence on this point.

62. For the temple, see *Archaeological Survey Reports,* XXI, pp. 90-95, Pls. XXV-XXVI; *The Classical Age,* pp. 501-06; Percy Brown, *Indian Architecture,* I, Buddhist and Hindu Period, Bombay, 1956, pp. 58, 60.

63. We get only the metronymic, not personal name, of this Vākāṭaka prince.

64. *CII,* V, pp. 93-100. Earlier only this charter and a single plate of the India Office grant of Deva Sena of the Vatsagulma branch were known. But in recent years quite a few charters and a lithic record of the last two members of this branch, viz. Deva Sena and Hari Sheṇa, have come to light.

65. Bhāraśiva king Bhavanāga was the father-in-law of Gautamīputra.

66. About this we cannot be sure, and it is not impossible that he was an important state official under Pṛithivī Sheṇa I.

67. Bhandarkar, Chhabra and Gai, *CII,* III, p. 213, line 21 *(ādy-aneka).*

68. Ajay Mitra Shastri, *Varāhamihira's India,* p. 50.

69. The inscription actually describes the Ḍabhālā-rājya (same as the Ḍāhala region) as included in the eighteen forest kingdoms *(s-āshṭādaś-āṭavi-rājy-ābhyantaraṁ Ḍabhālārājyam). Vide EI,* VIII, p. 267, line 9.

70. This alternative suggestion has emerged from our discussions with Dr. Chandrashekhar Gupta.

APPENDIX II

Bālāghāṭ Plates of Vakāṭaka Pṛithivī Sheṇa II: Some Aspects

(Pls. LXXXI-LXXXII)

Though the Bālāghāṭ plates, which are now known to contain so very important information about the reign of the Vākāṭaka king Prithivi Sheṇa II, were found some time before May 1893 when they were forwarded by the Deputy Commissioner of Bālāghāṭ to the Asiatic Society of Bengal,[1] they were first published together with facsimiles by F. Kielhorn in the *Epigraphia Indica,* Vol. IX, meant for 1907-08.[2] They were reportedly found 'hanging to a tree in the jungle'.

The set consists of five plates, but only the first three plates bear writing, the first and the third only on one side: first only on the inner side and the third only on the first side. The other two plates are left uninscribed, and similar is the case with the seal which is sliding on the ring but bears no writing or device or both. Then again, in the first line on the inscribed face of the first plate there is left uninscribed space for the word *dṛishṭam,* which, generally speaking, serves as authentication mark. The king's order just begins in line 35 which is the last line on the first side of the third plate, while the remaining plates including the second side of the third one are left blank. All these facts show that the charter is left unfinished deliberately for some unascertainable reason.

The extant text is engraved in the box-headed characters common to Vākāṭaka charters and is in Sanskrit prose the draft of which is mostly familiar from other charters of the branch of the dynasty to which the issuer, Pṛithivī Sheṇa II, belonged. However, before the discovery and publication of this charter we had the grants only up to Pravara Sena II. There is even now no grant available of his son and successor, Narendra Sena, and this was then the only known grant of his son Pṛithivī Sheṇa II. Naturally therefore the description of Narendra Sena and Pṛithivī Sheṇa II till the time of the issue of this charter had to be added.

And it is here, viz. the description of Narendra Sena and Pṛithivī Sheṇa II, that the importance of this charter lies primarily. In fact, we were not aware of even the names of these two kings who were brought to light for the first time by this charter. And for this reason the record is of great historical value despite the fact that it is left incomplete. And even now when we have as many as three other records of this king, which are complete,[3] this inscription is of great historical value for it brings to light a fact about his reign which is not known from any other source.

The charter was intended to be issued from the king's temporary residence *(vāsaka)* at Vembāra which V.V. Mirashi identifies with modern Bembāl, about twenty-eight miles east of Chāndā (Chandrapur) and two miles to the west of the river Waingaṅgā.[4]

Up to Pravara Sena II the description is fairly common and well-known from the grants of Pravara Sena II dated up to his thirty-second year.[5] But the description of Narendra Sena and his son Pṛithivī Sheṇa II is, or rather was, entirely new and a contribution of this charter. In connection with Narendra Sena some phrases occur the reading and interpretation whereof is a matter of controversy. Let us take note of them. The first phrase in the description of Narendra Sena was read as *pūrvv-ādhigata-guṇa-viśvāsād=apahṛita-vaṅ(ṁ)śa-śriyaḥ* doubtfully by Kielhorn[6] followed by Mirashi.[7] Kielhorn was very doubtful about the reading *viśvāsā* as would appear from the fact that he put an interrogation mark after the *akshara sā* which was followed by Mirashi as well. V.B. Kolte, while editing the Māhurjharī plates of this king,[8] also adopted this reading, perhaps without trying to verify it. The only thing he did was to drop the question mark following *sā*.[9] But while publishing the subsequently discovered Māṇḍhaḷ plates of his tenth year I discovered that this reading was erroneous and misleading as regards the five letters following *ṇa* and preceding *pa,* and that the correct reading of this portion was *vad=dāyādā* which revolutionised the interpretation of the entire passage which now became a source of highly invaluable historical information about king Narendra Sena. Therefore, the exact reading of the passage in question is *pūrvv-ādhigata-guṇavad=dāyād-āpahṛita-vaṁśa-śriyaḥ.*[10] On checking the facsimile of the first side of the third plate of the Māhurjharī charter accompanying Kolte's paper where this expression occurs in this charter I was simply astonished to find that the suggested reading was much clearer there and finally confirmed my reading. The Bālāghāṭ grant also appears to contain the same reading though it became uncertain and doubtful because of blurred engraving.

No doubt whatever exists regarding the reading of the portion *pūrv-ādhigata-guṇa.* The letter following it is apparently *va,* though the lower portion of the square of the letter has not been accommodated in the plate: what is read as medial *i* is but a meaningless inadvertent scratch. The next letter, though looking slightly like *śvā,* is in fact wrongly engraved *ddā* with its openings to right closed by oversight. The following *akshara* is clearly *yā,* and Kielhorn had read it as *sā* doubtfully in order to make the phrase yield some sense, and others merely followed in his footsteps. Thereafter in the facsimile accompanying Kielhorn's paper there is a meaningless scratch which is followed by *d* without a stroke for the medial *ā* and was correctly read by Kielhorn as *da.* However, the other two plates (Māṇḍhaḷ grant of his tenth year[11] and Māhurjharī charter of his seventeenth year[12]) show the *mātrā* of *a* very clearly, which demonstrates that the letter in question was there also intended as *dā.* We may thus conclude that the correct intended reading even in the Bālāghāṭ charter was *pūrvv-ādhigata-gunavad=dāyād-āpahṛita-vaṁśa-śriyaḥ,* and it is much clearer in the aforesaid two charters of his tenth and seventeenth years.

What is the most likely meaning of this expression? Kielhorn, who first edited the Bālāghāṭ charter, took the expression, as read by him, as alluding to a conflict for succession and felt that Narendra Sena took away the kingdom (probably from his brother).[13] To Mirashi, it meant that Narendra Sena 'from confidence in the excellent qualities previously acquired by him took away the (royal) fortune of (his) family'[14] and he observed that no reference to a disputed succession was intended and that this is only a poetic way to stating that Narendra Sena attracted royal fortune by his noble qualities.[15] According to A.S. Altekar, the compound meant that Narendra Sena 'took away the fortune of his family' and suggested a forcible seizure.[16] To him, it alludes to the restoration of family fortunes by Narendra Sena after defeating the Nalas of Bastar who had for some time been in possession of a sizeable portion of the Vākāṭaka kingdom.[17] Kolte followed this interpretation and felt that the expression *apahṛita-vaṁśa-śriyaḥ* denoted 'one who snatched away the fortune of his family'.[18]

This was the position till the said correct reading of the relevant phrase was pointed out by us on the basis of the aforesaid Māṇḍhaḷ and Māhurjharī plates, and, as we have just seen, is also the intended reading in the Bālāghāṭ charter. The compound thus restored becomes highly important historically in as much as it alludes to an hitherto unknown episode of the reign of Narendra Sena wherein his *dāyādas* were involved. The phrase may be split up as *pūrvam adhigatā (paśchād) guṇavatā dāyādena apahṛitā vaṁśa-śrīh yasya tasya*[19] which would indicate that Narendra Sena had at first succeeded to his family fortune, viz. ancestral kingdom, but was later deprived of it by his *dāyāda* or *dāyādas.* The word *dāyāda* primarily denotes 'heir or heirs to the property, viz. sons or brothers with reference to each other who are entitled to inheritance'. In case we were to adopt this primary sense, it would follow that Narendra Sena was divested of his kingdom or its major part by his co-sharers, i.e. brothers or other close relations, in the later part of his reign. We may therefore conclude that Pravara Sena II's demise was followed by a conflict for the throne in which his son (or one of the sons) Narendra Sena at first succeeded, but later some other *dāyāda* or *dāyādas* had an upper hand and seized the family fortune from him. But the word *dāyāda* has a secondary meaning as well, viz. a distant relative or kinsman,[20] and if this meaning is applied in the instant case, it may refer to some conflict between the two branches (the other branch being that founded by Sarva Sena I, viz. Vatsagulma branch) of the dynasty during Narendra Sena's reign wherein he was worsted.[21] It is very likely that this is the meaning intended here. The absence of more dependable evidence makes it difficult to be more precise on this point. There is, however, no doubt whatever that the phrase in question throws welcome light on the history of that branch of the dynasty whereto Narendra Sena belonged and gives a lie to the hitherto prevailing notion that the succession among the Vākāṭakas was peaceful and that the mutual ties between their two branches were always cordial. It also demonstrates that Narendra Sena's troubles were due much more to his own kinsmen than to any outside power. We are inclined to hold that while his succession was challenged by his unknown brothers, perhaps with the connivance and encouragement of the Vatsagulma branch, after Narendra Sena's success in ascending the throne, his contemporary ambitious king Deva Sena of that branch came out openly against Narendra Sena and occupied his kingdom or its major portion. Thus, the correct reading and interpretation of this passage shed a flood of light on an important critical phase in the reign of Narendra Sena in particular and the annals of the two branches of the dynasty in general.

The statement following this expression that his behests were obeyed by the rulers of Kosalā (Chhattīsgaḍh region), Mekalā (Amarkaṇṭak area) and Mālava (Mālwā) presently in Madhya Pradesh as well as that he kept in check the enemies humbled by his valour[22] look rather boastful in view of the critical situation he was put in by his own kinsmen. We may perhaps take the second statement to refer to his initial success against his kinsmen who had obstructed his accession. In any case at present we have absolutely no independent evidence to sustain the claim of his success in these regions put on his behalf in the records of his son. No records of the Vākāṭakas during this period have as yet been reported from the area north of the Narmadā[23] nor do the numerous inscriptions of other ruling families contain even the slightest hint of Vākāṭaka authority. In case of Mekalā this claim was till recently thought to find support on the basis of assumed allusion to Narendra Sena in the Bamhanī plates hitherto attributed to the Mekalā Pāṇḍava king Bharatabala who was taken to be his vassal.[24] This baseless assumption which was inspired by the claim of Narendra Sena's authority over the Mekalā king in this as well as other records of his son[25] has been knocked out of bottom by the recently reported Mallār plates of the Pāṇḍava king Śūrabala alias Udīrṇavaira. This charter contains a prose sentence introducing Bharatabala's son and successor Śūrabala[26] which is left out by inadvertence in the Bamhanī plates which too were issued not by Bharatabala, but his son Śūrabala. Moreover, as we have shown elsewhere,[27] Bharatabala and his son Śūrabala flourished considereably after the end of the Vākāṭakas and that consequently there could be absolutely no question of the two being connected in any manner. And as such it is difficult to sustain these claims and understand their true nature. We are aware, however, that the Gupta king Kumāra Gupta I was in great stress in the closing years of his reign, and it is possible that taking advantage of their sovereign's difficulties some of his vassals asserted their independence. In view of the cordial relations between the Guptas and the branch of the Vākāṭakas to which Narendra Sena belonged till the end of this branch,[28] it is likely that the Vākāṭaka king rendered valuable assistance to his Gupta cousin in curbing this rebellion and reasserting his authority over these recalcitrant chiefs. Narendra Sena may have played a vital role in these expeditions either as a prince-commander or after his accession, and this formed the basis of the claim of victory over these chiefs on his behalf in his son's records. It is also not impossible that taking advantage of his cousin's problems he carried out hurried raids in these regions.

With reference to Pṛithivī Sheṇa II, the donor of the charter, the record employs the expression *dvi-magna-vaṁśasy-oddhartṛi.*[29] Both Kielhorn and Mirashi, who edited this charter, surmised that the intended reading probably was *nimagna-vaṁśasy-oddhartṛi*[30] and took it to mean that Pṛithivī Sheṇa II had raised his sunken family.[31] It appears, however, that the proposed emendation of the reading is totally unwarranted and that the composer of this record deliberately added the word *dvi* with the object of referring to the sinking and retrieval of the family fortune *twice*, not *once*, by his patron. This finds support from a couple of Pṛithivī Sheṇa II's charters discovered thereafter. These are the Māṇḍhaḷ plates of his tenth year and Māhurjharī charter of his seventeenth year, both hailing from the Nāgpur district of Maharashtra.[32] Both these records contain this expression, but without the word *dvi* prefaced to it.[33] In these records the intention was to refer to Pṛithivī Sheṇa II as one who had rescued his sunken family. It is only in the Bālāghāṭ plates that we find the word *dvi* prefixed to *magna*, thereby conveying that the Vākāṭaka king had actually rescued his sunken family fortunes twice. It is thus clear that Pṛithivī Sheṇa II had retrieved the fallen family fortunes only once up to the seventeenth year of his reign and that sometime after that the family fortunes had sunk again and it became necessary for him to restore the same once again. This situation was sought to be reflected by adding the word *dvi* to the phrase which had already found a place in his copper-plate charters. It is difficult in the present state of inadequate information to determine as to what these two calamities were. But it may be reasonably surmised that the first catastrophe was apparently the one that had led to Narendra Sena's loss of his kingdom or its major portion due to a close or distant relation(s), and the first task before Pṛithivī Sheṇa immediately following his accession must have been the restoration of fallen family fortunes. This had obviously been achieved latest by the tenth year of his reign.[34] The second calamity was in all probability the Nala invasion resulting in the occupation of a large part of the realm including the erstwhile metropolis of Nandivardhana by the Nala king Bhavadattavaraman.[35] Needless to say that the Bālāghāṭ plates which as yet form the only record to have the word *dvi* prefixed to the expression in question must have been issued sometime after the seventeenth year of his reign.[36]

As we have seen above, the Bālāghāṭ plates have been left unfinished. There is, however, no doubt that they were issued later than the other charter of Pṛithivī Sheṇa II known to date. They contain an allusion to two calamities and following retrievals of family fortunes by him as against other two charters referring only to one such event. But exactly how much later cannot be ascertained as the portion giving the regnal year which is normally at the end of the record has been left unfinished.

V.B. Kolte, while editing the Māhurjharī plates, has taken a very serious note of the unfinished condition of this (Bālāghāṭ) charter. He feels that it could not be completed and had to be left unfinished because of a third disaster which again reduced the Vākāṭaka power to a shambles. And when the very existence of the kingdom was in doubt, the land-grant had no value. However, it need not, and perhaps could not, have been so. There could, and perhaps most probably, be some other reason for it. The king might have decided to abandon the grant when some unpalatable facts about the beneficiary/beneficiaries[38] or some points about the land to be donated[39] were brought before him or for such other cause. And only for this reason alone we need not assume another calamity befalling the Vākāṭaka kingdom. There are some other examples of unfinished charters among the Vākāṭakas. The solitary Durg (Mohalla) plate is one such example where also at the beginning (in line 1) space enough to accommodate the word *dṛishṭam* and space sufficient for five letters is available at the end of the fifth and last line.[40] If Kolte's explanation about the unfinished character of the Bālāghāṭ plates were to be accepted, some similar reason will have to be found out in this case also. Under the circumstances it is best to leave such reasons unspeculated.

The case is akin to numismatics where also scholars are in the habit of speculating some such reason as, for example, insecurity caused by some alien invasion for cause of interring hoards of coins underground and drawing some very important though totally unfounded historical deductions therefrom, forgetting that in the pre-banking days it was a common practice to bury coins, by themselves or in pots, underground and even after the banks came into existence, several people continued to bury their treasure under the earth, sometimes even currency notes with results disastrous to the owners. In any case, while in the field of numismatics it is common to draw such unfounded important historical deductions, in the field of epigraphy we are not aware of any other such inference.

It would be seen from the above that the Bālāghāṭ plates, though left unfinished, are of great value for the history of the branch of the Vākāṭakas to which Pṛithivī Sheṇa II, the donor, belonged.

Even though the charter under reference is left incomplete for some indeterminable reason which need not be speculated about, the condition in which the plates were found perhaps sheds some welcome light on the physical aspect of the preparation of a charter. After it was decided to issue a grant and after the text of the charter was finalised, the plates required for the purpose were strung together in a copper-ring to which the disc meant for the seal was also attached. The engraving then started. And when the entire text was incised, it was checked and as a mark of this final act the word *dṛishṭam* was finally engraved and the seal engraved on the metallic disc, turning it into a regular authenticated charter. And if in the course of engraving, some irregularity or fact going against the grant came to notice it was abandoned. Thus, so far as the Vākāṭaka copper-plate grants are concerned, this set of plates throws welcome light on the physical aspect of their preparation.

In resume we can say that

(i) The Bālāghāṭ plates were important when discovered because they first brought to light Narendra Sena and Pṛithivī Sheṇa II.

(ii) As indicated by two other charters of Pṛithivī Sheṇa II found subsequently, the correct reading of the expression read by Kielhorn followed by Mirashi as *pūrvv-ādhigata-guṇa-viśvāsād= apahṛita-vaṁśa-śriyaḥ* is *pūrvv-ādhigata-guṇavad=dāyād-āpahṛita-vaṁśa-śriyaḥ* which sheds welcome light on a crucial phase in the life of Narendra Sena by showing that the demise of Pravara Sena II was followed by a struggle for succession in which Narendra Sena succeeded but was later divested of his kingdom or its major portion by his relations, perhaps of the Vatsagulma branch.

(iii) In view of the difficult situation in which he was placed because of his kinsmen, the statement that Narendra Sena's behests were obeyed by the rulers of Kosalā, Mekalā and Mālava cannot be taken literally.

(iv) The expression *dvi-magna-vaṁś-oddhartuḥ* used with reference to Pṛithivī Sheṇa II does refer to two catastrophes from which he rescued his family. The first of these was that which had led to his father's deprivation of his kingdom or its major part from which he had rescued it before his tenth year and the second calamity, perhaps the invasion of the Nalas, took place after his seventeenth year.

(v) The charter throws new light on the preparation of the Vākāṭaka copper-plate grants.

Notes and References

1. See *EI*, IX, p. 267.
2. *Ibid.*, pp. 267-71 and plates between pp. 270 and 271. The charter has been re-edited by V.V. Mirashi in his *Inscriptions of the Vākāṭakas, CII*, V, pp. 79-81 and plates opposite pp. 80 and 81.

3. These are Māṇḍhal plates of his second and tenth years (Ajay Mitra Shastri, "Māṇḍhaḷ Plates of Pṛithivī Sheṇa II, Years 2 and 10", *EI*, XLI, pp. 159-80) and Māhurjharī grant of his seventeenth year (V.B. Kolte, "Māhurzarī Plates of Pṛithivī Sheṇa II", *ABORI*, LIII, pp. 183-94 and plates following p. 194).
4. *EI*, XXII, p. 210, fn. 6; *CII*, V, p. 80.
5. V.B. Kolte, "Pauni Plates of Pravara Sena II", *EI*, XXXVIII, pp. 53-56.
6. *Ibid*., IX, p. 271, lines 26-27.
7. *CII*, V, p. 81, lines 26-27.
8. *ABORI*, LIII, p. 193, lines 21-22. *Vide* also *Vidarbha Saṁśodhana Maṇḍala Vārshika*, 1971, p. 75, lines 21-22, especially line 22.
   I also had originally adopted this reading while editing the Māṇḍhal charter of Pṛithivī Sheṇa II's tenth year in *ibid*., 1977, line 7, and in my paper entitled "Bālāghāṭ Plates of Pṛithivī Sheṇa II" published in *Srīnidhiḥ: Perspectives in Indian Archaeology, Art and Culture: Shri K.R. Srinivasan Festschrift*, eds. K.V. Raman et al., Madras, 1983, pp. 443-49.
9. *Vide* references to Kolte's publications in the preceding fn.
10. Ajay Mitra Shastri, "Māṇḍhaḷ Plates of Pṛithivī Sheṇa II, Years 2 and 10", *EI*, XLI, p. 177, line 17. For discussion, see *ibid*., pp. 172-74; *AV*, pp. 241-42.
11. *EI*, XLI, pl. iib, line 17, opposite p. 177.
12. *Vidarbha Saṁśodhana Maṇḍaḷa Vārshika*, Nagpur, 1971, pl. VI, lines 21-22; *ABORI*, LIII, relevant plate and lines.
13. *EI*, IX, p. 269.
14. *CII*, V, pp. xxv and 79-81.
15. *Ibid.*
16. G. Yazdani (ed.), *Early History of the Deccan*, p. 182.
17. *Ibid*., pp. 182-83.
18. He rightly stressed that *hṛi*, when prefixed by *apa* as in this case, actually alluded to forcible seizure.
19. It can as well be split and explained as *pūrvv-ādhigatā guṇavato dāyādād=apahritā vaṁśa-śrīh yena tasya* or *pūrvv-ādhigatena gunavatā dāyādena apahṛitā vaṁśa-śrīh yasya tasya*. But they do not yield any satisfactory sense and consequently cannot be upheld.
20. For the connotation of *dāyāda*, see *Amara-kosha*, III, 3.89; Monier Monier-Williams, *A Sanskrit-English Dictionary*, p. 474, s.v. *dayāda*. See also P.V. Kane, *History of Dharmaśāstra*, III, pp. 543-44.
21. The employment of the word *guṇavat* as an adjective of the *dāyāda* who was the source of trouble to Narendra Sena is rather enigmatic. It may have perhaps been intended to aver that even though the *dāyāda* was endowed with virtues, he indulged in acts like seizing his relation's (Narendra Sena's) throne. Alternatively, and this is more likely, it may have been used in the sense of *gauṇa*, 'minor', a derivative from *guṇa*, with reference to a member of the Vatsagulma branch of the dynasty.
22. The expressions are *Kosalā-Mekalā-Mālav-ādhipatibhir=abhyarchchita-śāsanasya* and *pratāpa-pralāt-ārisanasya* (*CII*, V, p. 81, lines 28-29), the latter being apparently an error for *pratāpa-praṇat-āri-śāsansya* which is the restored corrected reading met with in the Māhurjharī plates (*ABORI*, LIII, p. 193, line 23).
23. The Nachnā-kī-talāi and Ganj inscriptions of Vyāghradeva belong to the reign of Pṛithivī

Sheṇa I and not his homonymous great great-grandson as believed by some scholars. See for our discussion, *AV*, pp. 10-12; supra, pp. 55-69.

24. This suggestion was floated by B.Ch. Chabra while editing the Bamhanī plates (*EI*, XXVII, pp. 137-38) and followed by V.V. Mirashi (*CII*, V, pp. 83-84). This was based on the word *narendra* in verse 11 of this record which was taken to make a veiled allusion to the Vākāṭaka king Narendra Sena. But the recently published Mallār plates of Bharatabala's son Śūrabala also contain this word and leave absolutely no doubt that there is no pun on this word which has the sense of 'king' only.
25. This claim is made in all his charters except only the Māṇḍhal plates of his second year which just name Narendra Sena without any reference to his achievements. See for these plates, *EL*, XLI, pp. 165-69.
26. The prose sentence in question is *tasya putras=tat-pād-ānudhyātaḥ parama-māheśvaraḥ parama-brahmaṇyaḥ parama-guru-devat-ādhidaivata-viśeshaḥ śrīmatyāṁ Mahādevyam= utpannaḥ śrī-mahārāja-Śūrabalaḥ*. See *vide* B. Sitaraman and M. Jayarama Sharma, "Malhār Plates of Pāṇḍava King Śūrabala, Year 8", *Studies in Indian Epigraphy (JESI)*, III, pp. 190-91, lines 26-28. These plates have been later edited by us in our *Inscriptions of the Śarabhapurīyas, Pāṇḍuvaṁśins and Somavaṁśins*, Part II, pp. 83-85.
27. "The Date of the Bamhanī and Mallār Plates of Śūrabala Udīrṇavaira", *Bhāratī-Bhānam: Dr. K.V. Sarma Felicitation Volume*, pp. 439-43; infra, pp. 80-84.
28. This is clear from the fact that marriage of Rudra Sena II with Prabhāvatī Guptā,

II, the last known member of this branch.

29. *EI*, IX, p. 271, line 33.
30. *Ibid.*, p. 271, fn. 15; *CII*, V, p. 81, fn. 7.
31. *Ibid.*, V, pp. xxvii, 81; *EI*, IX, p. 269.
32. *Ibid.*, XLI, p. 177, line 21; *ABORI*, LIII, p. 193, line 26.
33. The correct form of the expression in both these charters is *magna-vaṁś-oddhartuḥ*, the genitive singular of *magna-vaṁś-oddhartṛi*.
34. This is the date of his second set of Māṇḍhaḷ plates.
35. The Ṛiddhapur charter of the Nala king Bhavadattavarman (called Bhavattavarman in the record, which is perhaps an error or perhaps the popular spelling of the name) was issued from Nandivardhana (modern Nagardhan or Nandardhan) and registers the grant of land situated in the Yawatmāl district, showing that the occupied territory included the whole of the region extending from the Nāgpur district up to the Yawatmāl region. For the plates, *vide ibid.*, XIX, pp. 100ff.
36. The Māhurjharī charter was issued in this year.
37. *ABORI*, LIII, p. 189.
38. As the plates are left unfinished, it is difficult to ascertain if there was only a single donee or more.
39. It is difficult to determine, because of the incomplete nature of the charter, if one or more villages or piece/pieces of land were intended to be granted. The reason for giving up the grant could have been the earlier unknown fact that they were already donated to some other person/persons by some earlier king(s) of his own/another family.
40. *CII*, V, plate opposite p. 78.

APPENDIX III

The Date of the Bamhanī and Mallār Plates of Śūrabala Udīrṇavaira

The discovery of a copper-plate charter at a place called Bamhanī in the Shahḍol district of Madhya Pradesh in 1940 and its publication by B.Ch. Chhabra in *Epigraphia Indica,* Vol. XXVII, pp. 132-45 naturally attracted a good deal of attention as it brought to light the Pāṇḍava dynasty of Mekalā for the first time. For over three and half decades it remained the sole source of our information about this dynasty until another charter of the dynasty was found at Mallār in the Bilaspur district and published by B. Sitaraman and M.J. Sharma in the *Studies in Indian Epigraphy (Bhāratīya Purābhilekha Patrikā),* III, pp. 183-93 a few years ago.[1] The former grant was believed to belong to the fourth member of the dynasty, Bharatabala *alias* Indra until the latter record proved conclusively that, like it, the Bamhanī plates also belonged to Bharatabala's son and successor Śūrabala *alias* Udīrṇavaira. The misconception that the Bamhanī plates belonged to Bharatabala was due to the omission by oversight of a short prose passage introducing his son Śūrabala which is found at its proper place in the Mallār plates.[2]

As usual with copperplate inscriptions, both these charters are donative in nature and aim at recording land-grants. The Bamhanī charter purports to register the grant of the village Vardhamānaka situated in the Pañchagartā *vishaya* included in the Uttara-rāshṭra in Mekalā to Lohiasara-svāmin who belonged to the Vatsa *gotra* and the Madhyandina *śākhā* of the Śukla Yajurveda. The Mallār plates record the grant of a village named Saṅgama included in the Dikshiṇa-rāshṭra of Mekalā after receiving it from Narasimha, son of Boṭa and grandson of the merchant Manoratha, in favour of the god Jayeśvara-bhaṭṭāraka. The Bamhanī plates were issued on the 13th day of the dark fortnight of the month of Bhādrapada in the second year of the reign of Śūrabala Udīrṇavaira while the Mallār charter is said to have been given on Wednesday, the eleventh day of the dark fortnight of the month of Kārttika when the *nakshatra* was Pūrva-Phālgunī in the eighth year of the same monarch's reign. Both the records were composed by Śiva and engraved by Mihiraka (or Mahiraka as he is called in the Mallār plates).

The importance of these records lies in the fact that they form the only source of our information about the Pāṇḍavas of Mekalā.[3] And consequently the determination of the date of these records is most vital for ascertaining the chronology of the Pāṇḍava rule in Mekalā. But unfortunately the dates of these charters are given only with reference to the reign of the issuing chief, and not in a known reckoning which could enable us to determine their exact import. Therefore the dates, approximate indeed, of these records and the chronology of the Pāṇḍavas emerging therefrom have to be determined on other available grounds.

Chhabra found a veiled allusion to the Vākāṭaka king Narendra Sena in verse 11 of the Bamhanī plates and felt that the verse aimed at describing by *double entendre* the contemporary Pāṇḍava chief as a feudatory of Narendra Sena.[4] He tried to reinforce this conclusion by citing the statement in the Bālāghāṭ plates of Pṛithivī Sheṇa II that the commands of his father Narendra Sena were honoured by the lords of Kosalā, Mekalā and Mālava.[5] And on this ground he thought that Bharatabala was a contemporary of Narendra Sena and approximately equated the second year of the former's rule to 460 AD.[6] This suggestion was okayed by V.V. Mirashi who proposed to place Bharatabala's reign in *circa* 460-480 AD.[7] A slightly later date is favoured by D.C. Sircar who would prefer to place the reigns of Nāgabala and Bharatabala in the second half of the fifth century AD.[8] It is, however, difficult to accept these views in the light of the evidence now available. Firstly, as observed above, the Bamhanī plate, like the Mallār grant of the dynasty, was issued not by Bharatabala, but by Śūrabala *alias* Udīrṇavaira. Therefore, if the poet actually intended to refer to his Pāṇḍava chief's overlord, Śūrabala, not Bharatabala, would turn out to be Narendra Sena's feudatory. But actually no allusion, however indirect, seems to be intended in the verse in question and the word *narendra* has to be taken only in the sense of 'king' and it qualifies the Pāṇḍava king Udīrṇavaira who is mentioned by name just before this word. In fact, the notion that there is a veiled allusion in this word to the Pāṇḍava ruler's Vākāṭaka overlord would not have occurred to Chhabra and Mirashi but for the aforesaid assertion of Pṛithivī Sheṇa II's records with reference to his father Narendra Sena. That this notion is erroneous is indicated by the description, in the same stanza, of the Pāṇḍava king as a paramount ruler with a number of feudatory chiefs falling at his feet.

Thus, there is absolutely no reference to Vākāṭaka Narendra Sena in our records and the verse in question is therefore of no help in determining the period of the Pāṇḍava rule over Mekalā.

The evidence necessary for our purpose is, however, furnished by the statement in both these records that Lokaprakāśā, the queen of Bharatabala, was born in the Amaraja family in Kosalā. There can be no doubt that the Amārajakula is the same as the Amarārya-kula which is known from the Mallār plates of Vyāghrarāja[9] to have held sway over Kosalā for some time. This charter gives us the names of two rulers of family, viz. Jaya-bhaṭṭāraka and Pravara-bhaṭṭāraka, and the record is dated in the 41 or 4 of the reign of the latter. It is generally believed that Amarārya-kula was the name of what is popularly known as Śarabhapurīya. But as we have shown elsewhere,[10] this view is unconvincing. The fact appears to be that the Amarārya-kula chiefs were probably ruling contemporaneously with the later Śarabhapurīya chiefs in a part of Kosalā not under the Śarabhapurīyas and conquered the Mallār area taking advantage of the decline of the Śarabhapurīya power about the close of the sixth or the beginning of the seventh century A.D. The Śarabhapurīyas are known to have held sway over Kosalā up to about the close of sixth century AD.[12] Therefore, Bharatabala, who married a princess of the Amarārya-kula, cannot be placed earlier than the latter half of the sixth century AD. And even if the identification of the Amarārya-kula with the Śarabhapurīyas is accepted, this date will not be affected as, according to our view, Jayarāja (who is sometimes identified with Jaya-bhaṭṭāraka), ruled from *c.* 550 to *c.* 560 AD. If Lokaprakāśā was the daughter of Jayarāja, i.e. Jaya-bhaṭṭāraka, the rule of her husband Bharatabala cannot be placed earlier than the third quarter of the sixth century AD. And if she was the daughter of Pravararāja I—Pravara-bhaṭṭāraka, Bharatabala will have to be placed in the last quarter of that century and his son Śūrabala about the end of the sixth and the beginning of the seventh century AD. The reigns of the earlier members of the dynasty will then have to be placed from the close of the fifth or the beginning of the sixth to the middle of the sixth century AD.

The evidence afforded by the Malgā plates of Sāmunta Indrarāja[13] also leads to the same conclusion. We have shown elsewhere that regarding all formal matters including tthe list of addressees of the royal command about the grant, privileges and exemptions accompanying the grant, the manner of recording the date, general drafting and the formal features of the plates, this charter bears a very close resemblance to the copperplate charters of the Pāṇḍavas of Mekalā.[14]

And what is even more interesting is that the scribes of the two sets of records were related to each other as brothers. Sāmanta Indrarāja therefore was probably connected in some way or other with the Pāṇḍavas of Mekalā though at the moment it is not possible to ascertain the exact nature of this connection. The find-spots of the Malgā and Bamhanī plates are also situated close to each other in the Shahḍol district of Madhya Pradesh. On palaeographical grounds the Malgā plates have been dated about the first half of the seventh century AD.[15] D.C. Sircar and S. Sankaranarayanan surmised that Indrarāja ruled as a semi-independent chief either sometime between the death of Maukhari king Grahavarman about 605 AD and the establishment of Harshavardhana's power over the former Maukhari principality shortly thereafter or sometime after Harshavardhana's death in 647 AD.[16] Be that as it may, the fact remains that it cannot be doubted in view of the extremely close similarities between the two sets of inscriptions they could not have been separated by a long period and that the records of the Pāṇḍavas of Mekalā cannot be placed earlier than the close of the sixth or early yers of theollowing centry AD.

It will follow from the foregoing that the Bamhanī and Mallār plates of Śūrabala Udīraṇavaira have to be dated about the commencement of the seventh century AD. This conclusion is also supported by the discovery of a charter of Śūrabala and the identification of the village granted thereby not far from Mallār in the Bilāspur district of Madhya Pradesh that his dominions included the region round Mallār. This could be possible only after the end of Śarabhapurīyas whose numerous records have been found at Mallār. This event took place about the close of the sixth century AD.

The upshot of the above discussion is that the commencement of the Pāṇḍava rule in Mekalā cannot be placed earlier than about the beginning of the sixth century AD while the dynasty came to an end about the beginning of the following century AD.

Notes and References

1. A stray plate of another record of the dynasty has also been reported from Mallār. See *ABORI, Diamond Jubliee Volume*, pp. 433-37.
2. *Studies in Indian Epigraphy*, III, pp. 190-91, text-lines 27-28.
3. There is possibly a reference to the Pāṇḍava king Jayabala in Purāṇic texts. See S.N. Roy, *Historical and Cultural Studies in the Purāṇas*, p. 170.
4. *EI*, XXVII, p. 137.
5. *CII*, V, p. 81, text-line 28. This statement is also found in the Māhurjharī and one of

the Māṇḍhal plates of Pṛithivī Sheṇa II. See *Vidarbha Saṁśodhana Maṇḍaḷa Vārshika,* 1971, p. 75, text-line 22; 1977, p. 171, text-line 17.

6. *EI,* XXVII, p. 138.
7. *Studies in Indology,* I, second edition, p. 233.
8. *The Classical Age,* p. 223; *The Vākāṭaka-Gupta Age,* p. 92.
9. *EI,* XXXIV, pp. 45-50.
10. *Prāchya-Pratibhā,* V, Part-I, pp. 1, 27-32.
11. The charter, though dated in the reign of Pravara-bhaṭṭāraka, was issued by his younger brother Vyāghraraja.
12. For a discussion on the Śarabhapurīya chronology see *ibid.,* V, Part-I, pp. 20-25; "Were Mādhavavarman and Tīvaradera Contemporaries?" *JESI,* pp. 20-25.
13. *EI,* XXXIII, pp. 209.
14. See our paper entitled "A Note on the Malga Plates of Samanta Indrarāja", *Sri Venkateswara University Oriental Journal,* Vols. XXI-XXII, pp. 19-25.
15. *EI,* XXXIII, p. 209.
16. *Ibid.,* p. 211.

II

Recent Discoveries of Vākāṭaka Inscriptions

The period of a little over three decades of this century that has elapsed since the publication of V.V. Mirashi's corpus of the inscriptions of the Vākāṭakas[1] has been very prolific from the view-point of Vākāṭaka epigraphy, and we shall not be wide of the mark if we aver that more than half of the Vākāṭaka epigraphs as known at the time of the publication of that work have been discovered during this comparatively short interval.[2] The present author has been intimately associated with the discovery and publication of a large number of these inscriptions. While some of these inscriptions have been published in well-known periodicals, others have not been published in detail or reported in rather obscure publications not easily accessible to historians. Their publication in standard professional journals may take quite a few years. However, as all these inscriptions are of inestimable value for the history of the Vākāṭakas, students of early Indian history can ill afford to ignore the valuable evidence furnished by them. We are, therefore, discussing their contents and historical bearing in these pages. Hopefully, this account will serve as a summary supplement[3] to Mirashi's above-mentioned valuable work.

Barring a couple of exceptions,[4] all these epigraphs are copperplate charters. Three of these inscriptions, one lithic and two copperplate grants, belong to the Vatsagulma (wāshim) branch of the dynasty, while the rest, one lithic and the rest copperplate inscriptions, are claimed by the Padmapura-Nandivardhana-Pravarapura branch. We may deal with these inscriptions chronologically, taking up first those belonging to the latter branch.[5]

PADMAPURA-NANDIVARDHANA-PRAVARAPURA BRANCH

I. Māṇḍhaḷ Plates of Rudra Sena II, Year 5 (Pls. VII-IX)

Incised on a set of four plates, this record was discovered in 1982, while ploughing a field at Māṇḍhaḷ, a village about seventy-five km from Nāgpur in the Umred tahsīl of the Nāgpur district. It aims at registering that the Vākāṭaka monarch Rudra Sena II granted four villages, to wit, Selludraha, Achchhabhallikā, Suragrāmakā and Aragrāmakā, situated to the west of the village of Kurudumbhaka, to the north of the two villages named Śaṅkhikā,[6] to the east of Bābbaikā, and to the south of Phukudumbhaka,[7] and included in the eastern part of the administrative division of Padmapura,[8] barring the land earlier granted in favour of a couple of monasteries of the Sātvata school originally belonging to Vatsagulma[9] (modern Wāshim, Akolā district). The granted villages appear to have been turned into an *agrāhāra* (Brāhmaṇa settlement) which was placed under the charge of the Brāhmaṇas belonging to different *gotras* and *charaṇas* and engaged in study, and the grant carried with it the usual privileges and exemptions applicable to the *agrāhāra* villages.[10] The grant is said to have been made at the message or command (*sandeśa*) of god Vishṇu called Mondasvāmin and described as carrying a conch-shell, a wheel and a sword[11] and resting in the *yoga-nidrā* on the body of the snake-king called Ananta[12] in the ocean. The order about the grant is stated to have been issued by the king himself.[13] The record is dated the seventh day of the sixth fortnight of the rainy season during the fifth year, evidently of the reign of Rudra Sena II, the donor of the charter, and was written by *Senāpati* Vibhīshaṇa.

The inscription is of great value for more than one reason. Till now the fragmentary Deoṭek stone inscription of Rudra Sena[14] was regarded as the earliest Vākāṭaka epigraph. But besides being fragmentary, it does not afford definite evidence which could enable us to attribute it undoubtedly to Rudra Sena I or II, though it is generally attributed to the former. Viewed from this standpoint, this is the earliest definitely attributable inscription of the Padmapura-Nandivardhana-Pravarapura branch of the Vākāṭakas, and certainly the earliest known copperplate charter of this branch of the dynasty. Secondly, as no dated record of Rudra Sena II was known so far, there was no means of ascertaining the length of his reign which was conjecturally fixed variously by historians. But the present record, which was issued in the fifth year of his reign, shows that he ruled at least for five years. However, we still have no means to ascertain as to how long he continued to rule after the date of this record. Thirdly, the employment of the season date instead of the usual month date, which is so far met with only in a few Vākāṭaka records, is of considerable interest.[15] Fourthly, *Senāpati* Vibhīshaṇa has come to be known from this record for the first time. Fifthly, this inscription gives us an idea of the evolution of the draft of the official charters of this branch of the dynasty up to the time of Rudra Sena II.[16]

The present charter is of considerable interest for the religious history as well. That it is a Vaishṇavite record will be clear from its contents. The custom of naming a divine image or shrine after a personal or place name was quite popular in ancient India and continues to be so even now, and while names ending in Īśa, Īśvara and Śiva were popular among the Śaivas, the Vaishṇavas favoured *svāmin*-ending names. And since Monda does not look like a personal name, the god Mondasvāmin appears to have been named after the place where the temple was situated. It is noteworthy in this connection that there still exist villages named Maudā and Doṅgar Maudā in the vicinity of Māṇḍhaḷ, the provenance of the plates. It would, thus, follow that the temple of Mondasvāmin was situated in this area. Let us hope that future explorations will throw more light on this problem. It is also pertinent to note in this context that the excavations at Māṇḍhaḷ carried out under the present author's direction have thrown up some beautiful early Vākāṭaka Vaishṇava images.[17] We may, therefore, conclude that the region round Māṇḍhaḷ was an important centre of Vaishṇavism during the early Vākāṭaka period. Rudra Sena II alone among the early Vākāṭaka rulers was a devout votary of Vaishṇavism, and it is stated in our record as well as the later official charters of the family that his authority was established by the wheel-bearing god, i.e. Vishṇu.[18] It is very likely, therefore, that he played a pivotal role in popularising the Bhāgavata religion in this region.

The description of Śeshaśāyīn Vishṇu under the name Mondasvāmin is also of great iconographic interest. This is, to our knowledge, one of the oldest datable descriptions of this form, and it will be in the fitness of things to find its sculptural parallels answering the description in full. The well-known Bhītargāon and Deogarh Anantaśayana panels, which are the earliest known so far, are somewhat later than our inscription and do not tally with our account in so far as the *āyudhas* held in his hands are concerned.[19] The South Indian Śeshaśayana or Anantaśayana panels, popularly known as Raṅganātha Raṅgasvāmin, are of a considerably later period.

In ancient India a great controversy raged regarding the Vedic or non-Vedic character of the Sātvatas. Some of the Vaishṇava Āgamas adduce arguments to prove their Vedic affiliation. The reference to the Sātvata *charaṇa* seems to indicate that their Vedicism has become established, at least among the Pāñcharātras, by the Vākāṭaka period. As the two monasteries of the Sātvatas mentioned in our record were situated in the Māṇḍhaḷ region, this area was undoubtedly an important centre of their activities. And since these Sātvatas originally hailed from Vatsagulma or Wāshim, the Vatsagulma region also must have been an important centre of the school.

Before we conclude, reference may be made to the *pūrva-mārga* of Padmapura in which the donated villages were included. That the word *mārga* when joined to a place-name indicates an administrative unit is shown by the Māhurjharī plates of Pṛithivī Sheṇa II which record the grant of the village Jamalakheṭaka situated in the Jamalakheṭaka-mārga.[20] As will be seen in the sequel, the *aparamārga* of Padmapura is mentioned in the Māsod grant of the nineteenth year of Pravara Sena II.[21] It may, therefore, be concluded that the administrative unit named after Padmapura was divided into two parts—eastern (*pūrva*) and western (*apara*). Padmapura after which the district was named cannot be identified satisfactorily. However, since Matsyadraha or Māsod in the Kaṭol tahsīl of the Nāgpur district which was donated by the Māsod grant is said to have been situated in the Padmapura-apara-mārga, the Kāṭol region may be taken to have been included in this *mārga*, though we are unable to determine its extent. The Padmapura-pūrva-mārga was evidently situated to the east of the Māsod area, though how far east we cannot say. In view of these facts, Padmapura, the headquarters of the unit christened after it, should be looked for somewhere in the Nāgpur-Wardhā region.[22]

II. Māṇḍhaḷ Plates of Pravara Sena II, Years 16 and 17 (Pls. XIX-XXII)

While the aforementioned charter was found accidentally while ploughing a field at Māṇḍhaḷ, archaeological excavations at the same site yielded, *inter alia*, three sets of Vākāṭaka copperplate inscriptions intact with their rings and seals preserved in an earthen pot covered with a lid. One of these charters belongs to Pravara Sena II, and the rest to his grandson Pṛithivī Sheṇa.[23]

The grant of Pravara Sena II, which is incised on a set of five plates, was, like a majority of his records, issued from Pravarapura, generally identified with modern Paunār in the Wardhā district. It records his donation of the village Mayasagrāma included in the Aparapaṭṭa of Beṇṇātaṭa in favour of *Upādhyāya* Māṭrisvāmin, son of a certain *Upādhyāya* who is left unnamed and simply described as *apratigrāhaka* or non-acceptor of gifts,[24] who was a resident of Beṇṇataṭa and belonged to the Taittirīya *śākha* of the Black *Yajurveda* and the Kautsa *gotra.* The grant is stated to have been made on an evening during the month of Kārttika in the sixteenth year, and one-third of the religious merit accruing from the donation was to go to Ājñākabhaṭṭarikā, mother of a certain Narindarāja (Narendrarāja). The order in respect of the grant was given by the king himself.

The gift was accompanied by the usual privileges and exemptions. The charter was written when Chitravarman was *Senāpati* on the tenth day of the dark fortnight of the month of Kārttika in the seventeenth year, apparently of the grantor's reign.

The four-line seal inscription is the same as that found on other seals of Pravara Sena II and is singularly bereft of historical interest.

It will be seen that the record contains two dates, one when the grant was made and the other when the charter was written and issued. Though the details of the first date are lacking, the two dates are separated form one another by about a year, and the charter was issued a year after the donation was made. But there is nothing to be surprised about it as this phenomenon is noticed in several other cases also.

These dates throw welcome light on the history of the Vākāṭakas. The Jāmb plates of the second year[25] and both the Belorā grants of the eleventh year of Pravara Sena II's reign[26] were given from Nandivardhana, whereas the Chammak charter of the eighteenth year of his reign was issued from Pravarapura.[27] It is, therefore, believed that Pravara Sena II shifted his capital from Nandivardhana to Pravarapura sometime between the eleventh and eighteenth years of his reign. But the present record, which was issued from Pravarapura and registers a grant made in the sixteenth year, shows that the capital of what is generally designated as the main branch of the Vākāṭakas was shifted, if at all, from Nandivardhana to Pravarapura sometime in or prior to the sixteenth year of Pravara Sena II's reign.

Neither Narendrarāja nor his mother Ājñākabhaṭṭārikā, who is stated to have shared one-third of the merit accruing from the grant, is known from any other source. That they had some pretensions to royalty is indicated by the words *rāja* and *bhaṭṭārikā* respectively suffixed to their names. In case this Narindarāja is identified with Narendra Sena, son and successor of Pravara Sena II, the inscription would give us the name of Pravara Sena II's chief queen and Narendra Sena's mother. However, there can be no certainty about it as the relegation of just one-third of the merit to Narindarāja's mother Ājñākabhaṭṭārikā and the casual manner in which the mother and the son are mentioned seem to negate this conjecture.[28] It may, therefore, be concluded that one of them was the person at whose request the grant was made,[28a] although their identity does not admit of determination at present.

The administrative division of Beṇṇataṭa, in the Aparapaṭṭa or western part of which the donated village was situated is evidently the same as Beṇṇākaṭa referred to in the Tirodī grant of Pravara Sena II,[29] the employment of the word *taṭa* instead of *kaṭa* being interesting linguistically. Beṇṇātaṭa (or Beṇṇākaṭa), as indicated by the name, apparently denoted the area on the banks of the river Veṇā or Waingaṅgā, and the mention of its Aparapaṭṭa in this as well as in the Tiroḍī charter would seem to show that this district was divided at least into two parts, viz., eastern (Pūrva) and western (Apara), the river Waingaṅgā probably forming the dividing line. But we know from other records to be noticed later in this paper that the other division was known as Uttarapaṭṭa following the course of the Waingaṅgā. The donated village Mayasagrāma cannot be identified definitely, but the possibility of its identity with Māṇḍhaḷ, the find-spot of the inscription in question, cannot be ruled out.[29a]

III. Māsod Plates of Pravara Sena II, Year 19 (Pls. XXXVIII-XLII)

The set of five plates bearing this record was found over four and half decades ago while ploughing a field at the village of Māsod under Maujā Kāmaṭhi and Koṇḍhālī Police Station in the Kaṭol tālukā of the Nagpur district and was acquired for the Central Museum, Nāgpur, some twenty years earlier (1976). The seal was found missing.

The charter records the donation, by Pravara Sena II, of a piece of land to the north-west[30] of the village Matsakadraha in the low-lying area (*garttasabhā*) of the river Rājatintiṇika situated in the *apara-mārga* of Padampura in favour of a group of nineteen Brāhmaṇas named with their respective *gotras*. The donated land is mentioned as 'three hundred lands' (*bhūmi-śata-traya*) measured by the royal measurement (*rāja-mānika-mānena*).[31] Although the exact unit of measurement has been omitted by oversight, the intended unit appears to have been *nivartana* which is referred to in a few other Vākāṭaka records as well. Thus, in all three hundred *nivartanas* of land was given away. The grant was made at the request of the chief queen (*bhāryā-mahādevi*) who is, however, left unnamed. The granted land was split up into twenty-five plots (*vāṭaka*)[31a] which were variously given to a certain Mahāpurusha, curiously styled *apratigrāhin* (non-acceptor of donations) and nineteen other Brāhamṇas bearing *āryya*-ending names[32] and belonging to the Kauṇḍinya (4), Bhāradvāja (4), Pārāśara (2), Kāśyapa (3), Kauśika (3), Vatsa (1) and Gautama (2) *gotras*. Each plot appears to have consisted of twelve *nivartanas* and was, thus, of a very large size. The order in respect of the grant was given by the king himself and was executed when Kātyāyana occupied the office of *Senāpati*. The date is specified in accordance with the older system of naming the season instead of the month, and the record was issued on the fifth day of the second fortnight of the rainy season during the nineteenth year, apparently of Pravara Sena II's reign. This is one of the few season dates of the reign of Pravara Sena II, all the rest being specified in terms of months.[33]

We know of another record issued in the nineteenth regnal year of Pravara Sena II, viz., Ṛiddhapur plates of Prabhāvatī Guptā, which were given on the twelfth day of the bright fortnight of the month of Kārttika.[34] Our plates, therefore, preceded this charter by a few months.

We find mention of *Senāpati* Kātyāyana in the Paṭṭan plates of the twenty-seventh year of Pravara Sena II also.[35] This fact coupled with a few other similar references[36] would seem to indicate that there were different *senāpatis* appointed for the different regions of the kingdom. But more evidence would be required before we could arrive at any definite conclusion in this regard.

Of the localities specified in our record, Matsakadraha is evidently identical with Māsod, the find-spot of the plates. The *apara-mārga* of Padmapura, in which the granted village was situated, apparently comprised the Kāṭol region of the Nāgpur district and the Ārwī tahsīl of the Wardhā district, while its *pūrva-mārga* covered the region to its east in the Nāgpur and Wardhā tahsīls of the districts of the same names, though it is difficult, in the present state of inadequate knowledge, to be more precise regarding the area comprised in the *mārga* named after Padmapura, probably the capital of this branch before its shifting to Nandivardhana. The river Rājatintiṇika, which may now be represented by one of the small streams in the vicinity of Māsod, cannot be definitely identified.[37]

IV. Miregaon Charter of the Reign of Pravara Sena II, Year 20

A grant of Prabhāvatī Guptā engraved on a set of five plates is reported to have been found together with the ring and the seal a few years ago at Miregāon in the Sākolī tahsīl of the Bhaṇḍāra district. The inscription is similar in all respects to Prabhāvatī Guptā's Ṛiddhapur plates except technical details like the names of the donees and the donated village, etc. It was given by Prabhāvatī Guptā on the twelfth day of the bright forthnight of what is called Hemanta Pushyamāsa in the twentieth year of the reign of her son Pravara Sena II. The date, it would be noticed, is a combination of season and month dates, which is rather unique and in so far as Vākāṭaka charters are concerned this is the sole instance of its type. The donees were five Brāhmaṇas of Kāśyapa *gotra* and the Vājaseneya Mādhyandina *śākhā* of the *Yajurveda*, their names being Bhaṭṭārya, Svāmikārya, Govyārya, Śaṅkarārya and Dharārya. The grant was, like the Puṇe and Ṛiddhapur plates, made after breaking the fast observed on the previous day, though this time of the month of Pausha instead of Kārttika. The granted village was Jalapura-vāṭaka situated to the east of Śarkkara-grāma, south of Vaṭa-padraka, west of Tolaredrukā and north of Mallikāṅk(g)aṇa and included in the Sabhārāshṭra, which is sometimes mentioned as an ancient name of Maharashtra in some texts. It was drafted by Amātya (minister) named Chandra who is known only from this charter. The designation Amātya is also specified only in this Vākāṭaka charter.

It will be seen that in most of the general features it closely agrees with her Ṛiddhapur charter which was issued just in the previous year. The seal of the Riddhapur plates was lost, but since both the charters were issued by Prabhāvatī Guptā and are removed from one another just by about one year. We may reasonably assume that the seal of the Ṛiddhapur charter also bore the same inscription as that attached to the present plates. It runs as follows:

Vikrāntayor=jananyās=tu
Vākāṭaka-narendrayoḥ
Śrī-Prabhāvati(tī)guptāyāḥ
Śāsanaṁ ripu-śāsanam.

This stanza, couched in the *Anushṭubh* metre, describes Prabhāvatī Guptā as the mother of two powerful kings[38] and refers to her *śāsana* (rule or charter, preferably the latter as she was not ruling over the kingdom at the time of issuing the charter) as the chastiser of the enemies. The description of Prabhāvatī Gupta as the mother of two kings is of great historical value as it helps solve a riddle of the Vākāṭaka history. In the present as well as in the Ṛiddhapur charter Prabhāvatī Guptā is styled *Vākāṭakānām Mahārāja-Śrī-Dāmodarasena-Pravarasena-janani.*[39] This expression has been variously interpreted by historians, and according to some, Dāmadara Sena was just another, pre-coronation, name of Pravara Sena (II), the reigning monarch, and that the name Pravara Sena was assumed by him at the time of his coronation.[40] If Dāmodara Sena and Pravara Sena were different personages, it has been argued, the title *mahārāja* should have been prefixed to Pravara Sena also.[41] However, the use of the dual number in *vikrāntayoḥ and Vākāṭaka-narendrayoḥ* should leave no room for doubt that they were separate persons, the latter following the former, and that the title *mahārāja* and the honorific *śrī* are intended for both. Divākara Sena, who was apparently the eldest son of Rudra Sena II and Prabhāvatī Guptā and consequently the rightful claimant to the throne, is out of question in the present context, for, he remained a crown prince or *yuvarāja* for full thirteen years as we learn from the Puṇe plates of Prabhāvatī Guptā,[42] and there is no evidence to indicate that he ever became a crowned king (*mahārāja*) in his own right. On the other hand, we have the negative evidence against his accession as *mahārāja* in his non-mention among Prabhavatī Guptā's sons who rose to the status of *mahārāja*. It is thus clear that the two Vākāṭaka monarchs, whose mother Prabhavatī Guptā was, were no other than Dāmodara Sena and Pravara Sena II. It is worth noting in this connection that so far we have no definite indication that the Vākāṭakas followed the practice of adopting a new name at the time of coronation which was prevalent among certain other dynasties.[43] As a fall-out of this new evidence noticed here for the first time, provision will have to be made for the reign of Dāmodara Sena and the chronology of this branch of the Vākāṭaka dynasty will have to be somewhat modified.[44]

V. Indore Plates of Pravara Sena II, Year 23[45] (Pl. XLIII)

The last three plates of this charter had been known to historians for quite a long time,[46] but the first plate had been missing with the result that its place of issue was not known. However, a few years ago this missing plate was found in the collection of Dr Nagoo of Indore.[47] As expected, in keeping with the general format of the Vākāṭaka copperplate grants this plate begins with the word *dṛishṭam*[48] followed by reference to the issuing place which is specified as *Tripuri-vāsakāt.*[49] The remainder of the text on the plate forms part of the genealogical account of the family well-known from other records. The plates were thus issued from the king's residence at Tripurī which was an important ancient town of Central India going back to chalcolithic times and has been identified with the modern village of Tewar near Jabalpur to the north of the river Narmadā.[50] V.V. Mirashi, who edited this plate, took this expression to indicate that Pravara Sena II carried his arms north of the Narmadā into Dāhala or Baghelkhaṇḍ region of Madhya Pradesh and occupied Tripurī in the twenty-third year of his reign, viz., in *circa* 443 AD.[51] He invites our attention to verse 4 of Skanda Gupta's Bhītarī pillar inscription[52] which is generally taken to refer to the invasion of the Gupta empire by the Pushyamitras towards the close of the reign of Kumāra Gupta I in which the Guptas were reduced to such a precarious situation that Skanda Gupta, who was deputed to lead the defensive operations, had to spend a night on bare ground. However, as the reading *Pushyamitrāṁś=cha* is not beyond doubt, he prefers the alternative reading *yuddhy-amitrāṁś=cha* suggested by H.R. Divekar[53] and accepted by some other epigraphists[54] and holds that the enemies said to have been vanquished by Skanda Gupta during the lifetime of his father, Kumāra Gupta I, included the Vākāṭaka king Pravara Sena II who went all out to expand his kingdom north of the Narmadā at the cost of his maternal uncle.[55] And identifying as he does the Vākāṭaka monarch Pṛithivī Sheṇa mentioned as Vyāghradeva's sovereign in the latter's Nachnā[56] and Ganj[57] inscriptions with the second Vākāṭaka monarch of that name, he holds that the Baghelkhaṇḍ region, which was annexed by Pravara Sena II, continued under the Vākāṭakas till the close of Pṛithivī Sheṇa II's reign in *circa* 490 AD, i.e., up to the time of the Gupta emperor Budha Gupta.[58]

This line of argument is, however, beset with several difficulties. First of all, the term *vāsaka* does not necessarily denote a military camp, but refers only to a camp or temporary residence.[59] Taking the case of the Vākāṭakas themselves, the Waḍgaon grant of Pravara Sena II was given from the monarch's *vāsaka* on the river Hiraṇyā[60] which was situated very much within the Vākāṭaka realm and there could be no question of any military camp there. Moreover, if the intention were to refer to a military camp set up in course of an invasion of enemy territory, an expression with an explicit connotation like *skandhāvāra* or *jaya-skandhāvāra*, which is known to early Indian epigraphy,[61] would have been employed. It is, therefore, not necessary to assume that Pravara Sena II had been to Tripurī only for military purposes. Relations between him and the Guptas being very close and friendly, he could have gone to and stayed at Tripurī (and, for that matter, any place within the Gupta empire) for any purpose including pilgrimage, for, Tripurī appears to have been regarded as a holy place.[62] There would have been some justification for Mirashi's assumption had the localities mentioined in the charter in connection with the grant been situated in the Tripurī region, which, as admitted by him, is not the case. Moreover, had the Gupta-Vākāṭaka relations become that inimical during Pravara Sena II's reign as Mirashi would have us believe, the reference to the matrimonial alliance with the Guptas, which is certainly indicative of cordial relations, would have been dropped in subsequent records. However, the phrase expressing this relationship continues not only in subsequent records of Pravara Sena II himself, but to the very end of the dynasty.[63] And lastly, we have no evidence whatsoever to indicate the inclusion of the Baghelkhaṇḍ region in the Vākāṭaka kingdom during the reign of Pṛithivī Sheṇa II.

The identification of Pṛithivī Sheṇa mentioned in the Nachnā-kī-talāī and Ganj inscriptions with the second Vākāṭaka ruler of that name, which forms the basis of this hypothesis, rests solely on the assumed identity of his feudatory Vyāghradeva with Vyāghra, father of the Uchchakalpa chief Jayanātha who is known to have been ruling in Gupta years 174 and 177[64] and whose reign may have, thus, extended from *circa* 490 to the early years of the sixth century AD. If this identification were to be conceded, Vyāghra would have to be placed in *circa* 470-490 AD, when Pṛithivī Sheṇa II was on the throne. But such an important conclusion cannot be drawn merely on the basis of identity of names. Moreover, we now have unimpeachable epigraphic evidence to show that in 487-88 AD Harivarman was ruling in the Baghelkhaṇḍ area as a feudatory of the Gupta emperor Budha Gupta and was preceded by at least two other *Māharājas* who also appear to have ruled as Gupta feudatories.[65] It would thus follow that during the period in question the Baghelkhaṇḍ region of Madhya Pradesh was ruled by the vassals of the Guptas and, like other Uchchakalpa rulers, *Mahārāja* Vyāghra of the Uchchakalpa family also was a Gupta vassal. The Vākāṭaka expansion in Baghelkhaṇḍ from the time of Pravara Sena II onwards is, therefore, not supported by any dependable evidence and we are left with no alternative but to believe that the Gupta-Vākāṭaka relations continued to be cordial till the very close of the Nandivardhana branch of the Vākāṭakas. Pṛithivī Sheṇa II cannot, therefore, be identified with the homonymous Vākāṭaka chief mentioned in the Nachnā and Ganj inscriptions of his vassal Vyāghra. Consequently the only Vākāṭaka monarch who has to be identified with Vyaghra's suzerain known from these records is Pṛithivī Sheṇa I who ruled in the second half of the fourth century AD. It would thus follow that the Baghelkhaṇḍ area, which seems to have been included in the Vākāṭaka kingdom from the very start,[66] continued under the dynasty till the time of Pṛithivī Sheṇa I whereafter it seems to have come under Gupta supremacy.[66a]

VI. Yawatmāl Plates of Pravara Sena II, Year 26 (Pls. LV - LVI)

Only two plates of this charter could be rescued from a coppersmith's melting pot at Yawatmal, the chief town of the district named after it in Maharashtra, by Shri R.M. Saklecha from whom they were acquired by Shri Prashant P. Kulkarni whose collection they adorn at present. The ring and the seal, like the rest of the plates (two or three), are missing. On comparing with other Vākāṭaka grants we find that the plates in question represent the second and the last plates of a charter. Although the record is, thus, incomplete, nothing of importance except only the name of the place of issue[67] seems to have been lost as the missing portion of the genealogial account[68] and details regarding privileges and exemptions granted to the donees,[69] which must have been given on the missing plates, are known from numerous other records of the family.

The charter belongs to the reign of Pravara Sena II and aims at recording the renewal, by him, of the doantion of some land along with two house-sites (*nive-śana-dvaya*) in the village Lāṭakapallī included in the administrative unit named Shaḍgriśaka[70] in favour of Indrārya and Svāmideva who belonged to the Taittirīya *śākhā* of the Black *Yajurveda* and the Vatsa *gotra*. It is averred that the land was being already enjoyed by the donees (*i.e.*, it was in their possession) and that the grant was renewed by Pravara Sena II by means of a copperplate charter. The charter was given on the eleventh day of the fourth fortnight of the summer season in the twenty-sixth year, apparently of the donor's reign. It was written when Bāppadeva held the office of *Senāpati*.

It will follow from the foregoing that ours was only the renewal of an old grant, and in the whole of the known Vākāṭaka epigraphy this is one of the very rare instances of its kind, all the remaining charters recording fresh grants. Unfortunately we have no information as to who was the original donor and what made it necessary to renew the grant. It may be mentioned, however, that we have a few other cases when fresh copperplate charters were issued in place of earlier charters, sometimes written on palm leaves,[71] consequent upon the destruction of the latter for some reason or other.[72] The present renewal also must have been due to some similar reasons.

This is, again, the only example of the royal order in respect of the grant being addressed to the village as a whole, the rest of the charters containing orders addressed to government officials with jurisdiction over the granted villages and the administrative units of which they formed part.[73]

The season date recorded in accordance with the older practice prevalent in the Deccan is also interesting and shows the continuing popularity of this mode of dating. Equally interesting is the Prakritism noticed in connection with the season dates in this[74] as well as a few other Vākāṭaka grants[75] which are otherwise couched in Sanskrit. Like the season dates, this, too, appears to be a remnant of the older age characterised by the use of Prakrit.

While we know of several grants of Pravara Sena II issued during the second to thirty-second years of his reign, this is the first record of his twenty-sixth year to be reported so far.

The Siwanī[77] and Waḍgāon[78] grants of Pravara Sena II inform us that Bāppadeva held the office of *Senāpati* during the eighteenth and twenty-fifth years respectively of his regin. Our record indicates that he continued to enjoy this office during the twenty-sixth year as well.[79]

VII. Paunī Plates of Pravara Sena II, Year 32

This set of four plates together with the ring on which they were strung and the seal were found at Paunī in the Bhaṇḍārā district of Maharashtra.[80] Issued from Pravarapura, the charter incised on these plates registers the grant of a piece of land measuring fifty *nivartanas* by the royal measure (*rājanya-mānena*) by Pravara Sena II to one Duggāryya who was a student of the *Ṛigveda* (Bahvṛicha)[81] and belonged to the Aupamanyava *gotra*. The plot of land together with a house-site (*niveśana*) which was given in exchange for some other land (*bhūmiprativastu*) was situated at Achalapura[82] included in the administrative unit called Kṛishṇāleśāli-kaṭaka. The grant was written on the third day of the dark half of the month of Jyeshtha during the thirty-second year, undoubtedly of Pravara Sena II's reign, when Mādhappa was *Senāpati*.

The importance of this record lies primarily in the fact that it supplies the latest date for the reign of Pravara Sena II, viz., thirty-second year, the latest known year earlier being twenty-ninth when the Pāṇḍhurṇā (or Tigāon) plates were issued.[83]

As Mādhappa figures in the capacity of *Senāpati* in the Tigāon grant also, it will follow that he occupied this office at least from the twenty-ninth[84] to the thirty-second year of Pravara Sena II's reign.

Achalapura, where the donated land was situated, has been identified by V.B. Kolte, who edited the record,[85] with the present Achalpur (or Elichpur) in the Amarāwatī district, Maharashtra.[86] This does not, however, appear very likely. The plates were found buried at Paunī, a place of great antiquarian interest in the Bhaṇḍara district, and the word *śāli* forming part of the name of the administrative unit in which the Achalapura under reference was situated stands for paddy. In fact, the entire name of the *kaṭaka*, Krishṇāleśāli, reminds us of certain valued varieties of rice known as *kālī kamot* or *kālī mūṁchh* and seems to have been named after some such variety of paddy. Evidently the region was well-known for abundant paddy cultivation. It is interesting to note that the Bhaṇḍārā region is even now regarded as the rice-bowl of Maharashtra. Achalapura mentioned in our record must, therefore, be differentiated from the above-mentioned homonymous locality in the Amarāwatī district and should be looked for somewhere in the Bhandārā district in the proximity of Paunī.[87] The *kaṭaka* of Kṛishṇāleśāli also must be located somewhere in the same region.[88]

VIII. Māṇḍhaḷ Plates of Pṛithivī Sheṇa II, Year 2 (Pls. LXIX-LXXII)

The four plates bearing this record were found preserved in an earthen vessel recovered in the excavations at Māṇḍhaḷ along with the aforesaid Māṇḍhaḷ grant of Pravara Sena II and the charter of Pṛithivī Sheṇa II to be noticed hereafter in 1976. Prior to the discovery of these two grants, two copperplate inscriptions of Pṛithivī Sheṇa II were known, to wit, the Bālāghāṭ[89] and Māhurjharī[90] plates. Of these, the former was left incomplete for some reason which cannot be ascertained and the seal-disc, naturally, does not bear any writing. As to the latter, the seal was lost before the plates came to light. Fortunately, the smaller and the larger rings as well as the seals of both the Māṇḍhaḷ grants are preserved with the result that we now know the inscriptions on the seals of this ruler including those lost or left unincised. For, it can be presumed justifiably that the writing on all of his seals must have been identical. Secondly, while the date is left out in the Bālāghāṭ grant,[91] that on the Māhurjharī plates is of the usual type with specification of the month, fortnight and *tithi*. Both the Māṇḍhaḷ charters, on the other hand, contain season dates which indicate the continuing popularity of such dates along with the other mode of dating. It will, thus, follow that the Māṇḍhaḷ plates are the only two copperplate grants of Pṛithivī Sheṇa II complete in all respects and dated according to the older method.

The charter under reference was issued from Rāmagiristhāna[92] which is not referred to in any other hitherto known Vākāṭaka inscription. It is no doubt true that the Ṛiddhapur plates of Prabhāvatī Guptā were given from the footprints of Ramagirisvāmin,[93] but there also Ramagiri is not spoken of as a *sthāna*. The genealogy up to Pravara Sena II is practically the same as met with in the earlier records of the family, and only a small portion relating to Narendra Sena and his son and successor, Pṛithivī Sheṇa II, has been added. No regal title is applied to Narendra Sena who is merely described as Pravara Sena's son. This is evidently due to negligence on the part of the composer of the grant. Similarly, we find the next king and the donor of the charter, Pṛithivī Sheṇa II, described only as 'Narendra Sena's good son' (*Narendrasena-satputra*) and the '*mahārāja* of the Vākāṭakas.' The eulogistic account of these two monarchs met with in the other records of Pṛithivī Sheṇa II including the other Māṇḍhaḷ grant is missing here. It may indicate that the post-Pravara Sena II *praśasti* or draft was not yet standardised at the time of this charter; alternatively, this omission may have been due to oversight.

The object of the inscription is to record the grant, by the reigning chief, of the village Kurubhajjaka in favour of Maheśvarasvāmin, Agnisvāmin and Brahmasvāmin who were sons of Mātṛisvāmin and grandsons of Droṇasvāmin and belonged to the Taittirīya *śākhā* of the Black *Yajurveda* and the Kautsa *gotra*. Mātṛisvāmin, the father of the donees, was apparently the same as the homonymous donee of the Māṇḍhaḷ plates of Pravara Sena II. Accordingly, the name of Māṭṛisvāmin's father, who is mentioned in Pravara Sena II's grant under reference merely as *apratigrāhaka-upādhyāya*, was Droṇasvāmin. The grant is said to have been made by Pṛithivī Sheṇa II for the merit of his mother whose name is spelt as Ajjhikabhaṭṭārikā.[94] Though not stated explicitly, the grant was obviously made at her behest. The order in respect of the grant was addressed to the agriculturists and other residents of the donated village headed by the Brāhmaṇas.[95] The gifted village is said to have been included in the Uttarpaṭṭa and situated to the west of Lavaṇatailaka, north of Ishṭākapallī (or Ishṭākapa),[96] east of the river Beṇṇā, and south of Govasāhikā. All these villages can be identified satisfactorily to the north or rather north-east of the river Waingangā (ancient Beṇṇa) in the Bhaṇḍārā district.[97] The administrative unit Uttarapaṭṭa, in which these villages were situated, was, therefore, named with reference to the flow of the Waingaṅga even as Aparapaṭṭa was.

The grant was issued on the twelfth day of the seventh fortnight of the summer season during the second regnal year of Pṛithivī Sheṇa II. As stated above, of the two grants of Pṛithivī Sheṇa II known prior to the discovery of the present charter, the Bālāghāṭ charter remained incomplete and undated while the Māhurjharī plates were issued in the seventeenth regnal year. The second set of Māṇḍhaḷ plates was given in his tenth year. The present grant is, thus, the earliest known dated record of Pṛithivī Sheṇa II.

At the time of this charter Vishṇudatta held the office of *Senāpati*, while the inscription was written by Śarvvadatta. The former has come to be known for the first time from the Māṇḍhaḷ plates.

The seal-inscription, which has come to be known for the first time, refers to Pṛithivī Sheṇa II as the good son (*satsūnu*) of Narendra Sena, master of the royal fortune of the Vākāṭakas and as eager for conquests, and speaks of his rule as victorious.[98] It will be noticed that this inscription, though couched in the *Anushṭubh* metre like other known inscriptions on the copper seals of the Vākāṭakas, is somewhat different in nature and contents from its counterparts on the seals of Prabhāvatī Guptā and her son Pravara Sena II.

IX. Māṇḍhaḷ Charter of Pṛithivī Sheṇa II, Year 10 (Pls. LXXIII-LXXVI)

Incised on a set of four plates,[99] this charter was issued from Beṇṇātaṭasthāna, evidently the headquarters of the administrative unit known as Bennatata,[100] and records the donation of the village Govasāhikā to four Brāhmaṇas, viz., Maheśvarasvāmin, Brahmasvāmin, Harasvāmin and Varāhasvāmin. All these Brāhmaṇas were residents of Beṇṇāṭaṭa and belonged to the Kautsa *gotra*.[101] Though not stated explicitly in the present record, we learn from the above-mentioned Māṇḍhaḷ plates of Pravara Sena II and Pṛithivī Sheṇa II that they were students of the Taittirīya *śākhā* of the Black *Yajurveda*. The present inscription is reticent regarding the ancestry of the donees; but we learn from the previous grant of Pṛithivī Sheṇa II that Maheśvarasvāmin and Brahmasvāmin were sons and grandsons of Mātṛisvāmin and Droṇasvāmin respectively. Similar may have been the case with Harasvāmin and Varāhasvāmin as well. It would, thus, follow that the grants recorded in the three Māṇḍhaḷ charters of Pravara Sena II and Pṛithivī Sheṇa II were made in favour of two generations of the same family.[101a]

The donated village is said to have been included in the Uttarapaṭṭa, evidently in the district of Veṇṇātaṭa, and is said to have been situated to the west of Śulkavaṭa, north of Kurubhejñaka, east of the river Beṇṇā, and south of Piḍerikā. Of these, Govasāhikā and Beṇṇā figure in the previous record also and have been discussed in that connection, while Kurubhejñaka is apparently the same as Kurubhajjaka mentioned in the same inscription. As to Śulkavaṭa, it may have been named after a banyan tree close to an octroi post at the boundary of the village. Though it is difficult to identify it at present, a look at the map of the adjoining area indicates that it was situated approximately at the same place as modern Kosarā, which is exactly to the east of the villages identified with the ancient Govasāhikā. Piḍerikā, which is said to have been to the north of Govasāhikā, seems to be represented by the modern village of Petari whose location answers the description in the record.

The charter was given on the first day of the first fortnight of the summer season in the tenth regnal year of Pṛithivī Sheṇa II. It was written by Śarvvadatta when Vishṇudatta was *Senāpati*. The combined evidence of the present and the preceding records shows that Vishṇudatta continued to occupy this office from at least the second to at least the tenth year of Pṛithivī Sheṇa II's reign. The writer Śarvvadatta is also known from the previous grant.

The seal-inscription is literally identical with that of the preceding charter and calls for no further comments.

The post-Pravara Sena II genealogical account of the family, which was missing but for the names of the ruling chiefs in the preceding grant, is found in a fully developed form in the present inscription and was retained in the subsequent records of Pṛithivī Sheṇa II with only some necessary alterations.[102] We should, in particular, like to refer here to a couple of phrases occurring in these grants,[103] one each in connection with Narendra Sena and his son, Pṛithivī Sheṇa II. One of these expressions referring to the former has been read by F.

Kielhorn,[104] V.V. Mirashi[105] and V.B. Kolte[106] as *pūrvv-ādhigata-guṇa-viśvāsād=apahṛita-vaṅśa=śriyaḥ,*[107] which, according to Kielhorn meant that Narendra Sena, 'from confidence in excellent qualities[108] previously acquired by him, took away (or appropriated) the family's fortune.'[109]

This interpretation is followed by Mirashi who merely drops the alternative word 'appropriated' and replaces 'the (*royal*) fortune of (*his*) *family*' for 'the family's fortune'.[110] But while Kielhorn felt that this expression alluded to a scuffle for succession and that Narendra Sena took away the kingdom (probably from an elder brother),[111] Mirashi held that no reference to a disputed succession was intended and that this is just a poetic way of saying that Narendra Sena attracted royal fortune by his noble qualities.[112] Kielhorn's rendering was evidently influenced by the inadequate understanding of the evidence afforded by the Ajanta inscription of Varāhadeva, while Mirashi seems to ignore the fact that the root *apa-hṛi* is not normally employed in the sense of taking possession of something rightfully one's own. A.S. Altekar seems to have been nearer the correct interpretation when he took *apahṛita-vaṁśa=śriyaḥ* to mean 'who carried away the fortune of his own family' and suggested a forcible seizure.[113] According to him, it refers to the restoration of his family fortunes by Narendra Sena after defeating the Nalas of Bastar who had for some time been in possession of a sizeable part of the Vākāṭaka kingdom.[114] This interpretation is followed by V.B. Kolte also.[115] The present inscription, however, affords an entirely new dimension to the problem by offering the reading *pūrvv-ādhigata-guṇavad=dāyād-āpahṛita-vaṁśa-śriya* which we have to restore as *pūrvv-ādhigata-guṇavad=dāyād-āpahṛita-vaṁśa-śriyaḥ.* In fact, the correct reading of this phrase in the Māhurjharī plates also is, as will appear from a glance at the facsimile accompanying Kolte's paper, *pūrvva-ādhigata-guṇavad=dāyād-āpahṛita-vaṅ(ṁ)śa-śriya[ḥ*]*[116] which is better than that in the Māṇḍhaḷ grant. This was also the intended reading in the Bālāghāṭ plates though it is rather badly engraved. This phrase, as restored by us, is pregnant with great historical significance as it alludes to a hitherto unknown event during Narendra Sena's reign in which his own *dāyādas* were involved. We may break this phrase as *pūrvamadhigatā guṇavatā dāyādena apahṛitā vaṁśa-śrīḥ yasya tasya*[117] which, if accepted, would indicate that Narendra Sena had at first succeeded to his family fortune, viz., throne, but was subsequently deprived of it by a *dāyāda* or *dāyādas.* The word *dāyāda* primarily means 'heirs to property,' i.e., sons or brothers in relation to each other with a claim to inheritance. If we adopt this primary meaning, it would follow that Narendra Sena was divested of his kingdom (or a part thereof) by his cosharers (brothers or other close relations) during the later part of his career.

It would, thus, appear that the demise of Paravara Sena II was followed by a struggle for succession in which his son (or one of his sons) Narendra Sena was at first successful, but at a subsequent stage some other *dāyāda* got an upper hand and seized the family fortune. *Dāyāda* has, however, a secondary meaning also, viz., a distant relative or kinsman,[118] and if this were the intended meaning, it may as well refer to a feud between the two branches (Nandivardhana and Vatsagulma) of the Vākāṭakas during Narendra Sena's reign in which Narendra Sena was defeated and lost the kingdom or a major portion thereof.[119] It is difficult to be more definite on this point for want of necessary evidence, but there is no gainsaying the fact that the phrase in question sheds new light on the history of this branch of the family and knocks at the bottom of the unfounded belief that the succession among the Vākāṭakas was peaceful and that the relations between their two branches remained quite cordial.

In view of the precarious state to which Narendra Sena was subjected in the later part of his reign, the statement in this grant as well as the Māhurjharī and Bālāghāṭ plates that his behests were obeyed by the rulers of Kosalā (Chhattisgaḍh region), Mekalā (Amarkantak area) and Mālava (Malwa) in the present state of Madhya Pradesh looks somewhat boastful. In any case we have no independent evidence in support of this claim. Neither any record of the Vākāṭakas has been reported from these regions nor do the records of the ruling families of these regions contain any allusion to the Vākāṭakas. The claim in regard to Mekalā was till recently sought to be substantiated on the assumption that the Bamhani plates made a veiled allusion to Narendra Sena and that Bharatabala, the Pāṇḍava chief of Mekalā and the supposed issuer of these plates, was a vassal of Narendra Sena.[120] However, the recently published Mallār plates have demonstrated beyond doubt that these assumptions are erroneous. Furthermore, as we have shown elsewhere, Bharatabala and his son and successor Śūrabala Udīrṇavaira, the real issuer of the Bamhanī plates, were separated from Narendra Sena by a long period of time and consequently there can be no question of any one of them owing allegiance to him.[121] In view of these facts it is difficult to appreciate the exact significance of these claims. But we know that the Gupta emperor Kumāra Gupta I had to face a lot of difficulties during the closing years of his reign and some of his vassals in these regions may have exploited the situation to assert their independence. It is not impossible that in keeping with the closeness of their relations with the Guptas the Vākāṭakas rendered valuable help to the Gupta emperor in maintaining his hold in these areas. Narendra Sena, either as a prince-commander or after his accession may have played an important role in this matter, and this may have formed the basis of his claims in question made in the records of his son.[122] Alternatively, we may surmise that he took advantage of the precarious situation in which his Gupta cousin was placed to carry out hurried raids in these territories.

Our inscription describes Pṛithivī Sheṇa II as *magna-vaṁś-oddhartṛi*,[123] 'resurrector of the sunken family'. This phrase is repeated in his Māhurjharī plates also.[124] The incomplete Bālāghāṭ plates prefix to it the word *dvi*.[125] Kielhorn,[126] followed by Mirashi,[127] takes *dvi* to be a mistake for *ni* and thinks that the intended reading in the Bālāghaṭ grant was *nimagna-vaṁśasy-oddhartuḥ*.[128] However, the recently discovered Māṇḍhaḷ and Māhurjharī charters in question, which do not prefix *dvi* or *ni* to this expression, show that the addition of *dvi* was deliberate and that the composer of the Bālāghāṭ plates was eager to credit his master with the restoration of the sunken family twice in contrast to the remaining two charters which describe him simply as the resurrector of the sunken family. This second calamity evidently occurred sometime after the seventeenth regnal year of Pṛithivī Seṇa II, the date of the Māhurjharī plates. While we are at present not in a position to ascertain the exact nature of these two catastrophes, the first calamity, alluded to in the Māṇḍhaḷ and Māhurjharī plates, was apparently the one that had led to Narendra Sena's deprivation of his family fortune by his own relative (or relatives), and the restoration of the fallen family fortune was evidently the first task that his son Pṛithivī Sheṇa II must have taken upon himself immediately after his accession. The second calamity, referred to in the Bālāghāṭ grant, may have been caused by the invasion of the Nalas who had occupied a large part of the kingdom under Padmapura-Pravarapura branch of the Vākāṭakas.[129] It is hardly necessary to add that the Bālāghāṭ plates must be placed sometime after the seventeenth year of his reign.[129a]

X. Māhurjharī Plates of Pṛithivī Sheṇa II, Year 17 (Pls. LXXVII-LXXX)

The five-plate set bearing this charter together with the ring on which it is strung as well as the smaller ring meant for sliding the seal but without the seal-disc was found while ploughing in a field adjacent to the Māhurjharī village near Nāgpur. It has been edited by V.B. Kolte,[130] and some corrections have been suggested by us.[130a]

The plates were issued from Pṛithivīsamudra by Pṛithivī Sheṇa II, and their object is to register the grant of the village Jamalakheṭaka to the Brāhmaṇas Vishṇudattta and Bhavadatta who were residents of Pṛithivīpura and students of the Vājasaneyī *śākhā* of the White *Yajurveda* and had Kāśyapa for their *gotra*. It is noteworthy in this connection that this is so far one of the two indubitable references to the Vājasaneyī Saṁhitā in the Vākāṭaka records,[131] most other references being to the Taittirīya *śākhā* of the Black *Yajurveda*.

As already pointed out, Kolte, following Kielhorn and Mirashi, reads one of the phrases describing Narendra Sena as *pūrvv-ādhigata-guṇa-viśvāsad=apahṛita-vaṁśa-śriyah,* but the correct reading is *pūrvv-ādhigata-guṇavad=dāyād=apahṛita-vaṁśa-śriyaḥ*[132] and refers to a serious family feud wherein Narendra Sena was worsted. The expression *pratāpa-praṇat-āri-śāsanasya* in the description of Narendra Sena is found here for the first time and is thereafter repeated in the Bālāghāṭ plates; evidently here onward it became part of the standard *praśasti* of this king. Further on, the donor, Pṛithivī Sheṇa II, is described, as in the preceding record, as *magna-vaṁś-oddharttṛi*,[132] 'resurrector of the sunken family', which, as shown above, indicates that the addition of the word *dvi* before it in the draft of the Bālāghāṭ plates was deliberate. The significance of these phrases has been discussed above.

The charter was written under the supervision of *Senāpati* Ravidatta on the twelfth *tithi* of the bright half of Kārttika. As we have seen above, the office of *Senāpati* was occupied by Vishṇudatta till the tenth year of Pṛithivī Sheṇa II's reign and Ravidatta must have taken over sometime between that year and the seventeenth year.

The granted village, Jamalakheṭaka, is stated to have been situated in the *mārga* of the same name which itself formed part of the Ārambī-*rājya*,[133] which was evidently a larger administrative division. Its boundaries are given as follows: it was to the west of Somadarī, east of Nāndīpuraka, south of Ubbhilaka, and north of Jalakukubhaka. It may be reasonably assumed that Pṛithivīpura, where the donees resided, was also included in the Ārambī-*rajya*. And so must have been Pṛithivīsamudra, the place of the issue of the present charter. As indicated by the first part of their names, they must have been christened or rechristened by Pṛithivī Shena II after himself.

Kolte thinks that Pṛithivīsamudra was the capital of Pṛithivī Sheṇa II and that Prithivīpura may have been its another name. And since the dynastic capital was being shifted from east to west, viz., from Padmapura to Nandivardhana and from the latter to Pravarapura, because of mounting pressure from some aggressor, probably the Nalas, Pṛithivīsamudra (as well as Pṛithivīpura) must have been situated considerably to the west of Pravarapura or Paunār. And accordingly he proposes to identify it with the modern village of Samudrapura in the Hingaṇghāt tāluka of the Wardhā district.

We find it difficult to accept this suggestion. The key to the solution of this problem lies in the location of the Ārambī-*rājya*. We are inclined to identify it with the Ārammī-*rājya* mentioned in the Dudiā[134] and Tīgāon (Pāṇḍhurṇā)[135] plates of the twenty-third and twenty-ninth years respectively of the reign of Pravara Sena II, the slight difference in the spelling of the concluding *akshara* of the name of the *rājya* being of no significance as such minor differences are not uncommon in the Vākāṭaka records. It is pertinent to remember in this connection that the other two inscriptions referring to this *rājya* have been found in the Chhindwārā district of Madhya Pradesh, while Māhurjharī, the provenance of the present record is in the adjoining Nāgpur district. It is, therefore, not unlikely that the Ārammī-*rājaya* included parts of the Nāgpur and Kātol tālukās of the Nāgpur district and the adjoining part of the Chhindwara district. It may be pointed out in the present context that there is still a village named Arambhi near Kāṭol. It will consequently be worthwhile to try to locate the *rājya* in question in this area and look for the localities included in it there.[136] Viewing from this angle, Māhurjharī itself has a strong case for identification with Pṛithivīsamudra. It has even now a large water-reservoir which could be figuratively called *samudra.* It may have been in existence at the time of Pṛithivī Sheṇa or may have been excavated and named/renamed similarly.[137] The numerous megalithic stone circles adjoining the township show that its antiquity goes back to about mid-fifth century BC.[138] It must be mentioned that the two components of its present name also refer to two separate but connected things: *jharī*, the second component, to the water-reservoir and Māhur, a derivative from Māṭṛipura, to the township. In all probability Māṭṛipura is an ancient name going back to pre-Vākāṭaka times, indicating that the place was regarded as sacred because of being an abode of the mother goddess, and the tank, too, may have been regarded as sacred. It is, therefore, more likely that the township and the reservoir were renamed by Pṛithivī Sheṇa II. Because of the sanctity attached to the tank, Pṛithivī Sheṇa II may have gone over there on pilgrimage and issued the grant under reference after bathing in it. We have numerous other epigraphic references of this type. There is, therefore, no question of Prithivīsamudra being the new dynastic capital established by Pṛithivī Sheṇa II after deserting the earlier capital at Pravarapura. As for the non-retention of the newly given name, we must remember that more often than not older names persist and survive new names of which we notice numerous instances in our own times. And if the township and the tank were renamed by Pṛithivī Sheṇa II himself, we should not be surprised at this phenomenon as, in the present state of our knowledge, he seems to have been the last ruler of the Nandivardhana branch of the dynasty and there was none to enforce the perpetuation of these new names.

VATSAGULMA BRANCH

XI. Hisse-Borālā Stone-slab Inscription of Deva Sena, Śaka 380 (Pl. XC)

The slab bearing this four-line inscription was found accidentally amidst what may be regarded as the remnants of an ancient dam near the village of Hisse-Borālā, about $9^1/_2$ km south of Wāshim in the Akolā district. Ever since the discovery of this record there has been prolonged controversy regarding who deserves the credit of its location as well as the interpretation of a portion of the inscription, and a number of epigraphists including Shobhana Gokhale,[139] V.B. Kolte,[140] G.S. Gai and S. Sankaranarayanan,[141] D.C. Sircar,[141a] the present writer[142] and B.N. Mukherjee[143] participated in it. The latter controversy centres primarily around the interpretation of the initial portion of the inscription which is considerably damaged and has become unascertainable due to the breakage of the portion of the slab bearing it. But the main contents and purport are fairly clear.

The epigraph commences with the specification of date which is first indicated astronomically with reference to the position of the Saptarshis or Seven Bears and then in the Śaka era. The reading and interpretation of the astronomical portion are highly uncertain, and consequently subject of a wide difference of opinion among scholars, particularly Kolte and Gai and Sankaranarayan. This is, as pointed out above, due to the fact that the stone is broken away at this place. Thereafter we find mention of Śaka 380 (=458 AD). Even Kolte, who feels that there is no explicit reference to the Śaka date, holds that the astronomical details lead to the same Śaka year.[143a]

The object of this short epigraph is to record that a lake named Sudarśana was constructed by a certain *Āryya* Svāmilladeva, an obedient servant (*ājñākara*) of the Vākāṭaka king Deva Sena, for the benefit of all the creatures in Śaka 380, corresponding to 457-58 AD. One Bappa was the supervisor (*karmopadeshṭṛi*) of this work. A wish is expressed that this meritorious deed should last as long as the changes of the four aeons (*yugas*), the sun, the moon and the earth exist. The remnants of the ancient dam mentioned above evidently represent the construction referred to in this record.

This is the only lithic record and, for that matter, the only complete original inscriptions of Deva Sena, the penultimate member of the Vatsagulma branch, and by virtue of specifying a Śaka date, provides the so far only known definite date in the history of the Vākāṭakas. It is noteworthy that this alone of all the Vākāṭaka records is dated in the Śaka era, the rest being dated with reference to the years of individual reigns. The key to understand this strange phenomenon[144] is afforded by the name, Sudarśana, given to the lake, which was evidently borrowed from the well-known lake of that name near Girnār in the Jūnāgadh district of Gujarat which was originally constructed by Chandragupta Maurya and subsequently repaired and enlarged by Aśoka Maurya, Śaka *Mahākshatrapa* Rudrādaman I and the Gupta emperor Skanda Gupta and, thus, has a chequered history lasting nearly eight centuries. We may, therefore, resonably conclude that Svāmilladeva, who was responsible for getting this inscription engraved and, of course, for the excavation of the lake recorded in it, hailed from Gujarat where the Śaka era had been in use ever since its initiation. This date, it goes without saying, affords a *terra firma* for the chronology of the Vākāṭakas in general and of the Vatsagulma branch in particular.

The present inscription contains the earliest known specific mention of the Śaka era by name in so far as the Vidarbha region is concerned and the second oldest reference in the country as a whole. The earliest undoubted reference to the reckoning by name is met with in the Wāḍā (Ṭhāṇe district, Maharashtra) inscription of the Bhoja-Maurya chief Suketuvarman recording the consecration of god Koṭiśvara on the full-moon day of Vaiśākha when the Śaka year 322 was current.[145] The second reference is that found in our epigraph and the third one (Śaka 465) found in the Badami rock inscription of Chālukya Pulakeśin I is separated from it by a long gap of eighty-five years.[146]

XII. Bīdar Plates of Deva Sena, Year 5[147] (Pls. LXXXVI-LXXXVIII)

The original copperplates bearing this important record together with the ring which held them together as well as the seal sliding on the smaller ring are no longer traceable. But the original set was reportedly brought to a Bīdrī artist by some villager from the Bechchali tālukā of the Bīdar district of Karnataka who, however, did not want to part with it. The artist, realising its historical and resultant monetary value, prepared its exact replica on iron plates of the same size and thickness with holes for the ring as well as the seal (diameter $1^3/_4$") and sold it to the Birla Archaeological and Cultural Research Institute, Hyderabad, where it is presently deposited. It has since been published together with facsimile plates by P.V. Parabrahma Sastry, formerly Deputy Director (Epigraphy), Department of Archaeology, Government of Andhra Pradesh.[148]

The iron reproduction is so faithful that it looks just like a xerox copy of present-day paper documents, and there is absolutely no reason to doubt the genuineness of the record. Even otherwise we know of no other complete copper-plate charter of Deva Sena which could be used as the model so that there can be no question of anyone venturing a counterfeit.

The epigraph, though composed in Sanskrit, exhibits a great deal of Prakritism both in the genealogical and grant portions and thereby marks, linguistically speaking, an important hitherto missing transitional stage between the Wāshim plates of Vindhyaśakti II and the Thāḷner grant of the last known ruler of this branch, Hari Sheṇa, to be noticed hereafter. It commences with the invocation *siddhaṁ namaḥ*, the second component of this formula being hitherto unknown in so far as the Vākāṭaka epigraphy is concerned. The grant was issued from Vatsagulma (modern Wāshim, Akolā district, Maharashtra), the capital of the branch of the Vākāṭakas to which the issuer belonged. Next we find the genealogical account which begins with Vindhyaśakti who is described as the first (*adi*) *Dharmma-mahārāja* of the Vākāṭakas. The description bears a close similarity to that met with in the following Thāḷner plates of Hari Sheṇa and apparently forms the basis of the latter. His son Pravara Sena I is described in the same manner as in the Wāshim and Thāḷner plates including the application of the titles *Hāritīputra* and *Dharmma-mahārāja*. Next are mentioned his son Sarvva Sena and Vindhya Sena (same as Vindhyaśakti II), Pravara Sena (II) and Sarvva Sena, each succeeding monarch being the son of the preceding one. All these kings are given the regal title *Maharaja*, while the apparently more dignified title *Dharmma-mahārāja* is reserved only for Vindhyaśakti I, Pravara Sena I and Deva Sena, the issuer of the charter under reference. The last named monarch is described, rather strangely, as the great-grandson of the son of Pravara Sena's son, great-grandson of Sarvva Sena's son, grandson of Vindhya Sena's son, grandson of Pravara Sena and son of Sarvva Sena and is styled *Dharmma-mahārāja*. This description is met with in a summarised form in his son's Thāḷner grant. The object of this inscription is to record Deva Sena's grant of the village Velpakoṇḍā in favour of one Raddochha, a scholar of the four Vedas (*chātuvejja=Chāturvidya*), for the purpose of sacrificial offering (*charu*). The administrative division in which the village was situated is left unnamed, but the boundaries of the donated village are indicated by mentioning bordering villages. It lay to the west of Pasāpalakalla, to the north of Sirimandāpaka, to the east of Kreriñchakalla and to the south of Doṇiṭhoma. The grant, which was accompanied by the usual privileges and exemptions, was executed by Sāmilladeva,[149] who is evidently identical with Svāmilladeva known from the Hisse-Borālā inscription of the reign of Deva Sena himself and the Thāḷner plates of his son and successor, Hari Sheṇa. It was written by a certain Vammasvāmin's son whose name began with the letter *sa.*[150] The record ends with the date which is specified with reference to the issuer's reign and the season. The figure for the year has no parallel in the Vākāṭaka inscriptions, but is very much like the figure in the last line of the Malhārā plates of the Muṇḍaputra king Ādityarāja which has been taken as 5.[151] Accordingly, the regnal year should be read as 5. There is no doubt about the reading of the figures for the fortnight and the day which are clearly 8 and 1 respectively and the season is specified as *vāsa* or rainy. The grant was, thus, issued on the first day of the eighth fortnight of the rainy season in the fifth year of Deva Sena's reign.

The record is important in more than one respect. First of all, this is so far the only complete copperplate charter of Deva Sena, his only other known charter, viz., India Office grant, being represented only by a single plate. The Hisse-Borālā inscription of his time, though set up by one of his officials, cannot be regarded as an official record. Thus, this is not only his only known complete copperplate grant, but also his only complete official record. Secondly, this provides an important link for tracing the evolution of the draft of the copperplate charters of the Vatsagulma branch of the Vākāṭakas. Its draft marks a complete departure from the earlier Wāshim grant in the manner of specifying the genealogy which is given in a rather novel style. Even though all the rulers up to the donor are named, the relationship of Pravara Sena I and other members of the dynasty is indicated in a strange and unusual manner. This style was followed in the Thāḷner plates of his son, but with the omission of a large number of names. Thirdly, the title of *Dharmma-mahārāja* is applied only to three members of the family, viz., Vindhyaśakti I, Pravara Sena I and Deva Sena, while the style *Hārītīputra* is employed only for the first two. Other rulers are given only the title *Mahārāja*. It is interesting to note in this connection that these two titles are not used for Deva Sena in the only known copperplate (viz., Thāḷner grant) of his son and successor, Hari Sheṇa, who, too, is mentioned without these titles. Fourthly, the date of this record, which is given with reference to season following the earlier practice current in Western Maharashtra, is in keeping with the custom noticed in the other known complete copperplate grants of this branch which appears, for some reason, to have preferred this tradition.[152] Fifthly, the date would give us the only recorded year of Deva Sena and show that he ruled for at least five years, an information not so very important historically, for no historian of the Vākāṭakas ever proposed to allot him such a short reign.

And last but not the least, the provenance of the record, if reported correctly, is of utmost historical significance for historical purposes. If the plates originally belonged to the Bīdar region, they would indicate an extension of the dominions of the Vatsagulma branch of the Vākāṭakas into northern Karnataka. The place-names, particularly the name of the donated village, also seem to strengthen this surmise, for *koṇḍa*-ending place-names are common in the Andhra-Karnataka region. At the first sight this conjecture may look somewhat startling, but in reality there is nothing impossible about it. For we already know that the Nāndeḍ (mentioned as Nāndīkaḍa in the Wāshim plates)[152a] region was already included in its territory as early as the time of Vindhyaśakti II (Vindhya Sena of our record), and some of the finest paintings at Ajantā in the Aurangābād district were executed during Hari Sheṇa's reign. A little more southerly expansion so as to reach the Bīdar region of Karnataka is well within the bounds of probability. And, as if to put the final seal upon this conjecture, the Muḍigere (Chikmagalur district, Karnataka) plates of the Kadamaba king Siṁhavarman issued in his fifth regnal year tell us that he was anointed by Sarvvasena-*mahārāja*[153] who undoubtedly belonged to the Vatsagulma branch of the Vākāṭakas for the simple reason that during the period in question *sena*-ending names were borne mostly only by the Vākāṭakas and there were two kings named Sarvva Sena in their Vatsagulma branch. And we have shown elsewhere that in view of the chronological considerations the Sarvva Sena under reference could only be the second king of this name who was the father of Deva Sena.[154] We should not be surprised if this interference in the internal affairs of the Kadambas resulted in the military occupation of at least a part of northern Karnataka. And the present record should leave absolutely no doubt in the Vākāṭaka occupation of the region round Bīdar and other intervening areas of Andhra Pradesh by the fifth year of the reign of Deva Sena, if not earlier. How long this rule lasted is not ascertainable in the present state of indequate information.

The seal bears along the edge the legend *Vākāṭakānām=mahārāja-Śrī-Devasena*. The same must have been the legend on the seal attached to the India Office copperplates of Deva Sena. The difference between the legend of this seal and those of the rulers of the Padmapura-Nandivardhana-Pravarapura branch is noteworthy in that the legends on the latter are metrical and refer to the *śāsana* (rule or charter) of the issuing monarch.

XIII. Thālner Grant of Hari Sheṇa, Year 3 (Pls. XCI-XCII)

This charter is incised on a set of three plates which along with the ring but without the seal were acquired by a coppersmith of Dhule from a resident of Thāḷner (ancient Sthālakanagara) in the Dhuḷe (formerly West Khandesh) district and has been edited by D.R. Bhat[155] and V.V. Mirashi.[156]

Chronologically the third complete copperplate charter of the Vatsagulma branch of the dynasty and the only known official record of its last known member, Hari Sheṇa, it records his donation of a couple of villages and certain land in some other villages in favour of the Brāhmaṇas Devasvāmin, Gaṅgasvāmin, Varāhasvāmin, Bhaṭṭārasvāmin, Khūḍasvāmin, Dharasvāmin and others who were students of the *Sāmaveda* and belonged to the Padañchala *gotra*.

The granted villages and pieces of land in other villages were as follows:-

(i) Bhaṭṭikāpadra to the east of Jātīkkheṭaka and west of Vatālikā; (ii) Kumāradāsavāṭaka on the southern bank of the river Mayasinī in Vaṁśivahalī[157] and lying to the east of Chchhabilānaka and west of Bodrakānaka; (iii) 20 or 20½[158] *nivartanas*[159] of land in Kaṁsakāragrāma included in the Ānarttapura-*bhukti*; (iv) a piece of land measuring 20½[160] *nivartanas* in the Suvarṇṇakaragrāma; and (v) a plot of the same measurement in the village of Govachchhetaṭī. Some of these villages have been located in the Dhuḷe district.

As in other copperplate inscriptions of the family,[161] the present record also gives genealogical account in the beginning. But this portion differs from its counterparts in other records in contents and nature. In all the other official records the account begins with Pravara Sena I, and for information regarding his father, Vindhyaśakti I, we have to depend on the dynastic accounts found in some of the Purāṇas and Ajantā Cave XVI inscription of Varāhadeva, a minister of Hari Sheṇa.[162] However, the Thāḷner plates, like the above-mentioned Bīdar grant, begin their account with him and describe him as the first (*ādi*) *dharmma-mahārāja* of the Vākāṭakas.[163] It seems as if Vindhyaśakti, who was forgotten or ignored by all the earlier members of the dynasty whose records have come down to us, was remembered reverentially, for some reason which cannot be determined, during the reign of its last two known members. Next is described Paravara Sena I. But thereafter it takes a leap and skips over a number of the members of the Vatsagulma branch including Sarvva Seṇa I, its founder, and his son Vindhyaśakti II, who is known from his Wāshim plates which, for the first time, brought this branch of the dynasty to light. In a strange manner, as if in great haste, it describes Hari Sheṇa, the donor, as the great-grandson of the grandson of the son of Pravara Sena I, grandson of Sarvva Sena and son of Deva Sena. This description agrees with the genealogy reconstructed with the help of the Wāshim plates of Vindhyaśakti II, the Bīdar grant of Deva Sena and the Ajanta cave XVI inscription of Hari Sheṇa's minister Varāhadeva. However, the name of Deva Sena's father, which was lost in the Ajanta inscription, is supplied by this record as well as the Bīdar plates. It is Sarvva Sena which we may call Sarvva Sena II in order to distinguish him from that of the founder of this branch who should now be known as Sarvva Sena I. It is interesting to note that the titles *Dharmma-mahārāja* and *Hāritīputra* are applied only to Pravara Sena I, while his father Vandhyaśakti I is given only the first title. The rest of the kings including Hari Sheṇa are styled simply *Mahārāja*. In the Wāshim plates also Pravara Sena I alone is styled *Hāritīputra*; but the title *Dharmma-maharaja*, which is applied to his son Sarvva Sena I and grandson Vāndhyaśakti, is not given to him either by oversight or because *samrāt*, applied to him in all the records, was thought to be enough.[164] In any case, it is obvious that in the records of this branch the title *Hāritīputra* is employed only to Pravara Sena I and *Dharmma-mahārāja* to him as well as the first two members of this branch.[165] This difference cannot be satisfactorily explained for want of necessary evidence. It may be possible to get some light on this problem when some more official records come to light.

The grant recorded in this charter is said to have been made with the permission of a certain Gomikarāja (*Gomikarāj-ānujñātaṁ*). Who this Gomikarāja was, we have no means to know. Mirashi thinks that he was probably the local chief of the Dhule region belonging to the Kumbhakarṇa family brought to light by a couple of copperplate charters of king Bhānusheṇa with Sthālakanagara (modern Thāḷner) for his capital and owing allegiance to the Traikūṭakas. It has been surmised that he was vanquished by and submitted to Hari Sheṇa who launched on a campaign of victory and vengeance against the Traikūṭakas who had occupied a portion of the Vākāṭaka kingdom on the western boundary of Vidarbha. It is averred that in course of this expedition he defeated Gomikarāja but did not annex the territory under him. And as the donated villages were situated in his vanquished enemy's territory, he thought it necessary to formally obtain his new vassal's consent for the grant recorded in these plates. Unfortunately there is absolutely no evidence to support this reconstruction. The theory of the Traikūṭaka occupation of the Vākāṭaka territory is based solely on the find of a few silver coins of Dahra Sena in a small hoard at Dahigāon in the Malkāpur tālukā of the Bulḍhaṇā district. But as we have shown elsewhere,[166] the discovery of a single lot of coins of a chief in a territory outside his dominions cannot by itself be construed as an evidence of occupation. For in that case we shall have to believe that the Śaka Kshatrapas of Chashṭana's line ruled over the whole of Maharashtra and a considerable portion of Andhra Pradesh and Karnataka, not to speak of other regions, where hoards of their coins have been found in good numbers. There can, therefore, be no question of the Traikūṭaka occupation of a part of the Vākāṭaka territory and Hari Sheṇa's wreaking vengeance against the Traikūṭakas. Further, while we do not deny Hari Sheṇa's conquest of the Thāḷner region or, in case of its occupation by one of his predecessors, its retention by him, we have absolutely no indication that the grant was made immediately after his conquest of Thāḷnar as has been suggested. And but for the name-ending *rāja*, which cannot be taken as an indubitable indication of the regal status, there is nothing to suggest that Gomikarāja, with whose permission or consent the grant is stated to have been made, was a ruling chief, much less that he was the vanquished lord of Thāḷner. It is difficult to believe that the conqueror would ever feel it necessary to seek his vanquished enemy's or vassal's permission to grant land in the latter's territory. At least, to our knowledge, there is no such instance on record. An exactly parallel expression occurs in the Mālhārā plates of the Muṇḍaputra chief Ādityarāja which are said to have been given at the behest of Yajñarāja (Yajñarāj-*ānujñāta*)[167] who appears to have been an elderly revered member of the same family. The same may have been the case with Gomikarāja as well. Alternatively, it is not impossible that the composer of the record erroneously used the word *anujñāta* instead of *prārthanayā* and that the grant was actually made at the request of Gomikarāja. But this appears less likely.

The charter was registered on the twelfth day of the fourth fortnight of the rainy season in the third year of Hari Sheṇa's reign. As we have seen above, the two Māṇḍhaḷ charters of Pṛithivī Sheṇa II and the Bīdar grant of Deva Sena also contain season dates. The present record, which, in the present state of our information, furnishes the latest known instance of the use of the season date, evidences the continuity of this mode of dating till at least the close of the fifth century AD.

The *dūtaka*[168] or executor of the grant was Svāmiladeva, and it was written by Boppadeva. Whether this Svāmiladeva is to be identified with Svāmilladeva known as an officer of Deva Sena from the Hisse-Borāḷā inscription[169] and Bīdar plates, cannot be ascertained; but the possibility cannot be ruled out. Similarly Boppadeva of the present record may be identified with Bappā of the other inscription.[170]

Notes and References

1. *Inscriptions of the Vākāṭakas, CII*, V, Ootacamund, 1963.
2. Barring the Bamhanī plates (*ibid.*, pp. 82-88) of the Pāṇḍava king Śūrabala *alias* Udīrṇavaira (owing to the inadvertent dropping of a prose passage introducing Śūrabala, the inscription was earlier assigned to his father Bharatabala) which have nothing to do with the Vākāṭakas, Mirashi's *Inscriptions of the Vākāṭakas* included twenty-six Vākāṭaka records. In these pages we are noticing fourteen inscriptions discovered after its publication.
3. A detailed supplement is under preparation but will take some time.
4. Hisse-Borālā inscription of Deva Sena and Rāmṭek inscription mentioning Prabhāvatī Guptā which are engraved on blocks of stone.
5. It need hardly be added that all these (but one) inscriptions are incised in characters belonging to the box-headed variety of southern alphabets and composed in Sanskrit. The only exception, i.e., Rāmṭek inscription mentioning Prabhāvatī Guptā is engraved in nail-headed alphabet. Like already known Vākāṭaka copperplate grants, the copperplate inscriptions noticed here are also multi-plate charters. As the object of the present contribution is of a limited nature, technical details like the number and size of plates, the diameter of the ring, hole for the passage of the ring and the seal are deliberately dropped.
6. Two neighbouring villages with identical names are known to have been sometimes styled 'large' and 'small' as at present. But no such suffix or prefix is noticed in this case.
7. Most of the donated as well as the bordering villages have not been identified so far. However, two of the villages, viz. Aragrāma and Selludraha, may be identified with Āregāon in the Nagpur tahsīl of the district of the same name and Selḍoh in the adjoining Wardhā tahsīl of the Wardhā district respectively.
8. One of the incomplete Vākāṭaka copperplate grants is known to have been issued from a certain Padmapura (V.V. Mirashi, *op. cit.*, p. 78) which Mirashi proposes to identify with modern Padampur near Āmgāon in the Bhaṇḍārā district. However, this identification has been disputed by others, and nothing definite can be said about it at present. But as will be shown in the sequel, this Padampur has nothing to do with the district named after Padmapura mentioned in our inscription. Another district named after this place is mentioned in the Māsod plates of Pravara Sena II noticed in the sequel.
9. In the original we have *Vātsagulmakasya Sātvata-charaṇ-ādhivāsa-dvayasya* which would literally mean that the two monasteries were situated at Vatsagulma itself. But since the grantor belonged to the Nandivardhana branch, Vatsagulma was the capital of another branch of the dynasty which started ruling independently after Pravara Sena I and the temple of Mondasvāmin, at whose instance the grant is reported to have been made, appears to have been situated near Manḍhaḷ, these two monasteries were also probably situated in the same region. In view of this fact the expression *Vātsagulmakasya* seems to be intended as an adjective of *Sātvata-charaṇa* and not of *Sātvata-charaṇ-ādhivāsa-dvayasya,* used in the sense of one originally belonging to and hailing from Vatsagulma. Examples of such *sāpeksha-samāsas* are often met with in Indian epigraphy. However, if the expression is taken in its apparent sense, we shall have to believe that the grant

was made in favour of the monasteries situated at Vatsagulma. The phrase beginning with the word *Sārvata* may also refer to two temples of *Sātvata*, viz. Vāsudeva-Kṛishṇa, with his footprints installed in them at Vatsagulma. However, the first interpretation appears preferable.

10. *Chāturvvedy-āgrahāra-maryyadā-parihārān* in the original meaning 'exemptions of the *āgrahāras* of (the Brāhmaṇas) learned in the four Vedas.' These exemptions are enumerated as in other Vākāṭaka grants.

11. This is obviously the description of a four-armed image, and the fourth hand did not carry any object as it must have supported the head in a lying posture.

12. The description is obviously of the Śeshaśāyin form of Vishṇu. The name of the snake-king (*nāga-rājño*) looks like Nanna, but we have taken the second letter as *nta* as there is often confusion between the letters *t* and *n* and taking *nāgarājño Nantasya* together, we have split it up into *nāgarājñah Anantasya.* It is quite possible, however, that the intended reading was actually *nāgarājño Nannasya* as it is found. But it would also not make any difference in the meaning as Ananta is known to have been transformed into Nanna and in Nanna-Nārāyaṇabhaṭṭāraka who figures as the donee of the Khalimpur plate of the Pāla king Dharmapāla. See *EI*, IV, p. 250, text-line 50 and p. 254, note 3. This would show that the name Ananta had been corrupted into Nanna as early as the fifth century AD.

13. Literally 'an order from his own mouth' (*sva-mukh-ājñaptiḥ*).

14. V.V. Mirashi, *CII*, V, pp. 1-4; *Supra*, pp. 3-5. Mirashi is inclined to assign it to Rudra Sena I.

15. As will be seen in the sequel, most of the records noticed in these pages contain season dates. In view of the evidence that has come to light during recent years, the so-called rarity of season dates in the Vākāṭaka and contemporary records cannot be taken to indicate an early date for inscriptions containing season dates. For the use of season dates as a criterion of date, see *JESI*, V, p. 2; and for its critisim, see *ibid.*, IV, p. 34.

16. Barring a few minor variations in phraseology, the draft generally agrees with the charters of his son Pravara Sena II. The genealogy up to the reign of Rudra Sena II is also the same. Perhaps the beginnings go back to the reign of his father.

17. See my paper in the *VSMV*, 1977, pp. 142ff.

18. The wording in our record is *bhagavataś=chakkra-lakshma-pralishṭhita-śāsanasya*, while other inscriptions generally have *bhagavataś=chakra-pāṇeḥ prāsād-opārjjita-śri-samudayasya*, the latter being grammatically more acceptable.

19. For discussion, see Ajay Mitra Shastri, "Anantaśayana Viṣṇu: Earliest Epigraphic Evidence," *ABORI*, LXXV, 1994, pp. 11-20. For the Deogargh and Bhītargāon panels, see J.N. Banerjea, *The Development of Hindu Iconography*, second edition, Calcutta, 1956, pp. 406-07. In the Deogarh panel we find Chakrapurusha standing behind Lakshmī, and a few of what are taken to be attendants, it has been suggested, may represent personified *āyudhas.*

20. *VSMV*, 1971, p. 76, text-lines 27-28 and 33-34. *Mārga* (and *pathaka*) as an administrative unit is referred to in other Vākāṭaka records also.

21. *JESI*, X, p. 113, text-line 19.

22. See also under Māsod plates in the sequel. This record has since been published in Marathi. See Ajay Mitra Shastri and Chandrashekhar Gupta in *Saṁśodhanāchī Kshitie*, Nagpur, 1985, pp. 223-29. The plates are now prescribed in the archaeological museum of the Department of Ancient Indian History, Culture and Archaeology, Nagpur University.

23. These charters are now deposited in the archaeological museum of the Department of Ancient Indian History, Culture and Archaeology, Nagpur University.

24. We learn from the Māṇḍhaḷ plates of the second year of Prithivi Sheṇa II, which will be noticed in the sequel, that his real name was Dronasvāmin. It is difficult to determine as to why his real name is dropped and he is simply mentioned as *apratigrāhaka* which may have been his title.

25. *CII*, V, p. 12, text-line 1.

26. *Ibid.*, p. 18, text-line 1.

27. *Ibid.*, p. 23, text-line 1.

28. However, the possibility cannot be altogether ruled out.

28a. For similar other examples, *vide* D.C. Sircar, *Indian Epigraphy*, pp. 114ff.

29. Another administrative unit connected with the Waingaṅgā during the Vākāṭaka period was Beṇṇākārpara-*bhoga* which is mentioned in the Siwanī plates of Pravara Sena II (*CII*, V, p. 30, text-lines 17-18). Varāhamihira refers to Veṇātata (*Bṛihatsaṁhitā*, IV, 26) or the Waingaṅgā region as a source of diamonds (*ibid.*, IXXIX.6). See Ajay Mitra Shastri, *Varāhamihira's India*, pp. 62, 313, 374. But there the reference is to the region on the banks of the river Waingaṅgā and not to an administrative division named after it.

29a. This record has been edited by us in *EI*, XLI, pp. 68-76.

30. Text-line 19. But in text-line 29 the land is said to have been situated on the west of the village.

31. The mention of royal or standard measurement would reveal that in ancient India different measurements were in vogue in different regions during the same period. Ancient texts inform us that two standards of measurement, to wit, Māgadha and Kālinga, commanded great popularity in early times. *Vide* Ajay Mitra Shastri, *Varāhmihira's India*, p. 324. *Rāja-māna* is mentioned in some other records of Pravara Sena II also. See *CII*, V, p. 55, text-line 20 (Waḍgāon pls.); p. 60, text-lines 21-23 (Paṭṭan pls.; the expression here is *rājakya-māna* which is apparently an error for *rājakīya-māna*). The word *rāja-mānika* itself occurs in the Chammak grant (*ibid.*, p. 24, text-line 18).

31a. It may also mean a piece of land for garden or orchard.

32. These are Boppāryya, Vishnvāryya, Aratyāryya, Bhavāryya, Bhavaputrāryya, Golāryya, Śryāryya, Nārāyaṇāryya, Achalāryya, Devāryya, Dāmāryya, Keśavāryya, Kumārāryya, Koṭṭāryya and Rudrāryya. The names Boppāryya, Golāryya and Dāmāryya repeat themselves twice, thrice and twice respectively.

33. For a couple of other season dates of Pravara Sena II's reign, see *ibid.*, p. 46, text-line 28 (Dūdiā pls.), and p. 66, text-lines 27-28 (Tīgāon grant). The Yawatmāl plates (see below) of the same reign also contain season date.

34. *Ibid.*, p. 37, text-lines 30-31.

35. *Ibid.*, p.61, text-line 44.

36. The Siwanī (*ibid.*, p. 31, text-line 35) and Waḍgāon (*ibid.*, p. 56, text-line 42) plates of the eighteenth and twenty-fifth years respectively of Pravara Sena II have the same *Senāpati*, to wit, Bāppadeva, while in between these two dates we have another *Senapati*, named Namidāsa (Dūdiā plates, *ibid.*, p. 46, text-lines 28-29). However, the possibility of different personages bearing the same name holding the office in question at different dates cannot be ruled out.

37. These plates have been recently edited by me in collaboration with Chandrashekhar Gupta. See *JESI*, X, pp. 108-16. For date, see *ibid.*, XI, p. 114.

38. Note the use of dual number in *vikrāntayoḥ* and *narendrayoḥ*.

39 *CII*, V, p. 36, text-line 10.

40. *Ibid.*, V, pp. xi, 24 and 35. For a different view, see *ibid.*, p. vii.

41. *Ibid.*, pp. ix and 35.

42. *Ibid.*, pp. 7-8.

43. The Śarabhapurīyas, Pāṇḍuvaṁśins and Somavaṁśins had different personal and coronation names. See our *EHDPP*, pp. 258-67. However, we cannot rule out this possibility altogether in view of the facts that Pravīra and Pravara Sena were identical and *sena*-ending names appear to be royal names. However, this does not affect the main point.

44. This important record has not yet been published. The information has been kindly supplied by my friends Dr A.P. Jamkhedkar, Director of Archaeology and Museums and Shri K.D. Kawadkar, Deputy Director in the same Directorate of the Government of Maharashtra, Mumbai.

45. For the contents of the record, see *supra*, pp. 23-25.

46. *EI*, XXIV, pp. 52ff; *CII*, V, pp. 38ff.

47. For its text, see V.V. Mirashi, *Indological Research Papers*, I, p. 72.

48. It is generally taken to indicate the authorisation of the grant recorded in the charter by competent authorities and is found at the beginning of most of the complete Vākāṭaka copper-plate inscriptions.

49. V.V. Mirashi, *Indological Research Papers*, I, p. 72, text-line 1.

50. For a detailed account of the history of this town, see Ajay Mitra Shastri, *Tripurī* (Hindi), Bhopal, 1971.

51. V.V. Mirashi, *Indological Research Papers*, I, p. 69.

52. J.F. Fleet, *Inscriptions of the Guptas and their Successors*, *CII*, III, pp. 53-54.

53. *ABORI*, I, p. 103.

54. D.R. Bhandarakar, *Inscriptions of the Early Gupta Kings*, *CII*, III (eds. B. Ch. Chhabra and G.S. Gai), p. 315; B. Ch. Chhabra in *Dr. Mirashi Felicitation Volume* (eds. G.T. Deshpande and Ajay Mitra Shastri), p. 367.

55. V.V. Mirashi, *Indological Research Papers*, I, p. 70.

56. Fleet, *CII*, III, pp. 233f; V, pp. 89-91.

57. *EI*, XVII, pp. 12ff; *CII*, V, p. 92.

58. V.V. Mirashi, *Indological Research Papers*, I, p. 71.

59. Like *vāsa*, *vāsaka* also connotes an abode, dwelling or habitation. See Monier Monier-Williams, *A Sankrit-English Dictionary*, s.v. *vāsaka*, p. 947. But in inscriptions, when mentioned as the place of issue of a charter, it is generally used in the sense of a temporary residence.

60. *CII*, V, p. 54, text-line 1.

61. *Cf.* the Nasik inscription of the eighteenth regnal year of Gautamiputra Sātakarṇi (D.C. Sircar, *Select Inscription*, I, p. 198, text-line 1), which is in the nature of a copperplate charter, was issued from the *vijaya-khadhāvāra (vijaya-skandhāvara)* at Govardhana.

62. For references, see my *Tripurī*, pp. 167-68.

63. It is found in all the known copperplate inscriptions of the reign of Pṛithivī Sheṇa II.

64. Fleet, *CII*, III, pp. 118-19 and 122-23.

65. This is indicated by Harivarman's Shankarpur inscription dated in Gupta year 168. See *JESI*, IV, p. 64.

66. *Cf.* the name Vindhyaśakti of the founder of the Vākāṭaka dynasty and the name Vindhyaka employed for the dynasty in the dynastic texts of the Purāṇas. In our opinion the Vākāṭakas rose to power in the Vindhyan region of Central India and later migrated to the Vidarbha region. We have discussed this question at length earlier in this volume.

66a. *Vide* also *supra*, pp. 65-69 for discussion of Nachnā-kī-talāi and Ganj inscriptions. Also see G.S. Gai, "Note on the Indore Plates of Pravarasena II ", *IESI*, V, pp. 98-102.

67. It must have been given in the opening line on the inner side of the first plate. We must remember, however, that this item is omitted in some of the Vākāṭaka copperplate charters. The first known grant of the Nandivardhana branch of the dynasty (Māṇḍhaḷ plates of Rudra Sena II), for example, does not mention the issuing place.

68. This initial portion describing Pravara Sena I and the Bhāraśivas was evidently given on the inner side of the first plate.

69. These formed the content of the missing intervening plate/plates.

70. While Lāṭakapallī appears to be identical with modern Lāḍkheḍ, some twenty miles east of Dārwhā on the Dārwhā-Yawatmal road in the Yawatmāl district, Shaḍgriśaka has not been identified. It is not impossible that this was an administrative division comprising six units/villages.

71. The Kurud plates of the Śarabhapura king Narendra register the renewal of a grant originally recorded on palm-leaves (*tāla-patra-śāsana*). See Ajay Mitra Shastri, *Inscriptions of the Śarabhapurīyas, Pāṇḍuvaṁśins and Somavaṁśins*, Part II, p. 8, text lines 7-8.

72. The well-known Nidhanpur plates of Bhāskaravarman were intended to replace the original copperplate grant which was destroyed by fire.

73. The king's command regarding the grant recorded in the Pattan plates of Pravara Sena II is also addressed to the village, but there it is described as headed by the Brāhmaṇas. See *CII*, V, p. 69, text-line 21.

74. We have *savva* for *saṁvat* and *gi* for *grī* which is an abbreviation of *grīshma*.

75. This feature is noticed in the Māṇḍhaḷ plates of Pṛithivī Sheṇa II (*VSMV*, 1977, pp. 166 and 174) as well as the Malhārā plates of the Muṇḍaputra chief Ādityarāja belonging to the post-Vākāṭaka period (*JESI*, IV, p. 39, text-line 50).

76. His Jāmb plates were given in the second year (*CII*, V, pp. 12-13) while the Paunī grant was issued in the thirty-second year (*EI*, XXXVIII, pp. 53-56).

77. *CII*, V, p. 31, text-line 35.

78. *Ibid.*, p. 56, text-line 54.

79. These plates have been edited by me and C.S. Gupta in *VIJ*, XXI, pp. 78-84; *EI*, XLIII, pp. 30-34.

80. The ring is now lost, while the inscription on the seal is the same as that found on several seals attached to Pravara Sena II's charters.

81. V.B. Kolte erroneously takes Bahvṛicha as forming part of the name of the *gotra* (*EI*, XXXVIII, p. 54). For the meaning of this word, see Monier Monier-Williams, *A Sanskrit-English Dictionary*, p. 726.

82. Achalapuka engraved in the original appears to be an error for Achalapura, caused by the addition of an unnecessary cross-bar to the vertical of the letter *ra*. Such errors are noticed elsewhere in the record also. See text-line 30 where *parihāra* has been incised as *pakihāka*.

83. *CII*, V, pp. 63-68; *supra*, pp. 32-35.

84. *Ibid.*, p. 67, text-line 54.

85. *EI*, XXXVIII, pp. 53-56.

86. *Ibid.*, p. 54.

87. Another Achalapura (called an *agrahāra*) is referred to in the Nāgardhan plates of Svāmirāja (V.V. Mirashi, *Inscriptions of the Kalachuri-Chedi Era*, *CII*, IV, p. 616, text-line 16). Some of the localities mentioned in this record have been identified in the proximity of its provenance, and Achalapura, too, must have been situated nearby. This Achalapura may have been the same as the homonymous town mentioned in our record.

88. The first component of the name of the *kaṭaka*, Kṛishṇā, may also refer to the river Kanhān, and the name may connote the Kanhān valley which is even now well-known for its paddy cultivation. It may as well allude to the cultivation of paddy in the black cotton soil.

89. *EI*, IX, pp. 26ff.; *CII*, V, pp. 79ff; *supra*, pp. 70-79.

90. *VSMV*, 1971, pp. 53ff.; *ABORI*, LIII, pp. 183-94.

91. It was obviously to form part of the concluding portion which has not been engraved.

92. The word *sthāna* is apparently used in the sense of a sacred spot and is indicative of religious sanctity of Rāmagiri which is known from other sources also.

93. *CII*, V, p. 35, text-line 1.

94. In all other records her name is given an Ajjhitabhaṭṭārikā. She is not named in connection with the description of her son as in other grants. It is known from other charters that she was the daughter of a king of Kuntala, evidently of the Kadamba family.

95. Such addresses are rather rare in Vākāṭaka grants.

96. In the original we have *Ishṭākapalyāttarataḥ* which may be corrected either as *Ishṭākapallyā uttarataḥ* or *Ishṭākapasyottarataḥ*, the former being definitely more likely.

97. The granted village, Kurubhajjaka, is identifiable with modern Kurjjhā, and Lavaṇatailaka with modern Loṇārā. It is noteworthy that Kurjjhā is, in keeping with the specification in the inscription, actually situated to the west of Loṇārā. Ishṭākapa or Ishṭākapallī can be equated with modern Iṭgāon which is, as stated in the record, situated to the south of Kurjjhā. Not only does this identification agree with the locational directions, but finds support from the sameness of the meanings of the ancient and modern names. Goshī Khurd and Goshī Budruk to the north of Kurjjhā seem to represent the ancient village of Govvasāhikā. A little distance to the east of Goshi Budruk there is a village named Bāserā. Ancient Govvasāhikā probably comprised all the area now covered by these three villages. When this ancient village was divided into these two villages [Ghosī (Khurd and Budruk) and Bāserā], the first part of the ancient name was transformed into Goshi and the second into Bāserā. Geographically also this equation is in conformity with the description in the inscription. In view of the close agreement between the directional specifications as given in the inscription and the location of the modern villages proposed to be equated with the ancient villages in question, there can be absolutely no doubt about the correctness of the suggested identifications.

98. *Jaya-śāsana* in the original can also be rendered as a `charter of victory,' and it is actually described as a kind of royal decree in the Dharmaśāstras. But our charter does not tally with its definition. The description of Pṛithivī Sheṇa II as the `good son of Narendra Sena' (*Narendrasena-satsūnu*) is literally identical with that found in the grant itself where he is described as *satputra*, the replacement of *putra* by *sūnu* being due to metrical requirements.

99. An uninscribed plate was also found strung on the ring along with the inscribed plates.

100. *Sthāna* also indicates sanctity and the expression in question may refer to a spot of religious significance on the bank of the river Waingangā which was regarded as sacred. But the other sense, viz., administrative headquarters, looks probable here.

101. Maheśvarasvāmin is styled *Kautsa-sagotra* and, thereafter, Brahmasvāmin and Harasvāmin, *tat-sagotra*, whereas no such expression is employed for Varāhasvāmin.

101a. This explains why these three grants were preserved together in an earthen pot.

102. As will be seen below, the phrase *pratāpa-praṇat-ari-śāsanasya* is found applied for the first time to Narendra Sena in the Māhurjharī plates of the seventeenth year of Pṛithivī Sheṇa II and the word *dvi* was prefixed to the expression *magna-vaṁś-oddharttuḥ* describing Pṛithivī Sheṇa II for the first time in the Bālāghāṭ plates.

103. Māṇḍhaḷ (10th year), Māhurjharī and Bālāghāṭ plates.

104. *EI*, IX, p. 271, text-lines 26-27 and note 6. See also p. 269, note 2.

105. *CII*, V, p. 81, text-lines 26-27.

106. *ABORI*, LIII, p. 193, text-lines 21-22.

107. I, too, had adopted this reading at one stage. See *VSMV*, 1977, p. 171, text-line 17.

108. This is a literal rendering of *guṇa-viśvāsād* which, as will be seen in the sequel, is non-existent.

109. *EI*, IX, p. 269.

110. *CII*, V, p. 81.

111. *EI*, IX, p. 269.

112. *CII*, V, introduction, p. xxv.

113. G. Yazdani (ed.), *The Early History of the Deccan*, Parts I-IV, p. 182.

114. *Ibid.*, pp. 182-83.

115. *VSMV*, 1971, pp. 61-64; *ABORI*, LIII, pp. 186-87.

116. *VSMV*, 1971, pl. vi; *ABORI*, LIII, third plate, first side (between pp. 194 and 195), lines 21-22.

117. The phrase can also be split in some other ways, particularly mentionable ones being *pūrvv-ādhigatā guṇavato dāyādād-apahṛitā vaṁśa-śrīh yena tasya, purvv-ādhigatād=guṇaavato dāyādad=apahaṛitā vaṁśa-śṛiḥ yena tasya*, or *pūrvv-ādhigatena guṇavatā dāyādena apahṛitā vaṁśḥa-śṛiḥ yasya tasya*. But they do not yield any satisfactory meaning.

118. For the meaning of *dāyāda*, see *Amara-kosha* (Nirnaya Sagar Press, Bombay, 1944), III, 3, 89; Monier Monier-Williams, *A Sanskrit-English Dictionary*, p. 474, s.v. *dāyāda*. Also *vide* P.V. Kane, *History of Dharmaśāstra*, III, Poona, 1946, pp. 543-44.

119. The employment of the expression *guṇavat* as an adjective of the *dāyāda* who was a source of calamity to Narendra Sena is somewhat enigmatic. The intention may have been to avṛr that the *dāyāda*, though endowed with good qualities, indulged in a nefarious act like seizing his relative's (Narendra Sena's) throne. Alternatively, it may have been used in the sense of *gauṇa* (minor), a derivative from *guṇa*, with reference to a scion of the Vatsagulma branch of the family. The latter interpretation looks more probable.

120. *EI*, XXVII, pp. 137-38; *CII*, V, pp.83-84. This assumption has for its basis the word *narendra* occurring in the 11th verse of this charter which was taken as alluding, though in a veiled manner, to Narendra Sena. But we now know from the Mallār grant of Śūrabala *alias* Udīrṇavaira (*Studies in Indian Epigraphy*, III, pp. 183-93) that the Bamhanī charter also belongs to him and that the word *narendra* is employed in its common sense of 'king', there being no pun on it. The erroneous impression that the Bamhanī plates were given by Bharatabala was due to the inadvertent omission of a prose passage introducing Sūrabala after the description of Bharatabala. This passage is now supplied by the Mallār plates.

121. *Bhāratī-Bhānam* (*Dr. K.V. Sarma Felicitation Volume*), Hoshiarpur, 1980, pp. 439-43.

122. The continued friendship between the Vākāṭakas and the Guptas seems to be vouched for by the retention of reference to the marriage of Prabhāvatī Guptā to Rudra Sena II, even in the latest records of the Nandivardhana branch.

123. The expression in this record is somewhat corrupt.

124. *ABORI*, LIII, p. 193, text-line 26.

125. *EI*, IX, p. 271, text-line 33.

126. *Ibid.*, p. 271, fn. 15. Kielhorn was, however, not quite sure about it as would follow from the fact that he puts an interrogation mark after *ni*.

127. *CII*, V, p. 81, fn. 7. He removes the question mark.

128. It must be said to the credit of Altekar that he accepted the reading *dvi* as correct. See G. Yazdani (ed.), *The Early History of the Deccan*, Parts I-IV, p. 184. He, however, took

these two misfortunes to have been due to the Śarabhapurīya and Traikūṭaka invasions. This surmise lacks supporting evidence. Also see D.C. Sircar in *HCIP*, III: *The Classical Age* (ed. R.C. Majumdar), p. 184.

129. The Ṛiddhapur charter of the Nala chief Bhavadattavarman was given from Nandivardhana, the erstwhile Vākāṭaka capital. See *EI*, XIX, pp. 100ff.

129a. Both these grants from Māṇḍhaḷ have been published by us in *EI*, XLI, pp. 159-80.

130. *VSMV*, 1971, pp. 53ff.; *ABORI*, LIII, 1972, pp. 183-94.

130a. "Some observations on the Māhurjharī Plates of Vākāṭaka Pṛithivī Sheṇa II, Year 17," *ibid.*, LXXVI, 1995, pp. 35-49.

131. The other charter containing an explicit mention of this recension of the *Yajurveda* is the Miregaon charter noticed at *supra*, pp. 91-92 In a couple of records we find *vāji* prefixed to or forming part of the names of donees' *gotras*. *Vide CII*, V, p. 55, text-line 21; p. 66, text-lines 24-24 and 28. However, we cannot be quite sure if it really refers to the Vājasaneyī *śākhā*, though it is not improbable.

132. Orthographic errors have been ignored.

133. Kolte reads Surambi-*rājya* which is evidently incorrect as will follow from a glance at the facsimile plate accompanying his papers.

134. *CII*, V, p. 45, text-line 13.

135. *Ibid.*, p. 66, text-lines 26 and 29.

136. For a different view on the question, see Hiralal, *Inscriptions in the Central Provinces and Berar,* second edition, Nagpur, 1932, p. 93, no. 168. Our view is comparatively close to Mirashi's, but he proposes to identify Ārammi, the headquarters of this *rājya*, with Āmlā which is quite unlikely. See *CII*, V, p. 44.

137. It is difficult to ascertain if the king responsible for it was the first or second chief of this name. However, in all likelihood it was Pṛithivī Sheṇa II. Had his illustrious homonymous predecessor done so, there would have been greater chances of the continuation of the new names given by him, for these names would have been enforced by his successors.

138. For excavations of some of these circles, see S.B. Deo, *Māhurjharī Excavation,* Nagpur, 1973.

139. *EI*, XXXVII, pp. 1-4.

140. *Dr. Mirashi Felicitation Volume*, pp. 372-84; *VSMV*, 1964, pp. 137-56.

141. *EI*, XXXVII, pp. 5-8.

141a. "Date of the Hisse-Borālā Inscription of Vākāṭaka Deva Sena", *JAIH*, I, pp. 94-98.

142. *Dr. Umesha Mishra Commemoration Volume,* Allahabad, 1970, pp. 617-27.

143. *JESI*, VII, pp. 2-5. Also see Mitchiner in *Monthly Bulletin of the Asiatic Society,* August 1978, pp. 6-7,.

143a. Some scholars find in the inscription an allusion to the year 220 of a reckoning counted from the termination of the Andhra (Sātavāhana) rule (*ibid.*) or the commencement of the Vākāṭaka rule (*JESI*, VII, pp. 2-5).

144. A parallel, if one be needed, is furnished by the Tummalaguḍem plates of the Vishṇukuṇḍin

king Vikramendravarman II which alone of the fairly numerous epigraphs of the dynasty are dated in the Śaka era.

145. *Annual Report on Indian Epigraphy*, 1950-51, No. B 36, as cited in K.V. Ramesh, *Indian Epigraphy*, I, p. 80 *(Śaka-varshe dvātriṁśaty-adhike śata-traye vrajati Śaka-nara-nāthānām)*. "Vala (or Vada) Inscription of Suketuvarman, Śaka 322", *EI*, XL, pp. 37-54. However, in the Report (p. 13) itself the record is said to have been found at Vālā in Saurāshtra and to refer to Suketuvarman as *Dharmma-mahārāja*. On palaeographical grounds it is dated about the sixth century AD.

146. *EI*, XXVII, pp. 4-9; D.C. Sircar, *Select Inscriptions bearing on Indian History and Civilization*, I, p. 482.

147. The account here is a slightly improved and updated version of what was published in our *EHDPP*, pp. 71-74.

148. *JESI*, XIII, pp. 71-75, where it is published under the title "Hyderabad Plates of Vākāṭaka Deva Sena, Year 5" after the place of its deposit whereas it should actually be designated after 'Bidar' in which district it was reportedly discovered.

149. According to Parabrahma Sastry, who follows literally the wording of the record, the grant was made by Svāmilladeva. See *JESI*, XIII, p. 72. However, the wording of the inscription is defective and the grant actually appears to have been executed by Svāmilladeva.

150. While in the context, our statement appears to be very probable, it is difficult to explain as to what prevented the scribe from completing the name. It is as well possible that he started engraving *savvachhara* without realising that it could not be completed in that line and therefore re-engraved the entire word in the next line and forgot to efface the letter *sa* engraved in the previous line.

151. V.V. Mirashi, *The History and Inscriptions of the Sātavāhanas and Western Kshatrapas*, Pl. VII, Fig. 10, line 50.

152. One reason may have been the spatial closeness to western Maharashtra.

152a. *CII*, V, p. 96, text-line 5.

153. B.R. Gopal, *Corpus of Kadamba Inscriptions*, I, p. 141, text-line 13. *Vide* also EI, XLII, pp. 187-92. The actual wording of the relevant portion is *Sarvvasena-mahārājena mūrddh-ābhisheken-ābhyarchchitaḥ*.

154. *Vide* Ajay Mitra Shastri, "The Mudigere Plates of Siṁhavarman and Kadamba-Vākāṭaka Relations", *Indian Archaeological Heritage: K.V. Sundararajan Felicitation Volume*, eds. C. Margabandhu et al., Delhi, 1991, pp. 317-19. Also see our paper under publication in B.K. Thapar communeration volume. In view of this statement in the Mudigere plates we have got to fix earlier dates for the Kadamba kings instead of inventing a Sarvva Sena III who might have been a son of the last known king, Hari Sheṇa, of this branch of the Vākāṭakas.

155. *Saṁśodhaka* (Marathi Journal of the Rājavāḍe Saṁśodhana Maṇḍaḷa), XLVII (1980), nos. 1-2.

156. *Indological Research Papers*, I, pp. 78-87.

157. This was obviously an administrative unit.

158. In the original we have *viṁśati arddhaviṁśati* which gives no sense. It seems that as in

other subsequent cases *arddhaviṁśatiḥ* was expected; but by oversight the scribe first wrote *viṁśati* and then the intended word, *arddhaviṁśati*, but, again by oversight, forgot to cancel *viṁśati*. *Arddhaviṁśati* is an error for *sārddhavimśati*.

159. Though not named, this was a common measurement prevalent under the Vākāṭakas.

160. Mirashi takes the expression *arddhaviṁśati* to mean 'half of twenty' (*Indological Research Papers*, I, p. 80, i.e., 10). But in that case he would have used *daśa* or *viṁśatyarddha*. As stated above, the intended reading probably is *sārddhaviṁśati*. Mirashi also feels likewise, but, according to him, it would mean 30 (*ibid.*, p. 80, fn. 5), which does not appear to be correct.

161. With the solitary exception of the India Office plate of Deva Sena which straightaway mentions the issuing chief (Deva Sena) without referring to any of his predecessors. See *CII*, V, p. 102.

162. *Ibid.*, V, p. 107, verse 2. *Vide* also *supra*, pp. 42-44.

163. In the original we have *Vākāṭakānām=ādi-dharmmamahārāja-śri-Vinddhyaśakteḥ* which Mirashi proposes to restore as *Vākāṭakānām-ādirdharmmamahārāja-śri-Vinddhyaśakteḥ*. We feel that the initial portion should be restored as *Vākāṭakānām=āder* (instead of *Vākāṭakānām=ādir*) which would go well with *Vindhyaśakteḥ* which it qualifies. Alternatively, even *ādi* without any case-ending will also serve the purpose.

164. *CII*, V, p. 96.

165. In the Bīdar plates this title is applied to Deva Sena also.

166. *Numismatic Digest*, I (i), pp. 25-28; III (i), pp. 7-9.

167. *JESI*, IV, p. 38, text-line 31. Also see p. 37.

168. For its connotation, see D.C. Sircar, *Indian Epigraphical Glossary*, pp. 103-04, s.v. *dūtaka*.

169. *Dr. Mirashi Felicitation Volume*, p. 384, text-line 2.

170. For discussion of a few points concerning this record, see our paper in *JESI*, XI, pp. 15-20.

APPENDIX

Rāmṭek Prabhāvatī Guptā Memorial Stone Inscription[1]

(PL LXVIII)

This epigraph of an inestimable value for the Gupta Vākāṭaka history, though extremely fragmentary, is found incised on two rectangular blocks of stone placed below one another with the lower slab further broken into two vertically in the middle. The three stones measure altogether about 1.04 x 0.56 m and are fixed on the right wall inside the *maṇḍapa* (hall) of the Kevala-Narasiṁha temple at Rāmṭek, a well-known religious spot and pilgrimage centre in the Nagpur district popularly identified with the celebrated Rāmagiri immortalised by the poet-dramatist Kālidāsa in his *Meghadūta*. Even though a couple of Vākāṭaka charters are known to have been given at Rāmagiri,[2] this happens to be the only Vākāṭaka epigraph reported hitherto from Rāmṭek itself. It came to light in course of the cleaning operations undertaken by the Directorate of Archaeology and Museums, Maharashtra Government, about seventeen years ago.

The inscription is engraved in what is known among epigraphists commonly as the nail-headed variety with southern forms of characters topped by solid triangles instead of square (filled or hollowed) boxes common to most of the Vākāṭaka charters.[3] The language is, as in most of the Vākāṭaka copperplate and lithic records, Sanskrit.[4] However, it is couched entirely in verse and originally formed a beautiful specimen of ornate Sanskrit poetry.[5] There are, in all, fifteen lines of writing comprising thirty-four stanzas. Unfortunately, however, a considerable portion at the end of all the lines and often in the middle of many a line has been irretrievably damaged and lost for historical purposes, most probably owing to inadvertent strokes of hammer and other tools in course of cleaning operations[6] and partly due to its long age of over fifteen centuries. And what little has escaped the agencies of destruction makes little sense and gives only a faint general idea of its likely contents. The only thing that can be done under the circumstances is to indicate bits of historical information that can be gleaned, very doubtfully sometimes, from its preserved portion.

Reference may be made here briefly to a couple of important attempts in this connection. A.P. Jamkhedkar, to whose efforts we owe this important discovery, published, almost simultaneously with our earliest writing on the subject,[7] information about it and his reading and interpretation of the text.[8] Thereafter Hans Bakker gave us his reading of the text and interpretation and its bearing on the date of the Kevala-Narasiṁha temple.[9] And finally he jointly with Harunaga Isaacson (hereafter referred to as HB:HI) edited it with a translation and detailed notes on the text and their interpretation of the same.[10] The last is so far the best effort at this inscription and the problems raised by it. Admittedly even this attempt, the most strenuous so far, cannot make up for the great loss of the text, and differences on its interpretation and implications are bound to survive. But it must be stated that these authors have spared no pains to arrive at the best possible text and number the stanzas which are thirty-four in all.[11] Our references in this note appertain to this edition.

The record belonged to the reign of Pravara Sena II of the Padmapura-Nandivardhana-Pravarapura branch of the Vākāṭakas and purported to record most probably some pious acts of a daughter (name lost) of Prabhāvatī Guptā to perpetuate the latter's memory and was in all probability assisted by her brother, perhaps Pravara Sena II, in this venture. The act apparently consisted of the erection of the Kevala-Narasiṁha temple wherein the inscribed slabs are fixed and, of course, the installation of the image of the man-lion (Narasiṁha) manifestation of Vishṇu which is still extant. Some other pious acts were also recorded. It may be inferred from the reference to a *prāsāda* in verse 30. More about it in the sequel.

The opening stanza is an invocation to god Vishṇu or one of his manifestations as can be made out from his comparison (in colour) to the depths of water-laden rain-clouds (*sa-jal-āmbud-odara*) and the expression *sa jayati* ('he is victorious'). It is not unlikely that the man-lion (Nṛi-siṁha) form, whose image is enshrined in the temple, was invoked. The third stanza refers to a sovereign monarch whose feet were touched by the crest-jewels (*chūḍāmaṇi*) of the kings which served as his footstool (*pāda-pīṭha*). The description is obviously of the Gupta emperor Chandra Gupta II Vikramāditya who is mentioned by name in verse 9. The fifth stanza perhaps refers to his queen, most probably Kuberanāgā, mother of Prabhāvatī-Guptā, who is described as 'being worshipped in the residence of her father like a deity' and is said to have grown up like a flame of fire wherein abundant ghee has been poured. We learn from verse 7 that after sons (at least three)[12] had been born to them in succession, their younger sister resembling the lustre of the moon (*chandramasaḥ prabh-eva*) was born. Her name appears to have ended in *-muṇḍā* and HB:HI feel that the full name might have been Gomuṇḍā or Chāmuṇḍā. Such a name, however, looks incongruous with the fact that the Guptas were devout devotees of Bhagavat, viz. Vishṇu, and assumed the sectarian title *paramabhāgavata* while Chāmuṇḍā was a Śaivite name. It may have been perhaps due to the insistence of the queen who hailed from one of the Nāga ruling families which are known to have espoused Śaivism very vehemently.[13] It is not impossible if she was a daughter different from Prabhāvatī who was married to the Vākāṭaka king Rudra Sena II, especially in view of the fact that one stanza intervenes between it and the one alluding to the marriage in question.

Verse 9 refers to Chandra Gupta, evidently the homonymous Guptā emperor, viz. Chandra Gupta II Vikramāditya, who is spoken of as of 'perfect character' *(paripūrṇa-vṛitta)*, 'god of gods' (*dai(de)va-deva*)[14] and, what is most important historically, as 'the lord of the three oceans' (*tri-samudra-nātha*). The style one whose fame was tasted by the waters of the four oceans' (*chatur=udadhi-salil-āsvādita-yaśas*) is commonly applied to Samudra Gupta in later epigraphs[15] and is once transferred to his grandson Kumāra Gupta I.[16] The Mandasor inscription of the silk-weavers' guild speaks of Kumāra Gupta I as ruling over the earth girdled by the four oceans,[17] and the same description is found applied with an insignificant alteration in the wording to his son and successor Skanda Gupta.[18] However, these are merely conventional descriptions without much historical significance. But the same cannot be said about the title 'lord of the three oceans' which is not known to have been employed for any other Gupta monarch, not even to the mighty Samudra Gupta, in Gupta records and it does not appear to be totally bereft of historical value. It will be admitted on all hands that this title is pertinent only in a South Indian context and is applied in a somewhat different form (*ti-samuda-toya-pita-vāhana*, 'one whose chargers have drunk the waters of the three oceans') to the Sātavāhana emperor Gautamīputra Sātakarṇi in the Nāsik inscription of the nineteenth year of the reign of his son and successor, Vāsishṭhīputra Puḷumāvi.[19] As Gautamīpūtra Sātakarṇi controlled a considerable portion of the southern peninsula and was definitely the greatest ruler of it, the justification, at least to a great extent, of applying this title to him cannot be doubted. The employment of this style for the Gupta emperor Chandra Gupta II in this epigraph seems to indicate that at the time of its composition he was regarded, at least theoretically, as the overlord of a fairly extensive portion of the South Indian peninsula, which is reminiscent of Samudra Gupta's peninsular conquests described so very succinctly but beautifully by Hari Sheṇa in his Allāhābād pillar inscription the memory whereof lingered on for a considerably long period.[20] This claim becomes all the more significant coming as it does from an inscription of another dynasty.[21] Historically speaking, it is indicative of the tremendous influence verging on political hegemony wielded by Chandra Gupta II over a large part of the Deccan during the regency of his daughter Prabhāvatī Guptā covering the minority of her son Divākara Sena and the reigns of Dāmodara Sena and Pravara Sena II. This may perhaps explain as to why the Gupta-Vākāṭaka matrimonial alliance is invariably mentioned as a matter of pride in all the official charters of the Padmapura-Nandivardhana-Pravarapura branch of the Vākāṭakas. We are also reminded in this context of the reference, with pride, to the matrimonial alliance with the Guptas established by the Kadamba king Kākutsthavarman of Vanavāsī in Karnataka.[22] These facts should suffice to show that the statement of the Meharaulī iron pillar inscription that the southern ocean was rendered fragrant by the winds of the prowess of king Chandra,[23] identifiable with Chandra Gupta II,[24] is not an empty boast though, of course, somewhat exaggerated.

This stanza also refers to a *sena*-ending name, the initial part of which is damaged; however, it commenced with the syllable *ru* so that it can be restored fairly certainly as Rudra, and the intended name was undoubtedly Rudra Sena. As the name is given in dative singular and as the opening letter *su* of *sutā* (daughter) is clearly legible, it may be reasonably conjectured that the stanza in question contained a reference to the giving by Chandra Gupta II of his daughter to Rudra Sena II in marriage. The name of this daughter, according to the Vākāṭaka records, was Prabhāvatī Guptā. But the name of the youngest daughter of Chandra Gupta II born of an unspecified[25] queen of his ended, according to verse 7 of this record, into muṇḍā. But obviously she is different from Prabhāvatī Guptā married to Rudra Sena II unless we suppose that the muṇḍā-ending name was changed into Prabhāvatī after her marriage in keeping with the local custom.[26] Unfortunately no reference to Rudra Sena's family (Vākāṭaka) is legible in the preserved portion and the word following *Rudrasenāya* has been restored as *guṇānvitāya*, i.e. 'endowed with virtues' by HB:HI. The record next refers to some person who is described as bearing the entire burden of the great kingdom which was difficult to bear and as the best of the beasts of burden who is evidently Chandra Gupta II. Next is mentioned his son Ghaṭotkacha, who is styled as 'king of kings' (*rāja-rāja*) or a sovereign ruler.[27] The fact that he is mentioned after the reference to the marriage of, probably Prabhāvatī, and after a gap of a stanza (verse 10) may perhaps indicate that he was born after Prabhāvatī (or after her marriage) and perhaps of a different queen. Verse 13, which is almost fully preserved, refers to his (Ghaṭotkacha's) sister's daughter (*bhāgineyī*), i.e. niece, and her marriage. She is described as the goddess of her house (*veśma-lakshmī*). Ghatotkacha did something about her marriage. If the wordings of the inscription (*pāṇigrahaṇaṁ chakāra*) were to be taken literally, he actually married her, and there is nothing unusual in it as such marriages were quite common (as they are at present) to the south of the Narmadā. However, the question is, that Prabhāvatī had come from the north and so was the case with Ghaṭotkacha, and in north such a practice was highly abhored and condemned. Moreover, unless Ghaṭọtkacha was born after Prabhāvatī's marriage, there would have been quite a difference between the age of Ghaṭotkacha and his niece. In view of it we strongly feel that the verbal form actually is intended for a causative, viz. *kārayāmāsa*, 'caused her to be married'. Then, the nature of the expression in question, viz. *pāṇi-grahaṇaṁ chakāra*, instead of the common *pāṇiṁ jagrāha*, also violates against the idea of such a marriage. Metrical exigencies cannot be cited a reason for it as the poet responsible for composing the *praśasti* was highly accomplished. However, if the normal meaning were to be accepted, there remains no alternative but to admit that such a marriage did take place under southern impact even though two of the parents were from the north where such marriages were severely condemned.[28] However, the details like the name of the niece[28a] wedded to him and the circumstances leading to this matrimony cannot be ascertained owing to the loss of the relevant portion of the text. Whatever that be, if this marriage really did take place, it must have doubly affirmed the friendly relations of two great ruling families. Verses 14-16 probably referred to Ghaṭotkacha, and of these first and last are almost lost for historical purposes. The intervening stanza spoke of his qualities like faultless speech, pleasant manners and courtesies towards the ladies and his liberality to the good people.[29] The next verse most probably alludes to his demise and the brother bringing back forcibly (viz. by persuasion)[29a] his widowed sister to his own house.

It is certain that Rudra Sena II, the father of Ghaṭotkacha's wife, was already dead long before the time of her marriage and the crown prince Divakara Sena was also not alive then. The brother in question therefore may have been either Dāmodara Sena or his younger brother and successor Pravara Sena II, more probably the latter who ascended the Vākāṭaka throne in c. 421 AD and remained king for about thirtyfive years thereafter. It must have been for a short period.[30] She must have spent some time at her brother's residence at Pravarapura or perhaps the earlier capital at Nandivardhana.[31]

After some time another calamity took place. It was the demise of her mother Prabhāvatī Guptā which must have occurred some time after the twenty-third year of Pravara Sena II's reign when he did a pious act for his mother's merit.[32] This event must have been described in verse 20 now completely lost. The next stanza refers to the pious act performed by her in memory of her dead mother which was the execution of an image of 'the lord of the universe' (*loka-nātha*) and the erection of the temple for housing it appropriately christened Prabhāvatisvāmin. For it was a common practice in these days to install an image or symbolic representation of the favourite divinity in a shrine in memory of a beloved person and name it after him/her, and we have numerous such instances. And *svāmin*-ending names were quite popular among the Vaishṇavas as Prabhāvatī admittedly was. As stated clearly in this stanza it was done for the inexhaustible merit (*puṇyam=akshayam=uddiśya*) of her mother. Verse 24 speaks of the excavation of a tank called Sudarśana as well as the god looking beautiful (*devaṁ sudarśanam)* at the village of Kadalīvāṭaka. The name of the person reponsible for these pious acts was also given, but it is now damaged. Whether it was a male[33] or female[34] could not be ascertained earlier due to the rather uncertain nature of the preserved information in this respect. But we now feel that the inscription, or, to be more precise, its preserved portion, describes only the pious deeds of Prabhāvatī's daughter, most probably with the tacit support from her brother Pravara Sena II. We are told that half of the merit accruing from these acts was meant for the Brāhmaṇas[35] and the remainiing half for her parents (verse 27). Earlier probably, after her father Rudra Sena II's demise, a shrine for perpetuating his memory was built, most probably by her mother,[36] and it was probably in decay, and therefore she erected a strong lithic shrine for her mother only (verse 30). The deity, man-lion form of Vishṇu, whose temple was built and image erected, is eulogised as 'possessing infinite might' (*amitaujas)* and 'the cause of the endurance and annihilation of the world' (*jagatas=sthiti-*

saṁhāra-kāraṇa).[37] The hope of its lasting long (*chirāya*) is also expressed (verse 31).Stanzas 33-34 refer to the composition of this 'great poem' (*kāvyaṁ mahat*) eulogising 'this pious work' 'lasting as long as the world' by a poet engaged by her and obeying her orders.[38] The poet's name also must have been given as would appear from the wording of the preserved portion of the stanza; but it is now permanently lost. Whatever may have been his name, the text leaves no doubt regarding his great poetic skills and literary taste.

The village Kadalīvaṭaka, the venue of some of the pious acts of Prabhāvatī Guptā's daughter (and perhaps of Pravare Sena II also) cannot be identified definitely. There is, of course, a village, now deserted, named Kelāpur, a couple of km. north of Rāmṭek hill, which is identical in meaning, *kadalī* (plantain) being the original Sanskrit word for modern Hindi-Marathi *kelā*, only *vāṭaka*- being replaced by *pura*. It is located in the *nālā* (basin) of the rivulet Surā which flows into the artifical lake now called Khiṇḍsī or Rām Sāgar, now a well-known picnic spot, which probably represents ancient Sudarśana lake got excavated by Prabhāvatī's daughter in memory of her mother. Secondly, the name Sudarśana is very interesting. It seems to have been borrowed from the famous homonymous water-reservoir near modern Jūnāgaḍh (Gujarat) with the excavation, extension and renovation of which Chandragupta Maurya, his grandson Aśoka Maurya, Śaka Mahākshatrapa Rudradāman and the Gupta emperor Skanda Gupta were intimately associated during about eight centuries of its documented existence. Another indication of the knowledge of its existence under the Vākāṭakas is provided by the above-mentioned Hisse-Borālā inscription of Deva Sena's reign. The present inscription shows that this knowledge was not confined to the Vatsagulma branch of the Vākāṭakas and was brought much earlier to the Padmapura-Nandivardhana-Pravarapura branch by Prabhāvatī Guptā whose father Chandra Gupta II had annexed the Saurāshṭra region to the Gupta empire.

Another point, a very important one, that emerges from this record concerns the date of the Kevala-Narasiṁha temple, originally known, as we have seen above, as Prabhāvatīsvāmin. As shown above, the temple was erected after Prabhāvatī Guptā's demise by her unknown daughter with the object of perpetuating her mother's memory. And we learn from the Tiroḍī plates of her son Pravāra Sena II that she was alive at least up to his twenty-third regnal year. And the construction of the temple and carving the image enshrined in it must have taken a year or two. Thus, the Kevala-Narasiṁha temple must have been erected about the mid-fifth century. This is based on the assumption that the record is *in situ*.[39]

We have attempted above to present the best possible gist of what we feel to be the contents of the preserved or otherwise sensible portion of this record and allude to certain fall-outs from only such points about which we can be reasonably sure. However, in view of its pitiable state of preservation one should refrain from indulging in wild speculation based on conjectural restoration of the now lost text.

Notes and References

1. We had earlier given its tentative gist in our *EHDPP*, pp. 68-71, and in *The Age of the Vākāṭakas*, pp. 253-57. The alterations noticed here represent our latest position based mainly on the readings of Hans Bakker and Harunaga Isaacson (HB:HI).
2. Ṛiddhapur plates of Prabhāvatī Guptā and the Maṇḍhaḷ plates of Pṛithivī Sheṇa II issued in his second regnal year.
3. The only hitherto known exception is Prabhāvatī Guptā's Puṇe charter which is also engraved in nail-headed characters though of northern type.
4. The only exception is the Wāshim plates of Vindhyaśakti II whose donative portion is composed in Prakrit prose, while the initial portion describing the donor's genealogy is in Sanskrit prose.
5. In fact, it is styled a *mahat kāvya* or `great poem' in the closing stanza (34). The name of the poet responsible for composing it also was most probably given but is not traceable in the preserved portion.
6. This is also the impression of HB:HI. *Vide BSOAS*, LVI, Part I, 1993, p. 48 ("was discovered when the covering plaster was removed during restoration work of the Archaelogical Survey [sic], which unfortunately led to severe damáge").
7. *EHDPP*, pp. 68-71.
8. "Vaiṣṇavism in the Vākāṭaka Times", *Vaiṣṇavism in Indian Arts and Culture*, ed. Ratan Parimoo, Books & Books, New Delhi, 1987, pp. 335-41; "A Newly Discovered Vākāṭaka Temple at Ramtek, District Nagpur", *Kusumāñjali: New Interpretation of Indian Art and Culture: Sh. C. Sivaramamurti Commemoration Volume*, ed. M.S. Nagaraja Rao, Agam Prakashan, Delhi, 1987, pp. 217-23. *Vide* also his "Beginnings of North Indian Style: Early Vidarbha Style, *c.* A.D. 350-500: Vākāṭakas (Main Branch)", *Indian Temple Architecture*, American Institute of Indian Studies, Princeton University Press, II (I), pp. 59-72.
9. *Rāmṭek*, Groningen University, 1989, pp. 93-94; ``Rāmṭek: An Ancient Centre of Viṣṇu Devotion in Maharashtra", *The History of Sacred Places in India as Reflected in Traditional Literature*, ed. Hans Bakker, Leiden, 1990, pp. 62-85; "The Footprints of the Lord", *Devotion Divine: Bhakti Traditions from the Regions of India: Studies in Honour of Charlotte Vaudeville*, eds. Diana L. Eck and Francoise Mallidon, Groningen/ Paris, 1991, pp. 19-37; "Throne and Temple: Political Power and Religious Prestige in Vidarbha", *Sacred Centre as the Focus of Political Interest: Proceedings of the Symposium held on the Occasion of the 375th Anniversary of the University of Groningen.*

5-8 March. 1989, pp. 83-100; "Memorials, Temples, Gods and Kings: An Attempt to unravel the Symbolic Texture of Vākāṭaka Kingship", *Ritual, State and History in South Asia: Essays in Honour of J.C. Heesterman*, pp. 7-19.

10. "The Rāmṭek Inscription II: The Vākāṭaka Inscription in the Kevala Narasiṁha Temple", *BSOAS*, LVI (I), 1993, pp. 45-74.

11. The metres are: verses 1-2: *Pushpitagrā;* verses 3-20: *Upajāti;* verses 21-34: *Anushtubh.*

12. This is indicated by the employment of plural number, viz. *jāteshu.*

13. The Bhāraśivas, a branch of the Nāgas, with whom the Vākāṭakas had one of the closest relations and who most probably played an important role in the growth of their political power, are said to have pleased god Śiva by carrying his phallus over their shoulders. This is averred in practically all the official records of the Vākāṭakas of the Padmapura-Nandivardhana-Pravarapura branch.

14. This would show that in the Gupta-Vākāṭaka period the divinity of the king had firmly entrenched itself in public mind. Cf. Samudra Gupta's Prayāga *praśasti* which ascribes a totally divine character to him and speaks of him as the 'god residing on earth' (*lokadhāmno devasya*).

15. D.C. Sircar, *Select Inscriptions*, I, p. 285, line 1 (Bilsad pillar inscr. of Kumāra Gupta I); p. 321, line 1 (Bhītarī pillar inscr. of Skanda Gupta), etc. This expression is found used for Samudra Gupta even in his forged Nālandā and Gayā plates. *Vide ibid.*, p. 271, lines 1-2; p. 273, line 2. It is not impossible that this expression was employed for him in his Prayāga *praśasti* as well.

16. *Ibid.*, p. 290, line 2 (Karamdaṇḍā inscr. of Kumāra Gupta I, dated GE 117=438 AD). In the Tumain inscr. of the time of Kumāra Gupta I and belonging to Ghaṭotkacha Gupta, dated GE 116 (*ibid.*, p. 297, line 1) Chandra Gupta II is also said to have conquered the earth bounded by the ocean(s).

17. *Ibid.*, p. 304, verse 23.

18. *Ibid.*, p. 308, verse 3 (Jūnāgaḍh inscr.).

19. *Ibid.*, p. 204, line 3.

20. There was an interval of almost three quarters of a century between the close of Samudra Gupta's reign and the composition of this record.

21. As stated above, this record was set up after Prabhāvatī's demise during the reign of her son Pravāra Sena II.

22. B.R. Gopal, *Corpus of Kadamba Inscriptions*, I, Sirasi, 1985, p. 15, verse 31 (Tālguṇḍa pillar inscr. of Kākutsthavarman).

23. D.C. Sircar, *Select Inscriptions*, I, p. 284, verse 1. *Vide* also Ajay Mitra Shastri in M.C. Joshi and S.K. Gupta (eds.), *King Chandra and the Meharauli Pillar*, pp. 85-91.

24. S.R. Goyal is, however, inclined to identity king Chandra of the Meharauli pillar inscription with Samudra Gupta. *Vide ibid.*, pp. 75-81 and 207-37.

25. In the preserved portion.

26. The name of a girl is often completely changed after her marriage in many parts of Maharashtra including Vidarbha.

27. This is very important historically inasmuch as it proves that Ghaṭotkacha (or Ghaṭotkacha Gupta) of the Tumain inscription of GE 116 = 435-36 AD) was a brother (or step-brother) of Kumāra Gupta I and he did ascend the throne as an emperor, maybe for a while, before the date of the inscription in question. For Tumain inscription, *vide Select Inscriptions*, I, pp. 297-99.

28. Cf. HB:HI, pp. 66-67, insist that such a marriage did take place. P.V. Kane refers to the currency of such marriages in the south while citing the statements of numerous dharmaśāstra-writers prohibiting them. *Vide History of Dharmaśāstra*, II, Part I, pp. 452-71.

28a. According to HB:HI, p. 67, her personal name could have been Atibhāvatī which occurs in verse 24. However, it could as well (and more probably) be a descriptive adjective meaning 'extremely lustrous'.

29. HB:HI, p. 55, render *sādhūn* by 'mendicants' which is not quite appropriate.

29a. *Bhrātā balāt svaṁ griham=ānināya* (verse 17) of the original is rendered as 'brother brought... back to his own residence with force' by HB:HI (p. 56) who feel that it (Pravara Sena's move to bring his sister back to her paternal house) was resisted either by the princess herself, or by her Gupta relattives, or by both and this led to this worsening of the Gupta-Vākāṭaka relations (p, 71). And all this is based on the employment of the word *balāt* which also, and most probably in this context, means 'by persuasion', which would obviate all this speculation.

30. She must have gone back to her deceased husband's house after some time as the Dharmaśāstras do not permit a widow whose male relations are alive to live permanently in her parental house.

31. Sometime in or before his sixteenth regnal year Pravara Sena II had shifted his capital from Nandivardhana to Pravarapura. Till at least eleventh year Nandivardhana was his captial. According to HB:HI the capital continued to be at Nandivardhana which was renamed Pravarapura by Pravara Sena II after himself.

32. This is recorded in his Tiroḍī plates issued in that year.

33. We had earlier felt that there were in this inscription masculine forms like *kārayitā* and *kretā* which indicated that some male person had something to do with these pious acts. But we have now given up this position in the light of the excellent edition of HB:HI.

34. Cf. *Dayitā, agha-varjitā* (verse 30) and *tayā* (verse 33) which should leave no doubt regarding the involvement of a female, no doubt Prabhāvatī's daughter.

35. HB:HI (p. 54) render *ardhaṁ brahmārpaṇaṁ puṇyam* (verse 27) of the original by 'half of the merit assigned to the gods'. But looking to other such usages we are inclined to take *brahma* as standing for the Brāhmaṇas. We have yet to come across the employment of the word *brahma* for 'gods'. And what merit did they need?

36. I.e. Prabhāvatī Guptā. It depends on the meaning of the word *dhātṛi* which is taken as 'begetter' by HB:HI (p. 56).

37. Verse 28.

38. The original as restored by HB:HI runs as follows:

Ā-loka-sthāyiniñ=ch-emāṁ kirtiṁ prakhyāpayishyatā

Tayā parigṛihtena tad=ājñ-ānuvidhāyinā.

Here *ā-loka* stands for 'till the world lasts' and not 'so long as ther is light' as rendered by HB:HI (p. 56). Such expressions occur in many ancient records including lithic and metallic ones. Likewise, the term *kīrti* is here employed in the derivative technical sense of 'pious act' or 'construction' and not in its primary sense of 'fame' as understood by HB:HI.

39. A.P. Jamkhedkar (*Kusumāñjali*, p. 221) dates its construction in 419-20 AD and Hans Bakker places this event in the second quarter of the fifth century AD (*Rāmṭek*, p. 90).

III

Coins of the Vākāṭakas

(Pls. C-CII)

The Vākāṭakas, who rose to the status of one of the greatest political powers with a pan-India image and impact during the fourth and fifth centuries AD had pretty humble beginnings. They launched on their political career somewhere in the Vindhyan region of the present State of Madhya Pradesh, as is evident from a study of the Purāṇic evidence.[1] Later they shifted southwards as there was no scope for expansion in the North because of the rising power of the Imperial Guptas and the Nāgas with both of whom they appear to have had friendly relations, while in the Deccan there was no such potential power at that time. They carved out, in course of time, a substantial kingdom comprising the area of Madhya Pradesh to the south of the river Narmadā (viz., Betūl-Chhindwārā and Siwanī-Bālāghāṭ region),[2] the Vidarbha-Khāndesh-Marāṭhwāḍa region of the present State of Maharashtra and, perhaps, also some area of northern Karnataka in the proximity of Bidar,[3] the last one at a comparatively later stage of their career. They played an important role in contemporary Indian politics and maintained friendly relations with the Imperial Guptas and Nāgas on the North, the Vishṇukuṇḍins in the Eastern Deccan and the Kadambas in the Western Deccan. They were proud of their relationship with the Nāgas and the Imperial Guptas,[4] while most of the Vishṇukuṇḍin inscriptions mention with pride that one of the Vishṇukuṇḍin monarchs was born of a Vākāṭaka princess.[5] They became so very powerful at one stage as to be able to successfully intervene in the internal affairs of the Kadambas of Karnataka.[6] According to one view, they were at first on hostile terms with the Early Rāshṭrakūṭas of southern Maharashtra which later changed into cordiality, thanks to the well-meaning intervention of the Imperial Guptas.[7] There is absolutely no doubt that they were the greatest political power in the Deccan and Central India during the fourth-fifth centuries AD. They were great not only in politics, but in cultural life as well, and the period of their rule witnessed economic prosperity and the efflorescence of artistic activity, and some of the best preserved Mahāyāna Buddhist caves at Ajantā were executed with the active involvement of some of their ministers and feudatories,[8] evidently under the patronage of the kings themselves.

Barring only the Early Rāshṭrakūṭas, the aforesaid neighbours as well as some other contemporary powers,[9] some of them comparatively insignificant, are known to have issued their own coins. Of them, the coins of the Imperial Guptas, with whom the Vākāṭakas had most cordial relations up to the very end, are too numerous and varied to escape attention. The coins of the Nāgas, Ikshvākus, Vishṇukuṇḍins and the Kadambas, though not so numerous and artistically much inferior, are also fairly well-known. But till now no coins of the Vākāṭakas were known nor do we encounter any allusion, direct or otherwise, to coins in their fairly numerous inscriptions on stone and copperplates. Not that these epigraphs did not provide an occasion to mention coins: they could have well been referred to in connection with land-grants recorded in them. It was, therefore, popularly assumed, quite naturally of course, that the Vākāṭakas did not issue any coins of their own and met their monetary requirements by permitting the circulation of the coins of other contemporary powers.[10] While no coins of the Vākāṭakas were known, silver coins of the Śaka Kshatrapas of Malwa and Gujarat were reported off and on in large numbers, both in hoards as well as stray finds, in the territory under the Vākāṭakas. Consequently some scholars were inclined to explain this rather strange phenomenon by the assumption that as the Vākāṭakas themselves did not mint any coins, they allowed the Western Kshatrapa coins to circulate in their kingdom.[11]

This fond belief[12] has, however, been rudely shaken by the recent discovery of some Vākāṭaka coins which presently adorn the collections of my friends Shri Prashant P. Kulkarni and Shri Raghunath Sanghi of Nagpur who were kind enough to invite my attention to them and permit me to study and publish the same. These coins, all of which are in base metal with copper predominating, have been reportedly found in the Wardhā region which was undoubtedly under the Padamapura-Nandivardhana-Pravarapura branch of the dynasty and especially from Pauñar which is believed to represent the site of their later capital, Pravarapura. All these coins are minute in size, irregular in shape and lightweight. We may first refer to a unique piece that must justifiably clinch the problem of attribution.

I. Coin of Pṛithivī Sheṇa

Copper : Circular with a small portion along the top edge broken away and missing; diam. 0.9 cm; wt. 0.632 gm.

Obverse : Legend in bold characters in the box-hearded variety of Brāhmī, beginning at 8 o'clock *[Śri-Ma]hararaja-Pṛithivī* along the circular edge.

Reverse : In the centre, a device consisting of a circle with a smaller circle attached to its left portion; the whole within a beaded (or dotted) circle a part whereof is visible. Incuse marks visible along the edge. (Pl. C.I)

The obverse legend obviously gives the name of the issuer preceded by the honorific *śrī* and the regal style *Mahārāja.* The characters are exactly similar to those employed in a vast majority of Vākāṭaka inscriptions.[13] The concluding part of the legend giving the second component of the issuer's name has not been accommodated in the die, while the upper parts of the letters including the medial signs attached to the tops of some of the letters have remained off the flan as even with the exclusion of the second part of the name, the metallic blank was too small as compared to the die. In fact, the size of the letters was quite large as is clear from the alignment and size of the accommodatd letters which are fairly large in comparison with the rather minute size of the coin. As the concluding part of the legend is not accommodated[14] in the legend, it cannot be ascertained if the legend terminated merely with the name or ended in the genitive singular as was the case with the Sātavāhana and Kshatrapa coins with which the Vākāṭakas may be justly supposed to have been familiar.[15] However, the legend should leave no doubt that the coin in question was issued by a monarch whose name began with Pṛithivī.[16] During the period and area in question the only name commencing with this word was Pṛithivī Sheṇa which is known to have been borne only by a couple of Vākāṭaka kings of the Padmapura-Nandivardhana-Pravarapura line, viz. (i) Pṛithivī Sheṇa I, son and successor of Rudra Sena I, and (ii) Pṛithivī Sheṇa II, son and successor of Narendra Sena and the last known member of this branch of the family. The employment of box-headed characters as well as the title *Maharaja,* which was assumed by practically all the Vākāṭaka monarchs,[17] and the provenance (Paunār) strengthen this identification. The internal evidence of the coin does not permit us to determine as to which of these two Pṛithivī Sheṇas was responsible for issuing it. It may perhaps be argued that as Paunār (Pravarapura) attained the status of supposed capital under Pravara Sena II, its find at this place indicates that it belongs to the second king of this name. But this reasoning does not hold good as the excavation at the site has shown that it existed much prior to the foundation of the Vākāṭaka dynasty and enjoyed considerble prosperity during the entire period covered by the Vākāṭaka rule. A coin of an earlier ruler also could, therefore, be found at the place. Thus, in the present state of inadequate information it is not possible to decide its ascription.

II. Coins of Narendra Sena

A couple of coins attributable to Narendra Sena, though not accommodating his full name, has been found and may be described as follows :

A. Copper; almost circular; diam. 1cm; wt. 0.360 gm.

Obverse : Legend in similar characters which can be read as *rendra.*

Reverse : The word *Śri* along with some indistinct letter before it.

(Pl. C.II)

If the reading *rendra* is accepted, the first missing letter preceding it with which the name could have begun may be restored as *na* with the result that the first component of the name of the issuer of this coin could have been Narendra, the full name possibly being Narendra Sena. And as no other chief of this region whose name contained the *aksharas re* and *ndra* is known today, we may be sure of this attribution. We may, again, presume, we think with some justification, that, as on the preceding coin, the name was preceded by the regal title *Mahārāja* and, probably, the honorific *śrī.* There was only one king named Narendra Sena in the Vākāṭaka dynasty, viz., son and successor of Pravāra Sena II and father of Pṛithivī Sheṇa II. The coin may, therefore, be attributed to him. It must, however, be remembered that in view of the fragmentary character of the legend not giving even the first part of the king's name in full, this attribution is purely tentative and in need of further evidence for its confirmation.

We have some coins with only a single bold letter in the box-headed variety of Brāhmī centrally placed on the obverse. These *aksharas,* in all probability, stand for the initials of the names of the issuers. One such coin which is of considerable interest in the present context may be described here.

B. Copper; almost square; 0.8 x 0.6 cm; wt. 0.275 gm.

Obverse : Bold box-headed Brāhmī letter *na* within a partially accommodated border of dots, leaving no doubt that the legend contained nothing else. Incuse marks visible along edge on left and at the bottom.

Reverse : Partially accommodated conch-shell (only upper part). (Pl. C-IIB)

If the contention that this letter is the initial of the issuer's name is to be conceded, as appears pretty certain, this coin may also be ascribed to the Vākāṭaka king Narendra Sena for no other chief of the Vākāṭaka dynasty or, for that matter, of any other ruling family of the region in question with his name beginning with *na* is known so far. If this attribution is accepted, these two coins would become the only known records of Narendra Sena as no inscription of this king has been reported to date and he is known only from the four copper-plate charters of his son and successor, Pṛithivī Sheṇa II.[18]

Regarding the attribution of the above coins we are on fairly dependable grounds. However, the same cannot be said about a few other coins of similar fabric and bearing similar devices. The same may, however, be described here.

III. Coins with the Legend Jaya (2 coins)

Copper; round; diam. 1 cm; wt. (A) 0.249 and (B) 0.363 gm.

Obverse : Legend consisting of two bold letters in the box-headed variety of Brahmī; on coin A the legend is clearly readable as *Jaya;* on coin B also, the first *akshara* is undoubtedly *ja,* while the second letter looks like *ra* but appears to be intended for *ya.* The identity of the legend on the two coins is also suggested by the identity of reverse device.

Reverse : Boldly executed retrograde *svastika* within a beaded border. On coin B, we have a dot in each arm of the *svastika.*

(Pl. C.III A-B)

IV. Coins with the Legend Vṛiddhi

We have three coins with this legend. But they are of different weights, sizes and types and may be described in the ascending order of weights and sizes.

A. Irregular in shape; 0.9 x 0.8 cm; wt. 0.210 gm.

Obverse : Boldly executed legend *Vṛiddhi* in the box-headed characters of Brāhmī within a circular beaded border, showing that though the piece is of a non-descript shape, it was intended to be circular.

Reverse : Same as on the coin of Pṛithivī Sheṇa.

(Pl. CI.IVA)

The reverse device clearly links this coin with that of the Vākāṭaka king Pṛithivī Sheṇa and thereby indicates its Vākāṭaka affiliation.

B. Copper; round; diam. 0.23 cm; wt. 6.800 gm.

Obverse : Very boldly inscribed legend as on A, in the centre.

Reverse : Vividly depicted figure of running lion to right with gaping mouth and curled tail.

(Pl. CI.IV B)

The lion is obviously the prototype of that met with on the so-called Vishṇukuṇḍin coins.[19]

C. Copper; round; diam. 0.27 cm; wt. 8.100 gm.

Obverse : Legend as above.
Reverse : Crudely executed figure of humped bull walking to right.

(Pl. CI.IVC)

V. Coin with the Legend Vṛiddhaḥ

Copper; irregular in shape; diam. 0.7 cm; wt. 0.331 gm.
Obverse : Boldly executed legend *Vṛiddhiḥ* in the box-headed characters.
Reverse : Same as on Pṛithivī Sheṇa's coin.

(Pl. CII.V)

As in the case of IV-A above, the reverse device of this coin connects it with the definitely attributable coin of Pṛithivī Sheṇa.

It is at present extremely difficult to suggest any definite attribution of these coins. But the fabric, use of box-headed characters and the provenance leave no doubt about their belonging to the same region and period as represented by the coins of the Vākāṭakas described above. Reference may also be made to the sameness of the reverse device on a few coins bearing the legends *Vṛiddhi* and *Vṛiddhaḥ* with that on the only known coin of Vākāṭaka king Pṛithivī Sheṇa which closely links these coins with the Vākāṭakas. However, the names Jaya, Vriddhi and Vṛiddha met with on these coins are not known from any other source. We cannot be sure if these words are to be taken as *virudas* or titles employed by the Vākāṭaka kings instead of their usual names. We are reminded in this connection of the practice prevalent among some of the ruling families of the Deccan and South India of employing *virudas* on their coins,[21] and therefore, there should be nothing surprising if the Vākāṭakas, who were spatially and chronologically close to these powers, also did likewise. Moreover, as we have shown elsewhere,[22] the practice of adopting coronation names different from their personal names was in vogue among the Vākāṭakas also. Unfortunately, however, none of these *virudas* (or, for that matter, any other *viruda*) or personal names is known from any Vākāṭaka inscription, and consequentiy we cannot be sure if these coins were actually issued by the Vākāṭakas, not to speak of the individual members of the dynasty. But such a possibility cannot be ruled out wholesale, especially in view of the identity of the reverse device of the coin of Pṛithivī Sheṇa and of one coin each with the legend *Vṛiddhi* and *Vṛiddhaḥ*. It is equally possible that these coins were struck by some hitherto unknown subordinates under the Vākāṭakas with the authority delegated by the latter. The riddle posed by these specie may hopefully be solved in the light of future discoveries.

We should like to end with some other uniface coins closely allied with the Vākāṭaka coins in respect of fabric and devices, but without legends. These devices include that on Pṛithivī Sheṇa's reverse, a conch-shell (Pl. CII. VI), *śrīvatsa* within a beaded border (Pl. CII. VII), spoked wheel (Pl. CII. VIII), bull (Nandin) standing to right before a sacrificial post *(yūpa)*, Nandin seated facing right or left and the like. In view of the extremely fragmentary character of their legends or total absence thereof it is not possible to determine their issuers. But that they were struck by or at the behest of the Vākāṭakas may possibly be assumed.

It will be seen from the foregoing that the Vākāṭaka kingdom was not without its own coins, and the notion that in the absence of their own coins the Vākāṭakas were not left with any other option but to allow coins of other dynasties to circulate in their territory has to be abandoned. As these coins are lightweight and in base metal, we may reasonably assume that they were meant to help day-to-day market transactions and for other ordinary purposes. As in the Gupta empire, they probably supplemented the cowrie-currency.[23]

We have described in these pages only a select small fraction of the large quantity of Vākāṭaka or Vākāṭaka-like coins that have now come to light, and the large volume of base metal coins may justifiably be taken to reflect deep penetration of money economy and the use of coins on a large scale in day-to-day life. This is as it aught to be. For, we know that the immediately preceding period was also characterised by an extensive use of base metal coins for ordinary market transactions in the Deccan[24] as in North India.[25]

We are now sure that one of the kings named Pṛithivī Sheṇa and Narendra Sena of the Nandivardhana-Pravarapura branch of the Vākāṭakas struck coins in base metals in their own names. It is quite likely that other members of this branch and those of the Vatsagulma branch also struck their own coins. Study of so far untapped material as well as further discoveries of coins are likely to enlighten us on these and related issues.

Recent archaeological excavations in Vidarbha have lent support to the attribution of these coins to the Vākāṭakas. Coins of similar fabric and make have been recently reported from the excavations at Mansar near Rāmṭek in the Nagpur district conducted by the Archaeological Survey of India and at Wāshim in the Akolā district by the State Directorate of Archaeology.[25a]

However, being in cheap metal these coins could be depended upon only for ordinary transactions and apparently could not serve the purpose of higher trade as well as sale and purchase of costly objects. In this context we may make special mention of the purchase of land mentioned in a Vākāṭaka inscription: Indore plates of the twenty-third regnal year of Pravara Sena II recording the *purchase* and grant of half of a village *(vāṭaka)* by a merchant named Chandra.[26] Such transactions could hardly have been performed with the help of copper coins and must have required costlier coins of silver or gold. But so far we have no such coins of the Vākāṭakas though they may actually have minted at least silver specie. However, we should not discount the possibility of such specie not being issued by the Vākāṭakas as some of their contemporaries in the North and South also are not known to have minted silver or gold. What were the coins then that served the purpose of costlier transactions? There was actually no dearth of silver coins in the market. In ancient India coins once issued continued to circulate in the market for centuries unless they lost weight due to a long circulation. We have definite evidences to show that punch-marked silver coins were in circulation till at least the early mediaeval age and this phenomenon explains the non-issue of silver specie by many a dynasty and comparative rarity of such coins of other dynasties that issued them. They are referred to by the meaningful name *purāṇa* in inscriptions and literary works dated to the second century AD[27] while as *nīle-kahāpaṇa* at least up to the fifth century AD.[28] At a village called Chik Sandogi in the Kopal talukā of the Raichūr district in Karnataka a hoard of 5,534 silver punch-marked coins was found in a copper pot bearing a Brāhmī label datable to about the third century AD.[29] A hoard of 440 silver punch-marked coins in the Lucknow Museum in association with an Indo-Sassanian coin shows the popularity of these coins in the early mediaeval age.[30] V.S. Agrawala has rightly arrived at the conclusion that the silver punch-marked coins and the *kārshāpaṇa* tradition continued right up to the mediaeval period.[31] Then, there were Sātavāhana silver coins which also must have continued to circulate in the Vākāṭaka territory which was formerly under the Sātavāhaṇas.[32] And lastly, the Western Kshatrapa[33] coins were highly valued and hoards and stray finds of these coins have been reported from territories far away from the area under the Kshatrapa control. Also in use must have been Traikūṭaka silver coins as a hoard containing, *inter alia*, ten specimens of Dahrasena's species has been reported rather recently at the village of Dahigāon in Malkāpur tāluka of the Bulḍhāṇā district.[34]

To add to these, Gupta gold and silver issues also must have been available in abundance, more especially in view of the friendly relations and consequent movement of traders from one territory to the other. And lastly, the Traikūṭaka silver coins were also in use during this period. All these coins must have circulated during the Vākāṭaka period and freely used by the people including merchants and even kings.

To sum up, even though the Vākāṭakas had issued their own coins in cheap metals, earlier and contemporary costly metal coins also must have been in use for costlier transactions as the Vākāṭaka state did not disturb the free market process. This, of course, must have created the problem of adjustment of the complex currencies which must have been solved by the market circles by fixing their relative values.

Notes and References

1. In the historical portions of a few of the Purāṇas they are mentioned along with Central Indian dynasties and are styled Vindhyakas or 'the Vindhyan people'. See F.E. Pargiter, *DKA*, p. 50. The first king of the dynasty is called by the meaningful name Vindhyaśakti, 'powerful in the Vindhyas'.
2. As pointed out earlier, initially (up to the time of Pṛithivī Sheṇa I) they controlled the Vindhyan region of Madhya Pradesh as well.
3. Recently a copperplate grant of Deva Sena, the penultimate member of the Vatsagulma branch of the dynasty, has been reported from Bīdar and appears to record the grant of a village situated nearby. For details about this record, see our *EHDPP*, pp. 71-74; P.V. Parabrahma Sastry, "Hyderabad Plates of Vākāṭaka Deve Sena, Year 5", *JESI*, XIII, pp. 71-75.
4. In fact, these are the only two matrimonial relationships involving the marriages of the Nāga and Imperial Gupta princesses with two Vākāṭaka kings that are mentioned in all the known official records of the Nandivardhana-Pravarapura branch of the Vākāṭakas.
5. Several Vishṇukuṇḍin records aver that king Vikramendravarman I had adorned by his birth the twin families of the Vishṇukuṇḍins and the Vākāṭakas.
6. That the Kadamba king Simhavarman was anointed on the throne by the Vākāṭaka king Sarva Sena (II) has been clearly stated in his Mudigere grant of his fifth regnal year. For the record, see B.R. Gopal, *Corpus of Kadamba Inscriptions*, I, p. 141, text-line 13.
7. V.V. Mirashi, *CII*, V, Introduction, p. xxv.
8. *Ibid.*, pp. 103ff., 120ff.

9. E.g, the Ikshvākus of Andhra Pradesh. For the Ikshvāku coins, see R. Subrahmanyam, *A Catalogue of the Ikshvāku Coins in the Andhra Pradesh Government Museum.*

10. This conjecture is based on the discovery of the coins of these dynasties in the regions held by the Vākāṭakas. For references to these coins, see B.C. Jain, *Inventory of the Hoards and Finds of Coins and Seals from Madhya Pradessh (non-Muhammadan),* Numismatic Notes and Monographs, No. 5.

11. See V.V. Mirashi, *Studies in Indology,* III, pp. 95-96; IV, pp. 223-26. Surprisingly, the same conclusion is not drawn in respect of the Traikūṭaka coins which, too, have been recently reported from Vidarbha and have been taken by him to indicate the occupation of a part of Vidarbha by the Traikūṭakas. See V.V. Mirashi, *Literary and Historical Studies in Indology,* pp. 180-84.

12. It may be mentioned here that K.P. Jayaswal (*History of India : AD 150 to 350,* pp. 71-73, Pl. III) proposed to attribute three coins already published by Vincent Smith in his *Coins of Ancient India: Catalogue of the Coins in the Indian Museum,* Calcutta, I, Pl. XXII.15, Pl. XX.5 and Pl. XX.4, to the Vākāṭaka kings Pravāra Sena I, Rudra Sena I and Pṛithivī Sheṇa respectively. This suggestion, which is undoubtedly wild, has been examined at length and shown to be untenable by A.S. Altekar ("Some Alleged Naga and Vākāṭaka Coins", *JNSI,* V, pp. 130-34.)

13. The only exceptions are the Puṇe plates of the dowager queen Prabhāvatī Guptā and the recently discovered Rāmṭek stone-slab inscription recording some pious acts in her memory by her unknown daughter which are incised in nail-headed characters.

14. It is also possible that the non-inclusion was deliberate.

15. This is very likely in view of the discovery of numerous Sātavāhana and Western Kshatrapa coins in the region under their rule. It may be emphasised in this connection that the Vākāṭakas were the true successors of the Sātavāhanas in the Central Deccan.

16. The form of the king's name met with in the inscriptions has short medial *i* sign and not long which is the correct one. It is quite likely, nay almost certain, that on this coin also the same form was intended.

17. The only exception was Pravara Sena I who alone among all the Vākāṭaka kings is styled *samrāṭ* in all the official records of the Nandivardhana-Pravarapura branch of the dynasty.

18. These are his (i) incomplete Bālāghaṭ plates (*EI,* IX, pp. 267-71); (ii-iii) Māṇḍhaḷ plates of the second and tenth regnal years (*ibid.,* XLI, pp. 159-80); and (iv) Māhurjharī plates of the seventeenth regnal year (*VSMV,* 1971, pp. 53-77, Pls. III-X).

19. We had also attributed such coins to the Vishṇukuṇḍins over three decoder ago when the coins described here were not known. In view of the find of these and a few other coins a reconsideration of the problem of the so-called Vishṇukuṇḍin coins from Vidarbha is imperative.

20. Only the lower dot of *visarga* is visible, but there can be absolutely no doubt about the correctness of the suggested legend.

21. *Cf.* the legend *Vishamasiddhi* on Eastern Chālukya coins and some other *virudas* on the Kadamba coins.

22. "Some Aspects of Personal Names in the Vākāṭaka Inscriptions", *JOI*, XXXVI, pp. 257-64.
23. The Chinese traveller Fa-hien, who was in India during *circa* 400-11 AD, refers to heaps of cowrie shells in the markets of the cities of the Gupta empire.
24. We have in our mind the Sātavāhana base metal (copper, lead and potin) coins which have been found in thousands in the whole of the Deccan including the territory later occupied by the Vākāṭakas which has yielded enormous quantities of coins, especially in potin.
25. Kushāṇas and Maghas as well as other ruling powers of Northern India are known to have issued base metal specie on an extensive scale.

25a. On Mansar coins a paper was presented by Dr. Amarendra Nath, Superintending Archaeologist, Excavations Branch, Archaeological Survey of India, Nagpur, at the Kochhi Session of the Numismatic Society of India in September, 1995. The information about Wāshim coins is based on conversation with some of the excavators who would prefer anonymity.

26. V.V. Mirashi, *Inscriptions of the Vākāṭaks, CII*, V, pp. 38ff.
27. This name occurs in the Mathurā inscription (of the twenty-eighth year of what may be called Kushāṇa era) of the Kushāṇa king Huvishka and the *Manu-smṛiti* both of which are attributable to the second century AD.
28. Buddhaghosha in his *Sāmanta-pāsādika* mentions punch-marked silver coins as *nīla-kahāpaṇa* because of the bluish accumulation in course of time. See C.D. Chatterjee, "Some New Numismatic Terms in Pali Texts", *JUPHS*, VI, 1933, pp. 156ff.; "Some Numismatic Data in Pali Literature", *Buddhistic Studies*, ed. B.C. Law, Calcutta, 1931, Ch. XV.
29. Ajay Mitra Shatri, "Presidential Address", *PIHC*, 1978, II, pp. 968-69.
30. P.L. Gupta, "Fabrication of Ancient Punch-Marked Coins", *Indian Numismatic Chronicle*, III, p. 133.
31. "Coin Data in the Divyāvadāna", *ibid.*, pp. 148-50.
32. Quite a few Sātavāhana silver portrait coins have recently been reported from Vidarbha and are under study.
33. As far as Peṭlūrapalem in Andhra Pradesh and Ranjangāon near Puṇe in Maharashtra and some places in Karnataka hoards of Kshatrapa coins have been reported, while stray coins and moulds for counterfeiting them have been repored from several ancient sites.
34. For the coins, see V.V. Mirashi, "Dahigāon Hoard of Kshatrapa and Traikūṭaka Coins", *JNSI*, XXXV, pp. 118-22; *Literary and Historical Studies in Indology*, pp. 180-84; for discussion, *vide* Ajay Mitra Shastri, "Did Traikūṭaka Dahrasena Rule over Vidarbha?", *ND*, I (I), pp. 25-28.

Part II
HISTORICAL OUTLINE

I

Introduction

The Vākāṭakas or the Vindhyakas, as they are styled geographically in the Purāṇas, supplanted the Andhra-Sātavāhanas in the Vidarbha region around the close of the third century AD. The original centre of their power lay in the Vindhyan region of Madhya Pradesh to the north of the Narmadā from where they moved southward to Vidarbha and other regions of Maharashtra, Andhra Pradesh and Karnataka and exercised tremendous influence over wide areas of the Deccan. They had matrimonial relations with the Imperial Guptas, the Kadambas of Karnataka and the Vishṇukuṇḍins of Andhra Pradesh. The Vākāṭaka period lasting a little over two and half centuries from mid-third century to early sixth century AD provided peace and prosperity which resulted in literary and artistic efflorescence and witnessed great strides in the growth of Prakrit literature and the development of the Maḥāyāna phase at Ajantā and Gulwāḍā which represent the culminating fulfilment of this truly golden age.

Unfortunately, however, the absence of dependable information coupled with historians' prejudices has resulted into protracted and yet unsettled debate regarding even such basic issues as the Vākāṭaka original home and chronology not to speak of other comparatively minor details. All the same, it must be admitted, we are in a much better position and nearer the solution of these problems as compared to earlier writers on the subject, thanks to the discovery of some valuable material, especially the four Māṇḍhaḷ charters of Rudra Sena II, Pravara Sena II and Pṛithivī Sheṇa II (two), the Miregāon plates of Prabhāvatī Guptā, the Māhurjharī plates of Pṛithivī Sheṇa II, the Rāṃtek inscription commemorating the passing away of Prabhāvatī Guptā, the Bīdar charter and the Hisse-Borālā stone inscription of Deva Sena, the Thāḷner copperplate charter of Hari Sheṇa and the Muḍigere plates of the Kadamba king Simhavarman.[1]

We may now proceed to analyse the various problems concerning the history of the dynasty.

1. For a discussion of this material, see *supra*, pp. 88-146. Ajay Mitra Shastri, "The Muḍigere Inscription of Siṁhavarman and Kadamba-Vākāṭaka Relations", *Indian Archaeological Heritage: K.V. Soundararajan Felicitation Volume*, pp. 317-19, *infra*, pp. 228-32

II

Original Home

The determination of the region where the dynasty launched on its political career first has been debated for quite some time now but without reaching any finality. While, as will be seen in the sequel, the Purāṇic evidence clearly favours a Central Indian home, some scholars have postulated the theory of a South Indian origin which, being the latest in the field, may well be our starting point here. This view was first casually aired by R.P. Chanda[1] and later adopted and elaborated by V.V. Mirashi[2] and A.S. Altekar.[3]

The idea of the South Indian original home was evidently inspired by the mention of a *gahapati* (householder) named Vākāṭaka in a fragmentary votive inscription on an octagonal column dated palaeographically in the period from *c.* mid-second to mid-third century AD at the famous Buddhistic centre of Amarāvatī in the Guṇṭūr district of Andhra Pradesh. The epigraph records some pious act, probably the erection of the column itself, by Vākāṭaka together with his relatives and friends with the object of attaining longevity.[4] R.P. Chanda, while editing the record, took the name Pākoṭaka mentioned in another short record from the same place (no. 8) dating from *c.* mid-second century BC as identical with Vākāṭaka and felt that these records enabled one to trace the Vākāṭakas in the Deccan as early as about 150 BC.[5] He was, however, not sure if Vākāṭaka was a personal or clan name.[6] But Mirashi found in it a reference to the person whom he credited with the foundation of Vākāṭaka dynasty.[7] He felt that *gṛihapati* Vākāṭaka referred to in this inscription must have hailed from somewhere in South India.[8] This assumption, however, fails to carry conviction. First, the record refers to Vākāṭaka merely as a householder without any pretension to regal status, and secondly, it is known that Amarāvatī, like Bhārhut and Sānchī, had become an important pilgrimage-centre and as such attracted Buddhist pilgrims from far and wide. Inscriptions at Amarāvatī itself refer to pious donations made by pilgrims coming from numerous localities, some of them far off, including

Pāṭliputra and Rājagṛiha.[9] We cannot therefore be quite certain that Vākāṭaka known from this record hailed from some nearby locality as surmised by the protagonists of this theory. As in the case of some other donors coming from far off places, the possibility of his hailing from some distant locality far away from Andhra Pradesh cannot be overruled. Moreover, while Vākāṭaka under reference was a devout Buddhist, the Vākāṭaka kings, whose progenitor he supposedly was, were all staunch adherents of Vedic-Paurāṇic religions and some of them performed Vedic sacrifices. If one were to regard the *gṛihapati* Vākāṭaka of the said Amarāvatī inscription as the founder of the Vākāṭaka dynasty, one would have to postulate a sectarian catapult, quite unwarranted by the extant evidence. Thus not much can be built upon the mere identity of names which appears to be purely accidental.

Mirashi further draws attention to the great similarity between some of the technical terms occurring in the grant portions of the Wāshim plates of the Vākāṭaka king Vindhyaśakti II and the Hirahaḍagalli and Mayidavolu grants of the Pallava king Śivaskandavarman. It must be observed in this context that the grant portions of these charters are in Prakrit, and the occurrence of common revenue terms in the records of the two families ruling in almost adjacent territories in Southern Deccan is only natural. It is pertinent to note in this connection that such phrases are confined to the records of the southern (Wāshim) branch of the dynasty and are conspicuously missing from the fairly numerous grants of the northern (Padmapura-Nandivardhana-Pravarapura) branch. Had the Vākāṭakas been of southern origin, these expressions should have occurred in the records of this branch as well. Thus, not much need be made out of this similarity which is evidently born of regional proximity and necessity.

According to Mirashi, the use of the title *Hāritīpurtra* for Vākāṭaka king Pravara Sena I and of *Dharmamahārāja* for Sarva Sena I, the founder of the Vatsagulma branch, and his son and successor Vindhyaśakti II in the Wāshim plates of Vindhyaśakti II[10] also points to the southern origin of the Vākāṭakas as these titles are met with only in the charters of early South Indian dynasties like the Pallavas, the Kadambas and the Chālukyas of Bādāmī and are conspicuous by their absence from North Indian records. It must be pointed out in this context that, like the aforesaid revenue terms, these titles, which were popularly adopted by the members of some of the Deccanese dynasties, are found applied to a few Vākāṭaka rulers only in the charters of the Vatsagulma branch, while in fairly numerous inscriptions of the other branch of the dynasty they are not employed for any member, not even for Pravara Sena I. Had these titles been original to the Vākāṭakas and adopted by the members of the Padmapura-Nandivardhana-Pravarapura branch, we should naturally expect to find them in the records of this branch which give the genealogy of the family from the time of Pravara Sena I. It is obvious therefore that they were borrowed by the members of the Vatsagulma branch from their southern neighbours, viz. Kadambas of Vanavāsī, who are known to have adopted these titles. Consequently, the use of these titles does not lead us anywhere in regard to the original home of the dynasty.

Last but not the least, our attention is invited to a couple of records of a ministerial family at Ajantā (Cave XVI)[11] and Ghaṭotkacha Cave[12] belonging to the reign of Hari Sheṇa, the last known member of the Vatsagulma branch. The family in question was known as Vallūra, perhaps because it hailed from a place of that name which may be, as conjectured by Mirashi, represented by modern Velūr, about thirty miles north by east of Hyderabad in Andhra Pradesh.[13] The association of this family with the Vākāṭakas has been taken to strengthen the theory of the southern origin of the dynasty. But in spite of the common practice of employing officers including ministers from nearby localities which was quite natural, instances of appointment of ministers hailing from fairly distant regions are not unknown and are too numerous to be enumerated exhaustively. And as such, this argument is also completely irrelevant in the present context. Moreover, the Ajantā inscription of Varāhadeva mentions only the last two members of his family, to wit, Hastibhoja and Varāhadeva himself, as ministers of the last two members of the Vatsagulma branch, viz. Deva Sena and Hari Sheṇa, respectively.[14] It is, of course, true that the second member of the family, Deva, is described in the Ghaṭotkacha Cave inscription of Varāhadeva as a capable, learned and active statesman, depending on whom the king and the entire kingdom performed their religious duties well.[15] However, as the name of the king in question is not specified, one cannot be sure if a Vākāṭaka king was meant. Therefore the supposed association of this family with the Vatsagulma branch from the start as well as Pravara Sena I merely on the basis of supposed synchronism can at best be regarded as an unsubstantiated conjecture. Moreover, the predecessors of Hastibhoja, the eighth member of the line, had mainly Brahmanical attainments to their credit and can, at best, be taken to have been patronised by the kings of the Vatsagulma branch. There is absolutely no reason to believe that Pravara Sena I also had a member of this family as his minister.

It would thus follow that at the moment we have no evidence whatsoever to postulate that the original home of the Vākāṭakas lay in the South.[16] We may now proceed to take stock of the more dependable Purāṇic and epigraphic data which, when properly analysed, are likely to yield a more satisfactory answer to this vexed problem.

While describing the rulers of Vidiśā,[17] etc., who, from a general perusal, appear to have flourished in the post-Sātavāhana period, certain manuscripts of the *Vāyu, Brahmāṇḍa, Vishṇu* and *Bhāgavata* Purāṇas mention king Śisunamdin and his brother Nandiyaśas who flourished at the end of the lineage of the Śuṅgas. They then state that in Nandiyaśas's family were born three kings including Śiśuka, the daughter's son *(dauhitra)* of Nandiyaśas, who ruled over Purikā. Next is mentioned Pravīra, son of Vindhyaśakti.[18] Whether Pravīra and his father Vindhyaśakti were in any way related to the other kings mentioned in this passage is not clear, though the statement that there were three rulers in the family of Nandiyaśas and mention immediately thereafter of Śiśuka, Vindhyaśakti and Pravīra seem to suggest such a connection. However, in view of the utterly confused state of Purāṇic accounts at this place one cannot be quite sure on this point. Be that as it may, the description leaves no doubt that Vindhyaśakti and his son Pravīra were the first two members of the Vākāṭaka dynasty known from epigraphic records, the only difference being that Vindhyaśakti's son Pravara Sena I is here spoken of as Pravīra which was evidently his personal name or an epithet assumed by or given to him in allusion to his heroic deeds which made him the master of a vast area and enabled him to perform a large number of Śrauta sacrifices.[19]

According to Pargiter, the expression *Vaideśika* introducing these and other rulers mentioned earlier in the passage means 'of Vidiśā',[20] but as all the rulers are not known to have ruled from or over Vidiśā,[21] it may be more appropriate to take the expression in the sense of 'belonging to various regions'. That this should be the intended meaning is clear from the subsequent description of the Vākāṭaka kings as 'Vindhyakas' or 'belonging to the Vindhya region'.[22] It very closely resembles the mention of the Sātavāhanas as Andhras or Andhra-jātīyas in the Purāṇas which has also resulted in an equally great controversy about the original home of the Sātavāhanas. Thus the Vākāṭakas had their original home in the Vindhya region. However, there exists considerable uncertainty about the location of the Vindhya *vis-a-vis* the adjacent Ṛikshavat mountains both in ancient Indian tradition and among modern geographers. When used in a wider sense, the Vindhya denotes the entire mountain range spreading roughly from

Mirzapur in Uttar Pradesh to the Arabian Sea in Gujarat and includes the ranges of both these mountains which are regarded as *kula-parvatas.* But when distinguished from one another, the only point of unanimity is that the river Narmadā formed the dividing line between the two. However, there is a great controversy among Indologists about the designation of the mountains to the north and south of this river owing to confused ancient traditions. Some believe that when employed in a narrow sense the Ṛikshavat and Vindhya denoted the mountain ranges to the north and south respectively of the Narmadā.[23]

However, this position is totally untenable based as it is entirely on a confused statement of Nīlakaṇṭha, a mediaeval commentator of the *Harivaṁśa* and some confusion among the Bhuvana-kośa sections of the Purāṇas and ignores some vital points which establish that the position was just the otherwise, viz. Vindhya being the name of the range of mountains to the north and Ṛikshavat that of the ranges on the south of the Narmadā. This position finds support from overwhelming ancient literary and epigraphic tradition, and the name Vindhya is now commonly used in this sense. Without going into a detailed examination of the whole material bearing on this problem, we should like to invite attention here to some clinching evidences. First, Ṛikshavat is the ancient name of what is now commonly known as the Sātpuḍā range, the latter being a distant derivative of the former. The Nāsik inscription of the nineteenth year of Vāsishṭhīputra Puḷumāvi refers to his father Gautamiputra Sātakarṇi as the lord of a number of mountains including the Ṛikshavat mentioned in its Prakrit form Chhavata,[24] which marks an intermediate stage in the progress from Ṛikshavat to Sāta. The derivative of Chhavata would naturally be Chhāta by the replacement *va* by a which got assimilated itself with the preceding *a* which, following the normal practice, resulted in its lengthening. Thus was developed the form Chhāta. Then in southern Prakrit sibilants and *ch* and *chh* were interchangeable as we learn from inscriptions, coins and literary evidence. Thus *Chhimuka* becomes *Simuka,*[25] *Sānta* becomes *Chānta,*[26] *Sātakaṇi* becomes *Chātakani,*[27] and *Vāsiṭhī* turns into *Vāchiṭṭi.*[28] Conversely, *Chhāta* could turn into *Sāta*. And the terminal *puḍā,* which is apparently a much later accretion, was most probably suffixed to indicate layers.[29] Secondly, the reference to the Vindhya mountain and Vindhya forest *(Vindhy-āṭavi)* in Bāṇabhaṭṭa's *Harsha-charita* (Uchchhvāsas VII and VIII) in connection with Rājyaśrī's being traced by her brother Harshavardhana evidently cannot refer to the mountain-chain to the south of the Narmadā. Thirdly, there are numerous places associated with the Vindhya mountain in North India, e.g. Vindhyāchal and Vindhyavāsinī, whereas there is none to the south of the Narmadā. It is therefore obvious that Nīlakaṇṭha's erroneous statement, which is born of confusion and unintentional, by itself, cannot be made the basis of such an epoch-making theory on the location of the two mountains as is done by scholars like H.C. Raychaudhuri and D.C. Sircar. And this point is finally clinched by the stock-example *Uttaro Vindhyāt Pāriyātraḥ* on the *Vyākaraṇa* of Śakaṭāyana (II, 2.75),[30] Pāriyātra is to the north of the Vindhya which would be meaningless if the Ṛikshavat had intervened between them.

In connection with Pravīra or Pravara Sena I the reconstructed Purāṇic stanza runs as follows :

Vindhyaśakti-sutaś-ch-āpi Pravīro nāma vīryavān
bhokshyate cha samāḥ shashṭiṁ purīṁ Kāñchanakāṁ cha vai.[31]

It would normally mean that the valorous son of Vindhyaśakti named Pravīra would rule over the city of Kāñchankā for sixty years. This closely agrees with Pargiter's rendering.[32] K.P. Jayaswal, however, proposed to amend the reading of the relevant portion to *Purikāṁ Chanakāṁ cha vai* and took Pravīra (i.e. Pravara Sena I) to have ruled over the twin cities of Purikā and Chanakā.[33] This emendation has been endorsed by V.V. Mirashi on the ground that the adoption of Pargiter's reading would render the particle *cha* meaningless which would then have to be regarded as inserted in the line merely for completing the verse-quarter *(pāda-pūraṇa)*.[34] But it is worth remembering in this connection that not a single manuscript consulted by Pargiter contains the reading *Purikā* in this context,[35] and in the case of Purāṇic texts one should not stretch grammatical considerations beyond proportion as words like *hi, tu, cha* and *vai* are often employed as the compilers were unable to complete the stanzas otherwise and if one were to go in search of their meanings always one would be landing oneself in absurdities and disappointment.[36] So we prefer Pargiter's reading following which Pravīra or Pravara Sena I ruled from the town of Kāñchanakā which was evidently his capital.

If, however, we accept the amended reading, we must attempt the location of the cities of Purikā and Chanakā as it is very germane to the settlement of the problem of the original habitat of the Vākāṭakas. As per the *Harivaṁśa* (Vishṇuparvan, 38.22), the town of Purikā was situated at the foot of the Ṛikshavat mountain.[37] And as we have seen, Ṛikshavat was the ancient name of the mountain range to the south of the Narmadā known as Sātpuḍā which is its derivative. Purikā must therefore have been situated on the slope of the Sātpuḍā range and should be looked for not very far from the southern bank of the Narmadā. It is pertinent to note in this context that Varāhamihira's *Bṛihatsaṁhitā* locates Purikā in the south-eastern division of Bhāratavarsha,[38] which would be in agreement with this location.

However, as pointed out earlier, Purikā is not actually named in the context of Pravara Sena I and the reference to it is purely an invention born of wild imagination on the part of K.P. Jayaswal and hair-splitting argument of V.V. Mirashi in support of the amendment of the Purāṇic passage suggested by the former. So the only town referred to in the Purāṇas in connection with Pravara Sena I is Kāñchanakā. This town (or Chanakā if the amended reading is accepted) has been equated long back with the modern village of Nachnā or Nachnā-kī-talāi in the Pannā district of the Bundelkhaṇḍ division of Madhya Pradesh[39] and seems to satisfy all the conditions of identification. A number of early monuments including a couple of early Vākāṭaka lithic records[40] and an early Gupta-Vākāṭaka temple[41] standing here are quite well-known. It would thus follow that the Vindhyan tract including a major portion of the Bundelkhaṇḍ-Baghelkhaṇḍ region formed part of the Vākāṭaka kingdom during the reign of Pravara Sena I and continued under the dynasty for some more time as will be shown below. That the Vindhyan region formed the core of the Vākāṭaka kingdom initially is clearly vouched for by a couple of other considerations also. The name Vindhyaśakti adopted by its founder clearly shows that he had carved out for himself a kingdom in the Vindhyan region and considered the Vindhya mountain main source of his strength,[42] and Kāñchanakā (or Chanakā) was probably founded by him.

His son and successor Pravīra alias Pravara Sena I was very powerful as indicated by his performance of numerous Vedic sacrifices involving rich fees and his assumption of the supreme regal title of *samrāṭ*, and he could have hardly remained contented with a small principality confined to the Vindhyan region. By his extensive conquests he added fresh territories to his kingdom extending it as far in the south as Vidarbha and carved out a sufficiently large kingdom to be shared by his four sons as stated in the Purāṇas. If the emendation of the Purāṇic stanza suggested by Jayaswal were to be conceded, it is likely that Nachnā (ancient Chanakā) situated at its northern end could not conveniently serve as the imperial capital and Pravara Sena I established another capital at Purikā to the south of the river Narmadā. But the continued association of the Vākāṭakas with the Vindhyan region is clearly established by the meaningful name Vindhyaka (Vindhyan) used for the dynasty in the Purāṇic accounts immediately after the description of Pravīra (Pravara Sena I) and his four sons.[43]

We may thus conclude that the original territory of the Vākāṭakas lay in the Vindhyan region of the present State of Madhya Pradesh which, as we shall see, continued for a few generations under the Vākāṭakas. But before we conclude, attention must be invited to the interesting but apparently contradictory fact that the dynasty is mentioned as Vindhyaka in the Purāṇas whereas all the epigraphic records of the family refer to it as Vākāṭaka alone. This is, as stated above, analogous to the Sātavāhanas whose successors in the northern Deccan and Central India they were. And like Sātavāhana, Vākāṭaka was obviously the dynastic or family name while Vindhyaka, like Andhra or Andhra-jātīya, referred to the area where lay the original centre of their political authority. Like Sātavāhana again, the name Vākāṭaka appears to allude to the eponymous heir from whom the dynasty traced its origin. It is not impossible, though by no means certain, that Vindhyaśakti was only an appellation or secondary name of the first king of the dynasty while Vākāṭaka was his personal name. Alternatively, the family name may have been derived from a locality closely connected with the Vākāṭakas. Jayaswal invited attention to the modern village of Bāgāṭ in the northern-most part of the former Orchhā State, six miles east of Chirgāon in the Jhānsī district of Uttar Pradesh, and thought that the dynastic name was derived from it. He also felt that Vindhyaśakti himself adopted the name of the town as his dynastic appellation.[44] However, we must be prepared for the possibility of the similarity of the two names being purely accidental. And even if it is connected with the name Vākāṭaka, it is possible that the locality was named after the Vākāṭakas rather than otherwise being the case. It must be mentioned in this connection that there are a few such names in Vidarbha also.

It has been suggested by S.V. Sohoni that the expression *Vākāṭakānām* occurring in the Vākāṭaka inscriptions should be translated as 'of the Vākāṭaka territory' and not 'of the Vākāṭaka people'.[45] However, irrespective of the manner one derives the dynastic name, in the Vākāṭaka records it is undoubtedly used in the dynastic sense, and the word *Vākāṭakānām* has got to be rendered as 'of the Vākāṭakas' and certainly not as 'of the Vākāṭaka territory'. This is clearly indicated by the use of the plural number. If the territory were intended, number or an expression like *Vākāṭaka-rājyasya* would have been employed. The expression met with in the Vākāṭaka records is comparable to similar expressions in the epigraphs of the Kadambas and Pallavas and of the last Sātavāhana ruler Puḷumāvi where it has to be rendered similarly. And the word Vākāṭaka must have taken this implied dynastic meaning shortly after Vindhyaśakti, though it occurs in this sense first in the Nachnā and Ganj inscriptions of the reign of Pṛithivī Sheṇa I and in the Wāshim plates of Vindhyaśakti II of the Vatsagulma branch. In the recently discovered Bīdar plates of Deva Sena[46] and the Thāḷner plates of Hari Sheṇa[47] of the Vatsagulma branch the word is found used in this sense in connection with Vindhyaśakti I himself, and it may appear at first sight that the first king himself was styled as the king of the Vākāṭakas. But let us remember that these inscriptions are of a much later period when the word had already been crystallised in the dynastic sense. These records thus reflect the conditions of their own times and in no way prove that it had developed a dynastic significance right at the beginning.

The Vākāṭakas were Brāhmaṇas of the Vishṇuvṛiddha *gotra*[48] and followed Vedic-Paurāṇic religion, performing Vedic sacrifices and observing several Paurāṇic rites. Most of the Vākāṭaka monarchs about whom we have relevant information were devout Śaivas, only two of the members of the Padmapura-Nandivardhana-Pravarapura branch being Vaishṇavas. But they were away from sectarian bigotry, and some of their vassals and officers including ministers were adherents of Mahāyāna Buddhism and extended liberal patronage to Buddhist establishments at Ajantā and Ghaṭotkacha caves, evidently with the knowledge and encouragement from their masters.

Notes and References

1. "Some Unpublished Amarāvatī Inscriptions", *EI,* XV, pp. 260-61.
2. *Nagpur University Journal,* III, pp. 22ff.; *Inscriptions of the Vākāṭakas, CII,* V, pp. xi-xvi; *MSGH,* I, pp. 113-16; *CHI,* III, Part I, p. 130.
3. *NHIP,* VI: *Vākāṭaka-Gupta Age,* p. 96; *EHDY,* pp. 154-55. Altekar has only hinted at the likelihood of a South Indian origin merely on the basis of the Amarāvatī inscription in question and would prefer to keep the question open till it is settled by fresh discoveries. Mirashi developed it into a full-fledged theory and therefore we mainly aim at his views while discussing the South Indian origin theory.
4. *EI,* XV, pp. 267-68, no. 27.
5. *Ibid.,* pp. 260-61.
6. In *ibid.,* XV, p. 260, he speaks of it as a personal name and regards Pākoṭaka occurring in inscription no. 8 (p. 263) as identical with Vākāṭaka (*p* softened into *b* which was not always distinguished from *v*), while elsewhere (*ibid.,* p. 268) he takes it to be a clan-

name and not a personal name. C. Sivaramamurti (*Amarāvatī Sculputures in the Madras Government Museum, Bulletin of the Madras Government Museum*, New Series, General Section, IV, p. 304, no. 126) cites Chanda's latter opinion without any comment.

7. *Op.cit.* Also Altekar, *op.cit.*

8. The name of the locality from where Vākāṭaka hailed was mentioned in the inscription, but the relevant portion is damaged and lost.

9. *EI*, XV, p. 262, no. 3; Lüders' List, no. 1250. Kalingā referred to in an inscription from Amarāvatī *(ibid.*, no. 1251) appears to have, as indicated by her name, hailed from Kalinga.

10. *CII*, V, p. 96, lines 3-5. From the recently discovered Bīdar plates of Deva Sena (*AV*, pp. 248-51) and Thāḷner plates of Hari Sheṇa (*ibid.*, pp. 251-53) we learn that the title *Dharma-mahārāja* was employed for only three members of the dynasty, viz. Vindhyaśakti I, Pravara Sena I and Deva Sena, and Hāritīputra only for the last two.

11. *CII*, V, pp. 103-11, *supra*, pp. 42-44.

12. *Ibid.*, pp. 44-46; *CII*, V, pp. 112-19.

13. For reference to Vallūra, see *ibid.*, p. 115, line 3, verse 3; for proposed identification, pp. xv-xvi, 114-15.

14. *Ibid.*, p. 108, verses 12-18; pp. 116-17, verses 10-18.

15. *Ibid.*, p. 116, verse 5.

16. K.V. Ramesh ("On the Vākāṭakas and their Inscriptions", *AV*, pp. 29-30) points out that the Purāṇas actually describe the Vākāṭakas as 'of or belonging to or native to the respective regions' and that their original home should be traced in Vidarbha. In this connection he attaches great importance to the Vākāṭaka *gotra* Vishṇuvṛiddha and draws attention to a Purāṇic account according to which a certain usurper had forcibly abducted the wife of a king of Vidarbha and wifed her and that the progeny of this forced union came to be known as Vishṇuvṛiddha, indicating the Vidarbhite origin of the Vishṇuvṛiddha *gotra*. This view is further sought to be supported on linguistic grounds. It is pointed out that the name Vākāṭaka is totally inexplicable in Sanskrit whereas the middle portion, *kāṭa*, could actually be the Sanskritised form of the word *kādu* which in all Dravidian languages denotes 'a forest' or 'a thicket'. Vākāḍu might have been some forested region of this name in Vidarbha which was a part of South India linguistically. Likewise S.V. Sohoni (*ibid.*, pp. 33-35) would prefer to connect the Vākāṭakas with one of the four villages named Vākāḍ situated in the region Maheshwar in the Nīmāḍ district of Madhya Pradesh and the Ghaṭotkacha cave near Ajantā and is inclined to place the initial historical setting of the dynasty south of the Sātpuḍā hills and the Mahādeva range. See also his "A Note on the Original Territory of the Vākāṭakas", *JIH*, XLIX, pp. 135-42. However, both these views are at a variance with the Purāṇic description of the Vākāṭakas as Vindhyaka and consequently unacceptable.

As for the view of K.V. Ramesh regarding the derivation of the dynastic name Vāṭāṭaka, it must be pointed out that the linguistic figuration of Vidarbha is quite different from the Dravidian. Moreover, we need not go to any hypothetical word like Vākāḍu as the name of a forest which was later turned into Vākāṭaka. For, the dynastic name might as well be a contracted and slightly altered form of the Sanskrit words (or names) Varakaṭaka or more probably Vyāghrakaṭaka by the well-known linguistic process of elision and elongation. It must be remembered in this connection that the Vākāṭaka charters are familiar with names of localities and regions ending in *kaṭa* or *kaṭaka*. In that case it was primarily a local name later turned into a dynastic nomenclature. There a casual possible derivations emerge in course of discusion with Professor V.S. Pathak and Dr. Chandrashekhar Gupta in a casual discussion.

17. It would appear better to take the expression *Nṛipān Vaideśikān* of the Purāṇas in the sense of 'rulers of (or belonging to) various regions' instead of 'kings of Vidiśā' as proposed by F.E. Pargiter (*DKA*, p. 72 [Engl. tr.; also p. 42 where the relevant Purāṇic passages are captioned 'Dynasties of Vidiśā') as the kings referred to in these passages did not all belong to Vidiśā only and are known to have ruled in various regions.

18. *DKA*, pp. 50 (text) and 73 (translation).

19. For Vākāṭaka monarchs assuming coronation names which are different from their personal names, see Ajay Mitra Shastri, "some Aspects of Personal Names in the Vākāṭaka Inscriptions", *JOI*, XXXVI, pp. 254ff.

20. See note 17 above.

21. Nakhavān or Nakhapāna, who is identifiable with Kshaharāta Nahapāna, and his descendants or family members who are mentioned earlier in the passage, for example, had nothing to do with Vidiśā.

22. *Vindhyakānām kulasy-ānte*, *DKA*, p. 50, line 1 under 'Dynasties of the Third Century A.D.'.

23. H.C. Raychaudhuri, *Studies in Indian Antiquities*, pp. 108-14; D.C. Sircar, *Studies in the Geography of Ancient and Mediaeval India*, p. 57.

24. V.V. Mirashi, *HISWK*, p. 45, line 2.

25. Ajay Mitra Shastri, "Presidential Address", *PIHC*, 1978, pp. 969-70. The form Chhimuka is found on the coins issued by him whereas the other form is met with in a short label-inscription at Nāṇeghāṭ.

26. *Chāntasa* for *Śāntasya* on a copper-pot containing 5,534 silver punch-marked coins found at Chik Sandogi in the Dhārwāḍ district, Karnataka (*ibid.*, p. 969), and Chātamūla for Śāntamula met with in Ikshvāku inscriptions may be cited as examples.

27. This is the correct reading of the king's name in the reverse legend of Sātavāhana silver portrait coins.

28. This in our opinion is the correct reading of the first part of the metronymic in the legend on the reverse of the silver portrait coins of the Sātavāhana monarchs who were Vāsishṭhīputra.

29. In view of this the popular belief that Sātpuḍā means the seven sons or seven folds of Vindhya as recorded in the *C.P. District Gazetteer* for Betāl by Russel (1907, p. 258) must be discarded. This legend is evidently intended to explain the otherwise queer name, taking *sāt* in the sense of seven. For this reference, see H.C. Raychaudhuri, *op.cit.*, p. 112, fn.5.

30. *Vide* V.S. Agrawala, *Matsyapurāṇa—A Study*, p. 194.

31. Pargiter, *op.cit.*, p. 50.

32. *Ibid.*, p. 73.

33. *History of India: 150 AD to 350 AD*, p. 16, fn. 3. Also see p. 70. Jayaswal feels that Kāñchanakā and Chanakā were probably alternative names. He also invites attention to the mention of Kāñchanī purī as the capital of the Nāgas in the *Kalki-purāṇa*, III, 14.2-21. See *ibid.*, pp. 16-17, fn. 3. Even without this emendation it is possible to get this meaning as Purī could easily stand for Purikā.

34. *CII*, V, p. xii. Curiously enough, he has ignored similar meaningless usages of such particles elsewhere in the same passage. This point was stressed by Jayaswal also.

35. *DKA*, p. 50, fn. 33.

36. Not to speak of the occurrence of these adjuncts for the fulfilment of metrical requirements in the entire range of the dynastic texts of the Purāṇas, the immediately preceding quarter of the same line which refers to Kāñchanakā contains the unnecessary particle *cha (bhokshyate cha samāḥ shashṭim)*.

37. *Ṛikshavantaṁ samabhitas=tīre tatra nirāmaye nirmitā sā purī ramyā Purikā nāma nāmatah.*

38. Ajay Mitra Shastri, *Varāhamihira's India*, p. 90. J.F. Fleet tentatively located it in the open area on the south of the island-village of Onkār Māndhātā, where the map shows the villages called Godurpoora, Bainpoora, Baintanpoora and Dhooka (*JRAS*, 1910, p. 446). For inscriptional references to Purikā, see Lüders' list, nos. 782, 812, 838 and 839. *Vide* also P.K. Bhattacharya, *Historical Geography of Madhya Pradesh*, pp. 217-18.

39. K.P. Jayaswal, *op.cit.*, p. 16, fn. 3. As pointed out by Jayaswal, the transposition of syllables involved in the transformation of Chanakā (or Kāñchanakā) into Nachnā is a common phonetic phenomenon. This would, however, explain only the *aksharas cha* and *nā* which would exchange place. It is possible that in course of time both (initial and concluding) *kā-s* were dropped and the remainder-*ñchana*-got transformed into Nachnā. However, despite these possibilities, one cannot be sure regarding the identification, though it looks very probable not only because of some similarity of the two names but also due to its antiquity and find of a couple of Vākāṭaka inscriptions there.

40. *CII*, V, pp. 89-91.

41. For this temple, see *Archaeological Survey Reports*, XXI, Pls. XXV-XXVI; *HCIP*, III : *CA*, pp. 501-06.

42. Vindhyaśakti II, also called Vindhya Sena, of the Vatsagulma branch of the dynasty had nothing to do with the Vindhyas, and the name was simply repeated without any intentional significance.

43. *DKA*, p. 50 *(Vindhyakānāṁ kule=tite)*. The Vindhyaka-Vākāṭaka equation was pointed out long back by Jayaswal *(op.cit.*, pp. 55 and 66) and is accepted by some other historians as well. See D.C. Sircar in *HCIP*, II : *AIU*, p. 218.

The association of the Vākāṭakas with the river Kilakilā stressed by Jayaswal (*op.cit.*, pp. 66-67) is denied by Altekar (*NIHP*, VI: *VGA*, p. 96; *EHDY*, p. 154), but may be likely, particularly because of its location in the area in question and the mention of the Kolakilas or Kilakilas in connection with Vindhyaśakti who is actually said to have belonged to or born from the Ko(i)lakilas (*DKA*, pp. 48 [text] and 72 [Engl.tr.] where *tataḥ Kolakilebhyaś=cha-Vindhyaśaktir=bhavishyati* is rendered as 'Then after the Kilakilas Vindhyaśakti will reign').

44. Jayaswal, *op.cit.*, pp. 67-68.

45. "A Note on the Original Territory of the Vākāṭakas", *JIH*, XLIX, pp. 135-42.

46. P.V. Parabrahma Sastry, "Hyderabad Plates of Vākāṭaka Deva Sena, Year 5", *JESI*, XIII, p. 73, line 1.

47. V.V. Mirashi, *Indological Research Papers*, Vidarbha Sanshodhan Mandal, Nagpur, 1982, p. 85, line 1.

48. The *gotra* name is wrongly spelt as Vṛishnivṛiddha in the Wāshim plates of Vindhyaśakti II.

III

Chronology

It has been proposed by some scholars that the Vākāṭakas founded or at least were aware of some reckonings. K.P. Jayaswal suggested long back that the Kalachuri-Chedi era commencing 248-49 AD was initiated by Vindhyaśakti I.[1] But the view has naturally not found favour with the historians as the Vākāṭakas are not known to have employed any era in their fairly numerous records which are dated with reference to the reigns of individual rulers. Recently, B.N. Mukherjee has suggested that the Hisse-Borālā inscription of Deva Sena, the fifth member of the Vatsagulma branch, indicates the existence of a popular, though unofficial, reckoning counted from the time of the beginning of the dynasty 220 years prior to Śaka 380 (457-58 AD), which is the date of the record.[2] But this view is as unacceptable as the previous view as no other Vākāṭaka record shows awareness of any such reckoning and the reading of the relevant portion of the inscription whereupon this theory is based is highly uncertain.[3]

However, we have some general indications to fix, in a general way, the chronology of the Vākāṭakas. First, the Purāṇic texts mention Vindhyaśakti, the founder of the dynasty, as a ruler who flourished in the third century AD.[4] But the Purāṇic data are highly uncertain and controversial as regards chronology, and we must look for some other more dependable basis to fix the chronology of the Vākāṭakas, and such data are not wanting. The main plank of the general Vākāṭaka chronology is provided by the marriage of Prabhāvatī Guptā, daughter of the Gupta emperor Chandra Gupta II Vikramāditya (accession 376 AD), with the Vākāṭaka monarch Rudra Sena II, which would indicate that the predecessors of Rudra Sena II flourished in the pre-Chandra Gupta II period. This is reinforced by the statement met with in several copperplate charters of the Padmapura-Nandivardhana-Pravarapura branch that when the fifth member of the dynasty since Vindhyaśakti I, Pṛithivī Sheṇa I, ascended the throne the Vākāṭaka treasury and forces had been growing for a full century.[5] It would follow that Vindhyaśakti I had established regal power about a hundred years prior to Pṛithivī Sheṇa I's accession. A more precise chronological information is afforded by the Hisse-Borālā lithic record of the time of Deva Sena, fifth member of the Vatsagulma branch and seventh from Vindhyaśakti I, the founder of the dynasty. The only inscription dated in a well-known reckoning, it records the excavation of a lake called Sudarśana by the king's officer Svāmilladeva in Śaka 380 (457-58 AD). Unfortunately, the epigraph does not specify the corresponding regnal year.[6] But this also leads to the same general conclusion that Vindhyaśakti I came to power in mid-third century AD.[7]

We have also some general indications about the closing period of the Vākāṭaka rule. The Vishṇukuṇḍin king Vikramendravarman I is said to have adorned by his birth the twin families of the Vishṇukuṇḍins and the Vākāṭakas.[8] On the basis of the backward calculation from the eleventh regnal year of the last known Vishṇukuṇḍin monarch Vikramendravarman II ascertained from his Tummalaguḍem plates dated in expired Śaka year 488 corresponding to 566-67 AD,[9] he must have come to the throne in 555-56 AD. His father, Indrabhaṭṭārakavarman, is known to have ruled for at least twenty-seven years and consequently his accession cannot be dated later than 528-29 AD. No record of his father Vikramendravarman I has been reported so far but his assumption of the regal titles *rājan* and *mahārāja* leaves no doubt that he did come to the throne. Assigning him a brief reign of ten years, his accession cannot be dated later than 518-19 AD and his father Mādhavavarman II Janāśraya who had a long reign of not less than forty or forty-eight years,[10] must have come to power not later than 478-79 or 470-71 AD and should have concluded his reign not later than 518-19 AD. He was a very powerful ruler and we learn from his Polamūru plates that he had conquered all the territory up to the river Revā or Narmadā. It has been assumed, perhaps plausibly, that he regarded himself as the rightful successor of the Vākāṭakas and probably brought a large part of Maharashtra under his rule. Thus, the end of the Vākāṭaka rule cannot perhaps be dated much after *c.* 500 AD.[11]

To conclude, the period of Vākāṭaka authority has got to be placed between mid-third century and close of the fifth century AD.[12]

Notes and References

1. *Op.cit.*, pp. 109-11.
2. "A Note on the Hisse-Borālā Inscription of the Time of Vākāṭaka Devasena", *JESI*, VII, pp. 3-5. He follows the reading of J.E. Mitchiner, *Asiatic Society, Monthly Bulletin,*

August 1978, pp. 6-7. But this reading and interpretation are not accepted by scholars.

3. For a discussion on this inscription, see Ajay Mitra Shastri, "New Vākāṭaka Inscriptions", *AV*, pp. 246-47, *supra* pp. 106-07.

4. *DKA*, pp. 48 (text) and 72 (Engl.tr.). Though in general one may feel sure that the post-Andhra dynasties and rulers are mentioned in the passage, there are numerous exceptions also.

5. The relevant passage is *varsha-śatam=abhivarddhamāna-kośa-daṇḍa-sādhana-santāna-putra-pautriṇaḥ*. The expression *varsha-śata* is only a round figure and should not be taken as an exact figure. Moreover, it is not certain whether the passage refers to his accession or some period of his reign.

6. For the inscription, see Shobhana Gokhale, *EI*, XXXVII, pp. 1-4; V.B. Kolte, *Dr. Mirashi Felicitation Volume*, pp. 372-84; *Vidarbha Saṁśodhnana Maṇḍala Vārshika*, 1964, pp. 137-56. For discussion, *vide* G.S. Gai and S. Sankaranarayanan, *EI*, XXXVII, pp. 5-8; Ajay Mitra Shastri, *Dr. Umesha Mishra Commemoration Volume*, pp. 617-27; *AV*, pp. 246-47; *supra*, pp. 106-07; D.C. Sircar, *Journal of Ancient Indian History*, I, 1978, pp. 94-98.

7. This is an almost unanimous conclusion. But J.E. Mitchiner (*Asiatic Society, Monthly Bulletin*, August, 1978, pp. 6-7) and B.N. Mukherjee (*JESI*, VII, pp. 3-5) hold, basing on their reading of the date portion of the Hisse-Borālā inscription that in Śaka 380 (457-58 AD) 220 years had expired since the establishment of the Vākāṭaka rule. However, as the reading is extremely doubtful, this view cannot be taken seriously.

R.C. Majumdar (*Journal of the Royal Asiatic Society of Bengal, Letters*, XX, pp. 101-05) and D.C. Sircar (*ibid.*, XII, pp. 71ff.; XIII, pp. 75-78; *HCIP*, III: *CA*, pp. 180-81; *Select Inscriptions bearing on Indian History and Civilization*, I, p. 440, fns. 2-3) also date the commencement of the dynastic authority in c. 250 AD. But their views and reconstructions based on their interpretation of the expression *s-āgra-varsha-sata-d(j)īvaputra-pautrā* occurring in the description of Prabhāvatī Guptā in her Rithapur plates issued during the nineteenth year of her son Pravara Sena II's reign that the queen was more than a hundred years of age at that time lacks support. The whole compound has to be taken as a single expression describing her as endowed with sons and grandsons for whom she wished a long life of over a hundred years, and such expressions are common in ancient Indian literature. See Jagannath Agrawal, *PIHC*, IV, p. 59; *Researches in Indian Epigraphy and Numismatics*, pp. 27-28; Mirashi, *CII*, V, p. VIII. Likewise, the statement of Majumdar that Hari Sheṇa was a contemporary of Narendra Sena based as it is on wrong calculation and ignoring the likely unevenness of the length of individual reigns has nothing to commend itself.

8. *Vishṇukuṇḍi-Vākāṭaka-vaṁśa-dvay-ālaṅkṛita-janmanaḥ*, Chikkulla plates of Vikramendravarman II, Yr. 10, S. Sankaranarayanan, *The Vishṇukuṇḍis and their Times*, p. 169, line 10.

9. For the text of these plates, *vide ibid.*, pp. 172-74. This is the only Vishṇukuṇḍin record dated in the Śaka era, while the rest are all dated in the regnal years of individual rulers.

10. It depends upon the reading of the regnal year in his Polamūru plates, some reading it as forty-eight and others forty.

11. For elaboration of the chronological bearing of the Tummalaguḍem plates of Vikramendravarman II, see *EHDPP*, pp. 128-29.

12. It is sometimes argued that the Purāṇas are aware of three generations of the Vākāṭakas, whereas they mention the Guptas only in a general manner. However, the use of plural number *(Gupta-vaṁśajāḥ)* for the successors of Gupta would indicate that the compilers of the concerned section of the Purāṇas were aware of at least three generations, viz. Ghaṭotkacha, Chandra Gupta I and Samudra Gupta, and perhaps the reason behind the silence about the rich territorial additions made by Samudra Gupta was to stress their original territories. In the case of the Vākāṭakas also they mention only the Vindhyan region altogether ignoring the Vidarbha and intervening regions conquered by them, obviously for the same reason. It would be unfair to draw any chronological inference from this Purāṇic evidence as done by some scholars (e.g. D.C. Sircar in *HCIP, II : AIU*, p. 219).

IV

The Beginnings

With the above framework we may now proceed to outline the career of the Vindhyaka-Vākāṭakas.

Vindhyaśakti

A.S. Altekar feels that Vindhyaśakti I was a mere general as he was never consecrated to kingship by any formal religious coronation. This view was based on the fact that the Ajantā inscription of the time of Hari Sheṇa, which was till recently the only epigraphic source of our information about him, was not known to have employed any regal title for him.[1] However, besides the facts that the inscription is badly damaged and versified and that even other kings are not given regal titles, the recently discovered Bīdar plates of Deva Sena[2] and the Thāḷner plates of his son and successor Hari Sheṇa[3] describe him as the first *(ādi) Dharmamahārāja* of the Vākāṭakas *(Vākāṭakānām=ādir= Dharmamahārāja)*, leaving no doubt about his being coronated and assuming regal title. The Ajantā inscription gives a vivid but general account of his military successes. We are told that 'he augmented his valour by fighting great battles' *(mahā-vimarddeshv=abhivṛiddha-śaktiḥ)*, 'when enraged, he was irresistible even by gods' *(kruddhas=surair=apy-anivāryya-vīryaḥ)*, 'the masses of dust raised by (the hoofs of) his horses in wars obscured the sun' *(raṇeshu haryy-uddhata-reṇu-jāla-sañchhādit-ārkkaḥ)*, 'he had acquired the whole world by the prowess of his arms' *(sva-bāhu-vīryy-ārjjita-sarvva-lokaḥ)*, 'his majesty was comparable to that of Purandara and Upendra' *(Purandar-Opendra-sama-prabhāvaḥ)*, 'he had humbled his foes' *(vinivārit-āriḥ)*, etc.[4] However, all these praises are vague and unfortunately we have no specific references to the enemies defeated by him, but this should leave no doubt that he was constantly engaged in military activities for carving out and expanding his kingdom. In view of this account Altekar's view that diplomacy rather than military valour played a vital role in the creation of his kingdom[5] is inapt. Both appear to have supplemented each other.

Mirashi and Altekar, who believe in the southern origin of the Vākāṭakas, hold that these military expeditions led to the extension of the Vākāṭaka power towards the North. Altekar feels that the name Vindhyaśakti suggests that these victorious operations resulted in giving him control over a portion of the Vindhyan territory and that starting from Berar (Vidarbha), he conquered and annexed Betūl, Iṭārsī and Hoshangābād districts of Madhya Pradesh.[6] According to Mirashi, Vindhyaśakti, despite northward expansion of his kingdom, may have continued to rule from Chanakā which he is inclined to locate somewhere in the central part of Andhra Pradesh.[7] As we have seen, however, the original kingdom of Vindhyaśakti lay in the Vindhyan region and the expansion must have been southward, though, in the absence of any information, it is not possible to be specific. That the expansion was southward is clear from the fact that by the time of his son Pravara Sena I the kingdom had reached Vidarbha.

The mid-third century AD witnessed the rise of three political powers in Central India and Gaṅgā-Yamunā Doab. The Allāhābād-Ayodhyā region came under the Guptas, the Mathurā-Gwālior-Vidishā region saw the rise of Nāga houses, and the Bundelkhaṇḍ-Baghelkhaṇḍ region of the Vākāṭakas almost simultaneously, and in course of their long career all these dynasties came into contact with each other. Vindhyaśakti is described as *dvija (brāhmaṇa)* and said to have performed some religious rites in the aforesaid Ajantā inscription.[8] Some Purāṇas mention ninety-six years in connection with Vindhyaśakti[9] which, if correct, should refer to his long life. He may be assigned a reign of twenty-five years, viz. *c.* 250-275 AD.

Though an ambitious upstart, he laid the foundations of the Vākāṭaka power on a secure base which was developed into an empire by his able descendants.

Pravīra alias Pravara Sena I

Vindhyaśakti was succeeded by his son who is called Pravīra in the Purāṇas and Pravara Sena in inscriptions in *c.* 275 AD and closed his long eventful career about 335 AD after a rule of six decades according to the Purāṇas.[10] He was very ambitious and had the requisite strength to expand. But in the North there was no scope for expansion due to the rise of the Nāgas and the Guptas, and consequently he had to move southward to Vidarbha where an offshoot of the Śatavāhanas represented by Saka Sātakarṇi, Kumbha Sātakarṇi and Karṇa (or Kṛishṇa) Sātakarṇi known almost exclusively from their coins in the Tarhāḷā (Akolā district) hoard ruled up to about 300 AD.[11] It is difficult to identify the Ṣātavāhana king vanquished by Pravara Sena about the close of the third century AD for want of dependable evidence. But this was indeed a momentous event both for the Vākāṭakas as well as Vidarbha as from now on they became inseparably associated with each other. He must have annexed and brought some other regions also under his influence though at present we have no evidence to be more precise on this point. Earlier historians have made some guesses. Thus Altekar held that all th territories which are known to have been under the Vākāṭakas till their end were annexed by Pravara Sena I unless there is specific evidence of their addition by some later members. Basing on the *Śrīśaila-sthala-māhātmya* tradition that a daughter of Chandra Gupta named Chandrāvatī offered a garland of jasmine flowers daily to the god Mallikārjuna at Śrīśaila and identifying Chandrāvatī with Prabhāvatī Guptā he concluded that the *tīrtha* (Śrīśaila) was included in the Vākāṭaka empire and that all the territory right up to the Kurnool district fell within the Vākāṭaka sphere of influence, even if not actually under Vākāṭaka administration.[12] However, this tradition does not deserve the credence it is given, especially because the deity at Śrīsaila is Mallikārjuna Śiva whereas, like the imperial Guptas, Prabhāvatī Guptā was a staunch devotee of god Vishṇu. The same is true about his opinion regarding westward expansion under Pravara Sena I. It is pointed out that the end of the line of Chashṭana after Bhartṛidāman and the accession of Rudrasiṁha II, son of Svāmi-Jīvadāman and the non-assumption of the title Mahākshatrapa by him and his son and successor Yaśodāman II was due to the interference of Pravara Sena I into the affairs of the Western Kshatrapas. It is suggested that Pravara Sena I incited Rudrasiṁha II against the reigning king Bhartṛidāman on the stipulation that he would accept the Vākāṭaka suzerainty which explains the non-assumption of the now sovereign style Mahākshatrapa by him and his son all through their rule and payment of tribute which is represented by the Sonpur (Chhindwārā district, Madhya Pradesh) hoard containing, *inter alia*, their coins.[13] But this theory is as untenable as the previous one. For, the cessation of Chashṭana's line can be easily explained as on account of failure of a male child after Bhartṛidāman, especially as Rudrasiṁha II's coins show a continuity of numismatic and naming traditions, and the cessation of the style Mahākshatrapa was most probably due to the Sassanians who had about this time occupied Sind and might have prevented the two Kshatrapas from assuming the superior title.[14] The contention of Mirashi that the empire carved out by Pravara Sena I extended up to the river Tuṅgabhadrā in the south[15] fares no better. But by far the most exaggerated notion of Pravara Sena I's empire is that of Jayaswal who believed in its pan-Indian character and that he drove the Kushāṇas from the Punjab to Afghanistan and that the Pallavas were an offshoot of the Vākāṭakas, which is only a figment of imagination. As we have seen, Vindhyaśakti's kingdom included the Vindhyan region to the north of the Narmadā, while about any other territory we have no evidence at all. His son Pravara Sena I expanded southward and occupied Vidarbha and probably adjoining regions in the Deccan. It is likely that his sons made a few other conquests under him, but as of now we have nothing to define these additions precisely. It is possible that the neighbouring South Kosala or Chhattīsgaḍh region of Madhya Pradesh came under his influence though there is absolutely no indication at present of his exercising his authority there.[16] However, we can aver with confidence that the Vākāṭaka empire under him included all the territory from Bundelkhaṇḍ-Baghelkhaṇḍ region of Madhya Pradesh to the Vidarbha region of Maharashtra including all the intervening region of Madhya Pradesh. According to the Purāṇas, he had his capital at the city of Kāñchanakā identified with modern Nachnā in the Pannā district of Madhya Pradesh. And, if we were to concede the amendment of the reading suggested by Jayaswal, it is possible that he had established another metropolis at the town of Purikā on the slopes of the Ṛikshavat or Sātpuḍās near the southern bank of the Narmadā which has not been located satisfactorily.

Pravara Sena I entered into a matrimonial alliance with the Bhāraśiva Nāgas who were very powerful in Central India which proved to be a great source of strength and of momentous importance and is invariably mentioned in all the records of the Padmapura-Nandivardhana-Pravarapura branch. His son Gautamīputra was married to the daughter of the Nāga king Bhavanāga, whose family is said to have been created by god Śiva who was pleased with them because of their carrying his phallus *(Śiva-liṅga)* on their shoulders, to have been anointed with the pure waters of the river Bhāgīrathī obtained by their own valour and taken sacred ablution after performing ten *aśvamedhas*.[17] This matrimonial alliance appears to have played a significant role in strengthening the Vākāṭaka power and is, like the similar alliance with the imperial Guptas, invariably mentioned with a sense of pride in all the official records of the Padmapura-Nandivardhana-Pravarapura branch.

In consonance with his great power and authority and faith in Vedic religion

Pravara Sena I performed numerous *śrauta* sacrifices which are described in both the Purāṇas and Vākāṭaka records. The Purāṇas tell that he (viz. Pravira) performed several Vājapeyas or Vājimedhas attended by rich gifts.[18] From inscriptions we learn that he had performed all the Soma sacrifices *(sapta-soma-saṁstha)* including Agnishṭoma, Āptoryāma, Ukthya, Shoḍaśin, Atirātra, Vājapeya as well as Bṛihaspatisava, Sādyaskra and as many four Aśvamidhas.[19] Of these, Bṛihaspatisava could be performed only by the Brāhmaṇas.[20] The four Asvamedhas were evidently performed to celebrate as many victorious campaigns which resulted into the fructification of the seed sown by Vindhyaśakti into a mighty imperial fabric. It was after the performance of these sacrifices, especially the Vājapeya that he assumed the imperial title *samrāṭ,* which is employed only for him among the Vākāṭakas[21] and is known to have been borne, among the later rulers, only by Yaśodharman *alias* Vishṇuvardhana.[22]

In some grants of the Vatsagulma branch Pravara Sena I is styled *Dharmamahārāja,* but it is employed only because of the southern impact and there is absolutely nothing to suggest that the title was actually borne by him.

By his brilliant attainments Pravara Sena overshadowed only slightly less luminous successes of his father, and accordingly the genealogy in all but three Vākāṭaka records[23] begins with him. There is no doubt that he had consolidated these territorial gains and placed the Vākāṭakas on an imperial career next only to the Guptas in the North. The onward march continued unabated for a little over one and a half centuries before the decline set in.

The Purāṇas tell us that Pravīra=Pravara Sena I had four sons all of whom became kings.[24] Had it not been for the Wāshim plates of Vindhyaśakti II bringing to light his (Pravara Sena I's) son Sarva Sena, the founder of the now well-known Vatsagulma branch,[25] in addition to his other already known son Gautamīputra,[26] this Purāṇic statement would have been dismissed as a myth. Now, we know only two branches, viz. Padmapura-Nandivardhana-Pravarapura and Vatsagulma,[27] of the dynasty, the remaining two offshoots still remaining unknown. Some surmises have, of course, been made to locate the remaining two kingdoms,[28] but in the absence of any supporting evidence and presence of contradicting material these conjectures cannot be sustained, and one must await dependable discoveries in future.

We are inclined to believe that Pravara Sena I had partitioned the kingdom among three of his sons during his lifetime to avoid troubles later and kept with him a part of the kingdom because one of the sons, Gautamīputra, was too young to succeed. And therfore there is absolutely nothing to support the prevailing notion that Gautamīputra and his descendants represented the main or elder branch of the dynasty, and it would under the circumstances be most appropriate to call the two known branches after their respective capitals, viz. Padmapura-Nandivardhana-Pravarapura branch and Vatsagulma branch.

Notes and References

1. *NIHP,* VI : *VGA,* p. 97; *EHDY,* pp. 157 and 158.
2. *JESI,* XIII, p. 73, line 1; *AV,* p. 248; *supra,* pp. 107-11.
3. V.V. Mirashi, *Indological Research Papers,* I, p. 85, line 1; *supra,* pp. 111-14.
4. *CII,* V, p. 107, verses 2-5.
5. *NIHP,* VI : *VGA,* p. 97.
6. *EHDY,* pp. 157-58.
7. *CHI,* III, Part I, p. 131.
8. *CII,* V, p. 107, verses 2 and 5.
9. *Samāḥ shaṇ=ṇavatiṁ jñātvā (v.l. bhūtva) pṛithivīṁ tu smaeshyati, DKA,* p. 48 (text) and fn. 86 (variant).
10. *Bhokshyate cha samāḥ shashṭiṁ puriṁ Kāñchanakāṁ cha vai, ibid.,* p. 50.
11. For a detailed discussion, see Ajay Mitra Shastri, *EHDPP,* pp. 38-44.
12. *EHDY,* p. 159; *NIHP,* VI : *VGA,* p. 99.
13. *Ibid.,* pp. 58-59; *EHDY,* pp. 160-61. This suggestion is accepted by Shriram Goyal (*vide Gupta aura Vākāṭaka Sāmrājyoṁ kā Yuga* [Hindi], pp. 399-400). The inclusion of a few silver coins of Rudra Sena III in this hoard has not been explained satisfactorily. Actually, like silver punch-marked coins, Kshatrapa coins were also valued as treasure and their hoards have been reported from localities situated far away from their realm and not much historical significance should be attached to them.
14. There was no Mahākshatrapa during the period between Śaka 221 (299 AD) and 269 (347 AD), and kings Viśvasena, Rudrasiṁha II and Yaśodāman II had to remain satisfied with only the lower title Kshatrapa. The Sassanian emperor Varhrān II (267-93 AD), though facing trouble from the Roman emperors Marcus Aurelius, Carus and Diocletian, succeeded in crushing the rebellion of his recalcitrant brother Hormizd in the east and perhaps conquered and annexed Śakastān (Scythia) and Sindh and thereby deprived the Kārdamaka Kshatrapas of a part of their territory to the west and made his son Varhran III governor of this newly conquered territory. And in 293 AD Varhrān III was overpowered by his uncle Naresh, and the Kshatrapas appear to have maintained subordinate relations with him. Even up to the early years of the reign of Shāpur II (309-79 AD) Śakastān (and perhaps Sindh) formed part of the Sassanian empire as indicated by the Pahlavi Persepolis inscription dated probably in 310-11 AD. In view of these facts the view of E. Herzfeld (*Paikuli: Monuments and Inscriptions of the Early History of the*

Sassanian Empire, Berlin, 1924, pp. 41ff.) that the Sassanian sovereignty over the Indian parts of Śakastān was lost in 293 AD during the war between Varhrān III and Naresh and that these principalities regained their independence about this time needs a second thought. There is no doubt that the Sassanians deprived the Kārdamakas of the province of Sindhu-Sauvīra which might have continued under them since the reign of Rudradāman I and compelled them to adopt a lower title.

15. *CHI,* III, Part I, p. 133.

16. Mirashi thinks, without any evidence, that the Vākāṭaka rule in South Kosala was perhaps brought to an end by Mahendra who was a contemporary of Samudra Gupta. See *ibid.*, p. 134, fn. 45.

17. The relevant passage runs as follws : *aṁsa-bhāra-sanniveśtia-Śivaliṅg-odvahana-Śiva-suparitushṭa-samutpādita-rāja-vaṁśānāṁ parākkram-ādhigata-Bhāgīratthy-amala-jala-mūrddh-ābhishiktānāṁ daś-āśvamedh-avabhṛitha-snātānām Bhāraśivānām mahārāja-śrī-Bhavanāga-dauhitrasya Gautamīputrasya putrasya...* (description of Rudra Sena I), *CII,* V, p.12, lines 4-7 (Jāmb plates of Pravara Sena II). The description is met with in all the official records of the Nandivardhana branch. The Bhāraśivas perhaps had their original home in Vidarbha as indicated by the find of an early inscription of the Bhāra king Bhagadatta at Paunī (Bhaṇḍārā district). See V.V. Mirashi, "Pauni Stone Inscription of the Bhāra King Bhagadatta", *EI,* XXIV, pp. 11-14.

18. *Yakshyate Vājapeyaiś=cha samāpta-vara-dakshiṇaiḥ. DKA,* p. 50. *Vājimedhaiś* is a variant instead of *Vājapeyaiś* in a *Vāyu* manuscript called *e* by Pargiter. *Vide ibid.*, fn. 35. The same manuscript (*ibid.*, fn. 36) gives the reading *bahu* in place of *vara.*

19. *Agnishṭom-Āptoryyām-Okthya-Shoḍaśy Atirātra-Bṛihaspatisava-Sādyaskra-chatur=Aśvamedha-yajinaḥ* (Jāṁb plates), *CII,* V, p. 12, lines 1-2. This phrase is also repeated in all the official records of the dynasty. Of the seven Soma sacrifices, Atyagnishtoma is replaced by Sādyaskra.

20. This is an additional evidence for believing that the Vākāṭakas were Brāhmaṇas.

21. D.C. Sircar (*HCIP,* II: *AIU,* p. 220) is wrong in believing that the title is used in Vākāṭaka records for the Vākāṭakas, though with special reference to Pravara Sena I. It is used for Pravara Sena I only, and not for any other Vākāṭaka king. It must be mentioned in this context that he alone among the Vākāṭakas had performed the Vājapeya which, according to the *Śatapatha-brāhmaṇa,* entitled a king to assume this title.

22. See his Mandasor inscription (D.C. Sircar, *Select Inscriptions,* I, p. 418, verse 3). Mirashi (*Vākāṭaka Nṛipati āṇi tyāñchā Kāla,* Nagpur University, 1957, p. 32) is wrong in observing that this title is not known to have been borne by any other ruler either in North or South India.

23. These exceptions are the Bīdar or Hyderabad plates of Deva Sena, Thāḷner plates of Hari Sheṇa and Ajantā inscription of Hari Sheṇa's time, all the three belonging to the Vatsagulma branch.

24. *DKA,* p. 50.

25. *CII,* V, pp. 96-98.

26. It is only a metronymic, the personal name not being recorded in any record.
27. We are against calling the Padmapura-Nandivardhana-Pravarapura branch as the main or elder branch.
28. Altekar located them in Kosala and Andhra (*EHDY*, p. 163; *NHIP, VI : VGA*, p. 102-eastern provinces) and Mirashi in parts of South Kosala and Southern Maharashtra (*CHI*, III, Part I, p. 134). These views are, however, untenable as just a few years later we find in these areas other ruling families.

V

Padmapura-Nandivardhana-Pravarapura Branch[1]

Rudra Sena I

Gautamīputra married the daughter of the Bhārasiva Nāga king Bhavanāga who had perhaps no male issue and therefore his daughter's son from Gautamīputra, viz. Rudra Sena I, was to succeed him in his kingdom of Padmāvatī in addition to his own share of the Vākāṭaka kingdom. Gautamīputra predeceased his father Pravara Sena I who was consequently succeeded on the throne by his grandson Rudra Sena I. That he expected to succeed to his maternal grandfather's throne also is clearly indicated by his description as *Bhavanāga-dauhitra* in all the official records of his successors. *Dauhittra* is here employed most probably as a technical term as in *Lichchhavi-dauhitra* employed in referring to the Gupta emperor Samudra Gupta who inherited the joint Gupta-Lichchhavi kingdom which made substantial accretion to his power and dominion. Bhavanāga is known from his coins whereon he is styled as *Adhirāja* besides *Mahārāja*.[2] But probably ambitions of his other relatives did not permit this momentous event which would have united the Nāga and Vākāṭaka kingdoms turning this amalgamation into a mighty empire. That other Nāga rulers including Nāgasena and Gaṇapatināga ruled Padmāvatī is indicated by their coins[3] as well as their mention in the list of rulers vanquished by Samudra Gupta in his Allāhābād pillar inscription.[4]

Rudra Sena I came to throne around 335 AD. Even though the Purāṇas state that all the four sons of Pravara Sena I became kings, as his son Gautamīputra had predeceased him and he was therefore succeeded by his grandson Rudra Sena I, in this case we have to take this statement as actually referring to Rudra Sena I.

In the records of his successors Rudra Sena I is described as a staunch devotee of Svāmi-Mahābhairava *(atyanta-Svāmi-Mahābhairava-bhakta)*. It was the fierce form of Śiva, and it is possible that in this respect he was influenced by his maternal grandfather who loved him so much and intended to make him his successor.[5] Some scholars attribute to him a fragmentary inscription from Deoṭek (Chandrapur district).[6] This record refers to the construction of a *dharma-sthāna* by Rudra Sena at the place called Chikamburi (ancient name of Deoṭek). The word *dharma-sthāna* is commonly taken to mean a place of worship or shrine.[7] In that case it could be a shrine of Mahābhairava to whom he was devoted according to the charters of his descendents. However, as we have seen above, *dharma-sthāna* does not denote any religious structure and is used in ancient Indian literature in the sense of a court of justice and the same is perhaps intended here. We have no definite information about him except that his kingdom stretched from the Vindhyan region in Madhya Pradesh to the northern part of Vidarbha in the south and from the eastern limit of Khāndesh to the western limit of Kosalā. It is possible that he continued to rule from the same capital/capitals as his illustrious grandfather.

The period of his rule witnessed momentous political events and changes in North India where the mighty Gupta emperor Samudra Gupta was pursuing his victorious career taking his arms far and wide. It was held by some earlier historians like K.P. Jāyaswal[8] and S.K. Aiyangar[9] and recently by S.R. Goyal[10] that Rudra Sena I was defeated by Samudra Gupta and that he is mentioned under the name Rudradeva among the rulers of Āryāvarta (North India) extirpated by him.[11] But even though the Vindhyan region of Madhya Pradesh continued to form part of his kingdom, the main kingdom of Rudra Sena I lay to the south of the river Narmadā and therefore he could not be described as an Āryavarta ruler. Moreover, it is quite uncertain if Nachnā and Ganj in the Satna district where two records of a Vākāṭaka feudatory have been found was not technically included in the South. Then again, the kings of Āryavarta are said to have been extirpated by Samudra Gupta, whereas Rudra Sena's dynasty continued to rule for nearly a century and a half after him and a vassal of his son and successor Pṛithivi Shena I is known from a couple of records from Nachnā and Ganj. We are therefore convinced that Rudradeva of the Allāhābād pillar inscription of Samudra Gupta cannot be equated with Rudra Sena I. But at the same time it is likely that the impact of his widespread conquests was too much not to affect Rudra Sena at least psychologically. To add to it, some scholars believe that there was some opposition from the other branches of the dynasty to the succession of Rudra Sena[12] which further weakened the imperial position of the Vākāṭakas which was already undermined by the partition of the empire among his four sons by Pravara Sena himself. It is also pertinent that none of the successors of Pravara Sena bore the imperial title *samrāṭ* which was certainly due to their loss of imperial position. It is sometimes argued, rather naively, that the title was borne by Pravara Sena as he had performed the Vājapeya sacrifice which was not the case with any other Vākāṭaka ruler.[13] However, the same passage of the *Śatapatha-brāhamaṇa,* which observes that the performance of the Vājapeva results in the assumption of the title *samrāṭ* also states that one becomes *rājan* by observing the Rājasūya sacrifice.[14] And all the kings, including foreign rulers of India such as the Kshaharatas and Kārdamakas and followers of non-Brāhmanical religions like Jainism and Buddhism who cannot ordinarily be supposed to perform the *Rājasūya,* are known to have assumed the title *rājan.* Then, the Aulikara king Yaśodharman-Vishṇuvardhana is said to have assumed the imperial title *samrāṭ* even though his Mandasor inscription describing his achievements, even sundry, in detail,[15] contains no allusion to his performance of the Vājapeya. And if so many rulers could assume the title *rājan* without performing the Rājasūya and Yaśodharman-Vishṇuvardhana could become a *samrāṭ* without observing the Vājapeya, there was nothing to prevent the continuation of the title *samrāṭ* by the successors of Pravara Sena I if only they were sufficiently powerful, especially as it would have amounted only to carrying on a tradition. There is therefore no doubt that the imperial title *samrāṭ* was abandoned by Rudra Sena I because he was not powerful enough to warrant the use of this imperial title, particularly in the presence of the mighty Gupta emperor Samudra Gupta who had already crushed his Nāga relations in Central India. Even Mirashi, who is a staunch champion of the complete independence of the Vākāṭakas *vis-a-vis* the Guptas, concedes that Rudra Sena I had to acknowldege the superiority of Samudra Gupta and to permit him passage through his kingdom for his victorious expedition of Dakshiṇāpatha.[16] We may therefore hold that even though not actually defeated by Samudra Gupta, Rudra Sena I was compelled by circumstances to act like his subordinate ally.

Rudra Sena I ruled up to about 355 AD when he was succeeded by his son Pṛithivī Sheṇa I.

Pṛithivī Sheṇa I

Unfortunately we have no record of Pṛithivī Sheṇa I himself, but he is eulogised in the official records of his successors right from the time of his son and successor Rudra Sena II,[17] when going by the extant evidence, the draft of the official charters of the Vākāṭakas was finlised. This draft with certain insignificant modifications and necessary additions was continued till the very end of this branch. In these records he is described as a devout worshipper of god Maheśvara *(atyanta-Māhesvara)*[18] and endowed with various virtues like truthfulness, straightforwardness, mercy, valour, bravery, policies, humility, high-mindedness, intelligence, attachment to worthy people, the state of being a pious conqueror *(dhammavijayitva)*, purity of mind, etc. and as one who conducted himself like Yudhishṭhira. We are further told that 'he had sons and grandsons and a treasure and army which had been augmenting continuously for a hundred years'.[19]

The above is not a description of a very ambitious ruler but of a pious man, especially as he is compared to Yudhishṭhira who is known more for his righteousness and qualities of heart than as a great fighter. And to add to it, his contemporary Gupta emperor Samudra Gupta was busy with his victorious campaigns, and Rudra Sena I had already acquiesced in the position of his obliging ally. Pṛithivī Sheṇa I appears to have continued his father's policy and maintained a low profile. He continued to maintain his nominal authority over the Vindhyan region as indicated by the find of lithic records of a certain Vyāghradeva who meditated upon the feet of Vākāṭaka *Mahārāja* Pṛithivī Sheṇa at Nachnā-kī-talāi[20] and Ganj[21] in the Panna district of Madhya Pradesh.[22] There is a divergence of opinion regarding the identity of the Vākāṭaka king as there were two kings of this name in the dynasty, viz. Pṛithivī Sheṇa I, son of Rudra Sena I, and Pṛithivī Sheṇa II, the last known king of the branch represented by them. While several historians favour his identification with the first king of this name,[23] J. Dubreuil,[24] R.C. Majumdar,[25] K.N. Dikshit[26] and V.V. Mirashi[27] are inclined to equate him with the second monarch.[28] The latter flourished in the last quarter of the fifth century AD. The inscriptions are not dated and none of the champions of the latter view has cited any incontrovertible palaeographical[29] or other evidence against its ascription to an earlier period. Mirashi proposes to identify the Vyāghradeva of these epigraphs with *Mahārāja* Vyāghra, father of the Uchchakalpa *Mahārāja* Jayanātha mentioned in a few records of the family, who seems to have ruled almost simultaneously with Pṛithivī Sheṇa II according to his chronology. This theory, based as it is entirely on the identity of the names, is simply untenable.

The Nachnā and Ganj epigraphs give the name of the vassal as Vyāghradeva, while in the Uchchakalpa records the chief is called simply Vyāghra preceded by the regal title *Mahārāja* which is conspicuous by its omission in the two records in question. In view of these facts the identity of the Vākāṭaka vassal Vyāghradeva is not at all admissible besides being otherwise open to serious suspicion. As observed by H.C. Raychaudhuri,[30] the Bundelkhaṇḍ-Baghelkhaṇḍ region including Nachnā and Ganj was under the Gupta, not Vākāṭaka, supremacy for quite some time (to be precise, at least up to 528 AD) since the days of the mighty Gupta emperor Samudra Gupta. We learn from his Eraṇ inscription[31] that he had extended his direct rule at least up to Sāgar in the south. Further, as the Parivrājaka *Mahārājas* ruling to the west of the Uchchakalpa kingdom, clearly acknowledged the Gupta supremacy,[32] the Uchchakalpa *Mahārājas* must have, as a geopolitical compulsion, owned the Gupta suzerainty, even though their records do not aver it explicitly. Moreover, the recently reported Shankarpur (Sidhi district, Madhya Pradesh) charter of *Mahārāja Harivarman,* dated Gupta year 168, leaves no doubt that the Baghelkhaṇḍ region, where Ganj and Nachnā are situated, was ruled by Harivarman as a feudatory of the Gupta emperor Budha Gupta in 487-88 AD.[33] The record mentions a couple of generations preceding Harivarman which seems to show that the area in question formed part of the Gupta empire since a much earlier date. We may, therefore, conclude convincingly that the Nachnā and Ganj inscriptions in question belong to the time of Prithivi Shena I, and not Pṛithivī Sheṇa II, as commonly believed by historians. And this would prove the continuation of the Vākāṭaka control over the ancestral kingdom in the Bundelkhaṇḍ-Baghelkhaṇḍ region of Madhya Pradesh up to the early years of the reign of Pṛithivī Sheṇa I. This hold was definitely brought to an end by Samudra Gupta, as we have just seen. Whether it is mentioned specifically in his Allāhābād pillar inscription or this Vyāghradeva was one of the minor rulers of Āryavarta implicity alluded to among 'others' *(adi)*[34] is difficult to ascertain. It is possible, however, that he is identical with Vyāghraraja of Mahākāntāra mentioned as one of the kings of Dakshiṇāpatha (Deccan and South) defeated and reinstated by Samudra Gupta. The objection that Vyāghraraja is mentioned as a Deccanese ruler whereas Vyāghradeva was ruling over the Vindhyan region of the North can be easily met as ancient Indian writers like Varāhamihira include even the Chitrakūṭa hill in the Bāndā district, sixty-five miles west-south-west of Allāhābād in the southern division.[35] Mahākāntāra may in that case refer to the Aṭavi or forest region stretching from Jabalpur in

Madhya Pradesh to Mirzapur in Uttar Pradesh. And even if he, like other kings of the South, was reinstated by Samudra Gupta, his fief, like those of the Mālavas, Yaudheyas, etc., ceased to exist under the unbearable Gupta pressure. Later Pṛithivī Sheṇa I appears to have joined Samudra Gupta's southern expedition; for he claimed (or his successors claimed for him) to be a *dharma-vijayin* (pious conqueror who defeats and carries away the glory of his foes, not their territories), whereas, as we have seen, he does not appear to have achieved any conquest on his own and just maintained his territory in Vidarbha intact.[36] The friendship between the two royal families which were the most powerful then in the Indian subcontinent, was cemented by a matrimonial alliance. A little before the close of Pṛithivī Sheṇa I's reign (*c.* 380 AD) his son Rudra Sena II married Prabhavatī Gupta, daughter of Chandra Gupta II, son of Samudra Gupta, born of the Nāga princess Kuberanāgā, an event of momentous importance referred to with pride in all the subsequent official records of the Vākāṭakas.[37] Scholars have attributed a political motive to this alliance: Chandra Gupta's desire to secure the Vākāṭaka help in his projected campaign against the Western Kshatrapas.[38] But this is purely an unwarranted guess and has nothing to commend itself. For the Śakas of Western India were already humbled by Samudra Gupta and had become a petty state and Chandra Gupta II would not have been required to plan it some two decades in advance (Chandra Gupta II's victory over the Kshatrapas took place sometime between 409 AD and the close of his rule)[39] and to contract a matrimonial alliance with this object in view.

We know nothing about the capital of Pṛithivī Sheṇa I, and there is nothing to support Mirashi's conjecture that the capital was shifted to Nandivardhana during his reign,[40] for, as we shall see, there is reason to believe that his son Rudra Sena II had his capital at Padmapura. And it is not impossible that he abandoned his ancestral capital at Kāñchanakā putting it in charge of his vassal Vyāghradeva and established his own capital at Padmapura. And it is not impossible that the unfinished single plate purported to have been issued form Padmapura[41] actually belongs to him.

Rudra Sena II

Pṛithivī Sheṇa I was succeeded by his son Rudra Sena II around 385 AD. As stated above, he had married Prabhāvatī Guptā, daughter of the Gupta emperor Chandra Gupta II. While his father was a staunch devotee of Siva *(atyanta-Māhesvara)*, he was a devout Vaishṇava and believed that his authority was established by the favour of the wheel-emblemed god, i.e. Vishṇu.[42] It is commonly held that it was due to the great influence exerted by his chief queen Prābhvatī Guptā. But it is not correct as there was nothing like a family religion in ancient India and members of the family were free to adopt and are actually known to have adopted different religions according to their personal predilections.

Recently a copperplate charter issued by him has been found at Māṇḍhaḷ in the Nāgpur district.[43] Issued in the fifth year of his reign, it records grant of some villages to the Brāhmaṇas belonging to various *gotras* and Vedic *charaṇas.* The donated villages were situated in the eastern administrative division *(mārga)* of Padmapura. Earlier probably he had donated some land to the two monasteries of the Sāttvata *charaṇa* hailing from Vatsagulma, as the villages granted to the Brāhmaṇas are said to have excluded the lands earlier granted to the twin monasteries. The charter, in keeping with the king's freshly acquired Vaishṇavite leanings, is said to have been issued at the behest or message of god Mondasvāmin who is actually four-armed Śesha-śayana Vishṇu enjoying divine sleep on the body of the snake king Ananta in the ocean, carrying in his three arms conch shell, wheel and sword (the remaining arm actually supporting his head).[44]

Padmapura appears to have enjoyed great importance during his reign, and even after Pravarapura had become the capital of the family, it continued as an important administrative centre as indicated by the Māsod grant of Pravara Sena II purporting to donate some villages situated in its western division *(aparamārga).*[45] From the location of the villages named in these charters it is clear that this Padmapura has to be looked for somewhere in the Nāgpur-Wardhā region. This Padmapura must be the same as the homonymous locality wherefrom the unfinished (Mohallā) plate was issued.[46] This appears to have been the Vākāṭaka capital during the reign of Rudra Sena II.

The said plate can be attributed to any king only on the basis of palaeographical grounds as the plate containing the issuer's name is not forthcoming. Mirashi dates it in the reign of Narendra Sena. But the palaeograpical evidence is not decisive and we have reasons to date it earlier.[47] We prefer to place it in Pṛithivī Sheṇa I's time and feel that he had made Padmapura his capital. The only known date of Rudra Sena II is his fifth regnal year, and assuming that he continued to rule for another five years, the close of his reign may be placed around 395 AD.[48]

Yuvarāja Divākara Sena and Prabhāvatī Guptā's Regency

When Rudra Sena II passed away rather prematurely, all his three sons, viz. Divākara Sena, Dāmodara Sena and Pravara Sena, were minor. As Pṛithivī Sheṇa

I is said to have had within his lifetime son(s) and grandson(s), it is clear that at least the eldest (Divākara Sena) of them was born before he closed his reign. Thus, Divākara Sena may have been a little over ten years at the time of his father's death[49] and others, who might have been born after their grandfather's passing away, still younger. As none of them was major and capable of asscending the throne, their mother Prabhāvatī Guptā had to look after the kingdom on behalf of the eldest son, Divākara Sena, who was the crown prince *(yuvarāja)*. Whether Rudra Sena II had any younger brother and whether his claim to the throne was set aside in favour of Divākara Sena with the assistance and blessings of his maternal grandfather is something that cannot be determined in the present state of inadequate information. There is, however, no doubt that Prabhāvatī Guptā was naturally proud of herself and her paternal lineage and in the critical period of her life she naturally received substantial help from her father as well as brother. This is clearly indicated by her retention of her parental *gotra* (Dhāraṇa) as against the common practice of the wife changing over to her husband's after the marriage[50] and the fact that in both of her records she got her parental genealogy recorded instead of her husband's.[51] But this influence has been over-exaggerated by most of the historians of the Vākāṭakas who feel that even the scribes were imported from her father's kingdom which fact is thought to be responsible not only for the draft of her records but also for the use in one of them[52] of the nail-headed characters instead of the box-headed ones common to the Vākāṭaka charters. Had it been really so, the records would not have contained the serious factual errors from which the genealogical portion suffers.[53] As far as the employment of a particular variety of script is concerned, it depends on the type of training that a scribe receives and the rulers by and large have not much to do with it.

Divākara Sena was a *yuvarāja* for at least thirteen years as the Puṇe plates of Prabhāvatī Guptā were issued in the thirteenth year of her regency.[54] How much longer he continued as *yuvarāja* cannot be ascertained at present, but it must not have been much longer, for he had already attained the age of not less than twenty-three at the time the Puṇe plates were issued. That he passed away only as *yuvarāja* is certain as a stanza composed by Divākara Sena is cited in the *Sadukti-karṇāmṛita*, an anthology compiled by Śrīdharadāsa who mentions the composer as *yuvarāja* only.[55] So the close of his *yuvarāja*-ship can be dated around 410 AD. The Puṇe plates were issued from Nandivardhana identified with the modern village of Nandardhan or Nagardhan, some twenty-eight miles from Nagpur. It is apparent therefore that by this time the capital had been shifted from Padmapura to Nandivardhana: how much prior is difficult to ascertain for want of requisite evidence.

Dāmodara Sena

Divākara Sena was succeeded by his younger brother Dāmodara Sena about 410 AD. It is not impossible that for some time Prabhāvatī Guptā acted as regent on his behalf as well.[56] But there is now no doubt that he, as distinct from his younger brother Pravara Sena II, did succeed to the throne. There was a difference of opinion on this question till recently, and some scholars believed that Dāmodara Sena and Pravara Sena II were not two distinct personages and that Dāmodara Sena himself assumed the name Pravara Sena (II) after his illustrious homonymous ancestor (Pravara Sena I).[57] It is no doubt true that the Ṛiddhapur plates described Prabhāvatī Guptā as the mother of Dāmodara Sena and Pravara Sena *(Mahārājạ-śrī-Dāmodarasena-Pravarasena-jananī)*;[58] but as the title *Mahārāja* and the honorific *śrī* are used only once and the plates were issued during Pravara Sena II's reign, it was assumed that both these persons were one and the same as otherwise the omission of the regal title and honorific for the reigning king would be completely inexplicable.[59] But the seal-inscription of the recently discovered Miregāon (Sākolī tahsīl, Bhaṇḍārā district) plates of Prabhāvatī Guptā describing her as the 'mother of two kings' finally establishes that the two were separate and both ascended the throne.[61] We have absolutely no information about Dāmodara Sena's reign. Assigning him a brief reign of just a decade, we can place the close of his reign in *c.* 420 AD.

Pravara Sena II

Dāmodara Sena was succeeded by his younger and much more well-known brother Pravara Sena II for whose reign we have a large number of copperplate charters[62] and a lithic record.[63] As the latest of his copperplate charters (Paunī grant) was issued in his thirty-second year,[64] he may be taken to have ruled for about thirty-five years. Unlike his parents, he was a devout Śaiva, and he believed that by the favour of god Śambhu he had established Kṛita-yuga *(Śambhoḥ Prasada-dhṛita-kārtta-yugasya)*.[65]

His grants from the second to the eleventh year of his reign were issued from Nandivardhana which continued to be his capital at least till that year and sometime between this and his sixteenth year[66] his capital was shifted to Pravarapura generally identified with modern Paunār (Wardha district).[67]

Though we have more of his records than for any other Vākāṭaka king, they give us absolutely no information about his political career. In the grants of his grandson Pṛithivī Seṇa II we are told that he followed the conduct of earlier kings and had extirpated all his enemies by excellent policies, strength and prowess. These phrases also occur in the Siwanī grant of Pravara Sena II himself issued in his eighteenth year[69] while it is conspicuously absent in his Chammak grant issued a few months earlier in the same year.[70] If these references are of any historical value, the conquests mentioned in these grants may have occurred in his eighteenth regnal year between the months of Jyeshtha and Phālguna. The find-spots of his charters and the villages granted through them just indicate that he maintained intact the kingdom inherited by him.[71]

On the basis of the mention of *Tripurī-vāsaka* as the place of issue of his Indore plates of his twenty-third year,[72] Mirashi has concluded that Pravara Sena II's relations with his maternal relations (Kumāra Gupta I) had worsened and he had launched an invasion of the Ḍāhala (Baghelkhaṇḍ) region and that the charter was issued from his military camp at Tripurī (modern Tewar, Jabalpur district) to the north of Narmadā.[73] This is a purely gratuitous assumption. First, the word *vāsaka* denotes a temporary residence, not military camp, and is actually employed in this sense in the Waḍgāon plates of his twenty-fifth year issued from his *vāsaka* on the river Hiraṇyā *(Hiraṇyā-nadī-vāsakāt)*[74] which is definitely known to have been included in his own kingdom and where there could be no question of his invasion. Secondly, Pravara Sena II had high respects for his mother who exercised great authority and influence on Vākāṭaka administration all through her life. In Pravara Sena II's nineteenth and twentieth years she issued her Ṛiddhapur and Miregāon plates in her own right,[75] and the king himself gave his Tiroḍī charter for her merit in his twenty-third year,[76] when his Indore plates under reference were also given. In the Rāmtek stone inscription which was put up after the death of his mother towards the close of his reign, high praise is lavished on not only his maternal grandfather but also on his son Ghatotkacha Gupta.[77] That the relations between the Guptas and the Vākāṭakas continued to be friendly till the very end of this branch of the Vākāṭaka dynasty is inferable from the continuation of the reference in glowing terms to the marriage of Prabhavatī Guptā with Rudra Sena II in the records of Pṛithivī Sheṇa II, the last known member of this branch. Notwithstanding all these considerations, one might think of accepting this conjecture if only the villages mentioned in this charter were identified in the Baghelkhaṇḍ region. But as it is, these have been located in the Bālāghāṭ district of Madhya Pradesh. What therefore seems to be most probable is that Pravara Sena II had been to Tripurī for pilgrimage[78] and issued, perhaps after bathing in the Narmadā, the charter in question granting land in his own kingdom.[79] Alternatively, Tripurī being an important locality, he might have made a short stay there enjoying his maternal uncle's hospitality.

An important event which took place towards the close of Pravara Sena II's reign was the passing away of his mother Prabhāvatī Guptā who had played such a great role in maintaining intact the kingdom following her husband Rudra Sena II's premature demise which invested her with a very critical challenge. She was a great devotee of Vishṇu and all three of her grants were Vaishṇavite in nature. The Puṇe plates commence with well-known Vaishṇava formula *jitaṁ bhagavatā* and record a grant made by her to a Vaishṇava *(bhagavad=bhakta)* donee after presenting it first at the footprints of Vishṇu on the occasion of *pāraṇā* (fast-breaking) on the twelfth day of the bright fortnight of Kārttika.[80] The Ṛiddhapur charter, which also commences with the same formula, was issued from the footprints of Vishṇu at the celebrated Rāmagiri (modern Rāmṭek, Nagpur district), and the occasion of the grant was also the same. After a brilliant career she passed away in all the majesty at the ripe old age of about eighty-five.[81] It was commemorated by her unnamed daughter and son Pravara Sena II by building the Vishṇu (Narasiṁha) temple appropriately named Prabhāvatīsvāmin and excavating a tank called Sudarśana.[82]

Pravara Sena II was a man of literary taste and a great Prakrit poet, and his Prakrit epic named *Setubandha* or *Rāvaṇavaho*, based on the theme of Rāma's passage to Laṅkā and the killing of Rāvaṇa, achieved great fame among connoisseurs including Daṇḍin, Bāṇabhaṭṭa, Ānanda-vardhana, etc. But its attribution to Pravara Sena II cannot be regarded as certain as there were Pravarasenas in Kashmir, which is also known to have been a great literary centre, and some scholars are inclined to credit one of these Pravarasenas with the composition of this work. A later commentator, Rāmadāsa (c. 1875 AD), attributes its composition to the great Sanskrit poet Kālidāsa who, we are told, composed it for *Mahārāja* Pravara Sena at the behest of *Mahārājādhirāja* Vikramāditya.

In the colophon of each of the chapters *(āśvāsa)* it is described as 'composed' *(virachita)* by Pravara Sena and 'made' *(kṛita)* by Kālidāsa. It is supposed on the basis of this testimony that the poem was composed on behalf of Vākāṭaka Pravara Sena II by Kālidāsa on the orders of his patron Chandra Gupta II, who had assumed the *viruda* Vikramāditya.[83] However, one cannot be certain about this attribution in view of the facts that Chandra Gupta II is not the only Vikramāditya, that a persistent tradition places the original Vikramāditya in the first centruy BC, that the date of Kālidāsa himself is controversial with several scholars believing in a BC date and the recentness of the tradition recorded by Rāmadāsa which casts doubts regarding its trustworthiness. However, Pravara Sena's claim to poetic talent need not be doubted as a few of his *gāthās* are cited in the *Gāhāsattasaī* attributed to the Sātavāhana king Hāla.

Narendra Sena

Around 455 AD Pravara Sena II was succeeded by his son Narendra Sena. He is probably identical with Narindarāja, born of Ājñākabhaṭṭarikā known from the recently discovered Māṇḍhaḷ plates of Pravara Sena II. [84] He has left no record of his, and all our knowledge is derived from the four known charters of his son and successor Pṛithivī Seṇa II.[85] These records contain a very interesting compound while describing Narendra Sena. Till recently it was read as *Pūrv-ādhigata-guṇa-viśvāsād=apahṛita-vaṁśa-śriyaḥ* and commonly interpreted to mean that he had inherited regal power by virtue of his acquired virtues.[86] But the recently discovered Māṇḍhal grant of Prithivi Sena II's tenth year has enabled us to read it as *pūrv-ādhigata-guṇavad=dāyād-āpahṛita-vaṁśa-śriyaḥ* which means that Narendra Sena had first acquired the royal fortune which was stolen away later by his minor relations, even though possessed of virtues. This would show that the demise of Pravara Sena II was followed by a dispute about succession and Narendra Sena had at first succeeded in winning for himself the throne which had been later snatched away by his relations who may have been his brothers. If the word *guṇavad* is taken as synonymous with *gauṇa,* which is quite likely, it may refer to the feud with the Vatsagulma branch. This would then knock at the bottom of the unwarranted notion among historians that the relations between the two branches of the Vākāṭakas continued to be cordial all through. Whatever that be, there is no doubt that after initial success Narendra Sena was deprived of his kingdom or its major part by his relations.[87]

The statement in his son's records that Narendra Sena had held in check enemies subdued by his prowess (*pratāpa-praṇat-āri-śāsanas ya)* may probably refer to his initial success against the enemies who tried to obstruct his succession unsuccessfully. In view of the precarious condition to which Narendra Sena was subjected in the later part of his life, the claim that his commands were obeyed by the lords of Kosalā, Mekalā and Mālava must be taken with a grain of salt. At least at present we have no evidence to substantiate these claims. The claim in respect to Mekalā (the Amarakaṇṭak region, Madhya Pradesh) was till recently sought to be supported on the ground that the Bamhanī plates contained a veiled allusion to Narendra Sena and Bharatabala, the Paṇḍava king of Mekalā, who was till recently supposed to have issued these plates, was regarded as a vassal of Narendra Sena.[88] But the recent discovery of the Mallār plates has shown convincingly that these assumptions are completely unfounded. As we have shown elsewhere,[89] both the charters were issued by Śūrabala Udīrṇavaira,[90] who flourished considerably after Narendra Sena and there is absolutely no question of his owning the latter's suzerainty.[91] It is possible, however, that he participated in some of the campaigns of reassertion of Gupta authority in these regions which might have shown signs of rebellion during the reigns of Skanda Gupta and Budha Gupta and might have claimed success against these rulers as his own. It is also possible that he carried out hurried sallies in these regions during the troubled days of the Imperial Guptas.

Narendra Sena married a Kunatala princess Ajjhitabhaṭṭārikā who gave birth to the next king Pṛithivī Sheṇa II. Kuntala was the name of North Karnataka, and the princess was most probably a daughter or granddaughter of the Kadamba king Kākutsthavarman of Vanavāsī (Uttara Kannaḍa district, Karnataka) who is said to have married his daughters to the Gupta and other kings.[92] Looking to the friendly Gupta-Vākāṭaka relations that persisted all through it is quite likely that he had his daughters married to the Vākāṭaka kings as well.[93]

Till recently no coins of the Vākāṭakas were known. But recently some Vākāṭaka coins have been spotted at Paunār, and among them are two coins that can be attributed to Narendra Sena. One of these, both copper, has the legend *rendra* in box-headed characters on the obverse and *śrī* on the reverse and the other has a bold letter *na,* standing for Narendra Sena, on the obverse and partially accommodated conch-shell on the reverse.[94] These coins were apparently used for day-to-day transactions.[95]

Pṛithivī Sheṇa II

Around 480 AD Narendra Sena was followed by his son Pṛithivī Sheṇa II for whose reign we have four records, to wit, (1-2) Māṇḍhaḷ plates of the years 2 and 10,[96] (3) Māhurjharī plates of the year 17,[97] and (4) incomplete Bālāghāṭ plates.[98] Like his great-grandfather Rudra Sena II he was a devout Vaishṇava and is styled *atyanta-bhāgavata.*

He was indeed faced with the herculean challenge as his ancestral kingdom or a major part thereof was under the possession of his minor relations, probably of the Vatsagulma branch. But he proved equal to the occasion and restored the sunken family fortune (*magnavaṁś-oddhartuḥ*) which fact is referred to in his Māṇḍhaḷ and Māhurjharī grants of the tenth and seventeenth years respectively. In the subsequent Bālāghāṭ plates he is said to have extricated twice the sunken family fortunes (*dvi-magna-vaṁśasy-oddharttuḥ*).[99] This second calamity was most probably caused by the invasion of the Nala king Bhavadattavarman of the Bastar region of Madhya Pradesh and the adjoining territory of Andhra Pradesh. His Ṛiddhapur plates were issued from Nandivardhana, the earlier Vākāṭaka capital, and purport to grant a village in the Yawatmāl district.[100] Apparently a large part of the Vākāṭaka kingdom had fallen to the Nalas, especially their king Bhavadattavarman. This event must have taken place sometime after the seventeenth year of Pṛitivī Sheṇa II's reign, for his Māhurjharī grant issued in that year refers to only one calamity (*magna-vaṁś-oddharttuḥ*). Till the second year of his reign cartainly the Nandivardhana region formed part of his kingdom as indicated by his Māṇḍhaḷ grant of that year which was issued from nearby Rāmagiri (Rāmtek).[101] He appears to have lost this region to Bhavadaṭṭavarman after his seventeenth year. But obviously the whole kingdom was not lost as indicated by the unfinished Bālāghāṭ plates issued from his temporary residence at Vembāra (*Vembāra-vāsakāt*) which is perhaps identical with modern Bembāl, about 28 miles east of Chandrapur.[102] He may have ruled for some twenty or twenty-five years, and accordingly the close of his reign may be dated around 500/505 AD.

Recently a unique copper coin of Pṛithivī Sheṇa, most probably the second king of this name, has been found at Paunār.[103] It has on the obverse a circular legend in typical box-headed characters reading *śrī-Mahārāja-Pṛithivī* and a volute-like design within a beaded border on the reverse.

Pṛithivī Sheṇa II is the last known king of the Pravarapura branch of the Vākāṭakas. The end was most probably due to the insatiable ambition of the Vatsagulma branch of the dynasty or the occupation of the kingdom by the Nala king Arthapati or his father Bhavadattavarman who is known, as we have seen, to have issued his charter from Nandivardhana, or both. Only future discoveries can enlighten us on this intriguing point.

Notes and References

1. Most of the historians call it only Nandivardhana branch.
2. H.V. Trivedi, *Catalogue of the Coins of the Nagas of Padmavati,* pp. 27-37. See also pp. xviii-xx of the Preface.
3. *Ibid.*, pp. 49-54 (Gaṇapati Nāga).
4. D.R. Bhandarkar (Revisor), B.Ch. Chhabra and G.S. Gai (editors), *Inscriptions of the Early Gupta Kings, CII,* III, p. 212, line 13; p. 213, line 21.
5. We know absolutely nothing about the sectarian affiliation of Pravara Sena I as well as of his son Gautamīputra. But from the performance of numerous Soma sacrifices, the former appears to have been a follower of Vedic sacrificial religion.
6. *CII,* V, pp. 1ff.
7. *Ibid.*, p. 4.
8. *Op.cit.*, pp. 14 ff.
9. *ABORI,* IV, pp. 30-40.
10. *A History of the Imperial Guptas,* pp. 141-47; *Guptā Sāmrājaya kā Itihāsa* (Hindi), pp. 108-13; *Gupta aura Vākāṭaka Sāmrājyoṁ kā Yuga,* pp. 404-10.
11. Bhandarkar, Chhabra and Gai, *CII,* III, p. 213, line 21. Rudradeva heads the list of Āryāvarta kings vanquished by Samudra Gupta.
12. Altekar, *EHDY,* p. 171.
13. *Ibid.*, p. 169.
14. *Rājā vai Rājasūyen-eshtvā bhavati samrāḍ Vājepeyena, Śatapatha-brāhmaṇa,* V.1. 1.3. According to the *Aitareya-brāhmaṇa,* on the other hand, by performing the Rājasūya one could become *samrāṭ* (cf. N.N. Law, *Aspects of Ancient Indian Polity,* pp. 164ff.). There was thus no hard and fast rule about the relationship between the regal titles and these sacrifices.
15. D.C. Sircar, *Select Inscriptions,* I, pp. 412-20.
16. *Vākāṭaka Nṛipati āṇi tyāñchā Kāla,* p. 37.
17. Ajay Mitra Shastri and Chandrashekhara Gupta, "Dvitīya Rudrasenāchā Māṇḍhaḷa Tāmrapaṭa", *Saṁśodhanāchī Kshitje,* ed. B.L. Bhole, Ameya Prakashan, Nagpur, 1985, pp. 223ff.
18. A.S. Altekar (*EHDY,* p. 170) observed, prior to the discovery of the Maṇḍhaḷ plates of Rudra Sena II, that the text of the Vākāṭaka records was first finalised during Prabhāvatī Guptā's regency under the Gupta influence.
19. *Saty-ārjjava-kāruṇaya-śauryya-vikkrama-naya-vinaya-māhātmya-dhīmattva-pātra-gata-bhaktitva-dharmmavi jayitva-mano-nairmaly-ādi-guṇais=samupetasya varsha-śatam=abhivarddhamāna-kośa-daṇḍa-sādhana-santāna-putra-pautriṇaḥ,* Jāmb plates of Pravara Sena II, *CII,* V, lines 9-12.
20. *Ibid.*, pp. 89-91.
21. *Ibid.*, p. 92.

22. A.S. Altekar (*EHDY,* p. 172; *NHIP, VI : VGA,* pp. 109-10), on the other hand, in keeping with his theory of a southern origin, took these records as an evidence of the extension of the sphere of Vākāṭaka influence in the Vindhyan region.

23. K.P. Jayaswal, *op.cit.,* p. 73; H.C. Raychaudhuri, *PHAI,* pp. 541-42; A.S. Altekar in *NHIP,* VI: *VGA,* pp. 109-10 and *EHDY,* p. 173; D.C. Sircar, *HCIP,* III: *CA,* p. 179.

24. *IA,* LV, pp. 103ff.

25. *JRASB,* XII, pp. 1ff.

26. *EI,* XVII, p. 362.

27. *CII,* V, pp. xxvii-xxviii, 89-92; *CHI,* III, Part I, p. 141.

28. D.C. Sircar, who was earlier inclined to identify him with Pṛithivī Sheṇa I and adduced clinching palaeographical evidence in support of this contention (*HCIP,* III: *CA,* p. 179 and fn. 1), later gave this position up and favoured his equation with the second king of this name (*Select Inscriptions,* I, p. 456 and fn. 1) and felt that the Vākāṭakas ousted the Gupta rule from Bundelkhaṇḍ about the close of the fifth century AD, though he assigned the characters of the Ganj inscription to the box-headed variety of the Late Brāhmī of the Southern Class of the sixth century AD.

29. Normally palaeographical considerations, which are often resorted to in the absence of any other evidence, cannot give us absolutely dependable dates as is clear from several instances where dates fixed on such considerations had to be shifted earlier by several centuries.

30. *PHAI,* pp. 541-42.

31. D.C. Sircar, *Select Inscriptions,* I, pp. 268-70, which describes the city of Erikiṇa (modern Eraṇ) as his *sva-bhoga-nagara* (verse 7).

32. The Parivrājaka records commence with the expression *Gupta-nṛipa-rājya-bhuktau.*

33. B.C. Jain, "Shankarpur Plate of Budhagupta and Harivarman, Year 166", *JESI,* IV, pp. 62-66. The correct reading of the year, as pointed out by K.V. Ramesh (*ibid.,* p. 64, fn. 1 and p. 66, fn. 17), is 168. The supposed connection of Harivarman with the Maukharis can at best be regarded as a brilliant conjecture in the absence of any dependable evidence on the point. After the discovery of this plate Sircar feels that there is not much time available for the rule of Pṛithivī Sheṇa II which he regards as an unproved guess and also floats the conjecture that his vassal Vyāghradeva might have gone over to Nachnā and Ganj in course of a pilgrimage (see *AV,* pp. 47-49).

34. Bhandarkar, Chhabra and Gai, *CII,* III, p. 213, line 21 *(ādy-aneka).*

35. Ajay Mitra Shastri, *Varahamihira's India,* p. 51.

36. In view of this, the suggestion of A.S. Altekar that he aided his cousin Vindhya Sena of the Vatsagulma branch in his conquest of Kuntala, probably the Kadamba king Kaṅgavarman (*EHDY,* p. 172; *NHIP,* VI: *VGA,* p. 109), is problematic. For reference to Vindhya Sena's Kuntala conquest, see *CII,* V, p. 108, verse 8.

37. From the time of Pravara Sena II, all the official records of this Vākāṭaka line describe him as the son of Rudra Sena (II) born of Prabhāvatī Guptā, daughter of *Mahārājādhiraja* Deva Gupta or Chandra Gupta (II).

38. V.A. Smith, *JRAS*, 1914, p. 324; H.C. Raychaudhuri, *PHAI*, pp. 554ff.; R.C. Majumdar, *NHIP*, VI: *VGA*, p. 169; A.S. Altekar, *ibid.*, p. 110; *EHDY*, p. 174; Sudhakara Chattopadhyaya, *Early History of North India*, 2nd ed., pp. 203-04, etc. V.V. Mirashi (*CII*, V, p. XXIII; *CHI*, III, Part I, p. 136), however, feels that the marriage followed the alliance of Chandra Gupta II with Pṛithivī Sheṇa I both of whom acted jointly in the invasion against the Śaka Kshatrāpas. He places the close of Pṛithivī Sheṇa I's reign about 400 AD.

39. The date on the coins of Chandra Gupta II copied from the Kshatrapa issues has not been preserved fully; the only portion legible is the Gupta year 90=409 AD.

40. *CHI*, III, Part I, p. 136; *CII*, V, p. XXIII.

41. *CII*, V, p. 78.

42. *Bhagavataś=chakkra-pāṇeḥ prasād-opārijita-śrī-samudayasya*, is the expressioin used in the Jāmb and later charters, while in his own Māṇḍhaḷ grant it is *Bhagavataś=chaakkra-lakshma-pratishṭhita-śāsansya.*

43. Ajay Mitra Shastri and Chandrashekhar Gupta, *in Saṁśodhanāchī Kshitije*, pp. 223ff.

44. *Ibid.*, p. 227, lines 1-2. This is one of the earliest epigraphic descriptions of the Śesha-śayana Vishṇu. For a discussion, *vide* our "Śesha-śayana Vishṇu: Earliest Epigraphic Evidence", *Vishṇu in Art, Thought and Literature*, pp. 1-6; *ABORI*, LXXV, pp. 111-20.

45. Ajay Mitra Shastri, *AV*, pp. 231-33; *supra*, pp. 86-88.

46. Mirashi proposes to identify it with the village Padampur in the Gondiā tehsil of the Bhaṇḍārā district. See *CII*, V, pp. 77-78.

47. V.B. Kolte ("Mahurzari Plates of Pṛithivī Sheṇa II", *ABORI*, LIII, p. 129) also feels that the script belongs to the period prior to Pravara Sena II.

48. V.V. Mirashi (*CHI*, III, Part I, p. 137) argues that Divākara Sena was probably less than twelve years old at the time of his accession, and, as he was born prior to the demise of his grandfather, his father Rudra Sena II may not have ruled for more than eight years. This is based on the assumption that princes in ancient India attained age on completion of twenty-four years (*ibid.*, fn. 51) which itself is derived from the statement in his Hathigumphā inscription that Khāravela became full-fledged king, or received coronation as *Mahārāja*, on his completing full twenty-four years. But in practice there was no such rule, and Khāravela was coronated as *Mahārāja* on attaining twenty-four probably because his father passed away then.

49. As stated above, Mirashi feels that he was 'probably less than twelve years old at the time of his accession' (*CHI*, III, Part I, p. 137). It is likely but not the reason for this suggestion, as pointed out above.

50. The *gotra* of the Vākāṭakas, as seen above, was Vishṇuvṛiddha.

51. These records are her Puṇe and Ṛiddhapur plates issued respectively in the thirteenth year of her regency for Divākara Sena and in the nineteenth year of her son Pravara Sena II's reign.

52. Viz. Puṇe plates. The Ṛiddhapur plates are inscribed in the usual box-headed variety. Now we have another record, a stone inscription, from the Kevala-Narasiṁha temple at Rāmṭek, engraved after her death during Pravara Sena II's reign in nail-headed characters. For a discussion on this inscription, see *AV*, pp. 253-57; *supra*, pp. 125-35.

53. These mistakes include the description of Chandra Gupta I as *Mahārāja* (instead of *Mahārājādhirāja*), mention of Ghaṭotkacha (instead of Gupta) as the first Gupta king, and application of a few characteristic epithets of Samudra Gupta to his son Chandra Gupta II. The description of Samudra Gupta as *anek-āśvamedhayājin* (performer of several *aśvamedhas*), which is also supposed to be an error, is not really so as *aneka* in this expression appears to stand for 'more than one', not many, and the legends on Samudra Gupta's Asvamedha type coins leave no doubt that he had performed at least two horse sacrifices.

54. *CII,* V, pp. 7-8, especially line 22 (for date) and the seal-inscription at p. 8 which mentions him as *yuvarāja.* The inscription is apparently dated in the period of Divākara Sena's authority as crown-prince.

55. Edited by H.D. Sharma, II, 31.4.

56. If he was born two years before the close of the reign of his father Rudra Sena II, he may have been seventeen when his elder brother Divākara Sena passed away.

57. V.V. Mirashi, *Vākāṭaka Nṛipati āṇi tyānchā Kāḷa*, p. 43; *CII, V*, p. xxiv; *CHI*, III, Part I, p. 137.

58. *CII*, V, p. 36, line 10.

59. *Vākāṭaka Nṛipati āṇi tyānchā Kāla*, p. 43, fn. 2; *CII*, V, p. 35; *CHI*, III, Part I, p. 137, fn. 53. In support of this contention it is also argued that no records of Dāmodara Sena have been found and that the omission of Dāmodara Sena would also have to be explained otherwise. See *ibid.*

60. *Vikrāntayor=jananyās=tu*

Vākāṭaka-narndrayoḥ

Śrī-Prabhāvatiguptāyaḥ

Śāsanaṁ ripu-śāsanam.

AV, p. 233; *supra*, pp. 91-93. This important charter is yet to be published.

61. The omission of the title *Mahārāja* and the honorific *śrī* before the name of Pravara Sena can be easily explained by the fact that these are intended for both and have been used before the first name following the current grammatical rules.

62. So far as many as nineteen of his copperplate grants have been found. See *CII*, V, inscriptions nos. 3-16 and *AV*, pp. 230-38, inscription nos. II-IV and VI-VII. *Vide* also *supra*, pp. 88-98.

63. This is the stone-slab inscription found recently in the Kevala-Narasiṁha temple at Rāmṭek. See *ibid.* pp. 125-35, *AV*, pp. 253-57.

64. *Ibid.*, pp. 237-38; *supra*, pp. 97-98. Also see V.B. Kolte in *EI*, XXXVIII, pp. 53-56.

65. This phrase occurs in several grants of Pravara Sena II himself as well as in those of his grandson Pṛithivī Sheṇa II. The statement of A.S. Altekar *(NHIP*, VI, *VGA*, p. 114; *EHDY*, p. 178) that he was a Vaishṇava is evidently due to oversight.

66. This has come to be known from his recently discovered Māṇḍhaḷ plates of year seventeen issued from Pravarapura and recording a grant made in his sixteenth year. See *AV*, pp. 230-31. See also Ajay Mitra Shastri, "Māṇḍhaḷ Copperplate Charter of Pravara

Sena II, Year 16'', *EI*, XLI, pp. 68-76.

67. The exact date of transfer of capital cannot be determined at present, but this charter has narrowed the gap by a couple of years. For a description of the antiquities found at Paunār, see Chandrashekhar Gupta, ''Paunār under the Vākāṭakas'', *AV*, pp. 119-54.

68. Māṇḍhal plates of his tenth year, Māhurjharī plates of seventeenth year and undated Bālāghāṭ plates.

69. *CII*, V, p. 30, lines 14-15.

70. *Ibid.*, pp. 23ff.

71. In view of this A.S. Altekar's notion that he exercised sovereignty over the Vatsagulma branch of the dynasty (*EHDY*, p. 179; *NHIP*, VI: *VGA*, pp. 114-15) cannot be sustained.

72. The first plate of this charter was discovered recently, while the remaining plates were known earlier. See V.V. Mirashi, *Indological Research Papers*, p. 72 (first plate), and *CII*, V, pp. 40-41 (for remaining plates). For reference to *Tripurī-vāsaka*, see line 1.

73. *Indological Research Papers*, I, pp. 65-71.

74. *CII*, V, p. 54, line 1.

75. *Ibid.*, pp. 35-37 (Ṛiddhapur); *AV*, pp. 233-34; *supra*, pp. 91-93 (Ṃiregāon; only discussion).

76. *CII*, V, p. 50, line 16.

77. *Supra*, pp. 125-35, for a discussion of the contents of this unique record.

78. See Ajay Mitra Shastri, *Tripurī* (Hindi), Madhya Pradesh Hindi Grantha Academy, Bhopal, 1971, pp. 167-68.

79. This is comparable to the Kurud plates of the Śarabhapurīya king Narendra (Ajay Mitra Shastri, *Inscriptions of the Śarabhapurīyas, Pāṇḍuvaṁśins and Somavaṁśins*, Part-II, pp. 3-6) recording the land-grant in South Kosala by a Gupta emperor after bathing in the Gaṅgā.

80. The grant was obviously made on the day following the eleventh day of the bright half of Kārttika which is observed by the Vaishṇavas as the day when Vishṇu awakes after a four-month long slumber.

81. Based on the assumption that she was about twenty at the time of her marriage during the closing years of Pṛithivī Sheṇa I (*c.* 380 AD) and died about the twenty-fifth year of Pravara Sena II's reign (*c.* 445 AD). The view of R.C. Majumdar and D.C. Sircar that she was over 100 years at the time of issuing her Ṛiddhapur charter is based on a faulty interpretation as shown above.

82. *Supra*, pp. 125-35.

83. V.V. Mirashi, *Vākāṭaka Nṛipati āni tyānchā Kāla*, pp. 121-24.

84. Ajay Mitra Shastri, ''Māṇḍhaḷ Copper-Plate Charter of Pravara Sena II, Year 16'', *EI*, XLI, p. 74, lines 22-23; *AV*, p. 231. One-third of the religious merit accruing from this grant was meant for Ājñākabhaṭṭarikā, mother of Narinda (Narendra)rāja.

85. These charters are two Māṇḍhaḷ charters dated in second and tenth years, the Māhurjharī plates of the seventeenth year and undated and unfinished but definitely later Bālāghāṭ plates.

86. This was the reading of F. Kielhorn, V.V. Mirashi and V.B. Kolte. It was not clear in the Bālāghṭ plates and therefore Kielhorn doubtfully suggested this reading. But the Māhurjharī plates have the reading suggested by us even clearer than on our Māṇḍhaḷ plates, but V.B. Kolte merely followed the reading of Kielhorn.

87. See Ajay Mitra Shastri, "Māṇḍhaḷ Plates of Pṛithivī Sheṇa II, Years 2 and 10", *EI*, XLI, pp. 172-74; *AV*, pp. 241-42; *supra*, pp. 98-103. This most probably marks the beginning of the conflict between him and his contemporary Vākāṭaka king Deva Sena of the Vatsagulma branch which culminated in the next generation.

88. B.Ch. Chhabra, *EI*, XXVII, pp. 137-38; V.V. Mirashi, *CII*, V, pp. 83-84. This view was based on the assumption that the word *narendra* in the Bamhanī plates (verse 11) alluded to Narendra Sena.

89. "The Date of the Bamhanī and Mallār Plates of Śūrabala Udīrṇavaira", *Bhāratī-bhānam* (*Dr. K.V. Sarma Felicitation Volume*), pp. 439-43; *supra*, pp. 80-84.

90. The impression that the Bamhanī charter was issued by Bharatabala was caused by the omission of the prose passage introducing his son and successor Śūrabala Udīrṇavaira which is now supplied by the recently discovered Mallār plates.

91. Ajay Mitra Shastri, *Inscriptions of the Śārabhapurīyas, Pāṇḍuvaṁśins and Somavaṁsīns*, I, pp. 122-28.

92. Tālguṇḍa pillar inscription of Śāntivarman, D.C. Sircar, *Select Inscriptions bearing on Indian History and Civilization*, I, p. 478, verse 31.

93. We find it difficult to believe that the Rāshṭrakuṭas of Mānapura had been in any way related to the Vākāṭakas and that Ajjhitabhaṭṭārikā was the daughter of Avidheya as surmised by Mirashi (*CII*, V, p. xxv; *CHI*, III, Part I, p. 139), especially as Mānāṅka, is said to have invaded Vidarbha and it is uncertain if his dominions were included in Kuntala.

94. Ajay Mitra Shastri, "Vākāṭaka Coins", *AV*, pp. 287-88; also *supra*, pp. 139-40.

95. Recently a hoard containing, *inter alia*, ten coins of the Traikūṭaka king Dahra Sena was reported from the village of Dahigāon (Malkāpur tālukā, Bulḍhāṇā district). It has led V.V. Mirashi (*JNSI*, XXXV, pp. 118-22; *Literary and Historical Studies in Indology*, pp. 180-85; *ND*, III, Part I, pp. 4-6) to conclude that taking advantage of the weakness of Narendra Sena the ambitious Traikūṭaka king Dahra Sena raided and occupied some portion of western Vidarbha including the Bulḍhānā district. And as the Traikūṭaka coins in the hoard are better preserved than the accompanying Kshatrapa coins, he further concludes that the Traikūṭaka occupation was short-lived. But as we have shown elsewhere ("Two Numismatic Notes", *ibid.*, I, Part I, pp. 25-28; "Vidarbha and the Traikūṭakas", *ibid.*, III, Part I, pp. 7-9), it is hazardous and unsafe to draw so very important a conclusion merely on the basis of the find of coins of a ruler. Our conclusion has been supported by P.L. Gupta ("Bearing of Dahigāon Hoard on Traikūṭaka History", *ibid.*, III, Part II, pp. 42-51).

96. Ajay Mitra Shastri, "Māṇḍhaḷ Plates of Pṛithivī Sheṇa II, Years 2 and 10", *EI*, XLI, pp. 159-80.

97. V.B. Kolte, "Mahurzari Plates of Pṛithivī Seṇa II", *ABORI*, LIII, pp. 183-94.

98. *CII*, V, pp. 80-81.

99. *Ibid.*, p. 81, line 33. F. Kielhorn (*EI*, IX, p. 271, fn. 15), who first edited the inscription, suggested rather doubtfully that *dvi* here was perhaps an error for *ni*. But Mirashi took it as final (*CII*, V, p. 81, line 33) as would follow from his removal of the question mark after *nī* put by Kielhorn.

100. Y.R. Gupte, "Riddhappur Plates of Bhavattavarman", *EI*, XIX, pp. 100-04. The king's name is spelt both as Bhavattavarman and Bhavadattavarman.

101. Actually from Rāmagiri-sthāna or the holy temple at Rāmagiri.

102. *CII*, V, p. 80.

103. Ajay Mitra Shastri, "Vākāṭaka Coins", *AV*, pp. 286-87; *supra*, pp. 138-39. The letters bear a close resemblance to those met with in his inscriptions. As per our present knowledge, Narendra Sena, father of Pṛithivī Sheṇa II, was the first Vākāṭaka king to have issued his own coins and it is but natural that his son and successor carried this tradition forward.

VI

Vatsagulma Branch

This branch of the Vākāṭakas came to be known for the first time in 1939 as a result of the discovery of the Wāshim plates of Vindhyaśakti II.[1] It is no doubt true that the names of some of the rulers of this branch were mentioned in the Ajantā Cave XVI inscription, but the decipherment of this inscription was till then in a state of utter confusion.[2] Thanks to the subsequent discovery of two more records, viz. Hisse-Borālā stone inscription dated in Śaka 380 during the reign of Deva Sena,[3] the Bīdar plates of Deva Sena[4] and the Thāḷner plates of Hari Sheṇa,[5] and the reference to a king named Sarva Sena in the Muḍigere plates of the Kadamba king Siṁhavarman,[6] our knowledge of the history of this branch is much more fuller than what it was some quarter century ago.

Sarva Sena I

The founder of this branch was Sarva Sena, son of Pravara Sena I of the undivided Vākāṭaka dynasty. In order to distinguish him from his later namesake we may designate him as Sarva Sena I. He is known to us from his son Vindhyaśakti II's Wāshim plates and other subsequent records of his descendants, though we have no record of his own. In keeping with the geographical closeness to the Kadambas with whom this branch had close contacts he also assumed the title *Dharma-mahārāja* which is not known to have been borne by any ruler of the other branch. As we have seen above, it is very likely that Sarva Sena (I) rose to power during the lifetime of his father Pravara Sena I himself, perhaps in the territory conquered by him during the period he was a prince and was acting on his behalf. So his accession may be dated tentatively around 325 AD. We have no means to determine the length of his reign, but assuming that he ruled for about three decades, the close of his rule can be dated in *c.* 355 AD. We have absolutely no knowledge about his political activities. The Ajantā inscription of

Varāhadeva no doubt avers that he had defeated all the armies (verse 7), but unfortunately no further details are given. It is likely, however, that he conquered the adjoining region of Khāndesh and Marāṭhwādā.

Where his capital was located, we cannot be certain. But in all probability it was, as in later times, at Vatsagulma, identified with modern Wāshim in the Akolā district. It was a place of great religious and cultural importance in ancient times and it became much more well-known due to its association with the Vākāṭakas. It was regarded as a sacred pilgrimage centre (*tīrtha*), and according to the later *Vatsagulma-māhātmya*, it came to be so called in consequence of the sage Vatsa making by his austerities the assemblage (*gulma*) of divinities come over there and settle in his hermitage. Vātsyāyana in his *Kāma-sūtra* (V. 5.3) refers to the people inhabiting Vatsagulma as Vātsagulmaka.[7] And Yaśodhara in his commentary (Jayaṁangalā) calls the country round the town Vatsagulmaka and tells us that two uterine princes of Dakshiṇāpatha named Vatsa and Gulma settled in the country which received their name.[8] Due to the literary taste and patronage of the Vākāṭakas it became a great literary centre, and the Prakrit literary style developed here came to be known as Vāchchhomī (Vātsagulmī) which received general approval.[9] The celebrated Sanskrit-Prakrit polymath Rājaśekhara had great fascination for this town and in his *Kāvya-mīmāṁsā* describes it as the pleasure resort of the god of love where the mythical poetry-man (*kāvya-purusha*) married the literary lore.[10] According to Rājaśekhara, it was included in Vidarbha (*Vidarbheshu Vatsagulmaṁ nāma nagaram*), while Vātsyāyana appears to distinguish the two.[11] Sarva Sena was a great Prakrit poet, and his *Hari-vijaya*, which is unfortunately no longer extant, elicited great admiration from celebrated literary critics. It is eulogised by Daṇḍin in his *Avanti-sundarī-kathā*, by Ānandavardhana in his *Dhvany-āloka*, and by Kuntaka in his *Vakroktijīvita* which compares its author to Kālidāsa.[12] While this work is lost, a few of his Prakrit *gāthās* have found a place in the celebrated *Gāhā-sattasaī*.[13]

Vindhyaśakti II

Sarva Sena was succeeded by his son Vindhyaśakti, who may be styled second king of this name to distinguish him from his homonymous great-grandfather, in c. 355 AD. As he issued his Wāshim charter[14] in his thirty-seventh year, he may be supposed to have ruled for some forty-five years and the end of his reign may be dated about 400 AD. Like his father Sarva Sena I, he adopted the title *Dharma-mahārāja* which is found in his Wāshim plates.[15] The inclusion of the

Marāṭhwāḍā region in his kingdom is suggested by his Wāshim plates which record his grant of a village situated in the Nāndīkaḍa (Nāndeḍ) region. We have not much information about his political activities. But in the Ajantā inscription of the time of Hari Sheṇa, where he is mentioned as Vindhya Sena,[16] reference is made to his victory over the lord of Kuntala,[17] which appears to have denoted northern Karnataka ruled at this time by the Kadambas of Vanavāsī.[18] This event marked the beginning of Vākāṭaka interference in the internal affairs of the Kadambas which grew later when the Kadamba kingdom was divided between two factions one of which sought the support of the Vākāṭakas of the Vatsagulma branch. It also probably led to the occupation of the Bīdar region during or prior to the time of Deva Sena as we shall see later. The period of his rule was also crucial from the point of view of gradual replacement of Prakrit by Sanskrit as the language of the charters in the Deccan. For his Wāshim grant is couched in mixed Sanskrit and Prakrit, the genealogical portion being in Sanskrit and the grant portion, which was meant not only for the donee who must have been well-versed in Sanskrit, but also for many others who could not follow Sanskrit, in Prakrit.[19] The same is true about some other early Pallava charters also. Hereafter Prakrit was completely substituted by Sanskrit in the official records as it had become the official language of the states.

Pravara Sena II

Around 400 AD Vindhyaśakti (or Vindhya Sena) II was succeeded by his son Pravara Sena who may be called Pravara Sena II with reference to Pravara Sena I who was the common ancestor of both the known branches of the dynasty. In the Ajantā inscription he is described in very vague terms as 'exalted by his excellent, powerful and liberal rule' (verse 9), while the recently discovered Bīdar plates of Deva Sena mention him with the title *Mahārāja* in the genealogical portion as a routine matter.[20] Either he had a very brief reign or got his son very late in his life as the Ajantā inscription informs us that his son who followed him on the throne was only eight at the time of his accession.[21] We may not be far wrong if we allot him a reign of twenty-five years.

Sarva Sena II

Pravara Sena II was succeeded in *c.* 425 AD by his eight-year old son whose name has been lost in the Ajantā inscription which merely tells us that he ruled well. But his name has recently come to light as a result of the discovery of the

Bīdar plates of his son Deva Sena[22] and the Thāḷner plates of his grandson Hari Sheṇa.[23] But these records do not supply us any information about his life and are content merely by naming him. But we get a very important information about one of his political activities from quite an unexpected source. The recently discovered Muḍigere (Terikere taluk, Chikmagalūr district, Karnataka) plates of the Kadamba king Siṁhavarman, son of Vishnuvarman, inform us that he was 'honoured by *Mahārāja* (king) Sarva Sena by coronation'.[24] In view of the fact that *sena*-ending names were during this period and in the Western Deccan are known to have been borne mainly by the Vākāṭakas, all of whom invariably had such names, it may be reasonably concluded that *Mahārāja* Sarva Sena must have been a monarch of this dynasty. In the Padmapura-Nandivardhana-Pravarapura branch there was no king of this name, while in the Vatsagulma branch there were two kings bearing this name. The founder of this branch was Sarva Sena I, but as he ruled from about 325-355 AD, he was too early to be identified with the homonymous king who could have interfered in the internal affairs of the Kadambas in favour of the breakaway Siṁhavarman who can by no stretch of imagination be placed that early. In view of this fact B.R. Gopal, who has included this record in his *Corpus of Kadamba Inscriptions*, was constrained to observe that 'there are chronological difficulties that come in the way of such an identification'.[26] As till recently no other king of this name was known, it was found difficult to equate him satisfactorily. But now we know from the Bīdar plates of Deva Sena and the Thāḷner charter of Hari Sheṇa that the great-grandson of Sarva Sena I, whose name was damaged and consequently lost in the Ajantā inscription of Hari Shena's time, was also Sarva Sena. As we have seen, he came to throne approximately in 425 AD. And as he was just eight at the time of his accession, he must have ruled for a long period. And for the next king Deva Sena we have, as we shall see presently, the date Śaka 380 or 458 AD, the rule of his father Sarva Sena II must have come to a close before this year. It must have been this Sarva Sena who helped the Kadamba king Siṁhavarman in securing the throne. However, the earliest date suggested for Siṁhavarman is *c.* 490 AD.[27] So there remains a gap of about thirty-five years between the latest date for Sarva Sena II and the earliest suggested date of the Kadamba Siṁhavarman. It must be remembered, however, that the chronology of the Kadambas still rests on very uncertain grounds and but for the general period of their rule there is absolutely no certainty regarding the dates of individual rulers as the Kadamba inscriptions are all dated only in the years of individual reigns as most of the

Vākāṭaka records are. And let us realise that this is the only known Sarva Sena who could be a contemporary or near contemporary of the Kadamba king Siṁhavarman and should consequently be identified with the Sarva Sena mentioned in his only known record. This would indeed involve antedating the commencement of the reign of Siṁhavarman by a little over three decades which should not be difficult in view of the purely tentative nature of the Kadamba chronology. In fact, this statement contained in the Muḍigera plates of Siṁhavarman furnishes a very crucial evidence for the fixation of the date of his accession in particular and the Kadamba chronology in general. The description that the Kadamba king felt honoured by being coronated at the hands of Sarva Sena is indicative of the high esteem in which the former held the latter. Properly interpreted, it would mean that Siṁhavarman regarded himself as a subordinate ally, if not vassal, of the Vākāṭaka king Sarva Sena II. This serves as a useful commentary on the Vākāṭaka-Kadamba relations, the former ruling over the Vidarbha and adjoining region of Maharashtra extending at times their sway over the adjoining region of Andhra Pradesh and Karnataka and the latter over Kuntala region of Karnataka with some of the rulers acting as subordinates.

Sarva Sena II thus appears to have been a very powerful ruler of the Vatsagulma branch who not only maintained the paternal inheritance intact but added substantially to his as well as his house's prestige by a successful interference in the affairs of the neighbouring Kadamba kingdom. As we shall see presently, it was taken to a logical conclusion during the next reign.

Deva Sena

Deva Sena succeeded his father Sarva Sena sometime before 458 AD, say around 455 AD. For his reign we have three records, viz. (1) a stone inscription put up by his officer Svāmilladeva at Hisse-Borālā,[28] (2) an incomplete copperplate charter now deposited in the India Office, London,[29] and (3) an iron replica of a copper-plate charter issued in his fifth regnal year found near Bīdar (Karnataka) and now deposited in the Birla Archaeological and Cultural Research Institute, Hyderabad.[30] Of these, the India Office plate purported to be issued from Vātsyagulma (same as Vatsagulma) records just a village-grant without adding much to our knowledge about Deva Sena or his family. The other two records are quite important in their own way and supply valuable information about his time. The Bīdar charter informs us that he assumed the title *Dharma-mahārāja.*[31] He finds mention in the Thāḷner plates of Hari Sheṇa also as his father and is styled merely as *mahārāja*,[32] while from the Ajantā (Cave XVI) and Ghaṭotkacha cave inscriptions of Hari Sheṇa's minister Varāhadeva we learn that his father Hastibhoja belonging to the well-known Brāhmaṇa family of Vallūra was his minister[33] to whom he is said to have left all the administrative botherations and himself indulged in the pursuits of pleasure.[34] This statement need not, however, be taken in a literal sense and is meant only to heighten the importance of the ministerial line to which he belonged.[35]

The Hisse-Borālā stone inscription, which records the excavation of a tank called Sudarśana by an officer (*ajñākara*) of Deva Sena, Svāmilladeva, is of utmost importance for it provides us with the date Saka 380[36] or 457-58 AD, which is the only definite date not only for Deva Sena and the Vatsagulma branch to which he belonged but for the Vākāṭakas as a whole. Had the corresponding regnal year also been specified, it would have enabled us to fix the date of his accession precisely. As it is, we now know that this year fell in Deva Sena's time.

The Bīdar plates aim at recording Deva Sena's grant of the village Velpakoṇḍa to one Raddochha, a scholar of the four Vedas (*chātuvejja=chāturvidya*), for the purpose of sacrificial offerings. This grant was executed by Sāmiladedeva, apparently the same as Svāmilladeva known from the previous record, and concludes with the mention of the fifth year of his reign which must have fallen much prior to Śaka 380. The provenance of this record, if reported correctly, is of utmost historical value for historical purposes. If the plates originally hail from the Bīdar region, they would indicate the extension of the dominions of the Vatsagulma branch into northern Karnataka. The place names, especially the name of the donated village, also seem to strengthen this surmise, for koṇḍa-ending place-names are common in the Andhra-Karnataka region. At the first sight this conjecture may look somewhat startling, but in reality there is nothing improbable about it. For we already know that the Nāndeḍ (Nāndīkaḍa) region formed part of its territory as early as the reign of Vindhyaśakti II who is further said in the Ajantā inscription to have conquered Kuntala or northern Karnataka. We have already seen from the Muḍigere grant of the Kadamba king Siṁhavarman that he was installed on the throne by Sarvasena-mahārāja who, as we have seen, was none other than Deva Sena's homonymous father. One should not be surprised if this interference in the internal affairs of the Kadambas resulted in a military occupation of at least a part of northern Karnataka. And the Bīdar charter should leave absolutely no doubt regarding the annexation of the region round

Bīdar and other intervening areas of Andhra Pradesh by the fifth year of Deva Sena's reign, if not earlier, either in his own reign or that of his father. How long this occupation lasted is not ascertainable in the present state of inadequate information. This was indeed a very significant success of which the Vatsagulma branch could be justly proud.

Deva Sena was a contemporary of Narendra Sena of the other branch of the dynasty. As we have seen above, the latter had succeeded, despite opposition, in securing the throne for the time being but was ultimately divested of a substantial part of his inherited kingdom by his distant relations. It was evidently Deva Sena who was responsible for this catastrophe from which that branch could recover only at the commencement of the next reign. It is possible that his relations with the Kadambas and his cousin in the other branch of the dynasty were not unrelated altogether. We know that Narendra Sena had married a Kadamba princess who might have been either a daughter or granddaughter of Kākutsthavarman which might have annoyed Deva Sena who avenged it by occupying a substantial part of his territory. The exact course of events can be ascertained only when some fresh evidence comes to light. It was probably with a view to enlist support against Narendra Sena and the Kadambas that Deva Sena married his daughter to the most powerful Vishṇukuṇḍin king Mādhavavarman II Janāśraya, whose son Vikramendravarman I is said to have adorned the twin families of the Vishṇukuṇḍins and the Vākāṭakas by his birth. This relationship appears to have played an important role after the Vākāṭaka power ceased to exist.

The excavation of the Sudarśana lake during his reign is of great importance in-as-much as it reveals the interest the Vākāṭakas took in the welfare of their subjects and providing water for drinking and irrigation. The name reminds one of the well-known Sudarśana lake originally excavated during the reign and at the orders of Chandragupta Maurya and enlarged and beautified with conduits at the orders of his grandson Aśoka Maurya. It had been burst due to a very great storm during the reign of the Kārdamaka Mahākshatrapa Rudradāman I in 150 AD and was restored, enlarged and strengthened by him at huge expense.[37] Later again a great breach occurred in the fifth century AD during the Gupta emperor Skanda Gupta's reign and was restored by him as we learn from the Jūnāgaḍh inscription of his reign.[38] The name Sudarśana became very popular for lakes in the northern Deccan, and a lake excavated to commemorate Prabhāvatī Guptā, the chief queen of Rudra Sena II of the other Vākāṭaka branch, was also designated Sudarśana as we learn from the Kevala-Narasiṁha temple inscription at Rāmṭek.[39] Obviously Ārya-Svāmilladeva, who was responsible for the excavation of the lake recorded in the Hisse-Borālā inscription, hailed from the Saurāshṭra region where the original lake was situated. He employed the Śaka era for indicating the date of this record as the same was prevalent in his original home. Let us remember that this alone of the fairly numerous Vākāṭaka records is dated in the Śaka era, all the rest being dated with reference to the years of the reigns of individual rulers. The stone-slab bearing this inscription was found in the midst of what may be regarded as the remnants of the ancient lake.

Hari Sheṇa

Deva Sena closed his reign about 480 AD to be succeeded by his son Hari Sheṇa for whose reign we have as many as four inscriptions, the largest number for any member of this branch of the dynasty. One of them is a copperplate charter of his own and the rest in the caves at Ajantā (Caves XVI and XVII) and nearby Ghaṭotkacha. The only official charter is represented by his recently discovered Thāḷner (ancient Sthālakanagara, Dhule district) plates issued in the third year of his reign.[40] Of the remaining records, those in Cave XVI at Ajantā[41] and nearby Ghaṭokhacha cave[42] belong to his minister Varāhadeva, the last known member of the Brāhmaṇa family of Vallūra, and the third appears to belong to a vassal of Hari Sheṇa and is engraved in Cave XVII at Ajantā.[43] Thanks to these records, we have a good deal of information about the reign of this last known member of the Vatsagulma branch.

As the Thāḷner grant does not use the title *Dharma-mahārāja* for Hari Sheṇa, he evidently did not assume this title as some of his predecessors had done. Gomikarāja, with whose permission (*Gomikarāj-ānujñātam*) the grant is said to have been made, was evidently an elderly member of the family.[44] There is nothing to substantiate the suggestion that Hari Sheṇa had just conquered the Dhuḷe region after a memorable victory at Sthālakanagara (modern Thāḷner) and permitted the defeated ruler Gomika to continue to rule over this territory as his feudatory, and formally obtained the defeated and now-turned-feudatory ruler's permission to make this grant.[45] In fact, it need not be treated as a fresh conquest as it already appears to have formed part of the territory inherited by him. There is also nothing to show that it was preceded by the annexation of the Jaḷgāon region which too must have been included in his inherited kingdom.

Hari Sheṇa had a minister named Varāhadeva, son of Deva Sena's minister

Hastibhoja, who got cave no. XVI at Ajantā and the Ghaṭotkacha cave at nearby Gulwāḍa excavated and decorated with sculptures and paintings and whose records have been found in these caves. While the Ghaṭotkacha cave inscription furnishes an account of his own line from its inception and states that his father was a minister of Devarāja, the same as Deva Sena and he himself was a minister of Hari Sheṇa, the Ajantā inscription has turned out to be very important for the history of the Vatsagulma branch for it narrates its vicissitudes from the very beginning including the founder's two predecessors, viz. Vindhyaśakti I and Pravara Sena I, though due to mutilation at several places some of the vital information is lost. With reference to Hari Sheṇa it (verse 18) states that he had conquered Kuntala, Avanti, Kaliṅga, Kosala, Trikūṭa, Lāṭa and Andhra. Most probably Aparānta was also included in the list of the defeated countries.[46] Of these, Kuntala was at this time ruled by the Kadambas in whose internal affairs Sarva Sena had already intervened and Deva Sena had occupied a portion of northern Karnataka. It is likely that Hari Sheṇa assisted his father in this conquest. It must have been so in a few other cases as well though the *praśasti* is naturally reticent on this point. The Avanti region had slipped away from the Gupta hold and the Aulikaras of Daśapura, who were earlier vassals of the Guptas, had assumed full sovereignty in Avanti after Budha Gupta and brought the Maitrakas of Valabhi under their suzerainty.[47] It is possible, however, that Hari Sheṇa raided this region.[48] Kalinga now roughly connoted the area covered by the Purī-Ganjām region of Orissa and the Vishākhapaṭnam-Śrīkākulam region of Andhra Pradesh. Mirashi thinks that Hari Sheṇa had some role to play in the emergence of the Gaṅgas in Kaliṅga whose era started in 498 AD. Kosalā covered the Chhattīsgaḍh region of Madhya Pradesh, and it is possible that he raided it during the rule of the Śarabhapurīya upstart Śarabha. Trikūṭa obviously refers to the Traikūṭaka kingdom in North Koṅkaṇa, and the last known Traikūṭaka king Vyāghra Sena ruled up to 492 AD.[49] It is not unlikely that Hari Sheṇa took advantage of uncertain political conditions and fished in troubled waters there. Lāṭa is the ancient name of the Navsārī-Bharuch region of Gujarat, and it is possible that from the Khandesh region of Maharashtra which was already in his control he may have made a victorious march to it. As for Andhra, his brother-in-law Vishṇukuṇḍin king Mādhavavarman II Janāśraya was on the throne since at least 470-71 or 478-79 AD and continued far beyond his own reign[50] and also claims to have gone in course of his victorious expedition up the river Revā (Narmadā) and to have been lord of the mountains Trikūṭa and Malaya. It is supposed by some that

Hari Sheṇa's invasion in Andhra brought about a political revolution by putting an end to the rule of the Śālaṅkāyanas and installing Vishṇukuṇḍin king Mādhavavarman instead. This is just impossible in view of the facts noticed above, especially the fact that Vishṇukuṇḍins had come to power about the beginning of the fifth century AD.[51] This single example should suffice to militate against taking these claims at their face value. It is possible that he carried out hurried raids in some of these territories which the poet turned into full-fledged conquests and added to them some other regions where his relations were ruling or with which he had nothing to do militarily. It would therefore be wrong to assert merely on the basis of an otherwise unsubstantiated statement of a court-poet that 'Hari Sheṇa's supremacy was recognised throughout the Deccan extending from Mālwā in the north to Kuntala in the south, and from the Arabian Sea in the west to the Bay of Bengal in the east'[52] or to assert that 'he was the greatest ruler in the world'[53] in the late fifth century AD. What we can assert more reasonably is that he brought the process initiated by his father to a logical conclusion by establishing his authority over the territory of the other branch of the Vākāṭakas either by overthrowing Pṛithivī Sheṇa II, its last known member, or his successor, if any, or automatically without much resistance due to the failure of an heir. We can also conclude justifiably that for a time, howsoever short it may have been, he was a king who commanded a very high esteem among his contemporaries due as much to his great military strength as to his human qualities. Hari Sheṇa was a great patron of art, and a number of Buddhist caves at Ajantā were excavated and decked with sculptured figures and paintings by his minister Varāhadeva and his feudatory (name lost), perhaps of that region, evidently encouraged spiritually and materially by their enlightened master.[54] It is also possible that Hari Sheṇa had strong leanings towards Buddhism even though his only known charter registers village-grant to a few Brāhmaṇas.

Hari Sheṇa was the last known member of the Vatsagulma branch of the Vākāṭakas even as Pṛithivī Sheṇa II was of the other branch and closed his reign around 510 AD.[55] Both the branches thus came to an end within a few years of one another.

Notes and References

1. V.V. Mirashi and D.B. Mahajan, "Bāsim Plates of Vindhyaśakti II", *EI*, XXVI, pp. 137-55.
2. *CII*, V, pp. 103-11.
3. For references and discussion, are *supra*, pp. 106-07.

4. P.V. Parabrahma Sastry, "Hyderābād Plates of Vākāṭaka Devasena, Year 5", *JESI*, XIII, pp. 71-75 (for edition); Ajay Mitra Shastri, *EHDPP*, pp. 71-74; *AV*, pp. 248-51; *supra*, pp. 107-11 (for discussion). The editor in *JESI* refers to it as 'Hyderābād plates' as the plates are now deposited in the Birla Archaeological and Cultural Research Institute at Hyderabad where the record was reportedly brought from nearby Bīdar.
5. V.V. Mirashi, *Indological Research Papers*, I, pp. 78-87; Ajay Mitra Shastri, "Thāḷner Plates of Harishena: A Re-Appraisal", *JESI*, XI, pp. 15-20; *AV*, pp. 251-53; *supra*, pp. 111-14.
6. B.R. Gopal, *Corpus of Kadamba Inscriptions*, I, p. 145; Ajay Mitra Shastri, "The Muḍigere Plates of Siṁhavarman and Kadamba-Vakataka Relations", *Indian Archaeological Heritage: K.V. Soundarajan Felicitation Volume*, pp. 317-19; *infra*, pp. 228-32.
7. With Jaya-maṅgalā commentary of Yáśodhara, Kashi Sanskrit Series, No. 29, Varanasi, 1929, p. 261.
8. *Dakshiṇāpathe saudaryau rāja-putrau Vatsa-Gulmau tābhyām-adhyāsito des'o Vatsagulmaka iti pratītaḥ. Ibid.*
9. Rājaśekhara in his Prakrit play *Karpūra-mañjarī*, I.1.
10. *Kāvya-mīmāṁsā*, eds., C.D. Dalal and R.A. Sastry, p. 10.
11. Vātsyāyana describes sexual practices of Vatsagulma (V. 5. 33) and Vidarbha (V.5.34), while Rājaśekhara clearly states that Vatsagulma was situated in Vidarbha. So we can conclude that Rājaśekhara has used the name Vidarbha in a wider sense while Vatsyayana has employed it in a very narrow sense.
12. For references, see V.V. Mirashi, *Studies in Indology*, 1, 2nd. ed., pp. 114-19.
13. *Ibid.*, p. 119
14. *CII*, V, pp. 96-97.
15. *Ibid.*, p. 96, line 4.
16. *Ibid.*, V, pp. 108, verse 8. D.C. Sircar (*HCIP*, III: *CA*, p. 185), however, regards this reading (or rather correction of the earlier reading) as 'somewhat doubtful'. He feels that if the old reading Pṛithivī-Sheṇa is accepted, this Pṛithivī Sheṇa may be regarded as a brother of Vindhyaśakti II.
17. *CII*, V, p. 108, verse 8.
18. V.V. Mirashi (*ibid.*, V, pp. xxix-xxx; *CHI*, III, Part I, p. 143; *vide* also *Studies in Indology*, I, pp. 185-205) strongly advocates that by Kuntala was meant the southern Maratha country with Mānapura founded by the early Rāshṭrakūṭa king Mānānka and named after himself as the capital. The dynasty founded by Mānāṅka ruled over Kuntala and Mānāṅka himself was the Kuntala king who came into conflict with Vindhyaśakti II. And as Mānānka also claims to have defeated the Vidarbha king, he concludes that none of them achieved a decisive success. However, there is at present nothing to show that southern Maharashtra was known as Kuntala. The expression *Kuntalānāṁ praśāsitā* occurring in Avidheya's Pāṇḍaraṅgapallī grant with reference to Mānāṅka should, like the earlier description in the same stanza, be taken to mean 'the chastiser of the Kuntalas' as suggested by D.C. Sircar (*HCIP*, III : *CA*, p. 200) and not 'the ruler of the Kuntala country' as held by V.V. Mirashi (*Studies in Indology*, IV, p.

126). For, there was no necessity for a ruler, especially in the same stanza which refers to his successes against his enemies, to refer to the country which happened to be his home kingdom. This dynasty actually ruled over the country of Māṇadeśa comprising the Sātārā-Sholāpur tract of Maharashtra. As against this, some of the rulers of North Karnataka are clearly styled as rulers or lords of Kuntala in inscriptions.

19. *CII*, V, pp. 96-98. Lines 1-4 completely and line 5 partly are in Sanskrit while the rest of the charter is in Prakrit.
20. *JESI*, XIII, p. 74, line 7.
21. The former interpretation is very popular among historians all of whom have drawn such a conclusion from the statement in the Ajantā inscription that his son who succeeded him was eight when he came to power.
22. *JESI*, XIII, p. 74, line 8.
23. V.V. Mirashi, *Indological Research Papers*, I, p. 86, line 7.
24. *Tad=anu Sarvvasena-mahārājena mūrddh-ābhisheken-ābhyarchchitaḥ*, B.R. Gopal, *Corpus of Kadamba Inscriptions*, I, p. 141, line 13.
25. In fact, this name is not known in any other dynasty over the entire Indian subcontinent during the period in question.
26. *Ibid.*, p. 140.
27. *Ibid.*, Preface, p. xxx. For a discussion of the significance of this record, see *infea*, pp. 228-32.
28. For its contents, *vide supra*, pp. 106-07.
29. *CII*, V, p. 102.
30. *JESI*, XIII, pp. 73-75; AV, pp. 240-51; *supra*, pp. 107-11.
31. *JESI*, XIII, p. 74, line 8.
32. *Indological Research Papers*, I, p. 86, lines 7-8.
33. *CII*, V, p. 108, verse 12 (Ajantā); p. 116, verse 10 (Ghatotkacha). The latter inscription refers to Deva Sena also as Devarāja (*ibid.*, p. 119, verse 13).
34. *Ibid.*, p. 108, verse 16 (Ajantā inscription).
35. Hastibhoja is the first member of the family to be specifically brought into connection with the Vākāṭakas of the Vatsagulma branch. Whether his ancestors Yajñapati, Deva, Soma, Ravi, Pravara, Śrīrāma and Kīrti also were connected with the Vākāṭakas is something that cannot be ascertained in the present state of our knowledge. *Vide supra*, pp. 44-46.
36. Some astronomical details of this date are also mentioned which it is difficult to explain satisfactorily in the present damaged state of the record and have been sought to be explained variously.
37. Jūnāgadh inscription of Rudradāman I, D.C. Sircar, *Select Inscriptions*, I, pp. 175-80.
38. *Ibid.*, pp. 308-16.
39. See our discussion on this inscription, *AV*, pp. 253-57; *supra*, pp. 125-35.
40. V.V. Mirashi, *Indological Research Papers*, I, pp. 78-87; Ajay Mitra Shastri, "Thāḷner

Plates of Vākāṭaka Hari Sheṇa : A Re-Appraisal'', *JESI*, XI, pp. 15-20; *supra*, pp. 111-14

41. *CII*, pp. 103-11.
42. *Ibid.*, pp. 112-19.
43. *Ibid.*, pp. 120-29.
44. Mirashi regards him as the ruler of Sthālakangara defeated by Hari Sheṇa. See *Indological Research Papers*, I, pp. 79 and 85. But the wording of the inscription (*Gomikarājānujñatam*) does not support his contention as a victor would never seek the consent of the defeated enemy to make a grant in his kingdom. The name Gomikaraja is comparable to Pṛithivīrāja, Narindarāja and Devarāja which were the names of the members of the Vākāṭaka line.
45. See *JESI*, XI, pp. 17-18, for a detailed discussion.
46. Shobhana Gokhale, ''Epigraphical Evidence on Hari Sheṇa's Conquest from Kānheri'', *AV*, pp. 277-78.
47. Ajay Mitra Shastri, ''Overlord' of the Early Maitrakas", *JESI*, XVI, pp. 8-13.
48. Some scholars are of the opinion that as Hari Sheṇa had taken control of the territory of the Nandivardhana branch of the Vākāṭakas, it was easy for him to claim to have conquered Avanti as Narendra Sena of that branch had already conquered the Māḷavas. This, however, is simply ridiculous even if Narendra Sena's claim is taken at its face value because subjugation of new territory should not lead by itself to claim the achievements of its previous rulers.
49. V.V. Mirashi, *Inscriptions of the Kalachuri-Chedi Era*, I, p. xliii.
50. Up to about 518 AD. See *EHDPP*, pp. 128-29.
51. *Ibid.*, p. 129.
52. V.V. Mirashi in *CHI*, III, Part I, p. 144. See also *CII*, V, p. xxxi. *Vide* for a somewhat exaggerated account, *Vākāṭaka Nṛipatī āṇi tyāñchā Kāla*, p. 59.
53. Walter M. Spink, ''The Achievements of Ajantā'', *AV*, p. 117.
54. Caves XVI, XVII and XIX definitely belonged to his reign. According to the shorter chronology advocated by Spink, the entire Mahāyāna phase at Ajantā belonged to his reign.
55. This, with minor variations (500 to 510 AD), is the date commonly accepted by historians. Spink, however, dates it to 486 AD. See *AV*, p. 179.

VII

The End

It is impossible at present to ascertain the factors responsible for the abrupt end of the Vākāṭakas. Mark Collins felt that the Viśruta-charita (Uchchhvasa VIII) of Daṇḍin's *Daśa-kumāra-charita* contained the actual account of the political condition of Vidarbha,[1] and V.V. Mirashi concluded that it actually forms a running commentary on the fall of the Vākāṭakas following Hari Sheṇa's demise and tried to reconstruct the course of events related to it.[2] And this view has since been followed generally.[3] We are, however, inclined to reject this theory on the ground that the last Uchchhvāsa alone should not be singled out in distinction to the earlier sections describing the miraculous successes of the other *kumāras* who followed the mythical Rājavāhana, son of the equally mythical deposed king Rājahaṁsa of Magadha. In our opinion the story given in this section is as much a creation of Daṇḍin as other stories, and therefore is of no help at all in reconstructing the chain of events leading to the fall of the Vākāṭakas. We must therefore explain it otherwise with the help of available sources.

As we have seen above, Deva Sena had married one of his daughters (or the daughter) to the ambitious Vishṇukuṇḍin king Mādhavavarman II Janāśraya who ruled till about 518 AD. One of his inscriptions has been reported from Khānāpur,[4] and Vishṇukuṇḍin coins have been reported in numbers all over Maharashtra including territories that were under the Vākāṭakas.[5] It would therefore follow that the Vishṇukuṇḍins possibly regarded themselves as heirs to the Vākāṭaka kingdom which they occupied and held for some time.[6]

Nalas, who had created trouble to the Nandivardhana branch were also very powerful and continued so till at least the time of the Badāmī Chālukya king Kīrtivarman I (566-67 to 597-98 AD) who is described as a night of destruction (*kāla-rātri*) to, *inter alia*, the Nalas.[7] It is very likely that they occupied the Vākāṭaka kingdom or a large part thereof.

The Kadambas of Kuntala also, as we have seen, were often on hostile terms with the Vākāṭakas, and Hari Sheṇa himself had annoyed them by invading it. That they continued to be a power to reckon with is clear from the Aihoḷe inscription of Pulakeśin II which refers to his father, Kīrtivarman I, as a night of destruction to them.[8] It is not impossible that they too took advantage of the weakness of Hari Sheṇa's possible successors or failure of heirs and occupied some part of at least the territory of the Vatsagulma branch.

We have some evidence to show that at least parts of the territory under the two branches of the Vākāṭakas were occupied after them by the Muṇḍaputra and Kumbhakarṇa chiefs. The Malhārā (Achalpur tahsil, Āmrawati district) charters of the Muṇḍaputra king Ādityarāja have brought to light a Brāhmaṇa family the last three members whereof viz. Rāshṭra-mahārāja, Rājakula-mahārāja and Ādityarāja were powerful enough to celebrate their successes by observing a (or some) horse-sacrifice (sacrifices). These plates are not dated in any era but may, on some strong considerations, be placed in the post-Vākāṭaka period.[9] It is likely that the earlier members of the family were subordinates of the Vākāṭakas after whose fall they assumed regal power and occupied a large part of the territory under the Padmapura-Nandivardhana-Pravarapura branch. Five generations of the Kumbhakarṇa family have been brought to light by the Thāḷner plates of its last known member Bhānu Sheṇa who, like the preceding three members, is styled *maharaja*. Jayaraja, the first member of the dynasty is styled first *mahārāja* (*ādi-mahārāja*) and appears to have come to power after the end of the Vākāṭaka rule in Khāndesh region and the family was evidently uprooted by the Chālukyas of Badamī.[10] Finally, around the middle of the sixth century AD the territory of the Padmapura-Nandivardhana-Pravarapura branch appears to have been brought under his control by the first known early Kalachuri king of Māhishmatī, Kṛishṇaraja, and governed through his vassals. This is indicated by the Nagardhan plate of Svāmirāja dated Kalachuri-Chedi year 322 corresponding to 573 AD.[11] Whether they supplanted the Muṇḍaputra rule altogether or left some part of the erstwhile Vākāṭaka territory under them is not possible to ascertain at present. Coins of Kalachuri Kṛishṇrāja, called by the contemporaries as *Kṛishṇāraja-rūpaka* have also been reported from all parts of the territory of this branch of the Vākāṭakas.

Such tragic was the end of the glorious Vākāṭaka kingdom founded by Vindhyaśakti I[12] and nourished by a chain of able successors.

Notes and References

1. *Geographical Data of the Raghuvaṁśa and the Daśakumāracharita,* p. 21.
2. *Studies in Indology,* I, pp. 182-94; *CII,* V, pp. xxxii-xxxiii; *CHI,* III, Part I, p. 146.
3. Walter M. Spink, *AV,* pp. 183-84.
4. V.V. Mirashi and Y.R. Gupte, "Khānāpur Plates of Mādhavavarman", *EI,* XXVII, pp. 312-18.
5. Their attribution to the Vishṇukuṇḍins has been recently doubted but no other dependable attribution has been yet suggested.
6. *EHDPP,* pp. 132-37.
7. Aihole inscription of Pulakeśin II, D.C. Sircar, *Select Inscriptions bearing on Indian History and Civilization,* II, Motilal Banarsidass, Delhi, 1983, p. 445, verse 9.
8. *Ibid.*
9. Ajay Mitra Shastri, "The Malhārā Plates of Ādityarāja: A Re-appraisal", *JESI,* IV, pp. 30-41; "The Date of the Malhārā Plates of Ādityarāja", *ibid.,* VII, pp. 69-75.
10. Ajay Mitra Shastri, "A Note on the Thāḷner Plates of Bhānu Shena", *ibid.,* XII, pp. 53-58.
11. V.V. Mirashi, *Inscriptions of the Kalachuri-Chedi Era, CII,* IV, Part II, pp. 611-17.
12. Vindhyaśakti I is known from the Purnāṇas. Curiously enough, he is not remembered by the members of what is generally, though perhaps erroneously, regarded as the senior or main branch of the dynasty. It is only the inscriptions of Deva Sena and his son Hari Sheṇa of the Vatsagulma branch that remember him gratefully and call him *ādi-rāja* or the first king of the Vākāṭakas.

APPENDIX I

Genealogy and Chronology of the Vākāṭakas

Vindhyaśakti I
(*c.* 250-275 AD)
1
Pravīra *alias* Pravara Sena I
(*c.* 275-335 AD)
1

Gautamīputra I			Sarva Sena I
1			(*c.* 325-355 AD)
			1
Rudra Sena I			Vindhyaśakti II *alias* Vindhya Sena
(*c.* 335-355 AD)			(*c.* 355-400 AD)
1			1
Pṛithivī Sheṇa I			Pravara Sena II
(*c.* 355-385 AD)			(*c.* 400-425 AD)
1			1
Rudra Sena II			Sarva Sena II
(*c.* 385-395 AD)			(*c.* 425-455 AD)
1			1
(*Yuvarāja*) Divākara Sena	Dāmodara Sena	Pravara Sena II	Deva Sena
(*c.* 395-410 AD)	(*c.* 410-420 AD)	(*c.* 420-455 AD)	(*c.* 455-480 AD)
		1	1
		Narendra Sena	Hari Sheṇa
		(*c.* 455-480 AD)	(*c.* 480-510 AD)
		1	
		Pṛithivī Sheṇa II	
		(*c.* 480-500/505 AD)	

APPENDIX II

Capitals of the Vākāṭakas

The Vākāṭakas played a pivotal role in the politico-cultural history of the Deccan and Central India in particular and of India as a whole in general. They were a political power in importance next only to the Imperial Guptas from about mid-third century AD to about the close of the fifth century and had matrimonial relations with the Imperial Guptas, the Kadambas of Vanavāsī (Karnataka) and the Vishṇukuṇḍins of Andhra Pradesh, which may be taken as a measure of the high esteem and prestige enjoyed by them among their contemporaries. Under them literary and visual arts witnessed a great efflorescence and some of the Vākāṭaka monarchs themselves enjoyed a high reputation as Prakrit poets. However, the scarcity of source material makes a dependable reconstruction of their annals very difficult with the result that there are great controversies even about some of the vital problems concerning them.[1] Here it is proposed to discuss and give some finality to the question of their capitals. This is all the more necessary as they are known to have frequently shifted their capital from one place to another due to geopolitical reasons, and not just out of personal whims of the rulers. It is intended to remove some of the prevailing misconceptions basing on the reinterpretation of the extant evidence as well as discovery of fresh data.

Let us begin with the beginning. The dynastic sections of the Purāṇas[2] refer to the first two members of the family by name viz. Vindhyaśakti (I) and Pravīra who, as we know from inscriptions, was known more popularly as Pravara Sena (I). We are told that the latter ruled from the city of Kāñchanakā for six decades:

Vindhyaśakti-sutaś=ch-āpi Pravīro nāme vīryavān
bhokshvate cha samāḥ shashṭiṁ purīm Kāñchanakāṁ cha vai.[3]

Although in view of the clear wording of the passage there should be absolutely no doubt that the Purāṇas refer to Kāñchanakā alone as the capital of Pravīra, scholars like K.P. Jayaswal[4] followed by V.V. Mirashi[5] find it difficult to explain the occurrence of the particle *cha,* 'and', after Kāñchanakā and try to obviate this problem by amending the reading which they propose to split into *Purikāṁ Chanukām cha vai* and hold that in this passage we have actually an allusion to the two cities named Purikā and Chanakā both of which served as the two capitals of the Vākāṭakas during the reign of their second ruler Pravīra or Pravara Sena I. However, a close examination shows that there is not much strength in their arguments and that there is in reality mention of only one capital of Pravīra in this passage. First, even without amending the reading in the suggested manner it is possible to get what they want, for *Purī* by itself can denote the city of Purikā and there is therefore absolutely no necessity to amend and split the reading as surmised by these two historians. Secondly, particles like *hi, tu, cha* and *vai* are more often than not employed by the Purāṇa compilers merely due to metrical exigencies as they were not always skilled poets, and if everywhere we were to look for their meaning and interpret the Purāṇic statements, we shall be landing ourselves in a hopeless situation. Not to look for such instances in other places, in the instant case itself we have another *cha* following *bhokshyate* and a *vai* at the end which it would be difficult to explain except if we regard them as used as *pāda-pūraṇa.* Thirdly, if this were the intended reading, we should have expected to get at least a semblance of it in at least some manuscripts. But not one manuscript consulted by Pargiter gives this reading.[6] Thus, there should be no doubt whatever that the Purāṇa compilers had only the city of Kāñchanakā as the capital of Pravīra in their mind.

Where was this Kāñchanakā situated? To be able to answer this question one has to go into the question of the original centre of the Vākāṭaka power. The theory of southern origin doubtfully floated by A.S. Altekar[7] and turned into a full-fledged theory by V.V. Mirashi[8] has not much to commend itself as it has no real ground to stand upon.[9] On the other hand, the unimpeachable Purāṇic evidence clearly indicates that the original scene of the dynastic activities lay in the Vindhyan region of Madhya Pradesh. The founder of the dynasty, viz. Vindhyaśakti (I), had a meaningful name, signifying one whose strength lay in the Vindhyas.[10] Then, after referring to Pravīra and his four sons the Purāṇic text calls them Vindhyaka which is very significant meaning as it does 'belonging to the Vindhyas'.[11] The Purāṇas refer to the Vākāṭaka kings Vindhyaśakti, his son

Pravīra and the latter's four sons who rose to power in the list of kings 'belonging to various regions', and not of Vidiśā as held by Pargiter[12] and others who follow his interpretation. Here in the case of the Vākāṭakas apparently the Vindhyan region was meant. This region continued under the northern branch of the dynasty till at least the time of Pṛithivī Sheṇa I. That the *Purāṇakāras* show awareness of the Vākāṭaka hold over this region at least till the time of Rudra Sena I was first pointed out by us.[13] During the reign of Pravara Sena himself informally and after his death formally the dynastic kingdom was split into four parts as indicated by the Purāṇic statement that his four sons became kings. But in the case of the northern branch it was not son but grandson that was intended actually. For Pravara Sena's son Gautamīputra,[14] as admitted by all, passed away a minor and therefore Pravara Sena was succeeded by his grandson Rudra Sena I. What appears to have been the fact looks like this during his own long life time.[15] He divided at least informally his kingdom into four parts under his four sons; he gave the northern part to his son Gautamīputra and ruled it on his behalf as he was a minor; but he could not ascend the throne as he passed away prematurely during his own lifetime and it is possible that he had to carry on administration of the kingdom on behalf of his grandson Rudra Sena (I) also for some time before he himself ascended the throne. Thus in the case of this branch of the dynasty the Purāṇas could not have referred to his son Gautamīputra who never came to the throne, but only to his grandson Rudra Sena I. It is also possible that the Purāṇas were aware of the end of his reign though of this we have as of now no evidence. Thus, it is Vindhyaśakti, his son Pravara Sena and his grandson Rudra Sena who are described as Vindhyakas by the *Purāṇakāras*. Now, there is considerable uncertainty regarding the location of the Vindhya vis-a-vis the Ṛikshavat mountain. There is no doubt that the river Narmadā formed the dividing line between them; but the consensus ends here. Some scholars hold that the mountain ranges to the north of this river were known as Ṛikshavat and those to its south were called Vindhya. But as we have shown elsewhere,[16] there is no doubt that the actual position was just the reverse, viz. the Vindhya ranges lie to the north of the Narmadā. In fact, we have to look for the Vindhyan region in the former state of Vindhya Pradesh, now included in Madhya Pradesh, where there are still quite a few localities named after the Vindhyas. The early Vākāṭaka capital Kāñchanakā has therefore to be located in this region. And K.P. Jayaswal, who as we have seen above, proposed to split the relevant Purāṇic expression into Purikā and Chanakā, suggested the latter's equation with the modern village of Nachnā now included in the Pannā district of Madhya Pradesh.[17] But as we have seen above, the correct reading is Kāñchanakā, not Chanakā. We are firmly convinced that the identification proposed by Jayaswal is correct even though we do not agree with his emendation and interpretation of the Purāṇic passage. Then again, if we were to accept Jayaswal's view followed by Mirashi that the real name of the city was actually Chanakā, it would be difficult, nay impossible, to explain the initial *akshara na* of the name Nachnā. We feel that both the *kā*-s, initial and concluding, got dropped in course of time and the remainder, *ñchana,* got transformed into Nachnā. The identification is strengthened by the antiquity and importance of the locality during those days as indicated by the presence of an early Gupta-Vākāṭaka temple and a couple of inscriptions of one Vyāghradeva, described as meditating upon the feet of the Vākāṭaka king Pṛithivī Sheṇa who, we are convinced, must be identified with the first king of the name in the northern branch of the dynasty.[18] It meets all the requirements of the metropolis of a Vindhyan kingdom and apparently continued under the northern offshoot of the Vākāṭakas till at least the early years of the reign of Pṛithvī Sheṇa I who happened to be the last known Vākāṭaka king to hold the Vindhyan region of northern India under his control.

The southern expansion of the Vākāṭakas had commenced as early as the later part of the reign of Pravara Sena I, viz. end-third century AD.[19] The pressure of the Guptas from the North was growing and during the long reign of the ambitious Samudra Gupta the petty Gupta kingdom had turned into an empire. And his Vākāṭaka contemporaries Rudra Sena I and Pṛithivī Sheṇa I found it difficult to maintain their hold over the Vindhyan region of Bundelkhaṇḍ and had to abandon their capital at Nachnā along with their hold over the Bundelkhaṇḍ region. Even otherwise its location at the northern end and the full-grown Gupta pressure made it an inconvenient and unsafe place for the capital of a kingdom the major part of which lay to the south of the river Narmadā. In fact, it is difficult to explain as to why the shifting to a more convenient location was delayed so much. The reason simply is that no urgency was felt so long as there was no pressure from the Guptas. But now that the kingdom of the northern branch of the dynasty was confined to the south of the Narmadā the necessity of shifting it to a suitable location was urgently realised. And the choice appears to have fallen on a place called Padmapura. Pṛithivī Sheṇa I's son and successor Rudra Sena II definitely attached much importance to this city. His recently discovered Māṇḍhaḷ plates of his fifth regnal year record the grant of a few villages included in the *pūrva-mārga* of Padmapura.[20] The word *mārga* here denotes an administrative division, in this case named after Padmapura which must have been an important locality. That Padmapura continued to enjoy importance even after the capital had been shifted to other places (Nandivardhana and Pravarapura) is apparent from the Māsod plates of Pravara Sena II which refer to a land-grant in the *apara-mārga* of the division named after this town.[21] Padmapura was clearly the headquarters of this division of which the eastern part is referred to in the said Māṇḍhaḷ grant of Rudra Sena II and the western part is mentioned in the Māsod charter of his son Pravara Sena II. Thus, the administrative division or district of Padmapura appears to have been divided into eastern and western *mārgas* or something like modern tehsīls. Whether there were northern and southern *mārgas* also is something that cannot be decided in the absence of necessary evidence. The town of Padmapura after which the district was named defies identification at present. But as Matsya-draha or Māsod is said to have been situated in its *apara-mārga* or western division, and Māsod is a village in the Kāṭol tehsīl of the Nagpur district, it may be concluded that the Kātoḷ region was included in the western *mārga* of Padmapura, though it is not possible to determine its extent exactly. And its *purva-marga* was evidently situated to its east, though how far east cannot be ascertained for want of requisite evidence. We may thus sum up that the *apara-mārga* of this division comprised the Kāṭol tehsil of the Nagpur district and Ārvī tehsīl of the Wardhā district and the *pūrva-mārga* the region to its east in the Nagpur and Wardhā tehsīls in the districts of the same names. This reminds us of the Padmapura from where an unfinished plate was intended to be issued. This plate was found at Durg in the district of the same name in Madhya Pradesh.[22] Obviously, the two Padmapuras were identical. V.V. Mirashi had identified the Padmapura of the Durg plate with the village of Padampur near Āmgāon in the Bhaṇḍārā district, the only reason being the identity of the two names, and regarded it as of great importance in later times as well as due to its supposed connection with the great Sanskrit dramatist Bhavabūti.[23] But as the evidence of the Māṇḍhaḷ plates of Rudra Sena II and the Māsod charter of Pravara Sena II shows, we must look for Padmapura in the Nagpur-Wardhā region though at present it is difficult to locate it exactly. As for the attribution of the Durg plate in question, it is not possible to be sure as the preserved portion does not name the issuer and the text ends only with the expression *Bhavanāga-dauhitrasya* in description of Rudra

Sena I. So palaeography is our only guide in deciding its date. Mirashi felt that its characters agree with those of Pravara Sena II, but as his earlier grants are issued from Nandivardhana and later ones from Pravarapura, it should belong to his successor, Narendra Sena.[24] Padmapura was thus, according to Mirashi, the capital of Narendra Sena who had shifted his capital from Pravarapura to Padmapura because of the invasion and consequent occupation of a major part of the Vākāṭaka kingdom by the Nala king Bhavadattavarman and he chose Padmapura which is to the east as there he could count on the support of the loyal feudatories, the rulers of Mekalā and Kosalā.[25] It is impossible to concede this view for several reasons. First, there is nothing to show that the rulers of Mekalā, called Pāṇḍavas of Mekalā in historical parlance, were feudatories of the Vākāṭakas. As shown by us elsewhere,[26] the erroneous notion that the Pāṇḍuvamsin Bharatabala of Mekalā was a vassal of Narendra Sena was based on the occurrence of the word *narendra* in a stanza of the Bamhanī plates then attributed to Bharatabala which was taken to have the dual meanings of 'king' and a veiled allusion to his (Bharatabala's) supposed overlord Vākāṭaka Narendra Sena, and the recent discovery of the Mallār plates of his son and successor Śūrabala Udīrnavaira[27] has clearly established that the Bamhanī plates also belong to him only and not to his father and that the wrong impression about their being issued by Bharatabala is due to the inadvertent omission of the prose sentence introducing him (Śūrabala). Moreover, the Pāṇḍavas of Mekalā flourished considerably later than the Vākāṭakas and there could therefore be no connection whatever between the two dynasties.[28] Likewise Kosalā (Chhattīsgaḍh region) was at this time under the Imperial Guptas as clearly proved by the find of repoussé type coins issued by Kumāra Gupta I and Skanda Gupta under the alternative names or *virudas* Mahendrāditya and Kramāditya respectively who may have ruled it directly or through their vassals. Then, shifting the capital to this Padampur would have brought the Vākāṭakas closer to the Nalas who were their sworn enemies. And lastly, at the time when the Durg plate was published and Mirashi wrote no copperplate charter earlier than the Puṇe plates of Prabhāvatī Guptā and those of her son Pravara Sena II were known for a palaeographic comparison. But now we have the Māṇḍhaḷ plates of Rudra Sena II, and the characters of the Durg plate can no longer be regarded as later than those of these plates. We are therefore inclined to believe that the Durg plate was intended to be issued from Padmapura by either Rudra Sena II himself or by his father Pṛithvī Sheṇa I, who might have shifted his capital from the city of Kāñchanakā in the Vindhyan region to Padmapura in Nagpur-Wardhā region as his ancestral possessions in the North had been slipping from his control. It is possible, though by no means certain, that the capital of the northern branch was shifted to Padmapura considerably earlier.

We do not know how long Padmapura continued to serve as the capital of the Vākāṭakas; but when the curtain rises again in the thirteenth year of the regency of Prabhāvatī Guptā for her minor son *Yuvarāja* (Crown Prince) Divākara Sena we find Nandivardhana occupying this position: her Puṇe charter of this year was granted from this place.[29] It has been correctly identified with modern Nagardhan, also called Nandardhan,[30] some forty km to the north of Nāgpur in the Nāgpur district. It was thus to the east of Padmapura according to our location. What was the necessity of shifting the capital to this place cannot be determined, especially because it is not possible to identify the location of Padmapura exactly. However, it may be argued that for some unknown reasons Nandivaradhana might have been found more convenient. It was definitely situated on the high-way that linked it to Tripurī and through the latter to important locations in North India. Its location also placed it in a close proximity of the important religious centres of Rāmagiri and Mansar.[31] There is a mediaeval fortification of the Goṇḍs which, it is possible, may have been raised at the site of an old fort. It in those days included the area now occupied by some adjacent villages including Hamlāpurī which has yielded some bronzes and lithic sculptures dating from the Vākāṭaka period.[32] Its total extent in those days may have been two-three km.

Nandivardhana definitely continued to serve as Vākāṭaka capital till at least the eleventh year of the reign of Pravara Sena II[33] sometime whereafter but by his sixteenth year[34] he shifted it to another locality called Pravarpura from where most of his subsequent charters are issued. It continued to be his capital till the end of his long reign.[35] It has been identified generally with modern Paunār in the Wardhā district, and the excavations and explorations have given a good yield of Vākāṭaka material.[36] This includes the coins of Narendra Sena and Pṛithivī Sheṇa, perhaps the second king of this name and the last known monarch of this branch.[37] Being situated on the bank of the river Dhām, it had the advantage of a dependable water supply. Moreover, the shifting might have been inspired by another consideration. Nandivardhana might have been found rather inadequate and not too far to defend against the growing pressure from the Nalas. The town, which must have existed much earlier as indicated by the archaeological excavations there,[38] was most probably renamed by one of the two Pravara Senas after himself. It was quite prosperous during the Vākāṭaka period as revealed by numerous archaeological finds there. However, its identity with Pravarapura is denied by some scholars on not quite absurd grounds.[39]

It is not known how long Pravarapura continued as the capital of this branch of the Vākāṭakas. No record of Narendra Sena has to date been reported.[40] And none of the four charters of Pṛithivī Sheṇa II known so far has been issued from this place. They are issued from Rāmagiristhāna,[41] Beṇṇātaṭa-sthāna,[42] Prithivisamudra[43] and the temporary residence *(vāsaka)* at a place called Vembāra.[44] While editing the Māhurjharī plates of his seventeenth year V.B. Kolte pleaded that most probably the Vākāṭaka capital Pravarapura was also in danger from enemies and therefore Prithivi Sheṇa II had to shift his capital to another locality called Pṛithivīsamudra–Pṛithivīpura.[45] And of the three places in the Nagpur-Wardhā districts containing in their names the word *samudra,*[46] he proposes to identify it with Samudrapura in the Hinganghāṭ tehsīl of the Wardhā district in view of the fact that the capital was being shifted from east to west.[47] This view, however, cannot bear a close scrutiny. Let us examine it at some length. Kolte reads the name of the *rājya* (district) in which the smaller administrative division called Jamalakheṭaka-*mārga* (Jamalakheṭaka tehsil, to use the modern terminology) was situated as Surambi,[48] whereas it is actually Ārambi. The location of this district is crucial to the correct identification of Pṛithivīpura or Pṛithivīsamudra. This *rajya* is named in a slightly changed form Ārammi-*rājya* in the Dudiā[49] and Tigāon (Paṇḍhurṇā)[50] plates of Pravara Sena II issued during twenty-third and twenty-ninth years respectively of his reign. It must be noted that both these charters mentioning Ārammi-*rājya* have been reported from the Chhindwārā district of Madhya Pradesh and record grants of villages located nearby, while Māhurjharī, the find-spot of the charter of Pṛithivī Sheṇa II, is situated in the adjacent Nāgpur district. It is therefore almost certain that the Ārammi(mbi)-*rājya* comprised parts of the Nāgpur and Kāṭol tehsils of the Nāgpur district and the adjoining region of the Chhindwārā district. Although attempts have been made to locate Ārammi variously,[51] it may be pointed out that there is still a village called Ārambhi near Kāṭol and it is actually the Ārambi or Ārammi mentioned in these records. It is therefore in the fitness of things to locate the Āramm(mb)*ī-rājya* in this region and look for the localities described as situated in it there. Viewing from this angle, Māhurjharī, the provenance of the plates in question, itself has a very strong case for identification as Pṛithivīsamudra. There is here even now an extensive water-reservoir which could have been figuratively styled *samudra* (ocean). It must have been in existence at the time of Pṛithivī Sheṇa II or even earlier or, alternatively may have been excavated and re-named/named by him after himself.[52] The numerous megalithic stone circles adjoining the township prove that its antiquity goes back to at least the sixth century BC.[53] Māhurjharī was in those days a prominent centre of bead-making industry, and old beads of numerous varieties are still found in quantities. It is noteworthy in this connection that the two components of its present name also allude to two separate though connected phenomena: *jharī*, the second component, to the water-reservior, and *māhur*, a derivative from its ancient name Māṭṛipura,[54] to the township. In all probability Māṭṛipura is an ancient name going back to pre-Vākāṭaka period, indicating that the spot was regarded as sacred on account of being traditionally an abode of the mother goddess *(māṭri)*, and the tank, too, must have been so treated and held in high esteem.[55] It is therefore more likely that the township and the tank were renamed as Pṛithivīpura and Pṛithivīsamudra respectively by Pṛithivī Sheṇa II. In view of the sanctity attached to the tank which might have been treated as an important pilgrimage centre, Pṛithivī Sheṇa II may have visited it on pilgrimage and made the grant recorded in the plates in question after bathing in it. We have some other epigraphic references of this type. There is therefore no question of Pṛithivīsamudra or Pṛithivīpura being the new dynastic capital founded by Pṛithivī Sheṇa II after deserting the earlier capital at Pravarapura which might have after all continued as the capital till the end of this branch of the dynasty; at least till now we have no evidence to suggest otherwise.

Let us, however, strike a note of caution against dogmatism in this respect. The view set forth in these pages is based squarely on the common assumption among historians and epigraphists that normally when the place of the issue of a charter is mentioned by itself, viz. without any other word following it, in ablative singular, it should denote the dynastic capital at the time. It is on this basis that the shifting of the capital of the northern branch of the Vākāṭakas from Kāñchanakā at first to Padmapura and thence to Nandivardhana and Pravarapura in that order is propounded. The only place which can be said to be documented as capital is Kāñchanakā which is clearly referred to as the centre of authority of Pravīra or Pravara Sena I in the dynastic texts of the Purāṇas. However, when the gravity of Vākāṭaka power shifted southward, it would have been found difficult to administer the kingdom from this place situated in the

Bundelkhaṇḍ region of Madhya Pradesh, and it would have been rendered impossible to retain it, not to speak of continuing to have it as metropolis, during the later part of the rule of Pṛithivī Sheṇa I when the Vākāṭaka rule in that area was wiped out by the Gupta emperor Samudra Gupta. The Vākāṭakas must have therefore been compelled to shift their capital somewhere in their territory in the Vidarbha region. The first such capital must have been Padmapura followed by Nandivardhana and Pravarapura. But as regards the last two localities, except the use of these names by themselves as the places of issue of official records, there is nothing to compel us to treat them as capitals. Some scholars feel, perhaps not quite without basis, that Nandivardhana continued to be the capital of the dynasty till its end after which it continued in the same status under the Nalas who replaced them.[56] In that case Pravarapura is just mentioned as an important locality in Pravara Sena II's official records. But one will have to explain as to why after the eleventh year and definitely by the sixteenth year of this king's reign Nandivardhana was replaced as the place of issue of the charters by Pravarapura which by itself continued to be the issuing place of his records till the last recorded year of his reign.[57] What is interesting to remember in this connection is that Nandivardhana does not figure even once after the eleventh year of the reign of Pravara Sena II as the issuing locality of the charters of the dynasty. We are therefore inclined to hold that Nandivardhana ceased to be the capital and was substituted in that position by Pravarapura sometime in or after the eleventh and in or by the sixteenth year of Pravara Sena II's reign, though there is no doubt that the former continued to be an important administrative centre thereafter even though of this we have no direct evidence.

We do not definitely know about the capital of the dynasty during post-Pravara Sena II period. We have no record yet of his son and successor Narendra Sena, and the four known records of the latter's son and successor Pṛithivī Sheṇa II are, as we have seen above, issued from various places which were either important religious centres or temporary residences and so they supply absolutely no information about the dynastic capital during their respective reigns. But we may tentatively conclude that during this period also Pravarapura continued to serve this purpose till some definite evidence comes to light to disprove this assumption.

The only other known branch of the Vākāṭakas, which ruled over southern Vidarbha, Marāthwāḍā and Khāndesh regions of Maharashtra and at times succeeded in establishing its hold over northern Karnataka and perhaps North

Konkan region up to Kānherī near Mumbai had its capital at Vatsagulma (modern Wāshim, Akolā district, Maharashtra) and is in consequence known among historians as the Vatsagulma branch. The name is by itself mentioned as the place of issue in the first known charter of the branch, viz. Wāhsim plates of Vindhyaśakti II,[58] its second member, and both the grants of Deva Sena, viz. Bīdar plates of the fifth year[59] and the incomplete India Office charter.[60] So there should be no doubt that at least from the time of Vindhyaśakti II till the reign of Deva Sena Vatsagulma served as the capital of this branch of the dynasty. We have no record of the founder of the branch, viz. Sarva Sena, and the only known official record of the last king Hari Sheṇa, viz. Thāḷner plates,[61] does not mention the place of issue. But in the absence of any evidence to the contrary it may be reasonably presumed that Vatsagulma continued to be the capital of this branch from the beginning to the end.

It was regarded as a sacred pilgrimage centre *(tīrtha)*, and there are various myths and traditions about its foundation and nomenclature. The later *Vatsagulma-māhātmya* would have us believe that it got this name because of the sage Vatsa who, by his penance, caused the assemblage *(gulma)* of divinities come over there and settle in his hermitage. The *Kāmasūtra* (V. 5.3) of Vātsyāyana speaks of the residents of Vātsagulma as Vātsagulmaka,[62] while the mediaeval commentator Yaśodhara in his commentary (Jayamaṅgalā) calls the country round the town Vatsagulmaka and records the tradition that the region came to be so called in consequence of being settled by two uterine princes of Dakshināpatha named Vatsa and Gulma.[63] Rājaśekhara in his *Kāvya-mīmāṁsā* describes it as the pleasure-resort of the god of love where the mythical poetry-man *(kāvya-purusha)* married the literary lore,[64] indicating its great reputation as a prominent centre of learning and literature. As for its location, there appears to have been difference of opinion among ancient writers. While Vātsyāyana appears to draw a line of demarcation between the people of Vatsagulma and Vidarbha,[65] Rājaśekhara regards it as a part of Vidarbha *(Vidarbheshu Vatsagulmaṁ nāma nagaram)*.

Under the Vākāṭakas it became a prominent literary centre, and the Prakrit literary style developed here came to be known as Vāchchhomī (Vātsagulmī) which was widely appreciated.[66] The famed Prakrit epic called *Hari-vijaya*, which is unfortunately no longer extant, of one of the two kings named Sarva Sena of this branch, is showered with high encomium by such literary critics as Daṇḍin, Ānandavardhana and Kuntaka.[67]

The recently conducted small-scale excavations at Wāhsim have given some evidence of the life of ancient times there. Though nothing has been found to support its fairly certain identification with ancient Vatsagulma, the site has yielded some coins which are stylistically allied to the Vākāṭaka specie known from Paunār a few years ago.[68]

Notes and References

1. We have discussed some of these problems threadbare and attempted a dependable account of the Vākāṭakas above.
2. Those accounts have been compiled after comparing several manuscripts by F.E. Pargiter under the title *The Purāṇa Text of the Dynasties of the Kali Age.*
3. *Ibid.*, p. 50.
4. *History of India: 150 A.D. to 350 A.D.*, Lahore, 1933, p. 16, fn. 3. Also see p. 70. Jayaswal feels that Kāñchanakā and Chanakā were alternative names. He also draws attention to the mention of *Kāñchanipurī* as the capital of the Nāgas in the *Kalki-purāṇa*, III, 14.2-21.
5. *Inscriptions of the Vākāṭakas*, *CII*, V, p. xii; *Maharashtra State Gazetteer, History I: Ancient Period*, p. 114 and fn. 5; *A Comprehensive History of India*, III (I), eds. R.C. Majumdar and K.K. Dasgupta, p. 131, where it is taken for granted.
6. *DKA*, p. 50, fn. 33. Mirashi's statement that a reading of a manuscript of the *Vāyupurāṇa* cited by Pargiter in note 33 at p. 60 (*Maharashtra State Gazetteer, History I*, p. 114, fn. 5) suggests this amended reading is due to oversight as at p. 60 there is no such reference. The variants are cited by him at p. 50, fn. 33 and there is no such reading.
7. *A New History of the Indian People, VI : The Vākāṭaka-Gupta Age*, eds. R.C. Majumdar and A.S. Altekar, p. 96; *Early History of the Deccan*, ed. G. Yazdani, Oxford, 1960, pp. 154-55.
8. *Nagpur University Journal*, III, pp. 22ff.; *CII*, V, pp. xi-xvi; *Maharashtra State Gazetteer, History I*, pp. 113-16; *A Comprehensive History of India*, III, I, p. 130.
9. For a detailed examination of the basis of this theory, see *AV*, pp. 3-6; *supra*, pp. 150-53.
10. Vindhyaśakti (II) of the Vatsagulma branch, also called Vindhyasena, just bore this name without any such significance as a matter of naming tradition. Whether this was the proper name or title is not possible to determine at present.
11. The relevant Purāṇic passage is *Vindhyakānāṁ kule'tīte*. *Vide DKA*, p. 50 (under 'Dynasties of the Third Century A.D.').
12. *Ibid.*, pp. 48 (text) and 72 (Engl. tr.). The actual expression is *nṛipāu Vaidesikān* where the second word should be split as *vai deśikān* which should give the correct meaning.
13. *AV*, pp. 11-12.
14. This is only a metronymic and we do not know the personal name of this personage.
15. According to the Purāṇas, he ruled for sixty years.
16. *Ibid.*, pp. 7-9.

17. Jayaswal, *op.cit.*, p. 16, fn. 3. His explanation of the transformation of Chanakā into Nachnā is quite unsatisfactory.

18. *AV*, pp. 10-12; *supra*, pp. 55-69.

19. As we have shown elsewhere (*EHDPP*, pp. 38-44), Vidarbha continued to be under the Sātavāhanas till about the close of the third century AD when it was occupied by Pravara Sena I.

20. *AV*, pp. 227-30; *supra*, pp. 86088 (for discussion of its contents). The inscription has since been edited by us and Chandrashekhar Gupta in *Saṁśodhanāchī Kshitije*, pp. 223-29 (Marathi) and a detailed paper in English by us is under publication in *EI*, Vol. XLIII.

21. These plates have been edited by us together with Chandrashekhar Gupta in *JESI*, X, pp. 108-16; XI, p. 114. For its contents, see *AV*, pp. 231-33; *supra*, pp. 90-91.

22. *CII*, V, pp. 16-18; for discussion, *vide supra*, pp. 6-8.

23. *Ibid.*, pp. xxvii, 77; *CHI*, III, Part I, p. 140; *Bhavabhūti*, Delhi, 1974, Ch. III.

24. *CII*, V, p. 77.

25. *Ibid.*

26. "The Date of the Bamhanī and Mallār Plates of Śūrabala Udīrṇavaira", *Bhāratī-Bhānam: K.V. Sarma Felicitation Volume*, pp. 493-43; "A Note on the Malgā Plates of Sāmanta Indrarāja", *Śrī Venkaṭeswara University Oriental Journal*, XXI-XXII, pp. 19-25.

27. This charter was originally published by B. Sitarman and M.J. Sharma in the Studies in Indian Epigraphy *(JESI)*, III, pp. 183-92. It was re-edited by us in our *Inscriptions of the Śarabha-purīyas, Pāṇḍuvaṁśins and Somavaṁśins*, Part II, pp. 80-85.

28. For a historical account of the dynasty, see *ibid.*, Part I, pp. 117-32.

29. *Ibid.*, pp. 7-8. Here the name is spelt as Nāndivardhana. Such minor differences of spelling are not that uncommon in Vākāṭaka records. *Vide, supra*, pp. 8-11.

30. This is a descendant of ancient Nandivardhana and establishes its identity with this place beyond doubt. The claim of adjacent Nandapura has not much support.

31. Its ancient name was Maṇisara found in the Mahānubhāva literature.

32. Information kindly supplied by Dr. Chandrashekhar Gupta.

33. His Belorā charter of this year was issued from this place. *Vide ibid.*, pp. 18ff; *supra*, pp. 13-16.

34. His Māṇḍhaḷ plates of this year were given from Pravarapura. *Vide* Ajay Mitra Shastri, "Māṇḍhaḷ Copper-Plate Charter of Pravara Sena II, Year 16", *EI*, XLI, pp. 68-76; *AV*, pp. 230-31; *supra*, pp. 88-90.

35. Paunī plates of his latest known year (32nd) were issued from here.

36. See for this material, Chandrashekhar Gupta, "Paunār under the Vākāṭakas", *AV*, pp. 119-53.

37. Ajay Mitra Shastri, "Vākāṭaka Coins", *ibid.*, pp. 285-94; *supra*, pp. 136-46.

38. Its antiquity goes back to the first millenniuṁ BC. *Vide* S.B. Deo and M.K. Dhavalikar, *Paunar Excavations*, Nagpur, 1968, pp. 6-7.

39. Brahmananda Deshpande (*Bhāratīya Itihāsa āṇi Saṁakṛiti* [Marathi]), XXV, no. 100 (January-March, 1989, p. 5) feels that Paunār may be a corrupt form of Pravarasenapura, while A.P. Jamkhedkar thinks that it represents ancient Padmanagara. The whole problem is caused by the fact that in the inscriptions it is described as Pravarapura, but the identified place (Paunār) has its second component which can be a derivative only of *nagara.*

40. As stated above, the attribution of the unfinished Durg plate to him is based on very doubtful presumptions.

41. Ajay Mitra Shastri, "Māṇḍhaḷ Plates of Pṛithivī Sheṇa II, Years 2 and 10", *EI,* XLI, pp. 165-69.

42. *Ibid.*, pp. 175-80.

43. V.B. Kolte, "Mahurzari Plates of Pṛithivī Seṇa II", *ABORI,* LIII, pp. 192-94. For a discussion of these plates, *vide AV,* pp. 238-46; *supra,* pp. 103-06.

44. *CII,* V, pp. 80-81.

45. Both the localities are mentioned in the record though the charter itself is said to have been issued from Pṛihtivīsamudra.

46. These places are (i) Samudrī (Sāoner tāluk, Nāgpur district), (ii) Kshīra Samudra (Wardhā tāluk, Wardhā district), and (iii) Samudrapura (Hinganghāt talūk, Wardhā district).

47. Kolte, *op.cit.*, pp. 190-91.

48. *Ibid.*, p. 193, line 27.

49. *CII,* p. 45, line 13.

50. *Ibid.*, p. 66, lines 26 and 29.

51. Hiralal proposed to identify Ārammi with Ārvi, the chief town of the tehsil of the same name, in the Wardhā district. See his *Inscriptions in the Central Provinces and Berar,* 2nd ed., p. 93, no. 168. Mirashi (*CII,* V, p. 44) identified it with Āmlā, some forty miles north by west of Pāṇḍhurṇā in the Chhindwārā district. Our identification is spatially closer to Mirashi's, though his view identifying it with Āmlā is not likely.

52. It is difficult to decide if Pṛithivī Sheṇa responsible for it was the first or second king of this name. However, in all likelihood, it was Pṛithivī Sheṇa II. Had his illustrious homonymous predecessor done so, there would have been greater chances of the survival of these names given by him as there would have been in that case his numerous successors to perpetuate and enforce them.

53. For excavations of some of these burials, *vide* S.B. Deo, *Mahurjhari Excavations,* Nagpur, 1973.

54. The suggestion of some scholars to derive it from Mātāpura does not appear quite likely besides derivational difficulties.

55. There is another place called Māhur in the Nānded district sacred to the mother goddess who is worshipped in the name of Renukā. From Mahurjhari have been reported some figurines of the headless nude mother goddess commonly called Lajjāgaurī.

56. This is also the view of Hans Bakkar and Karunaga Issacson ("The Rāmṭek Inscriptions II: The Vākātaka Inscription in the Kevala-Narasiṁha Temple", *BSOAS,* LVI, Part I,

1993, p. 69, fn. 62) and H.S. Thosar, ("Re-examination of the Historical Contents of the Nāgardhan Plates of Svāmirāja and the Rithapur Grant of the Nala King Arthapati", *JESI*, XX (1994), p. 24; "Royal Seats of the Vākāṭaka", *SIPN*, XVI, 1996, pp. 31ff:).

57. I.e. Paunī plates of his thirty-second year. For its contents, see *AV*, pp. 237-38; *supra*. pp. 97-98.

58. *CII*, V, p. 96, line 1.

59. P.V. Parabrahma Sastri, "Hyderabad Plates of Vākāṭaka Devasena, Year 5", *JESI*, XIII, p. 73, line 1. The plates are styled "Hyderabad" only because they are now deposited in the Birla Archaeological and Cultural Research Institute, Hyderabad, though they were brought there from Bīdar in North Karnataka. We prefer to call them Bīdar plates, *AV*, p. 248.

60. *CII*, V, p. 102, line 1. It is called here Vātsyagulma.

61. V.V. Mirashi, *Indological Research Papers*, I, pp. 78ff.

62. With Jayamaṅgalā commentary of Yaśodhara, p. 261.

63. *Dakshiṇāpathe saudaryau rāja-putrau Vatsa-Gulmau tābhyām=adhyāsito daśo Vatsagulmaka iti pratītaḥ. Ibid.*

64. Ed. by C.D. Dalal and R.A. Sastry, p. 10.

65. Vātsyāyana describes sexual practices of Vatsagulma (V. 5.33) and Vidarbha (V. 5.34) separately, indicating that he has used the two names in a very restricted sense, perhaps in accordance with the prevailing connotations, and Rājaśekhara probably shows awareness of the extended sense of the name Vidarbha.

66. See his Prakrit play *Karpūra-mañjarī*, I, 1.

67. For references, see V.V. Mirashi, *Studies in Indology*, I, 2nd ed., pp. 114-19.

68. See Ajay Mitra Shastri, "Vākāṭaka Coins", *AV*, *Vākāṭakas*, pp. 285-94; *supra*, pp. 136-46.

APPENDIX III

The Mūḍigere Plates of Siṁhavarman and Vākāṭaka-Kadamba Relations

(Pls. XCVII-XCIX)

This record of the Kadamba monarch Siṁhavarman of the Triparvata branch was found together with another inscription of the ninth year of the reign of his father, Vishṇuvarman,[1] at Mūdigere in the Tarikere taluk of the Chikmagalur district of Karnataka, in 1983, and first published in the Kannada daily *Kannaḍa-prabhā* dated 7th August, 1983, by A. Sundara. Later, it was included in Volume 1 of his *Corpus of Kadamba Inscriptions* by B.R. Gopal.[2] However, the importance of the record from the point of view of Vākāṭaka-Kadamba relations has yet to be fully realised, and here is an attempt in this direction.

This 19-line inscription engraved on a set of four plates of copper is in Sanskrit, which is faulty, and is incised in box-headed characters which are somewhat different from the usual type. It is dated in the fifth year of the reign of the issuing chief[3] and aims at registering the grant of a piece of land measuring five *nivertanas*[4] situated to the down south of the Āsandī tank[5] in Āsandyāluru included in the Sendraka-*vishaya* to provide for the worship at a temple of the Arhats (viz., Jain temple) by him. The monarch is described as the dear grandson of the Kadamba king Kṛishṇavaraman[6] and dear son of Vishṇuvarman who is in turn referred to as a sovereign monarch *(sārvvabhauma)*.[7] He is said to have been born of a queen hailing from the Rāmeya family which is compared to the mountain Himavat, his own mother being compared to the river Gaṅgā originating from the Himalayas and described as the mother of the world *(jagan-māṭri)*. Nothing is known about the Rāmeya family from any other source.[8] Siṁhavarman is bestowed with high conventional praise and is described as anointed *(abhishikta)* by a Maisava chief or the Maisavas.[9]

What is of special interest to us in the present context is the statement that 'thereafter (after his anointment by the Maisavas or a Maisava chief) he (viz., Siṁhavarman) was honoured by king Sarva Sena by coronation':

Tad=anu Sarvvasena-mahārājena mūrddh-ābhisheken-ābhyarchchitah[10]

In view of the fact that *sena*-ending names were borne during this early period mostly only by the Vākāṭakas all of whom invariably had such names, we may reasonably conclude that *mahārāja* Sarva Sena must have been a monarch of this dynasty. And we are not disappointed in our search for such a name among the Vākāṭaka kings. The founder of the Vatsagulma (Wāshim) branch of the dynasty was known by this name. But he is too early for identification with the homonymous chief mentioned in the record under consideration, the commencement of his reign being generally dated about 330 AD,[11] while Siṁhavarman can by no stretch of imagination be placed that early. In view of this fact Gopal was constrained to observe that 'there are chronological and other difficulties that come in the way of such an identification.'[12] Till recently no other chief of this name was known and therefore it was found difficult to identify him. However, the name of the great-grandson of this Sarva Sena and father of Deva Sena was not known though it was given in the Ajantā (Cave XVI) inscription of Varāhadeva, a minister of the last king Hari Sheṇa, due to the mutilation of the relevant portion.[13] But we learn from the recently discovered Thāḷner plates of Hari Sheṇa that the lost name was Sarva Sena. He has to be distinguished from his homonymous predecessor, the founder of the Vatsagulma branch, and has therefore to be styled Sarva Sena II.[14] The beginning of the reign of this king, till then of unknown name, is dated by historians in *c.* 410 AD, while its close is placed around 450 AD.[15] Now, the earliest date suggested for the commencement of Siṁhavarman's reign is about 490 AD.[16] Thus, there is a gap of some four decades between the suggested dates for the end of Sarva Sena II's rule and the beginning of Siṁhavarman's reign. It must be remembered, however, that the chronologies of both the Vākāṭakas and the Kadambas rest on very uncertain grounds and as such all the suggested dates should be regarded as purely tentative. The only certain point as regards the chronology of the Vatsagulma branch of the Vākāṭakas is furnished by the Hisse-Boralā stone inscription of the time of Deva Sena dated Śaka 380 or 458 AD,[17] which should suffice to show that he (Deva Sena) must have come to throne sometime in or before that date. In other words, the reign of Sarva Sena II must have come to a close by this date. And he is the only Sarva Sena known to us who could be a contemporary or near contemporary of the Kadamba king Siṁhavarman and should consequently be identified with the Sarva Sena mentioned in the latter's only known record. This would of course involve antedating the accession of Siṁhavarman by about half a century or some four decades which should not be difficult in view of the purely tentative nature of the Kadamba chronology. The Mūḍigere plates, thus, provide an important point for the fixation of the date of Siṁhavarman's accession in particular and the Kadamba chronology in general.

The description that Siṁhavarman felt honoured by being coronated at the hands of Sarva Sena is indicative of the high esteem in which the former held the latter. Properly interpreted, it would mean that Siṁhavarman regarded himself as a subordinate ally of the Vākāṭaka king Sarva Sena II. This serves as a useful commentary on the nature of the Vākāṭaka-Kadamba relations, the former ruling over the Vidarbha region of Maharashtra extending their sway at times over the adjoining region of Andhra Pradesh and Karnataka[18] and the latter over the Kuntala region of Karnataka.

POSTSCRIPT

After the above was published[19] G.S. Gai edited this inscription afresh with illustrations.[20] He corrected a few readings and interpretations offered by B.R. Gopal. He is critical of our suggestion regarding the identification of the Sarva Sena-mahārāja who had anointed Siṁhavarman with the second king named Sarva Sena of the Vatsagulma branch of the Vākāṭakas brought to light for the first time by the Thāḷner charter of his grandson and the last known king of this branch, viz. Hari Sheṇa. He seems to follow Mirashi in identifying Kuntala with southern Maharashtra and equating the Kuntalādhipati whose daughter Ajjhitabhaṭṭarikā was married to the Vākāṭaka king Narendra Sena with a Rāshṭrakūṭa king of Mānapura (Satārā region) and argues that the Kadambas had nothing to do with the Vākāṭakas. He further argues that the *sena*-ending names were not a monopoly of the Vākāṭakas and such names were prevalent among other ruling families also. He further points out that some of the queens of the Kadamba kings hailed from the Kaikeya lineage and a chieftain of the name Chitra Sena is known from some records. And finally it has been concluded that Sarva Sena-mahārāja also *may have hailed* from the Kaikeya family and may have anointed his sister's son Siṁhavarman.[21]

We, however, are inclined to hold that the Kuntala princess married by Narendra Sena was a Kadamba princess, for the kingdom of the Kadambas was popularly known as Kuntala which connoted Northern Karnataka round Vanavāsī and the adjoining region of Maharashtra. But in the present context we are concerned with the Vatsagulma branch of the Vākāṭakas which was the northern neighbour of the Kadambas of Vanavāsī. There is dear evidence of the Kadamba impact on this branch of the dynasty as some of its members are known to have assumed typical Kadamba titles like Dharma-mahārāja and Hāritīputra besides employing some common revenue terms in their records. We too were aware of the fact that there were some kings with *sena*-ending names earlier and during the period in question. Besides Chitra Sena we can refer in this context to the Vidarbha kings Yajña Sena and Mādhava Sena and their cousin Vīra Sena who are known from Kālidāsa's play *Mālavikāgnimitra* to have been contemporaries of the Śunga kings Pushyamitra and Agnimitra and played a pivotal role in the episode forming the central theme of the drama. What was intended to be argued by us was that during the period in question it was only among the Vākāṭakas that *Sena* was employed like a surname as *Gupta* was among the Imperial Guptas of the North. And we now had a king named Sarva Sena who was almost a contemporary of the Kadamba king Siṁhavarman. Moreover, there was reason for him to take pride in being anointed on the throne by a powerful king like the Vākāṭaka king Sarva Sena. There would hardly have been any justification to feel proud in being anointed by a maternal uncle, particularly a petty chief, and that too for a king who styled himself as a sovereign ruler (*sārvabhauma*). Moreover, no chief named Sarva Sena is known among the Kaikeyas, while we know of a Vākāṭaka king of this name who was almost a contemporary and very powerful neighbouring ruler. It is for readers to judge whether we should search for an unknown petty chief or go in for a well-known powerful king for this purpose. As for us, one should definitely prefer a known king to an unknown hypothetical chief. We therefore stick to our earlier opinion in this matter. And the Bīdar (now Birla Archaeological and Cultural Research Institute, Hyderabad, collection) plates of Sarva Sena II's son and successor Deva Sena showing the southward expansion of the authority of this branch of the Vākāṭakas afford additional support for this view.

Gai has committed a number of errors in his short paper which need not detain us here any longer.

Notes and References

1. B.R. Gopal, *Corpus of Kadamba Inscriptions,* I, pp. 132-35.
2. *Ibid.*, pp. 139-43. However, the record has not been illlustrated by facsimiles and

consequently we are unable to check the readings. The same is true of other epigraphs also and is a great handicap.

3. The details of the date are given as the tenth day of the month of Pausha in the fifth year of his own rule *(svarājya-pañchame saṁvatsare)*.
4. According to the royal measure *(rāja-māna)*.
5. *Āsandī-taṭākasya dakshiṇa-pālyāḥ adhastāt*, i.e., below the southern bank of the Āsandī tank.
6. He is styled *dharmma-mahārāja*, a title denied to his son and grandson, and is described as belonging to the Mānavya *gotra* and as an embodiment of the fame of (performing) the *aśvamedha* sacrifice or sacrifices *(aśvamedha-yajña-yaśomaya-pratikṛita (e/h)*.
7. This title is applied in this record only to Vishṇuvarman, and even his son Siṁhavarman, the issuer of the grant, is not so styled and had to content himself by the simpler title of *mahārāja*.
8. The reading of the family-name appears to be doubtful as would follow from the interrogation mark against it by Gopal (*op.cit.*, p. 140; but the question mark is absent in the text-line 7 where the name actually occurs). Is it possible that her name was Gaṅgā?
9. Both the reading and interpretation are doubtful. The actual reading in the text is 'Maisada' which is proposed to be doubtfully corrected to 'Maisava' (Gopal, *op.cit., p.* 141, text-line 13). The interrogation mark is also used in the translation *(ibid.*, p. 143) where it is rendered as 'Maisavās'.
10. *Ibid.*, p. 141, text-line 13.
11. V.V. Mirashi, *Inscriptions of the Vākāṭakas, CII,* V, pp. vi-vii, ... 325 A.D.
12. Gopal, *op.cit.*, p. 140.
13. V.V. Mirashi, *Inscriptions of the Vākāṭakas, CII,* V, p. 108, verse 10.
14. For the text of the Thāḷner plates, see V.V. Mirashi, *Indological Research Papers,* i, Nagpur, 1982, pp. 78-87. For an analysis of the contents, see Ajay Mitra Shastri, 'Thāḷner Plates of Vākāṭaka Hari Sheṇa', *JESI,* xi, pp. 15-20.
15. V.V. Mirashi, *Inscriptions of the Vākāṭakas, CII,* V, pp. vi-vii.
16. B.R. Gopal, *op.cit.*, p. xxx. For a detailed discussion of the genealogy and chronology summarising different views on the subject, see *ibid.*, pp. xxiii-xxx.
17. Ajay Mitra Shastri, *EHDPP,* pp. 64-65; *supra*, pp. 106-07.
18. This southward extension of the Vākāṭaka power is clearly indicated by the recently discovered Bīdar plates of the fifth year of Deva Sena. For this record, see P.V.P. Sastry, 'Hyderabad Plates of Vākāṭakas', *JESI,* XIII, pp. 71-73.
19. *Indian Archaeological Heritage: Sh. K.V. Soundararajan Felicitation* Volume, pp. 317-19.
20. "Mūḍigere Plates of Kadamba Siṁhavarman, Year 5", *EI*, XLII, 1992, pp. 187-92.
21. *Ibid.*, pp. 189-90.

Bibliography

ORIGINAL SOURCES

I. LITERATURE

Joshi, Lakshmanshastri (ed.): *Dharmakósa*, Vyavahāra-kāṇḍa, Prājña Pratishṭhāna, Wai, 1941.

Pargiter, F.E.: *The Purāṇa Text of the Dynasties of the Kali Age*, Oxford, 1913.

Rajaśekhara: *Kāvya-mīmāmsā*, eds. C.D. Dalal and R.A. Sastry, Gaekwad's Oriental Series, No. 1, 3rd ed., Oriental Institute, Baroda, 1934.

Śrīdharadāsa (Compiler): *Saduktikarṇāmṛita.*

Vātsyāyana: *Kamasūtra* with Yaśodhara's Jayamaṅgalā commentary, Kashi Sanskrit Series, No. 29, Chowkhamba, Varanasi, 1929.

II. EPIGRAPHY

Agrawal, Jagannath; "Epigraphic Notes", *PIHC*, IV, 1940, p. 58-59.

Altekar, A.S.: Patna Museum Plate of Pravarasena II," *JBORS*, XIV, pp. 465-75.

Bakker, Hans and Isaacson, Harunaga, "The Ramṭek Inscriptions II: The Vākāṭaka Inscription in the Kevala-Narasiṁha Temple", *BSOAS*, LVI, Part I, 1993, pp. 46-74.

Bhandarkar, D. R. (Revisor), B. Ch. Chhabra and G.S. Gai (eds.): *Inscriptions of the Early Gupta Kings*, *CII*, III, Archaeological Survey of India, New Delhi, 1981.

Biswas, A.C.: "A Note on the Ajantā Inscription of the Vākāṭakas", *IC*, VII, pp. 372-75.

Bose, Sushil Kumar: "Indore Plates of Pravārasena II," *EI*, XXIV, pp. 52-56.

Bühler, G.: "The Ilichpur Grant of Pravārasena II of Vākāṭakas," *IA*, XII, pp. 239-47.

Chakravarti, N.P.: ''Some unpublished Amaravati Inscriptions'', *EI*, XV, pp. 260-61.

Chhabra, B.Ch: ''Beauties of the Bhitari Pillar Inscription,'' *Dr. Mirashi Felicitation Volume*, eds. G.T. Deshpande, Ajay Mitra Shastri et al., Vidharbha Samshodhan Maṇḍaḷ, Nagpur, 1965, pp. 362-71.

: ''Bamhanī Plates of Pāṇḍava King Bharatabala: Year 2'', *EI*, XXVII, pp. 132-45.

Cunningham, A.: *Reports of the Archaeological Survey of India*, XXI, 1885.

Daji, Bhau: ``Ajanta Inscriptions'', *JBBRAS*, VII, 1862, pp. 53-74.

Deshpande, Y.K. and Mahajan, D.B.: ``The Earliset Capper Grant of the Vākāṭaka Dynasty,'' *PIHC*, III, pp. 449-60.

Dikshit, K.N:. ''A Note on the Vākāṭaka Inscription From Ganj'', *EI*, XVII, pp. 362.

Dikshit, M.G: ''Two Charters of Bhānushesa, Year 30,''*EI*, XXXVIII, pp. 69-75.

Divekar, H.R.: ``Pushyamitras in Gupta Period'', *ABORI*, I, pp. 99-103.

Fleet, J.F.: *Inscriptions of the Early Gupta Kings and their Successors*, *CII*, III, Calcutta, 1888.

: ''Spurious Indian Grants'', *IA*, XXX, pp. 201-25.

Gai, G.S.: *Inscription of the early Kadambas*, Indian Council of National Research, New Delhi and Pratibha Prakashan, Delhi; 1996.

: ''Mūḍigere Plates of Kadamba Siṁhavarman, Year 5'', *EI*, XLII, 1992, pp. 187-92.

Gai, G.S. and Sankaranaryanan, S.: ''Note on the Date of Hisse-Borala Inscription of the Time of Vākāṭaka Devasena'', *ibid.*, XXXVII, pp. 5-8.

Gokhale, Shobhana: ''Hisse-Borala Inscription of Devasena, Śaka 380,'' *ibid.*, XXXVII, pp. 1-4.

Gopal, B.R.: *Corpus of Kadamba Inscriptions*, Sirsi, 1985.

Gupte, Y.R.: ''Prabhāvatīguptenī dilele Eka Śāsana'' (Marathi), *Bharata Itihasa Saṁśodhaka Maṇḍaḷa Traimāsika*, III, pp. 89-92.

: ''Riddhapur Plates of Bhavattavarman'', *EI*, XIX, pp. 100-04.

: ''Ṛiddhapur Plates of the Vākāṭaka Queen Prabhāvatī-guptā of the 13th Year'', *JASB*, NS, XX, pp. 53-62.

Herzfeld, E.: *Paikuli: Monuments and Inscriptions of the Early History of the Sassanian Empire*, Berlin, 1924.

Hiralal: *Inscriptions in the Central Provinces and Berar,* 2nd ed., Government Press, Nagpur, 1932.

: "Betul Plates of Sankshobha, the Gupta year 199," *EI,* VIII, pp. 284-88. Postscript by F.Kielhorn, pp. 288-90.

Indraji, Bhagvanlal: *Notes on the Baudha Rock-Temples of Ajanta,* Pamphlet No. 9 of Archaeological Survey of Western India, Bombay, 1881.

Jain, B.C.: "Shankarpur Plate of Budhagupta and Harivarman", *JESI,* IV, pp. 62-66.

Kielhorn, F.: "Inscriptions from Khajuraho, II: Stone Inscription of Yaśovarman, of the year 1011," *EI,* I, pp. 122-35.

: "Bilhari Stone Inscriptions of the Rulers of Chedi", *ibid.,* I, pp. 251-70.

: "Dudia Plates of Pravāra Sena II", *ibid.,* III, pp. 258-62.

: "Bālāghāt Plates of Pṛithivīṣena II", *ibid.,* IX pp. 267-71.

Kolte, V.B.: Vākāṭakā michā Hisse-Bōralā Yethila Śilālekha" *VSMV,* Nagpur, 1964, pp. 137-56.

: "Hisse Borala Inscription of Vākāṭaka Devasena"; *Dr. Mirashi Felicitation Volume,* eds. G.T. Deshpande, Ajay Mitra Shastri et.al., Vidarbha Samshodhan Mandala, Nagpur, 1965, pp. 372-84.

: "Divitiya Pṛithivīsheṇāchā Māhurajharī Tāmrapata", *VSMV,* 1971, pp. 53-77.

: "Mahurzari Plates of Pṛthivīṣeṇa II", *ABORI,* LIII, 1972, pp. 183-94.

Lüders, H.: A List of Brāhmī Inscriptions up to circa 400 A.D. with the Exception of those of Aśoka, Appendix to *EI,* X.

Mirashi, V.V.: *Inscriptions of the Kalachuri-Chedi Era, CII,* IV, Government Epigraphist for India, Ootacamund, 1955.

: *Hyderabad Archaeological Series,* No: 14, Hyderabad, 1941.

: Inscriptions of the Vākāṭakas, *CII,* V, Archaeological Survey of India, Ootacamund, 1965.

: *The History and Inscriptions of the Sātavāhanas and the Western Kshatrapas,* Maharashtra State Board of Literature and Culture, Mumbai, 1981.

: Tiṛodī Plates of Pravarasena II, *ibid.,* XXII, pp. 167-76.

: "Pattan plates of Parvarasena" *EI,* XXII, pp. 81-88.

: "An Unfinished Vākāṭaka Plate from Durg", *ibid.,* XXII, pp. 207-12.

: "Pauni Stone Inscription of the Bhāra King Bhagadatta" *ibid.*, *XXIV*, pp. 11-14.

: "Two Incomplete Grants of Pravarasena II", *ibid*, XXIV, pp. 260-67.

: "Kothuraka grant of Pravarasena II", *ibid*, XXVI, pp. 155-61.

: "Waḍgāon Plates of Vākāṭaka Pravarasena II," *ibid*, XXVII, pp. 74-79.

: "A Note on the India Office Plate of Devasena", *NIA*, II, pp. 721-23.

Mirashi, V.V. and Gupte, Y.R.: "Khanapur Plates of Mādhava varman", *EI* XXVII, pp. 312-18.

Mirashi, V.V. and Mahajan, D.B.: "Basim Plates of Vindhyaśakti II", *ibid*, XXVI, pp. 317-35.

Mitchiner, J.E.: "Note on Hisse Borālā Inscription of Vākāṭaka Devasena", *Asiatic Society, Monthly Bulletin*, August, 1978, pp. 6-7.

Mukherjee, B.N.: "A Note on the Hisse-Borālā Inscription of the Time of Vākāṭaka Devasena", *JESI*, VII, pp. 3-5.

Pathak, K.B.: "A Gupta-Vākāṭaka Copperplate Grant", *IA*, XLI, pp. 214-15.

Pathak, K.B. and Dikshit, K.N.: "Poona Plates of the Vākāṭaka Queen Prabhavatigupta, the 13th Year", *EI*, XV, pp. 39-45.

Randle, H.N.: "An Unpublished India Office Plate of the Vākāṭaka Mahārajā Devasena", *NIA*, II, pp. 177-80.

Sastry, P.V. Parabrahma: "Hyderābād Plates of Vākāṭaka Devasena, Year 5", *JESI*, XIII, 1986, pp. 71-75.

Shastri, Ajay Mitra: *Inscriptions of the Śarabhapurīyas, Panduvaṁśins and Somavaṁśins*, 2 Parts, Indian Council of Historical Research, New Delhi, and Motilal Banarsidass, Delhi, 1995.

: "Hisse-Borālā Inscription of Vākāṭaka Deva Sena: Some Observations", *Dr. Umesh Mishra Commemoration Volume*, Ganganatha Jha Research Institute, Allahabad, 1970, pp. 617-27.

: "New Vākāṭaka Inscriptions", *AV*, pp. 227-68.

: "Māṇḍhaḷ Copperplate Charter of Pravārasena II, Year 16", *EI*, XLI, pp. 68-76.

: "Māṇḍhaḷ Plates of Pṛithivīsheṇa II, Years 2 and 10", *ibid.*, pp. 159-80.

: "The Malhārā Plates of Ādityarāja: A Re-Appraisal", *JESI*, IV, pp. 30-41.

: "The Date of the Malhārā Plates of Ādityarāja", *ibid.*, VII, pp. 69-75.

: "Mallār Plates of Vyāghrarāja: A Re-Appraisal", *ibid.*, IX, pp. 40-47.

: "Thāḷner Plates of Harisheṇa: A Re-Appraisal", *ibid.*, XI. pp. 15-20.

: "A Note on the Thāḷner Plạtes of Bhānusheṇa", *ibid.*, XII, pp. 53-58.

: "Nachnā-kī talāi and Ganj Inscriptions of Vākāṭaka Pṛithivīsheṇa: Some Observations", *ibid.*, XXI, pp. 1-13.

: "An Unissued Vākāṭaka Plate from Mohallā: Problem of Attribution", *ibid.*, XXII.

: "A Note on the Malgā Plates of Sāmanta Indrarāja", *Sri Venkateswara University Oriental Journal*, XXI-XXII, pp. 19-25.

: "The Mūdigere Plates of Siṁhavarman and Kadamba-Vākāṭaka Relations", *Indian Archaeological Heritage: K.V. Soundararajan Felicitation Volume*, eds. C. Margabandhu et. al, Agam Kala Prakashan, Delhi, 1991, pp. 317-19.

: "Some Observations on the Māharjharī Plates of Vākāṭaka Pṛthivīṣeṇa II," *ABORI*, LXXXVI, 1995, pp. 35-49.

Shastri, Ajay Mitra and Gupta, Chandrashekhar: "Dvitīya Rudrasenāchā Māṇḍhaḷa Tāmrapaṭa" (Marathi), *Saṁśodhanāchī Kshitije*, ed. B.L. Bhole, Ameya Prakashan, Nagpur, 1985, pp. 223-29.

: "Māsod Copperplate Charter of Pravarasena II, Year 19", *JESI*, X, 1983, pp. 108-16; XI, 1984, p. 174.

: "Yawatmāl Plates of Pravara Sena II, Year 26," *EI*, LXII, pp. 30-34.

Sircar, D.C.: *Select Inscriptions bearing on Indian History and Civilization*, I, 2nd ed., University of Calcutta, Calcutta, 1965.

: *Select Inscriptions bearing on Indian History and Civilization*, II, Motilal Banarsidass, Delhi, 1983.

: "Date of the Hisse Borālā Inscription of Vākāṭaka Deva Sena", *Journal of Ancient Indian History*, I, Deptt. of Ancient Indian History and Culture, University of Calcutta, Calcutta, 1978, pp. 94-98.

: "The Vatsagulma Copperplate Grant of Vākāṭaka Vindhyaśakti, Regnal Year 37", *IHQ*, XVI, pp. 182-86.

: "The Vatsagulma Copperplate Grant of King Vindhyaśakti II", *ibid.*, XVII, pp. 110-16.

Sircar, D.C. and Bhattacharyya, G.: "Mallār Plates of Vyāghrarāja", *EI*, XXXIV, pp. 45-50.

Sircar, D.C. and Sankaranarayanan, S.: "Malgā Plates of Sāmanta Indrarāja", *ibid.*, XXXIII, pp. 209-14.

Sitaraman, B. and Sharma, M.J.: ''Malhār Plates of Pāṇḍava King Śūrabala, Year 8'', *Studies in Indian Epigraphy (Bhāratīya Purābhilekha Patrikā)*, III, pp. 183-93.

Srinivasan, P.R., ''Māsod-Kāmpṭī Plates of Vākāṭaka Pravarasena II, Year 19'', *EI*, XXXIX, pp. 199-204.

Sukthankar, V.S.: ''A Vākāṭaka Inscription from Ganj'', *ibid.*, XVII, pp. 12-14.

III. NUMISMATICS

Agrawala, V.S.: ''Coin-Data in the Divyāvadāna'', *INC*, III, pp. 155-54.

Altekar, A.S.: ''Some Alleged Nāga and Vākāṭaka Coins'', *JNSI*, V, pp. 130-34.

Gupta, P.L.: ''Fabrication of Ancient Punch-Marked Coins'', *INC*, III, pp. 121-34.

: ''Bearing of Dahigāon Hoard on Traikūṭaka History'', *ND*, III, Part II, pp. 42-51.

Jain, B.C.: *Inventory of the Hoards and Finds of Coins and Seals from Madhya Pradesh (non-Muhammadan)*, Numismatic Notes and Monograph Series No. 6, Numismatic Society of India, Varanasi, 1957.

Mirashi, V.V.: ''Dahigāon Hoard of Kshatrapa and Traikūṭaka Coins'', *JNSI*, XXXV, pp. 118-22.

Shastri, Ajay Mitra: ''Two Numismaics Notes'', *ND*, I, Part I, pp. 25-28.

: ''Vākāṭaka Coins'', *AV*, pp. 285-94.

Subrahmanyam, R.: Ikshvāku Coins in the Andhra Pradesh Government Museum, Hyderabad, 1962.

Trivedi, H.V.: *Catalogue of the Coins of the Nāgas of Padmāvatī*, Department of Archaeology and Museums, Gwalior, 1957.

B. MODERN WORKS

Agrawala, J.N.: *Researches in Indian Epigraphy and Numismatics*, Sundeep Prakashan, Delhi, 1986.

Agrawala, V.S.: *Matsya Purāṇa–A Study*, All India Kashiraja Trust, Varanasi, 1963.

Altekar, A.S.: ''The History of the Vākāṭakas'', *Early History of the Deccan*, ed. Yazdani, Oxford, 1960, pp. 149-200.

: Ch. II: ''The Sātavāhana Empire and its Feudatories'', *MSGH*, I, Government of Maharashtra, Mumbai, 1967, pp. 57-100.

: Ch. IV: ''The Western Kshatrapas'', *ibid.*, I, pp. 143-68.

Aiyangar, S.K.: "Vākāṭakas and their Place in the History of India", *ABORI*, V, pp. 31-54.

Bakkar, Hans: *Rāmṭek*, Gronigen University, Leiden, 1989.

: "The Antiquities of Rāmṭek Hill, Maharashtra" *South Asian Studies*, V, 1989, pp. 79-102.

: "Rāmṭek: An Ancient Centre of Viṣṇu Devotion in Maharashtra", *The History of Sacred Places in India as reflected in Traditional Literature*, ed. H. Bakker, Leiden, 1990, pp. 62-85.

: "The Footprints of the Lord", *Devotion Divine: Bhakti Traditions from the Regions of India: Studies in Honour of Charlotte Vaudeville*, eds. Diana, L. Eck and Francoise Mallison, Groningen/Paris, 1991, pp. 19-37.

: "Memorials, Temples, Gods and Kings: An Attempt to Unravel the Symbolic Texture of Vākāṭaka Kingship", *Ritual, State and History in South Asia: Essays in Honour of J.C. Heesterman*, eds. A.W.von den Hoek et al., Leiden, 1992, pp. 7-19.

: "Throne and Temple: Political Power and Religious Prestige in Vidarbha", *The Sacred Centre as the Focus of Political Interest: Proceedings of the Symposium held on the Occasion of the 375th Anniversary of the University of Groningen*, 5-8 March, ed. H. Bakkar, Groningen, 1990, pp. 83-100.

Bhandarkar, R.G.: *Early History of the Deccan, Collected Works of Sir R.G. Bhandarkar*, III, ed. N.B. Utgikar, Bhandarkar Oriental Research Institute, Pune, 1927, pp. 1-99.

Bhattacharya, P.K.: *Historical Geography of Madhya Pradesh*, Motilal Banarsidass, Delhi, 1977.

Chattopadhyaya, Sudhakara: *Early History of Northern India*, 2nd edition, Academic Publishers, Calcutta, 1968.

Collins, Mark: *The Geographical Data of the Raghuvaṁśa and Daśakumāracharita*, Leipzig, 1907.

Deo, S.B.: *Māhurjharī Excavations*, Nagpur University, 1973.

Deo, S.B, and Dhavalikar, M.K.: *Paunar Excavations*, Nagpur University, 1967.

Dubreuil, J. "Vyāghra, the Uchchakalpa", *IA*, LV, p. 103.

: *Ancient History of the Deccan*, Pondicherry, 1920.

Gokhale, Shobhana: "Epigraphical Evidence on Harisheṇa's Conquest from Kānherī," *AV*, ed. Ajay Mitra Shastri, pp. 269-78.

Goyal, Shriram: *Gupta Sāmrājya kā Itihāsa* (Hindi), Kusumāñjali Prakāshan, Meerut (now Jodhpur), 1988.

: *Gupta aura Vākāṭaka Sāmrājyoṁ kā Itihāsa* (Hindi), Kusumāñjali Prakashan, Meerut (now Jodhpur), 1988.

: *A History of the Imperial Guptas,* Central Book Depot, Allahabad, 1967.

Gupta, Chandrashekhar: "Paunār under the Vākāṭakas," *AV,* pp. 119-53.

Jamkhedkar, A.P.: "Vaiṣṇavism in the Vākāṭaka Times", *Vaiṣṇavism in Indian Arts and Culture,* ed. Ratan Parimoo, Books & Books, New Delhi, 1987, pp. 335-41.

: "A Newly Discovered Vākāṭaka Temple at Rāmṭek, District Nagpur", *Kusumāñjali: New Interpretation of Indian Art and Culture: Sh. C. Sivaramamurti Commemoration Volume,* ed. M.S. Nagaraja Rao, Agam Kala Prakashan, Delhi, 1987, pp. 217-23.

: "Discovery of Vākāṭaka Temples at Rāmṭek" *AV,* pp. 155-64.

: "Beginnings of North Indian Temple Architecture, Early Vidarbha Style, c. A.D. 350-500: Vākāṭakas (Main Branch)", *Indian Temple Architecture,* II (I), American Institute of Indian Studies, Princeton University Press, pp. 59-72.

Jayaswal, K.P.: *History of India: 150 A.D. to 350 A.D.,* Motilal Banarsidass, Lahore, 1933.

Joshi, M.C. and Gupta, S.K. (eds.): *King Chandra and the Meharaulī Pillar,* Kusumanjali Prakashan, Jodhpur, 1991.

Kane, P.V.: *History of Dharmaśāstra,* III, Bhandarkar Oriental Research Institute, Pune, 1941.

Law, N.N.: *Aspects of Ancient Indian Polity,* Orient Longmans, Mumbai, 1921.

Majumdar, R.C.: "Note on the Genealogy and Chronology of the Vākāṭakas", *JRASB,* XII, pp. 1-5, *Vide* also *ibid.,* XX, pp. 100-05.

Majumdar, R.C. and Altekar, A.S. (eds.): *A New History of the Indian People,* IV: *The Vākāṭaka-Gupta Age,* Reprint, Motilal Banarsidass, Delhi, 1960.

Majumdar, R.C. and Dasgupta, K.K. (eds.): *A Comprehensive History of India,* III, Peoples Publishing House, New Delhi, 1981.

Majumdar, R.C. and Pusalkar, A.D. (eds.): *A History and Culture of the Indian People,* II: *The Age of Imperial Unity,* second ed., Bharatiya Vidya Bhavan, Mumbai, 1953; III: *The Classical Age,* 1954.

Mirashi, V.V.: Ch. III, "Successors of Ṣātavāhanas in Maharashtra", *MSGH*, I, Government of Maharashtra, Mumbai, 1967, pp. 101-42.

: *Vākāṭaka Nṛipati āṇi tyāṁchā Kāḷa* (Marathi), Nagpur University, 1957.

: Ch. VII: "The Vākāṭakas and Other Contemporary Dynasties", *CHI*, III, Part I, Peoples Publishing House, New Delhi, 1981, pp. 128-72.

: *Studies in Indology*, 1, 2nd ed., Vidarbha Samsmodhan Mandala, Nagpur, 1968; IV, Tara Prakashan, Varanasi, 1966.

: *Literary and Historical Studies in Indology*, Motilal Banarsidass, Delhi, 1975.

: *Indological Research Papers*, I, Vidarbha Samshodhan Maṇḍaḷ, Nagpur, 1982.

: "A Note on the Dates of Uchchakalpa Kings", *EI*, XXIII, pp. 171-74.

: "Dahigāon Hoard and Traikūṭaka Rule over Vidarbha", *ND*, III, Part I, pp. 4-6.

Ramesh, K.V.: "On the Vākāṭakas and their Inscriptions", *AV*, pp.

Raychaudhuri, H.C.: *Political History of Ancient India*, 5th ed. Unversity of Culcutta, 1953.

: *Studies in Indian Antiquities*, 2nd ed., University of Calcutta, 1958.

Sankaranarayanan, S.: *The Vishṇukuṇdis and their Times*, Agam Prakashan, Delhi, 1977.

Shastri, Ajay Mitra: *Tripurī* (Hindi), Madhya Pradesh Hindi Grantha Academy, Bhopal, 1971.

: *Early History of the Deccan: Problems and Perspectives.* Sundeep Prakashan, Delhi, 1987.

: (ed.): *The Age of the Vākāṭakas*, Harman Publishing House, New Delhi, 1992.

: *Varāhamihira's India*, Aryan Books International, New Delhi, 1996.

: *Sātavāhanas and the Western Kshatrapas—A Historical Framework*, Dattsons, Nagpur, 1997.

: "Some Aspects of Personal Names in the Vākāṭaka Inscriptions", *JOI*, XXXVI, pp. 254-63.

: "Vākāṭakas: Original home and other problems", *AV*, pp. 3-20.

: "Original home and nomenclature of the Sātavāhanas", *BDCRI*, Sir William Jones Special Issue.

: "Presidential address", *PIHC*, 1978, pp. 965-81

: "The Vākāṭaka Kings Dāmodara Sena and Pravarasena II," *JESI*, XIV, pp. 38-40.

: "The Mūḍigere Plates of Simhavarman and Kadamba-Vākāṭaka Relations", *Indian Archaeological Heritage: K.V. Soundararajan Felicitation Volume*, eds. C. Margabandhu et. al., Agam Kala Prakashan, Delhi, 1991, pp. 317-19.

: "Śesha-śayana Vishṇu: Earliest Epigraphical Evidence", *Vishnu in Art, Thought and Literature*, Birla Archaeological and Cultural Research Institute, Hyderabad, 1993, pp. 1-6.

: "The Date of the Bamhani and Mallār Plates of Śūrabala Udirnavaira", *Bhāratī-Bhānam: Dr. K.V. Sarma Felicitation Volume*, Vishveshvaranand Indological Research Institute, Hoshiarpur, 1980, pp. 439-43.

: "Vidarbha and the Traikūṭakas", *ND*, III, Part I, pp. 7-9.

: "The Śarabhhapurīyas", *Prāchya Pratibhā*, V, Part I, pp. 1-40.

: "Capitals of the Vākāṭakas," *Quarterly Journal of the Mythic Society*, LXXXV, Part 3, Sept. 1994, pp. 17-37.

Sircar, D.C.: *Indian Epigraphy*, Motilal Banarsidass, Delhi, 1965.

: Indian Epigraphical Glossary, Motilal Banarsidass, Delhi, 1966.

: *Studies in the Geography of Ancient and Mediaeval India*, 2nd ed., Motilal Banarsidass, Delhi, 1972.

: "A Note on the Vākāṭakas", *JRASB*, XII, pp. 71-73; XIII, pp. 75-78.

: "Vākāṭaka Occupation of Baghelkhaṇḍa-Bundelkhaṇḍ Region", *AV*, pp. 47-49.

Sivaramamurti, C.: *Amaravati Sculptures in the Madras Government Museum, Bulletin of the Madras Government Museum*, New Series, General Series, IV, Madras, 1956.

Smith, V.A.: "The Vākāṭaka Dynasty of Berar in the Fourth and Fifth Centuries A.C.", *JRAS*, 1914, pp. 317-38.

Sohoni, S.V.: "A Note on the Original Territory of the Vākāṭakas", *JIH*, XLIX, pp. 135-42.

Thosar, H.R.: "Re-Examination of the Historical Contents of the Nagardhan Plates of Svāmirāja and Rithpur Grant of the Nala King Arthapati", *JESI*, XX, 1994, pp. 19-25.

: "Royal Seats of the Vākāṭakas", *SIPN*, XVI, 1996, pp. 27-35.

Yazdani, G. (*ed.*): *Early History of the Deccan*, Oxford, 1960.

Index*

*The following abbreviations have been used in the Index : a = author; *ad* = administrative division; *d* = dynasty; *l* = locality; *m* = mountain, o = office; q = queen; r = river; *s* = sacrifice; *t* = text.

Illustrations

Pl. I. Deotek Stone Inscription of Aśoka's Dharmamahāmātra

Pl. II. Deoṭek Stone Inscription of Rudra Sena I or II

Pl. III. Nachne-kī-Talāi Stone Inscription (No. I) of Vyāghradeva, Reign of Pṛithivī Sheṇa I

Pl. IV. Nachne-kī-Talāi Stone Inscription (No. II) of Vyāghradeva, Reign of Pṛithivī Sheṇa I

Pl. V. Ganj Stone Inscription of Vyāghradeva, Reign of Pṛithivī Sheṇa I

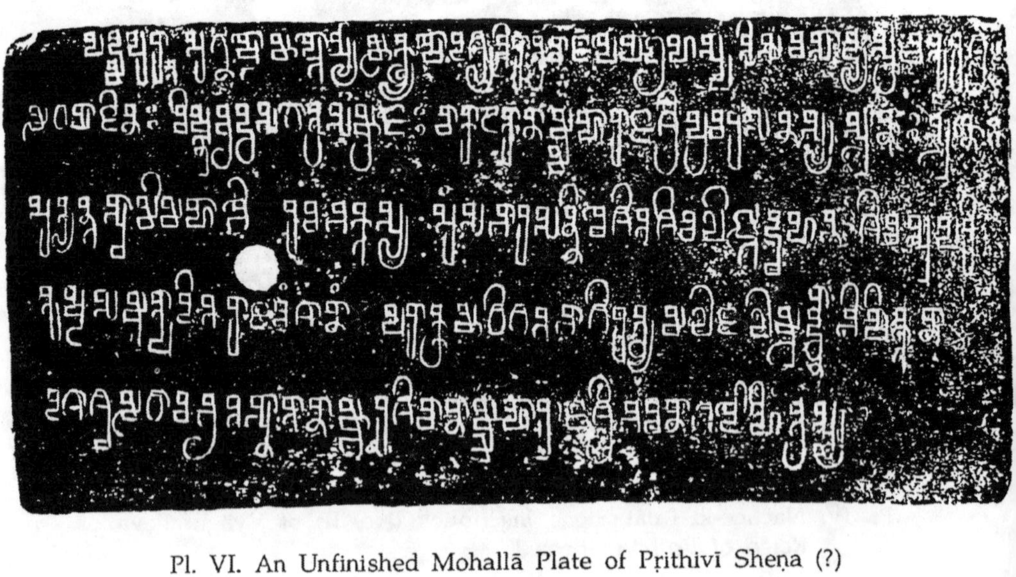

Pl. VI. An Unfinished Mohallā Plate of Pṛithivī Sheṇa (?)

Pls. VII-IX. Māṇḍhaḷ Plates of Rudra Sena II, Year 5

i

ii,a

ii,b

14

16

18

iii,a

20

22

24

iii,b

iv

IX

Pls. X-XI. Pune Plates of Prabhāvatī Guptā, Year 13

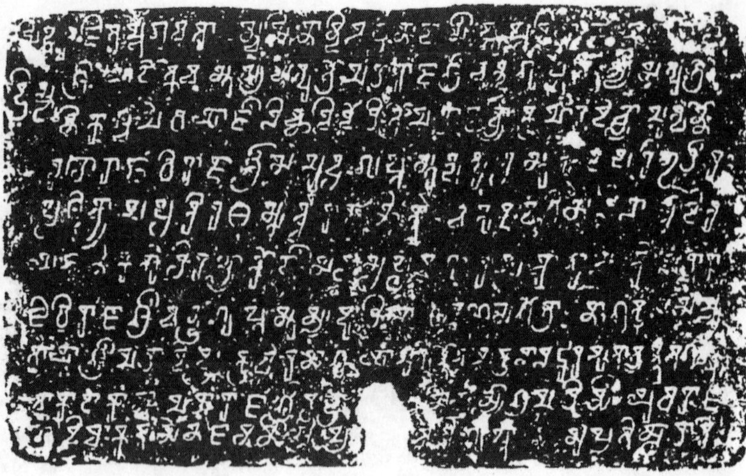

X

ii

Seal

XI

Pls. XII-XIV. Jāmb Plates of Pravara Sena II, Year 2

i

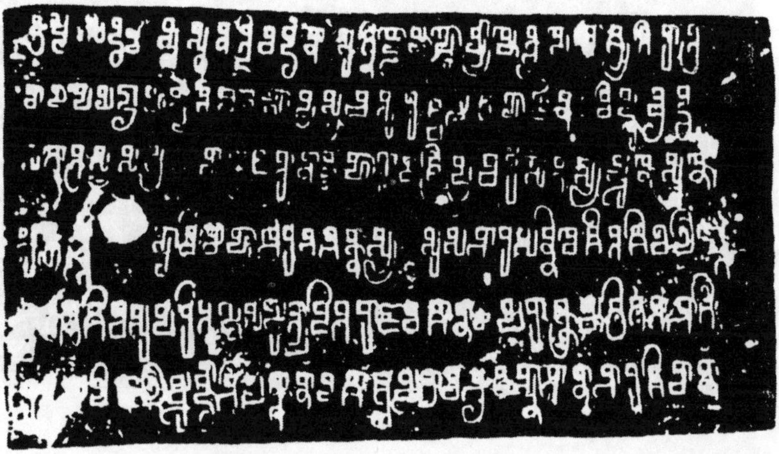

ii,a

ii,b

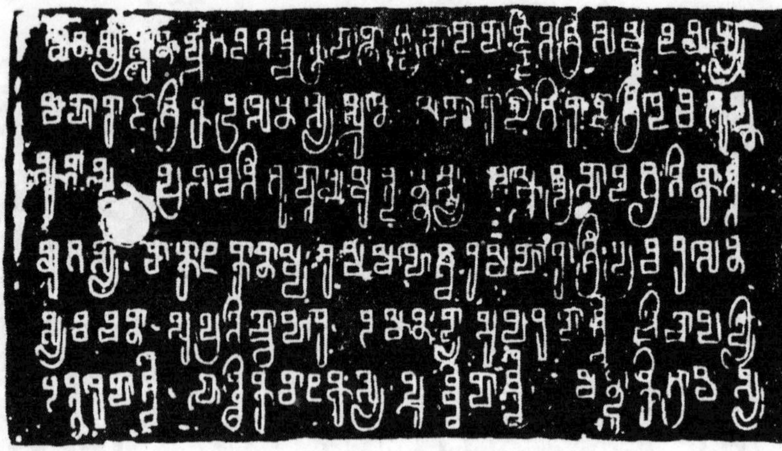

iii,a

iii,b

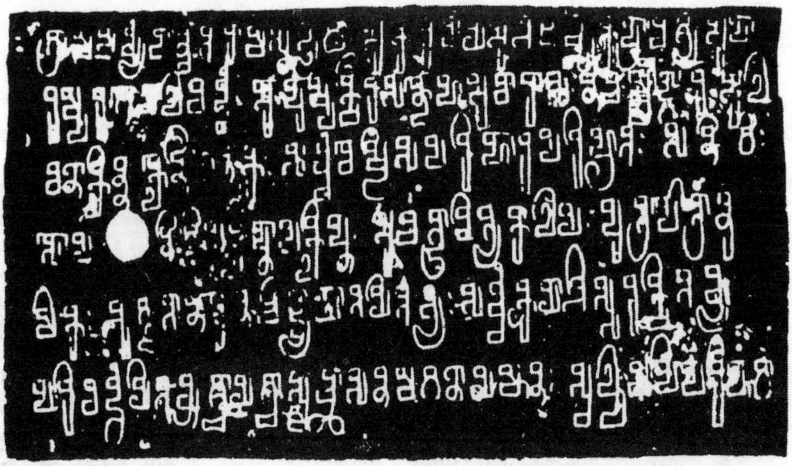

iv

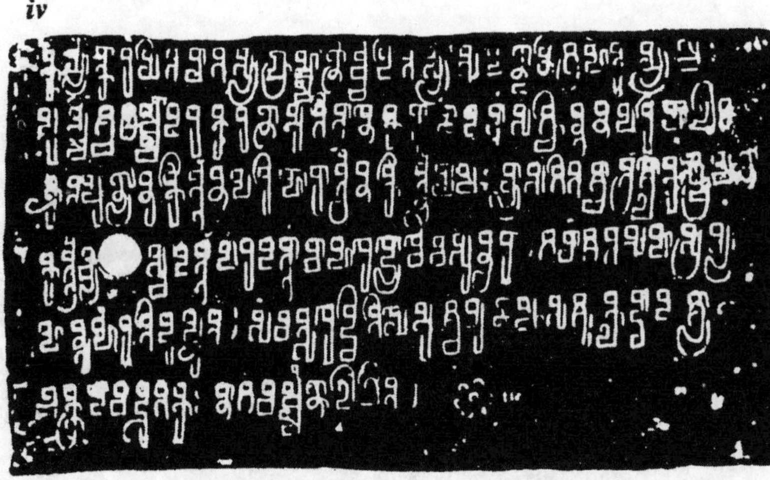

Pls. XV-XVII. Belorā Plates of Pravara Sena II, Year 11

i

ii,a

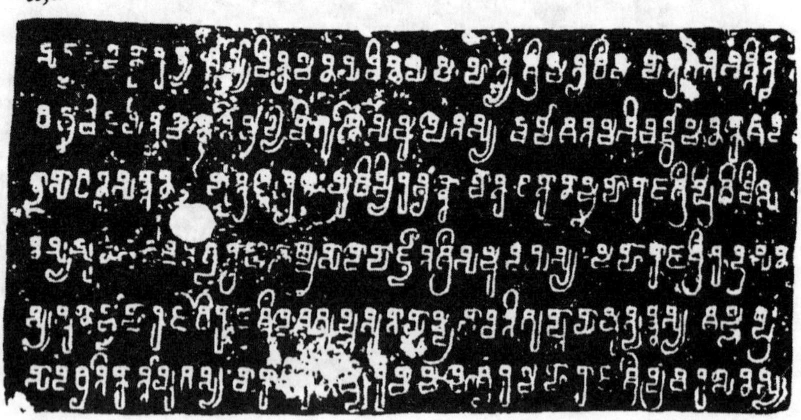

ii,b

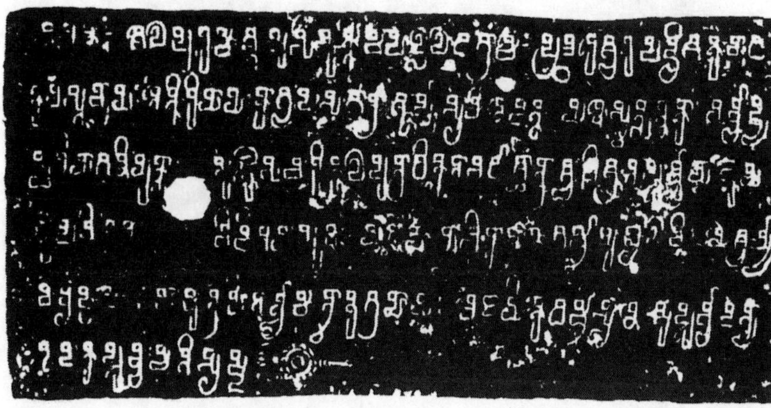

iii,a

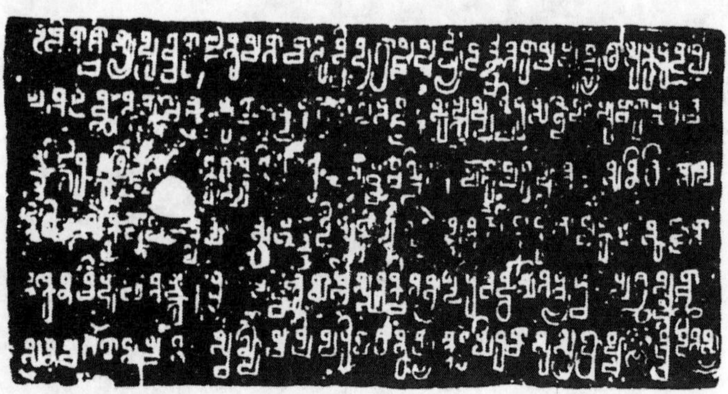

iii,b

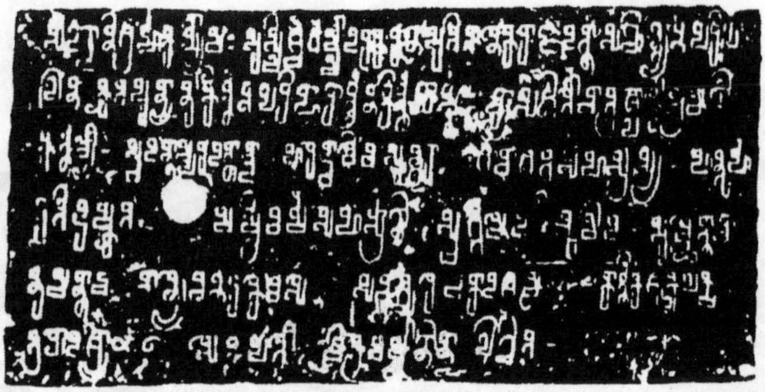

XVII

i,a

i,b

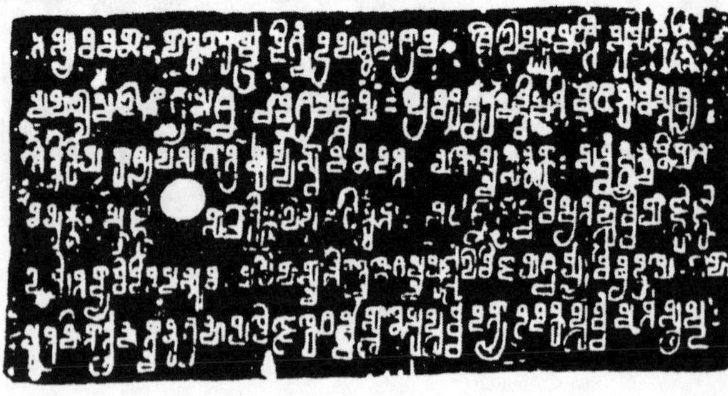

Pl. XVIII. Forged Belorā Plate of Pravara Sena II

Pls. XIX-XXII. Māṇḍhaḷ Plates of Pravara Sena II, Years 16 and 17

i

ii,a

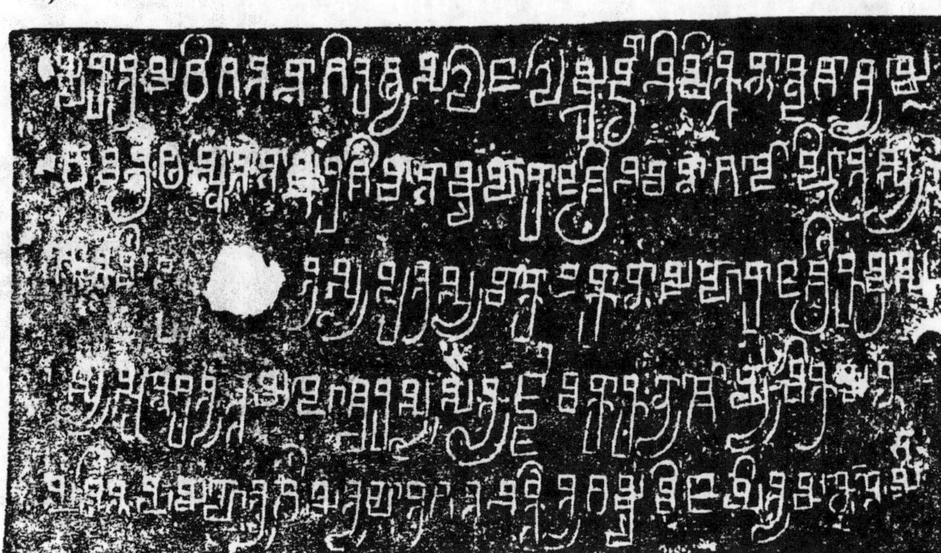

ii,b

iii,a

iii,b

iv,a

iv,b

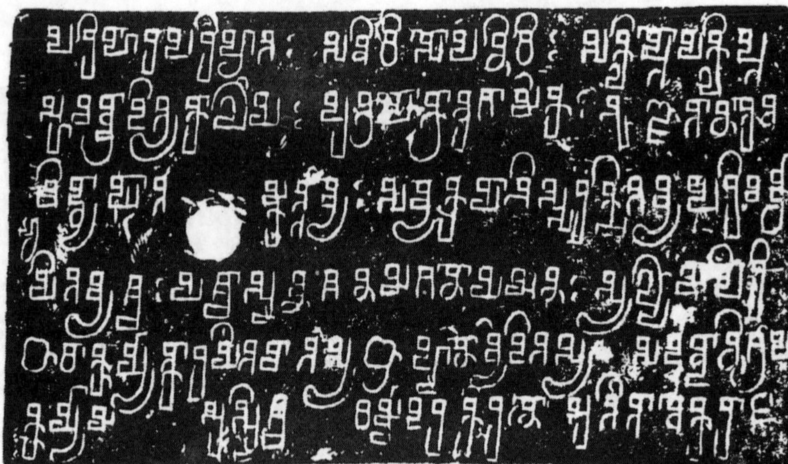

v

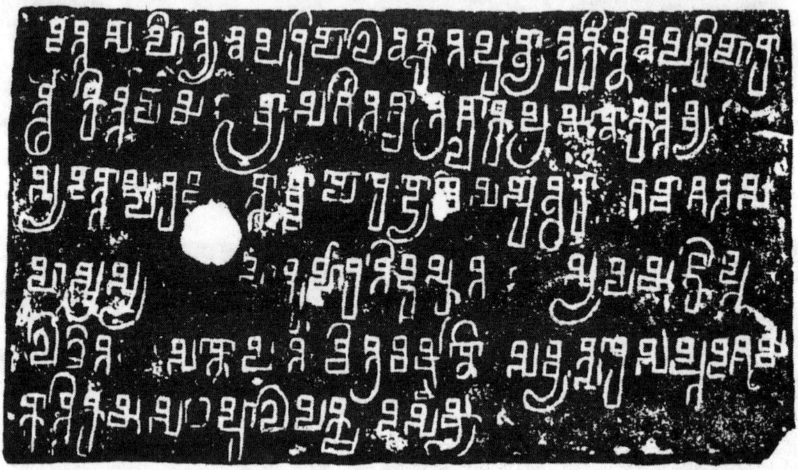

SEAL

Pls. XXIII-XXIX. Chammak Plates of Pravara Sena II, Year 18

i

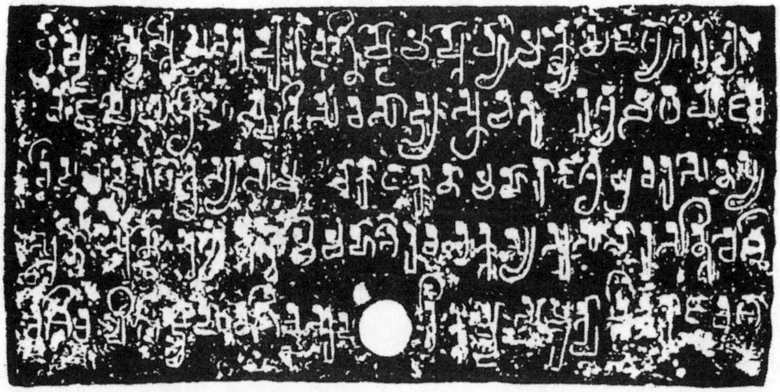

ii,a

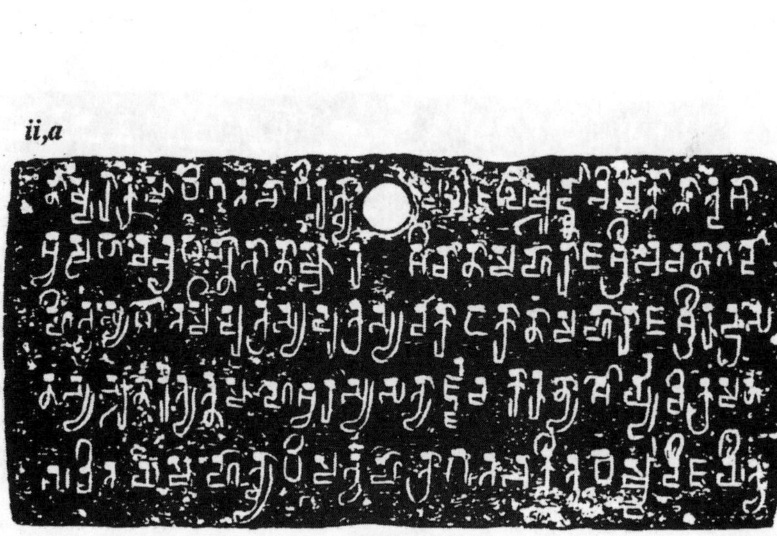

XXIII

ii,b

iii,a

XXIV

iii,b

iv,a

iv,b

v,a

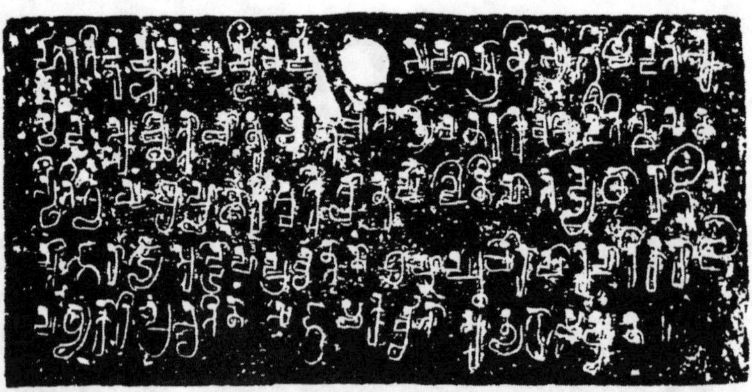

v,b

44 46

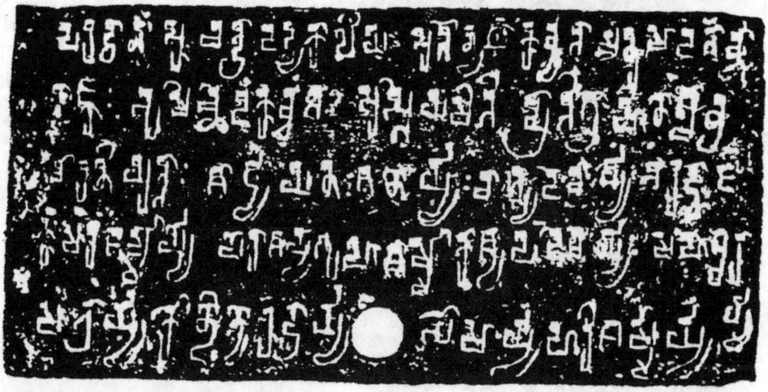

vi,a

48 50 52

vi,b

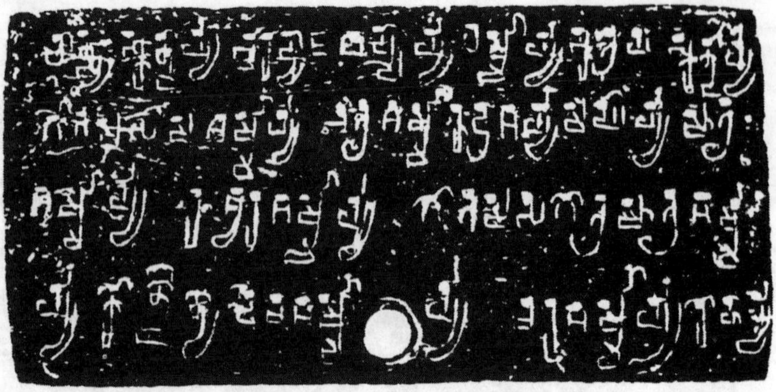

vii

XXVIII

XXIX

Pls. XXX-XXXIV. Siwanī Plates of Pravara Sena II, Year 18

i

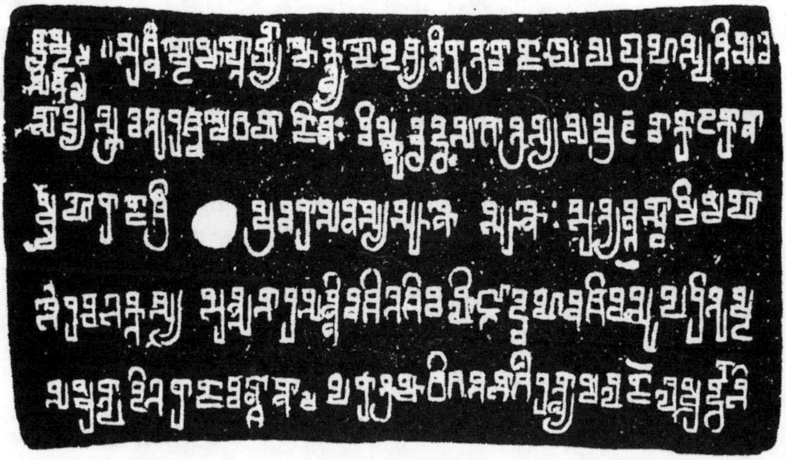

ii,a

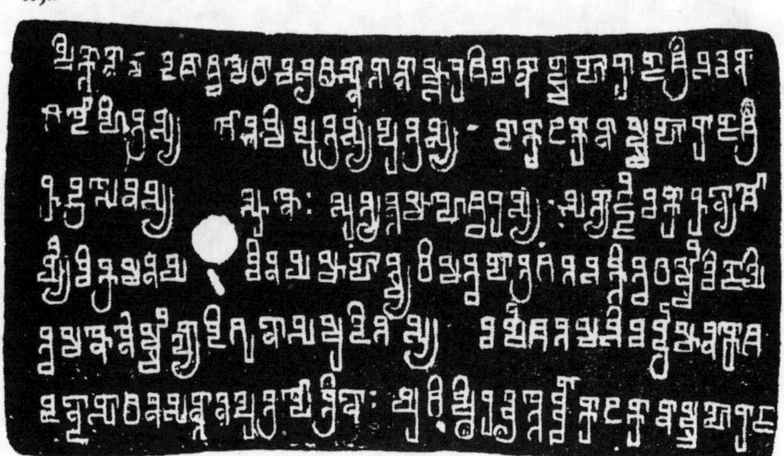

ii,b

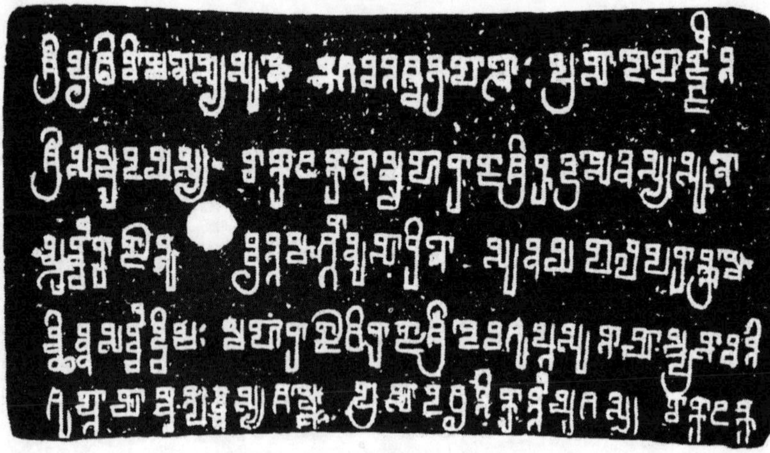

iii,a

iii,b

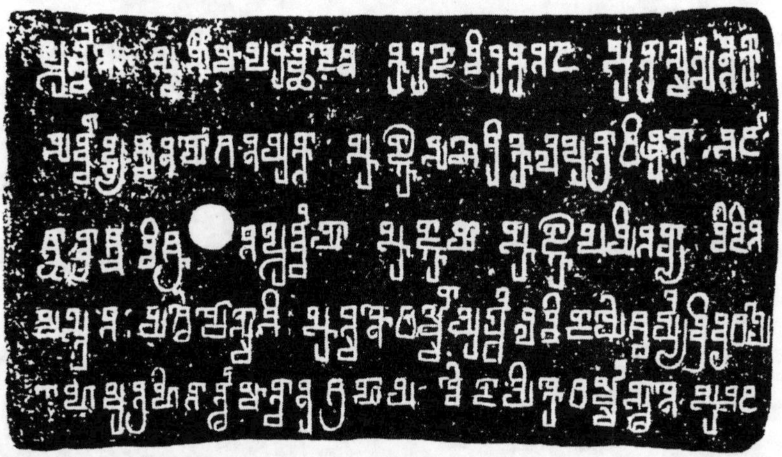

iv,a

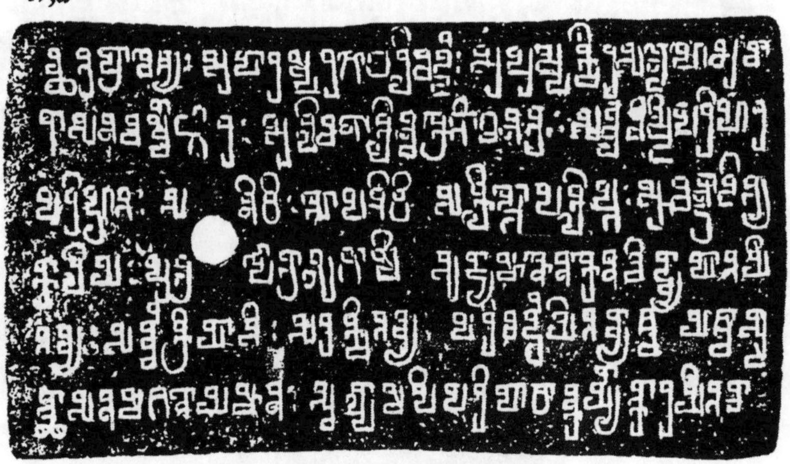

iv,b

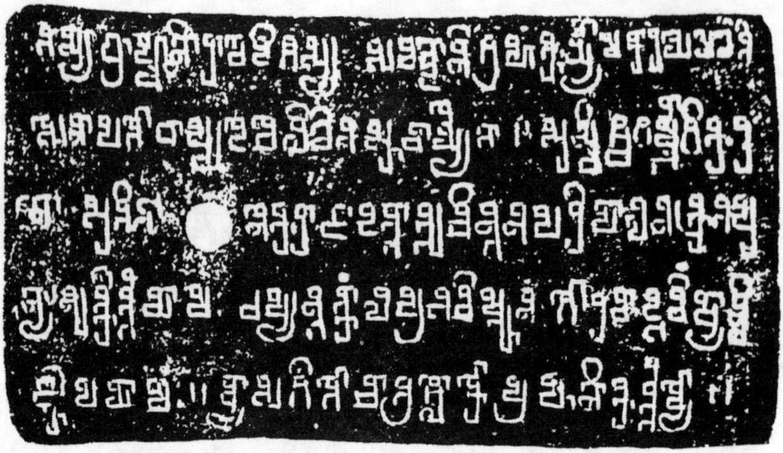

v

XXXIII

XXXIV

Pls. XXXV-XXXVII. Riddhapur Plates of Prabhāvatī Guptā, Year 19 of Pravara Sena II

i

ii,a

ii,b

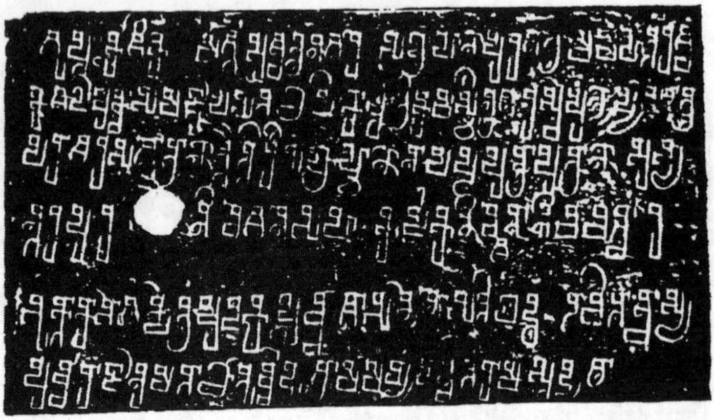

iii,a

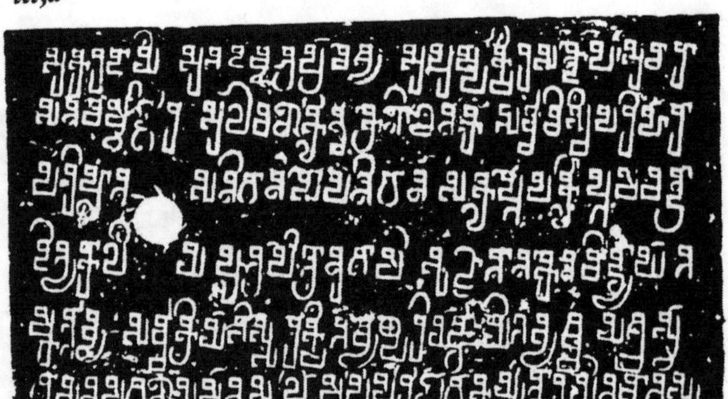

iii,b

iv

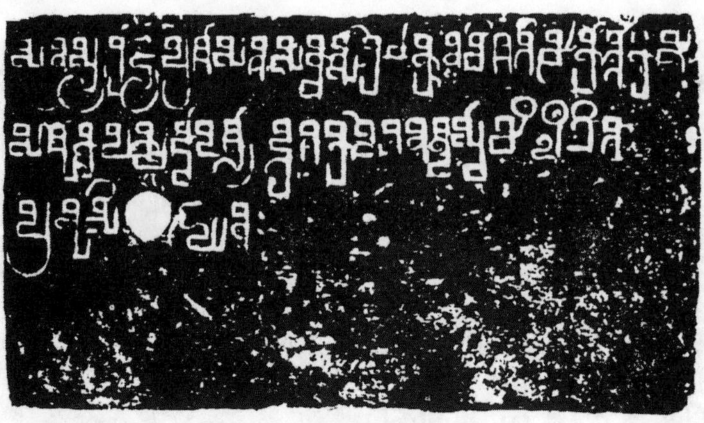

XXXVII

Pls. XXXVIII-XLII. Māsoda Plates of Pravara Sena II, Year 19

i

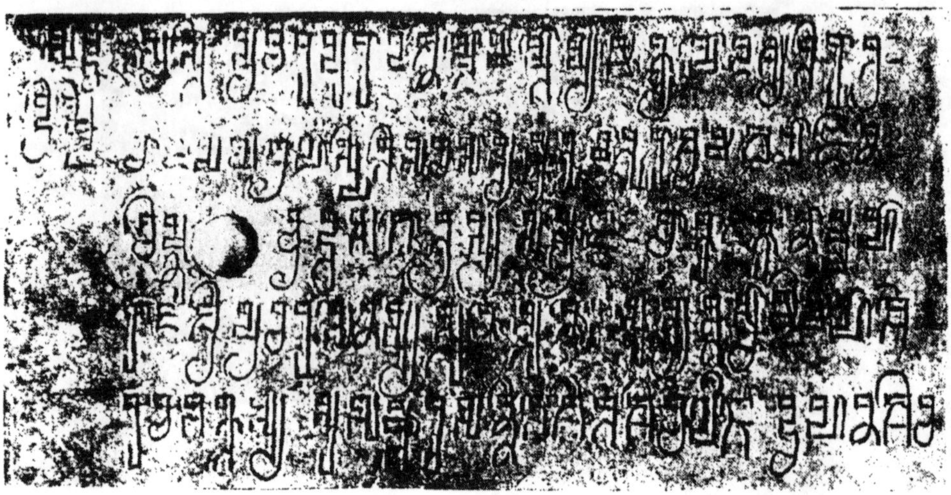

ii,a

ii,b

iii,a

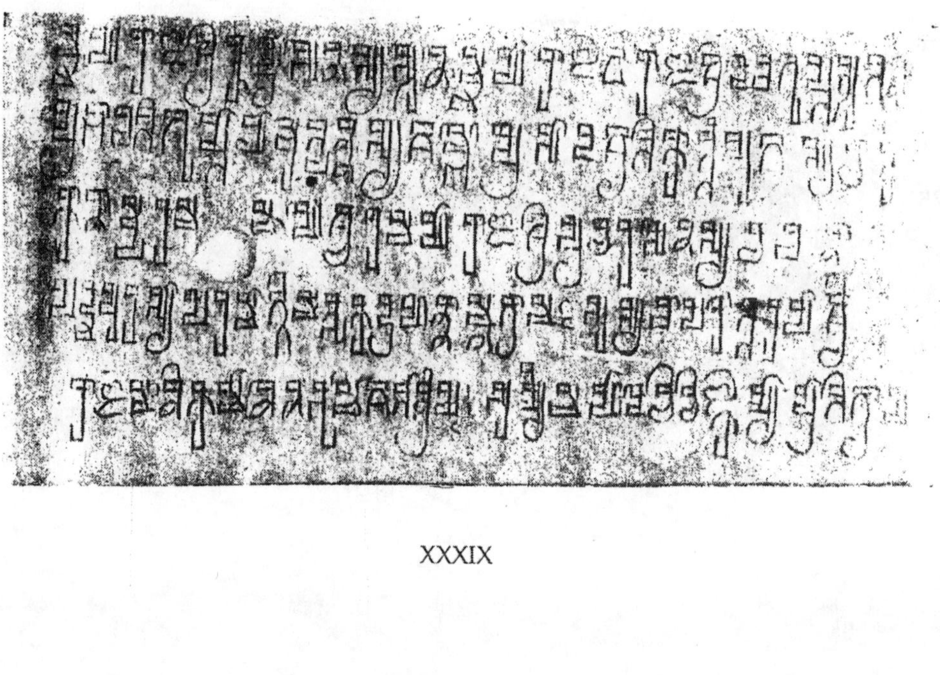

iii,b

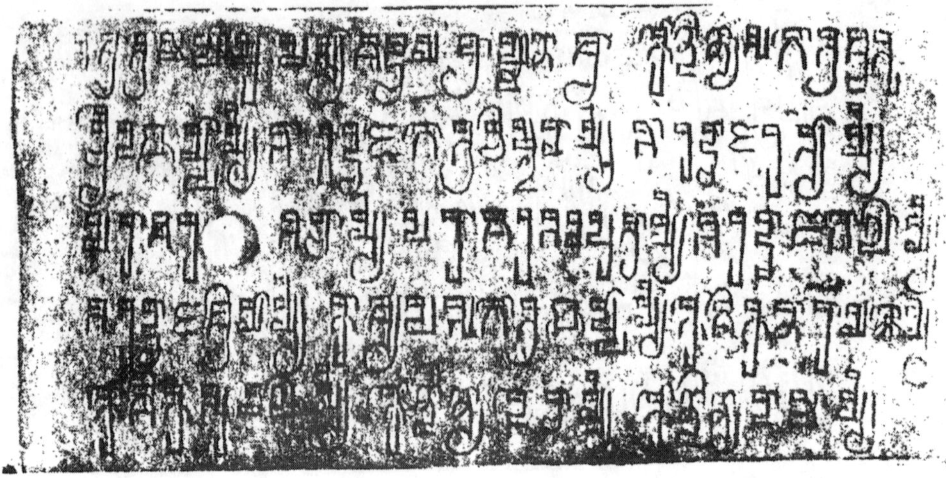

iv,a

iv,b

v,a

XLI

v,b

XLII

Pls. XLIII-XLV. Indore Plates of Pravara Sena II, Year 23

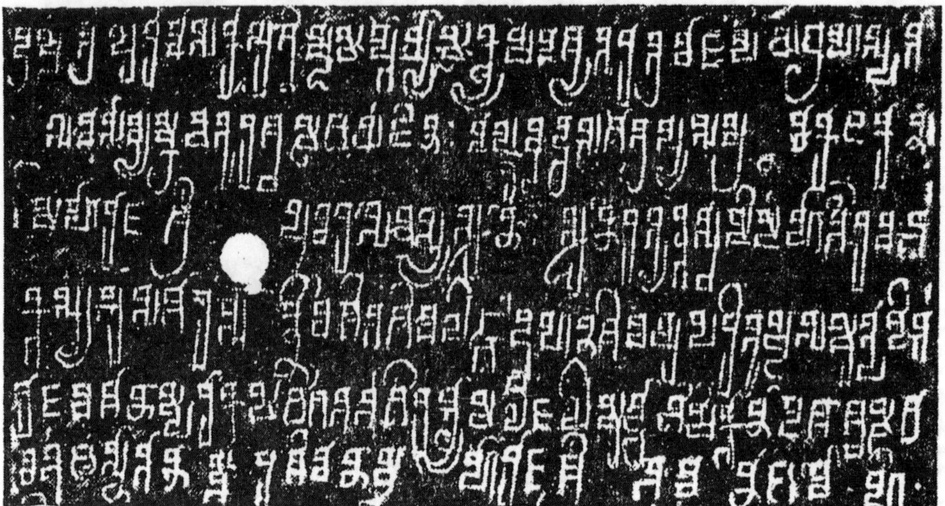

XLIII

ii,b

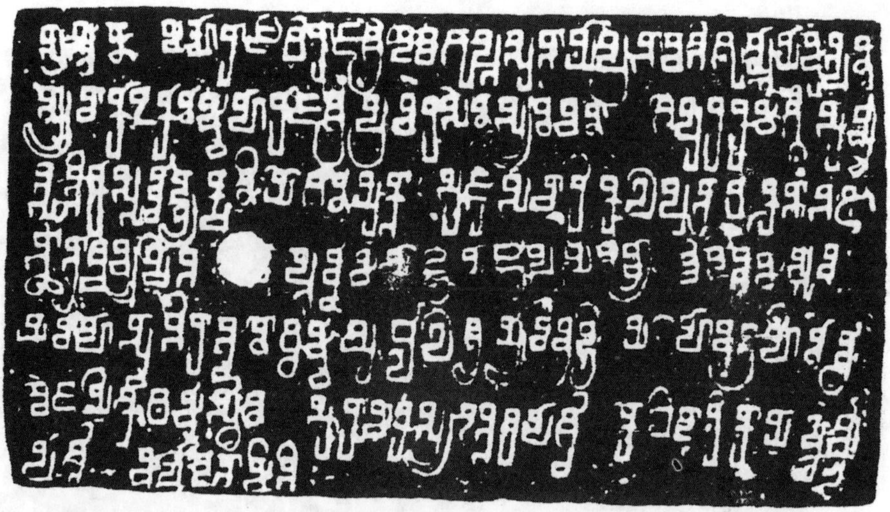

iii,a

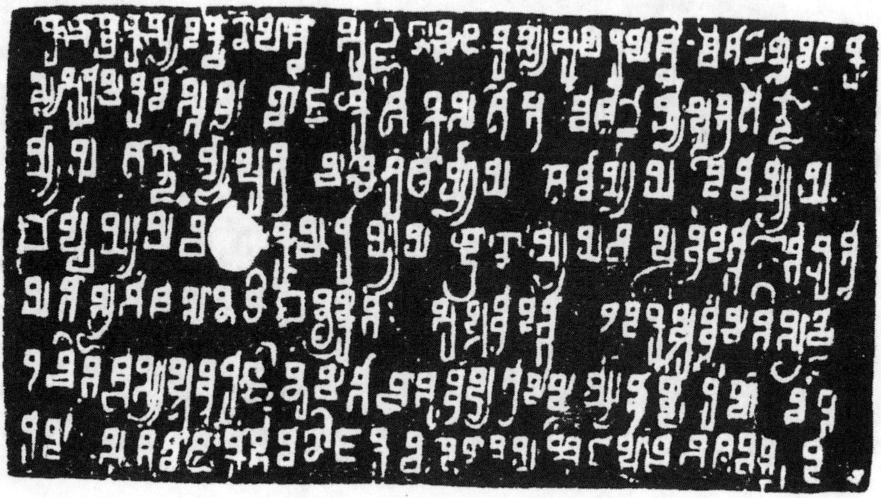

iii,b

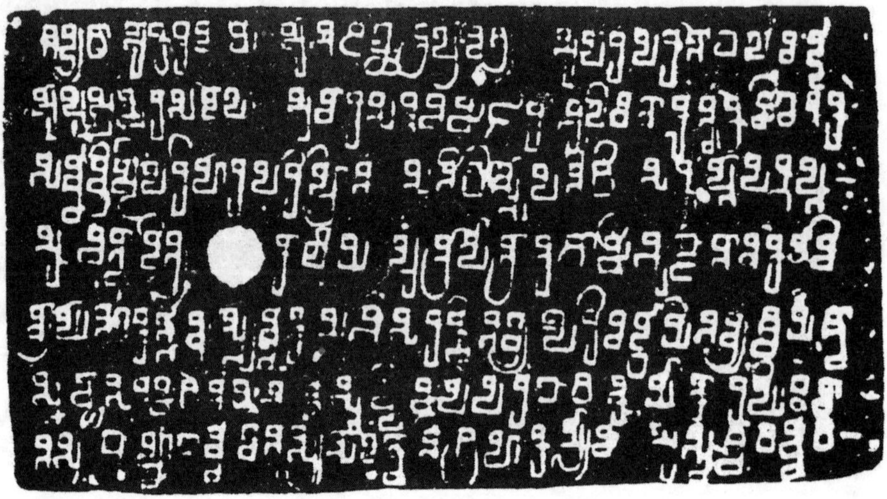

iv

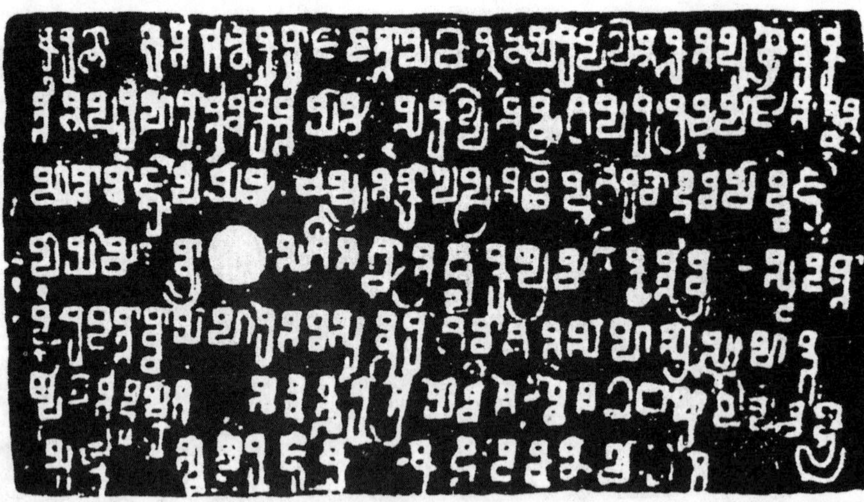

Pls. XLVI-XLVIII. Dudiā Plates of Pravara Sena II, Year 23

i

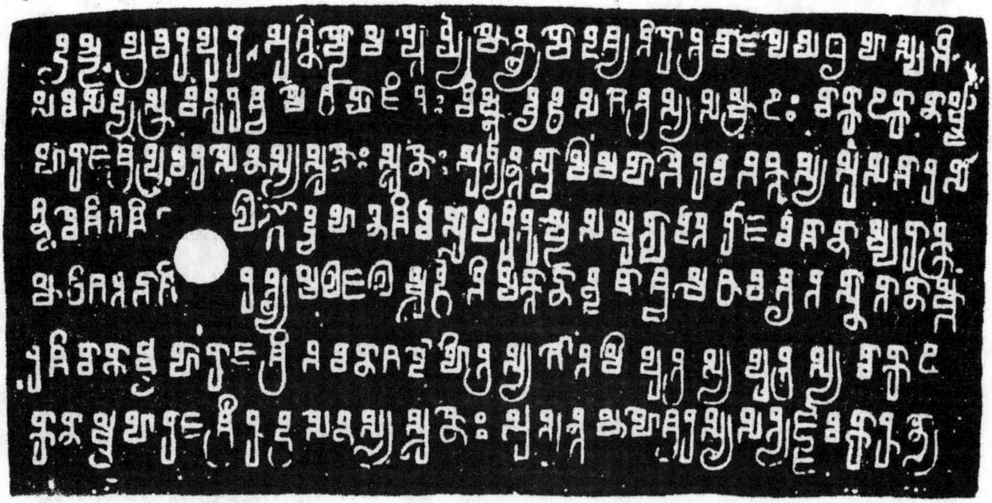

ii,a

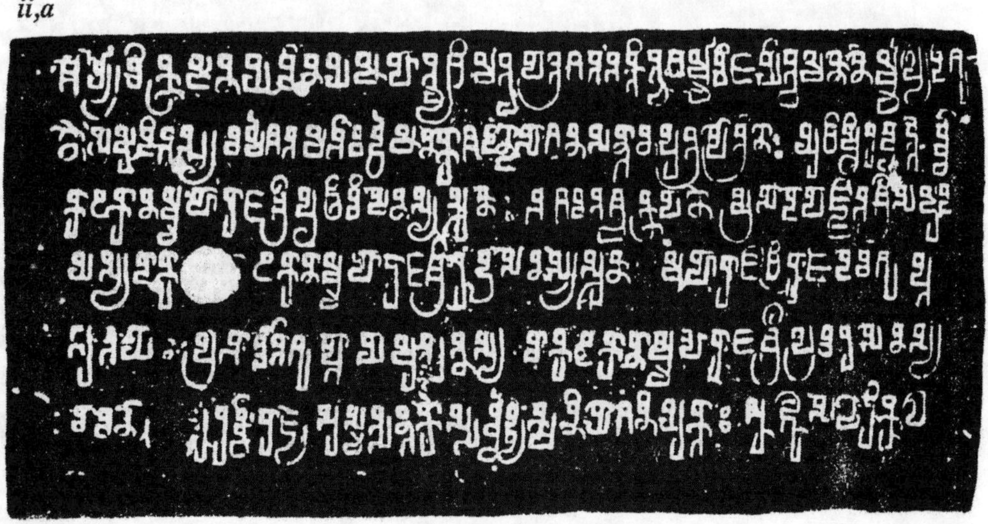

ii,b

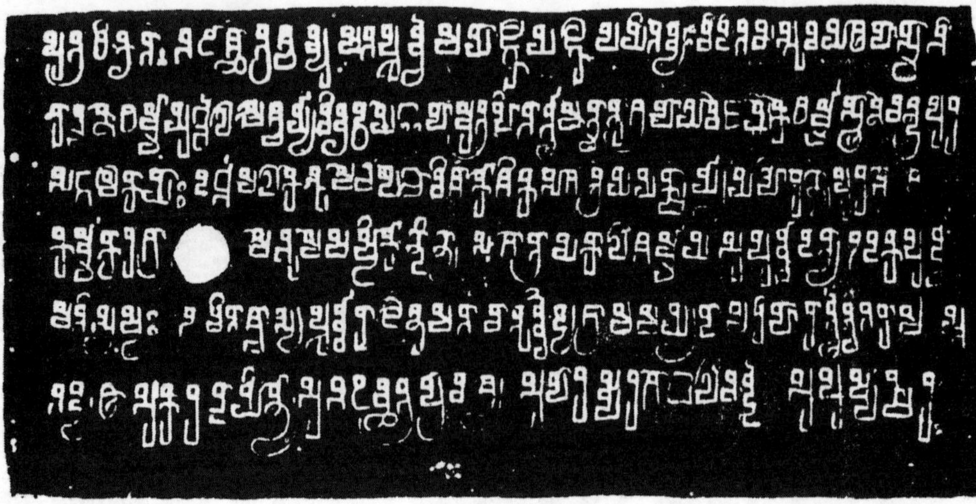

iii,a

iii,b

26

28

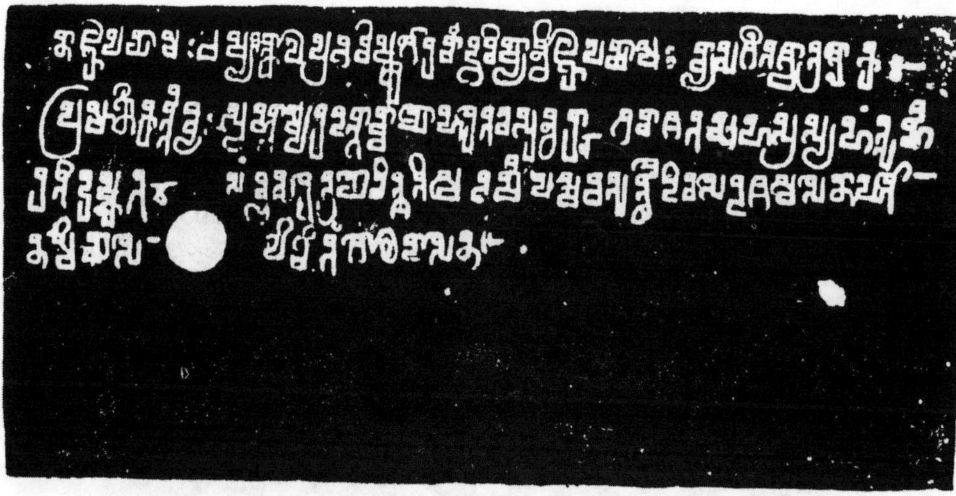

Seal

2

4

XLVIII

Pls. XLIX-LI. Tiroḍī Plates of Pravara Sena II, Year 23

i

ii,a

ii,b

iii,a

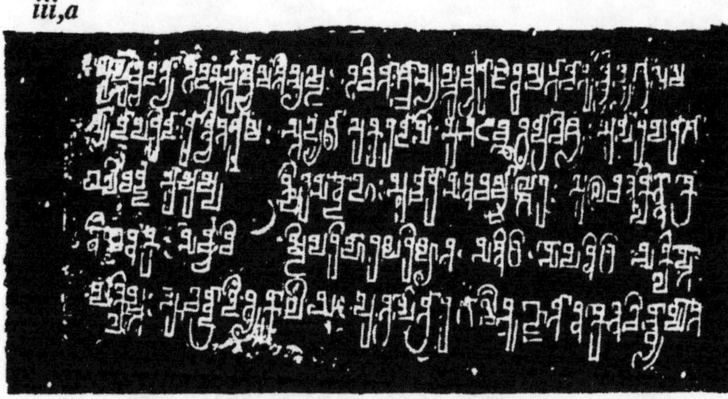

iii,b

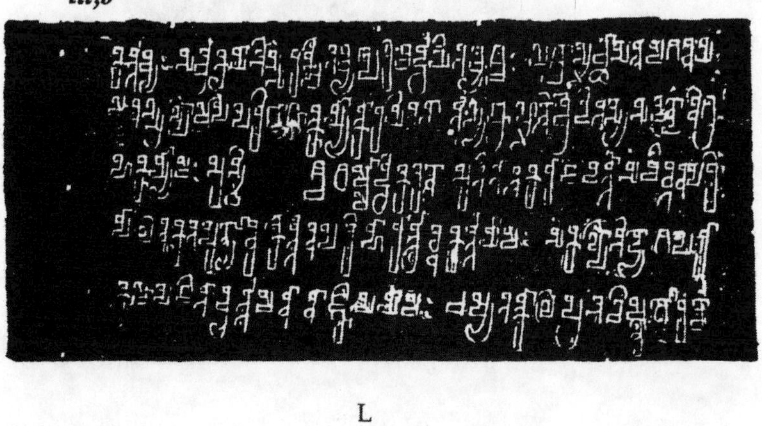

iv

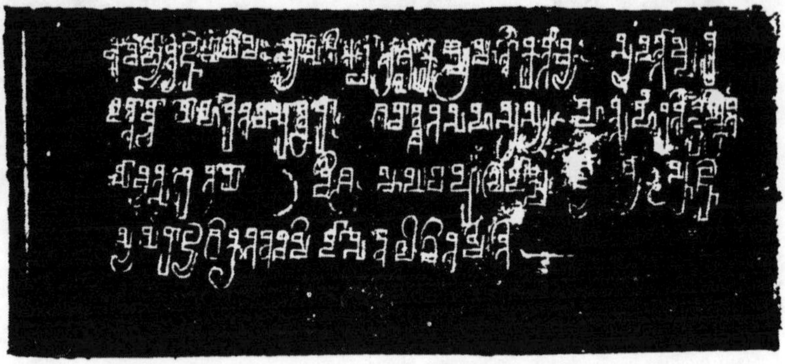

Pls. LII-LIV. Waḍgāon Plates of Pravara Sena II, Year 25

i

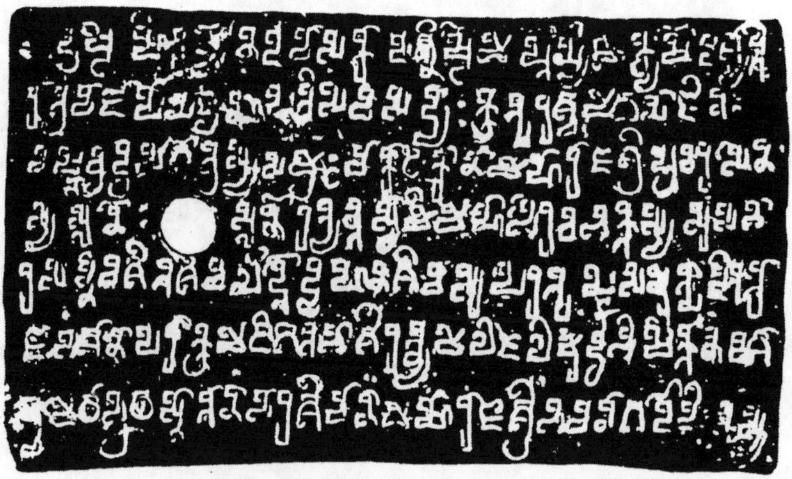

ii,a

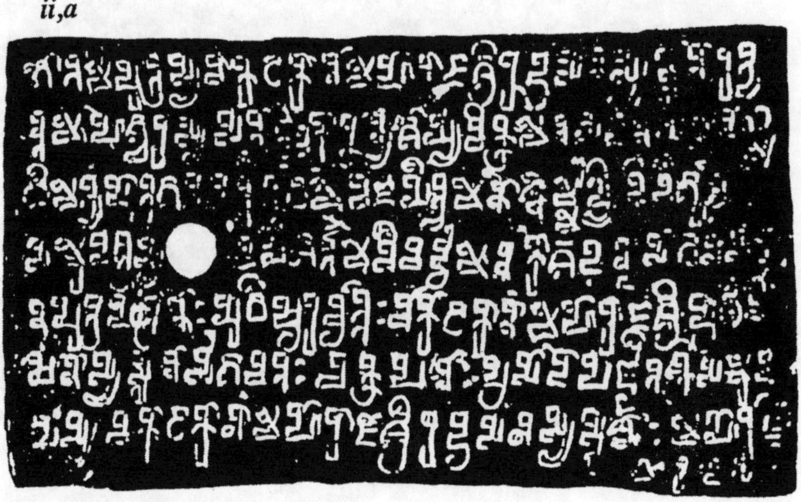

ii,b

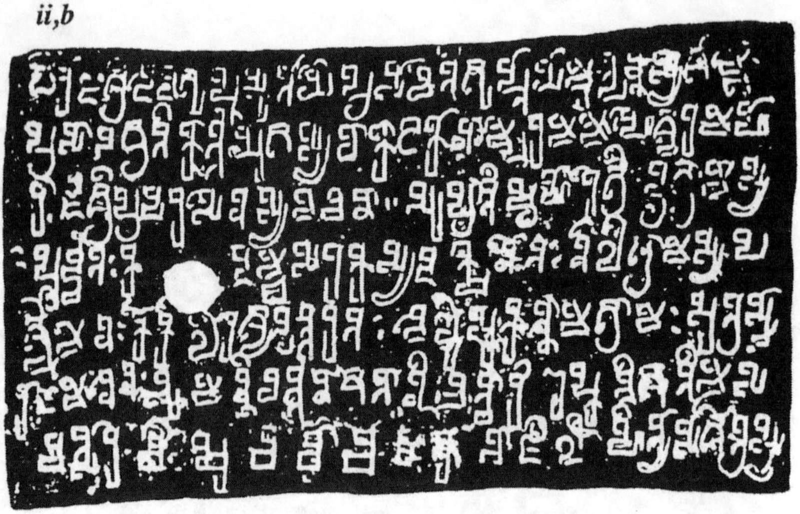

iii,a

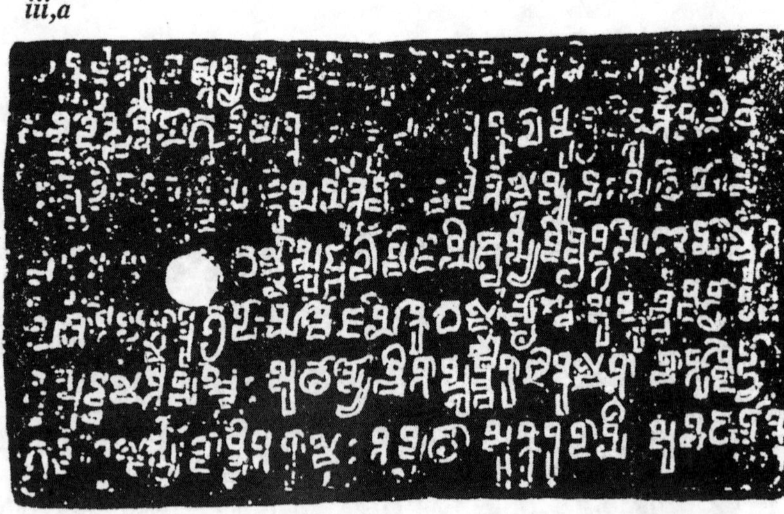

LIII

iii,b

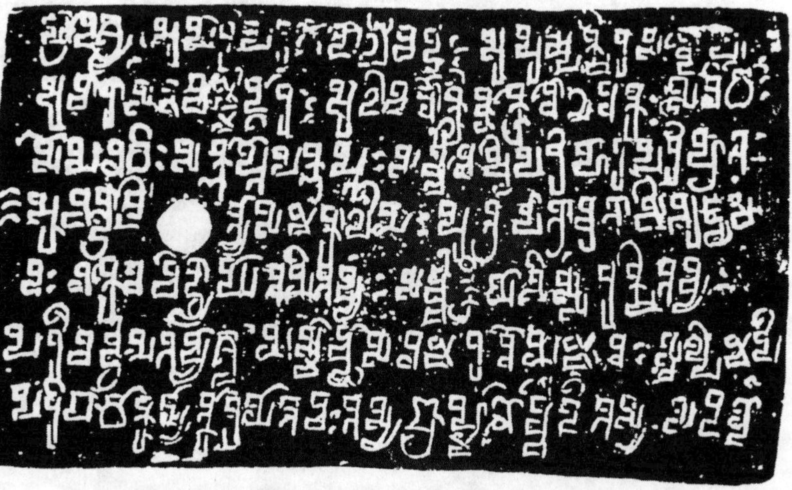

iv

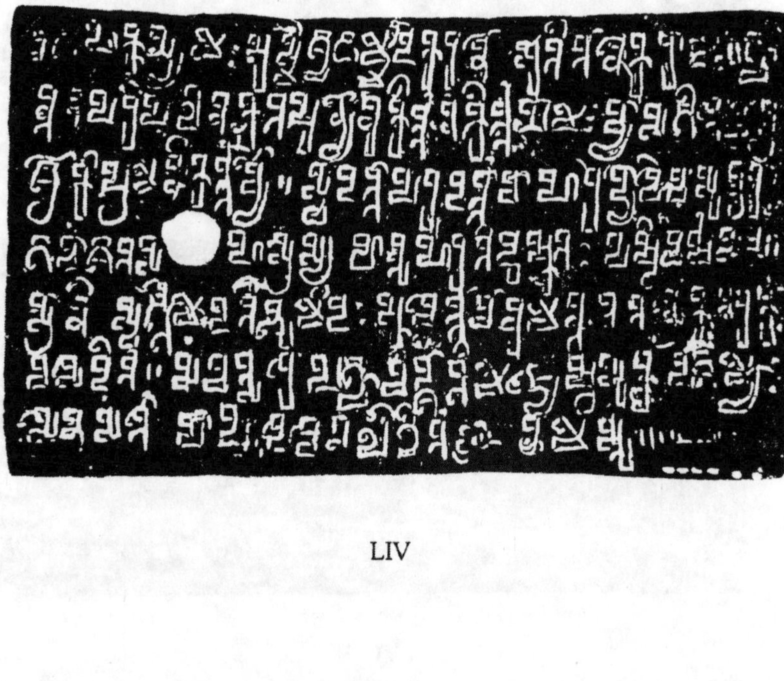

Pls. LV-LVI. Yawatmāl Plates of Pravara Sena II, Year 26

i,a

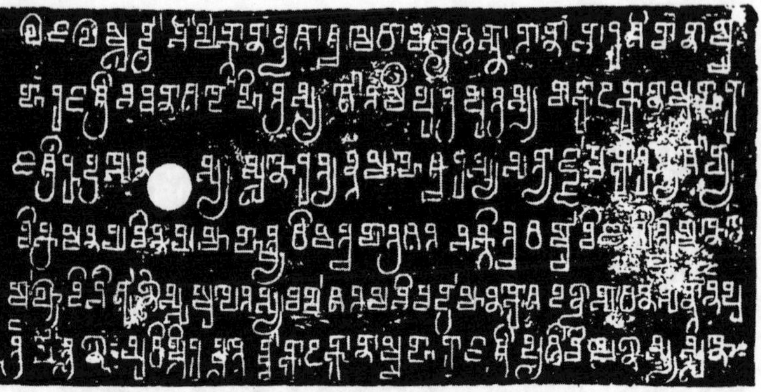

i,b

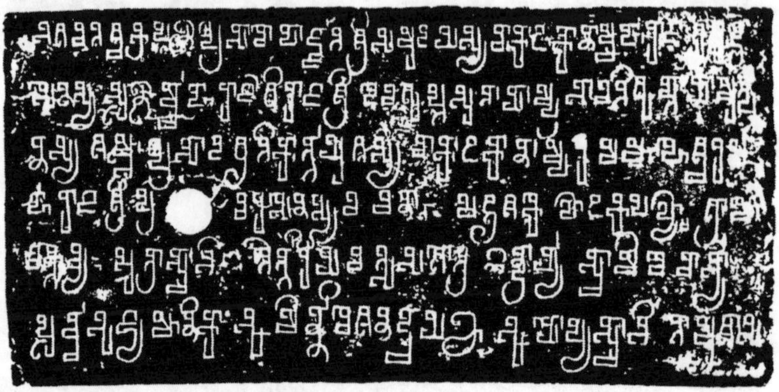

LV

ii

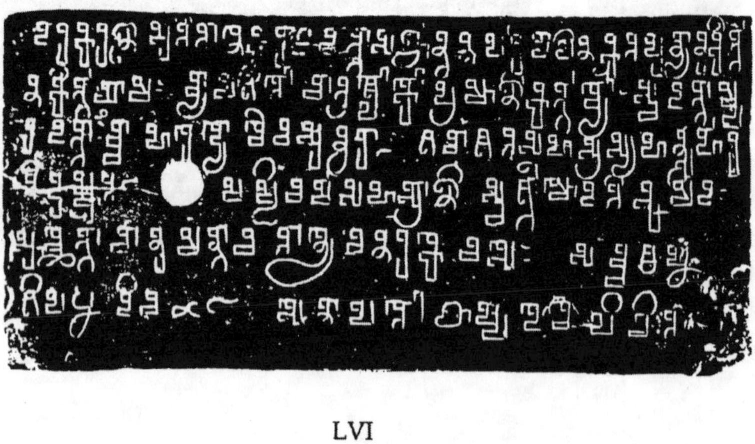

LVI

Pls. LVII-LXI. Paṭṭan Plates of Pravara Sena II, Year 27

i

ii,a

ii,b

14
16
18

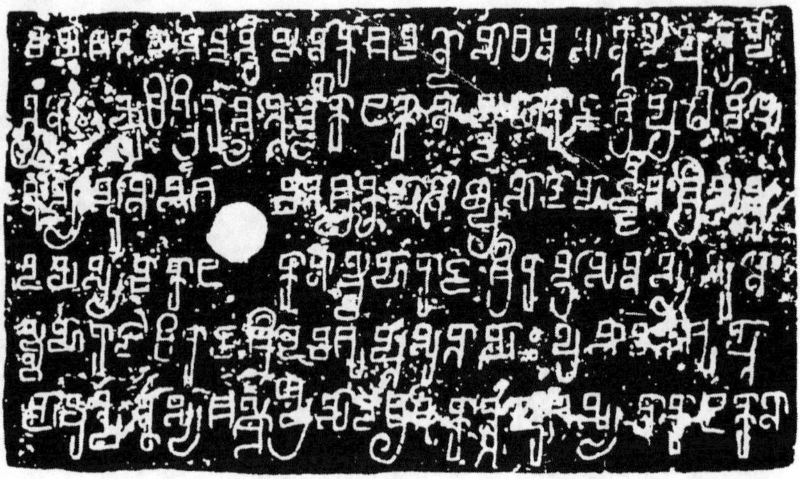

iii,a

20
22

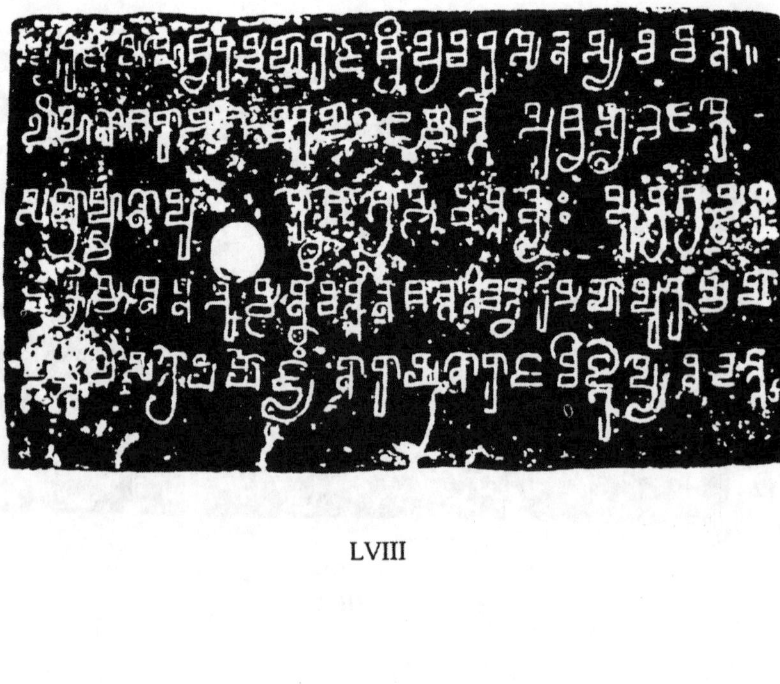

iii,b

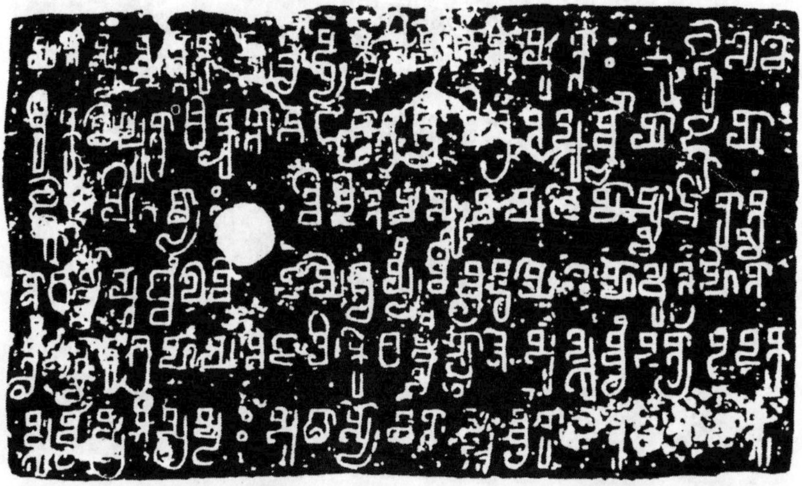

iv,a

iv,b

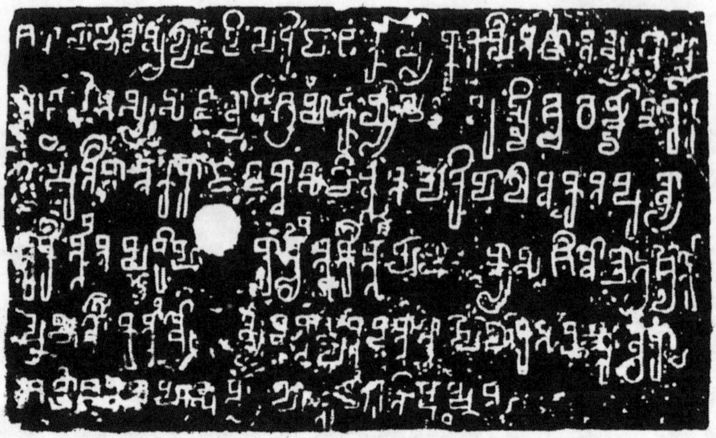

v

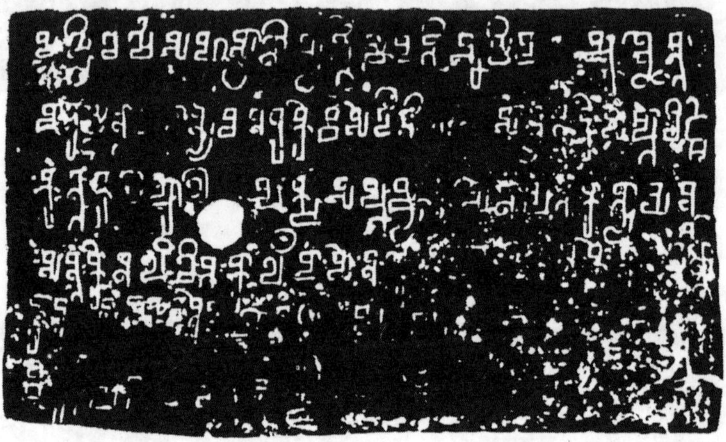

LX

Seal

LXI

Pls. LXII-LXIV. Tigāon Plates of Pravara Sena II, Year 9

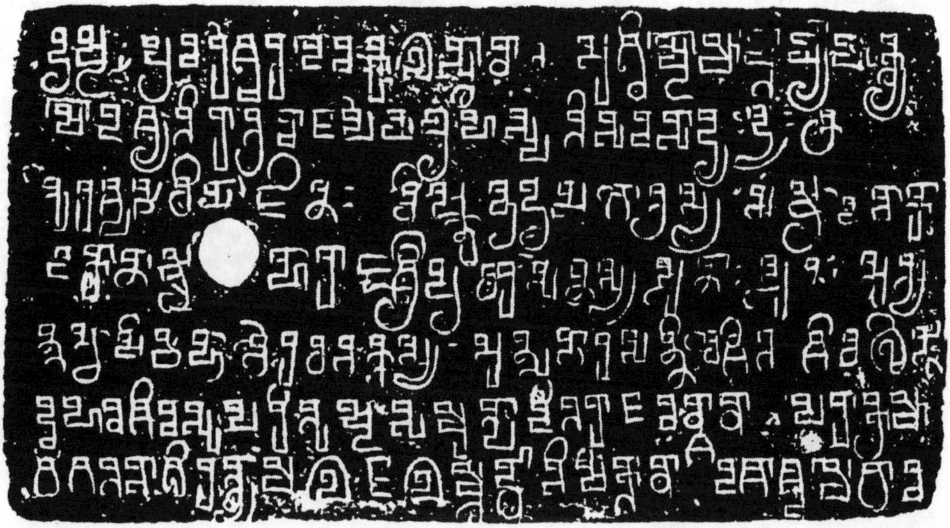

ii,a

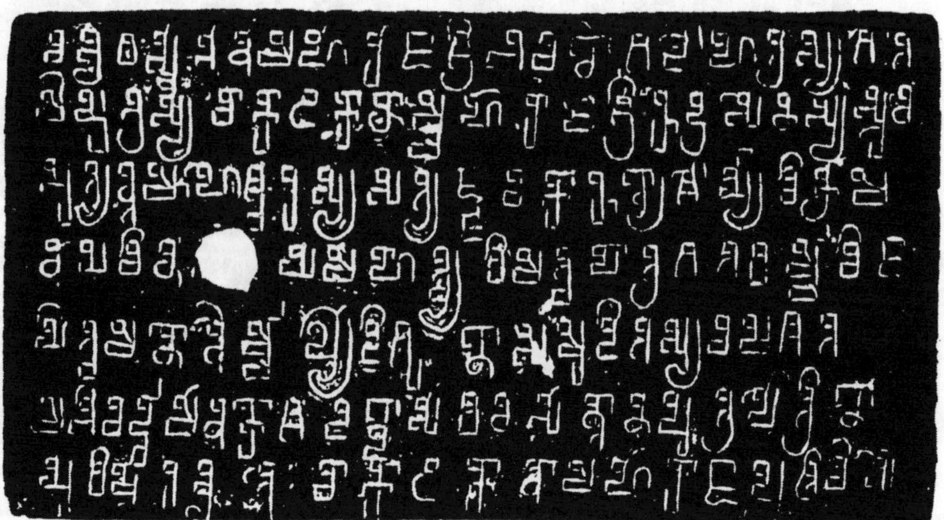

ii,b

iii,a

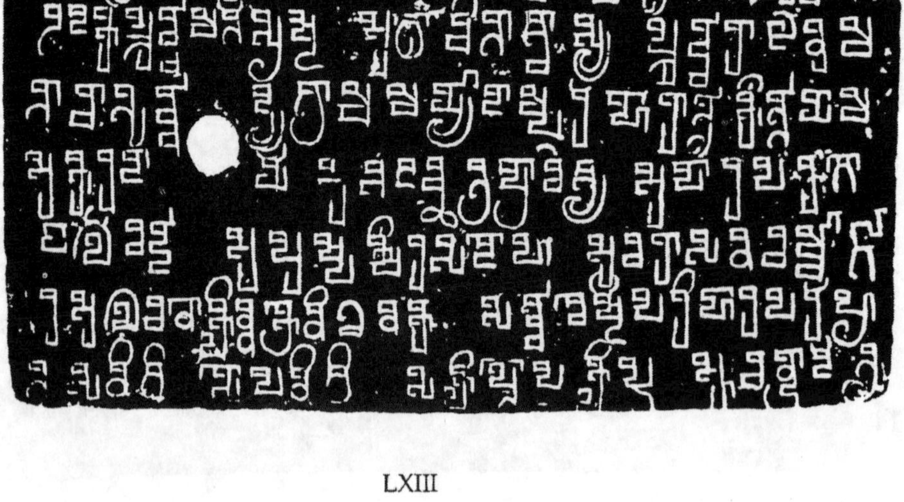

LXIII

iii,b

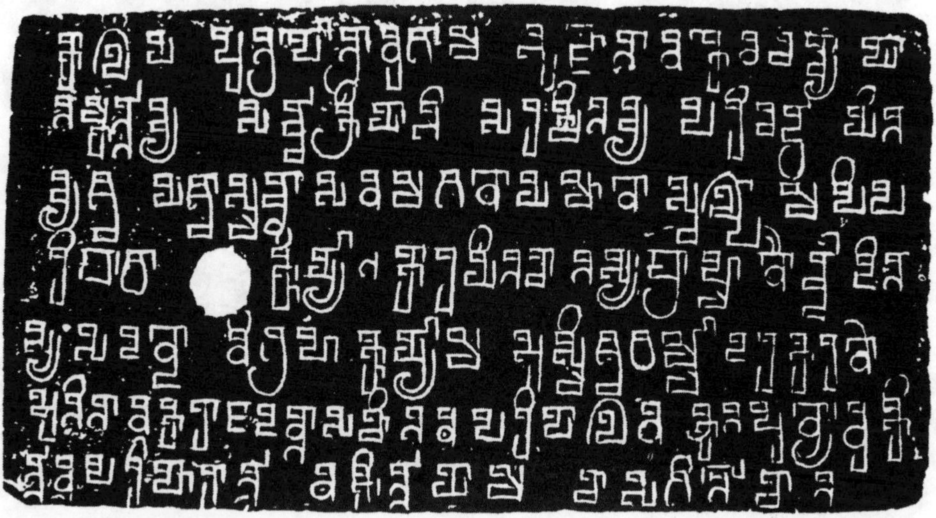

30
32
34
36

iv

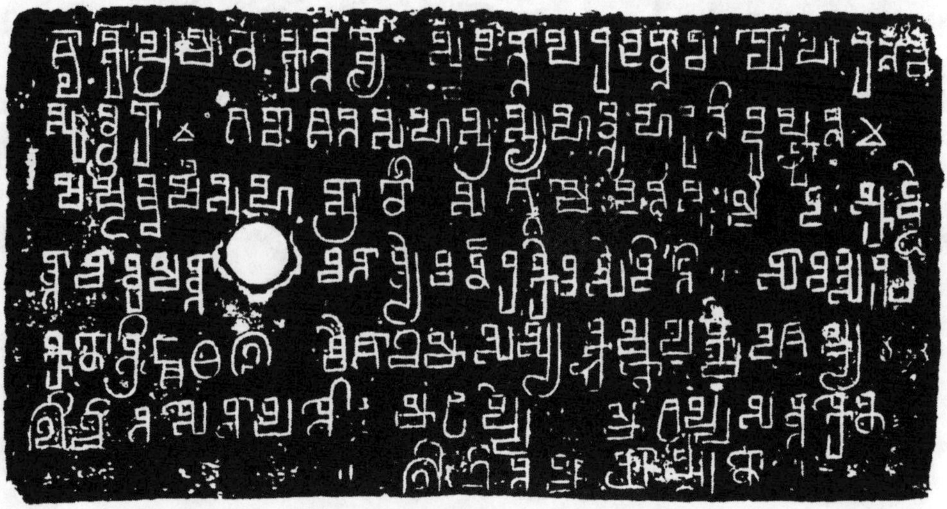

38
40
42

ii,a

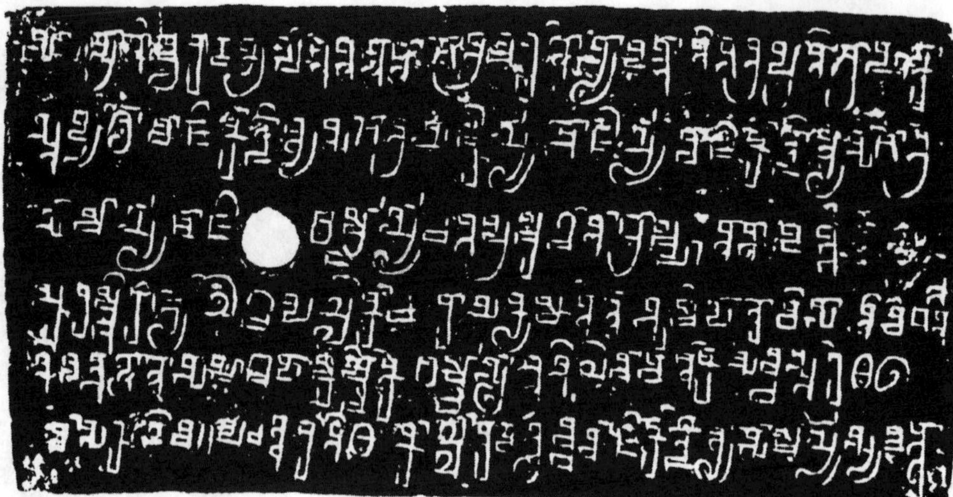

ii,b

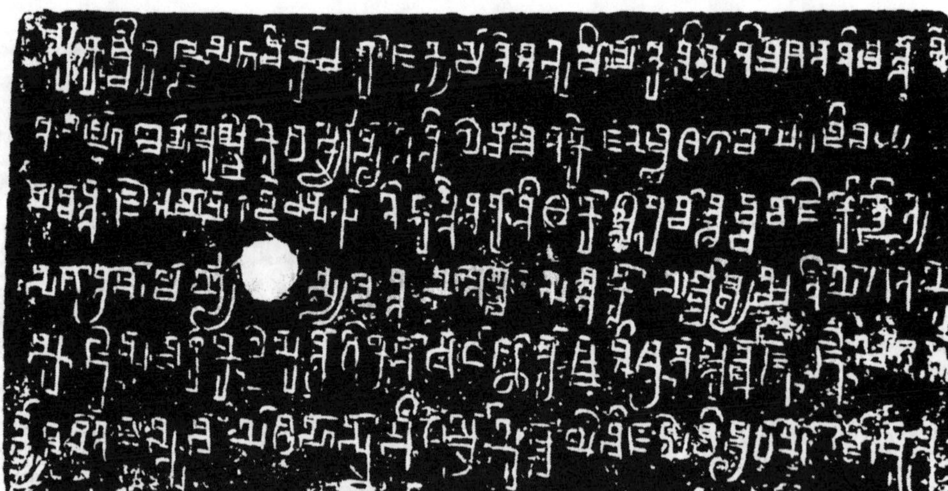

Pl. LXV. Forged Tīgāon Plate of Pravara Sena II

iii,a

iii,b

Pl. LXVI. Bālāghāṭ Plate of Pravara Sena II

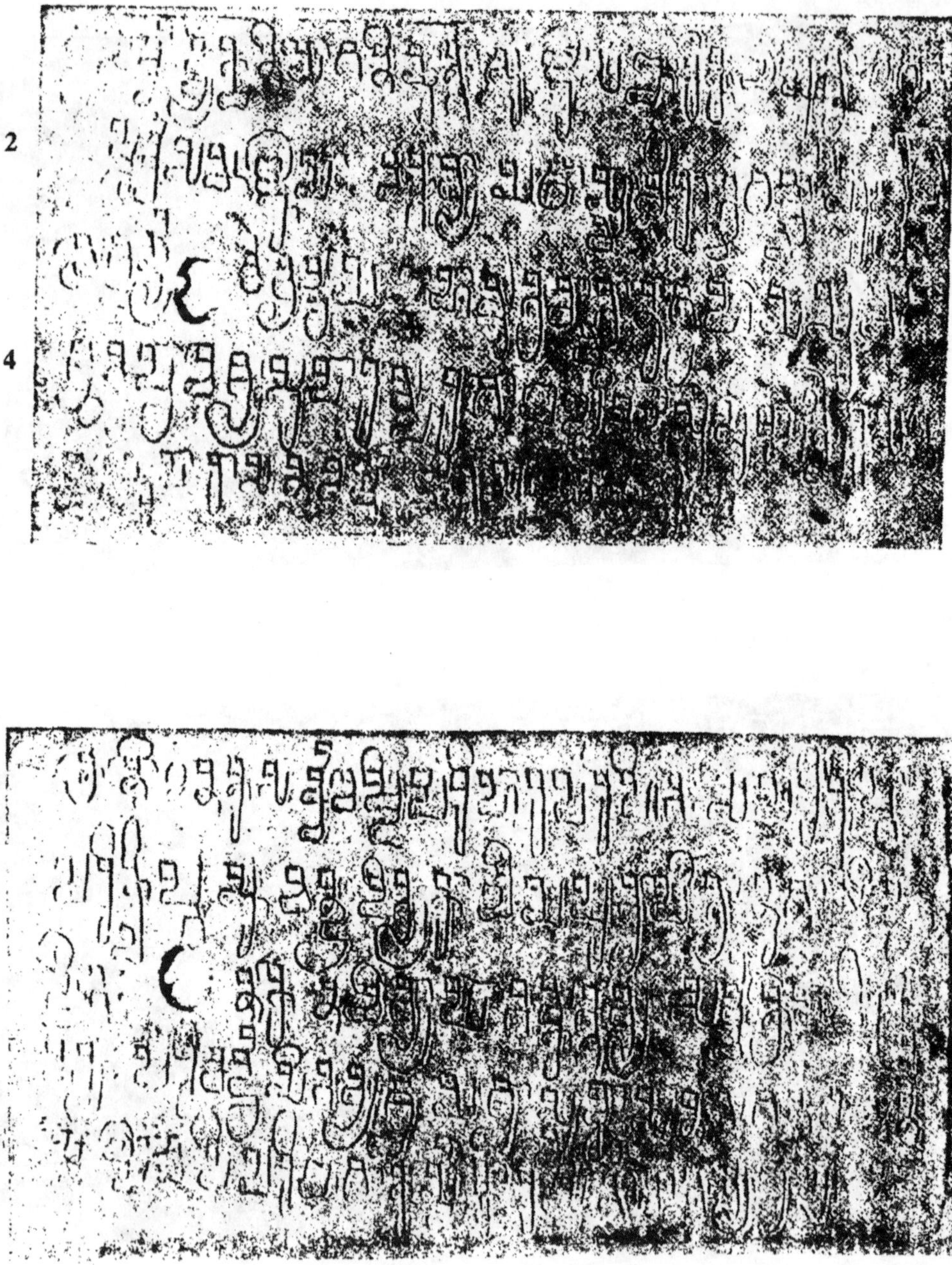

Pl. LXVII. Mansar Plate of Pravara Sena II (?)

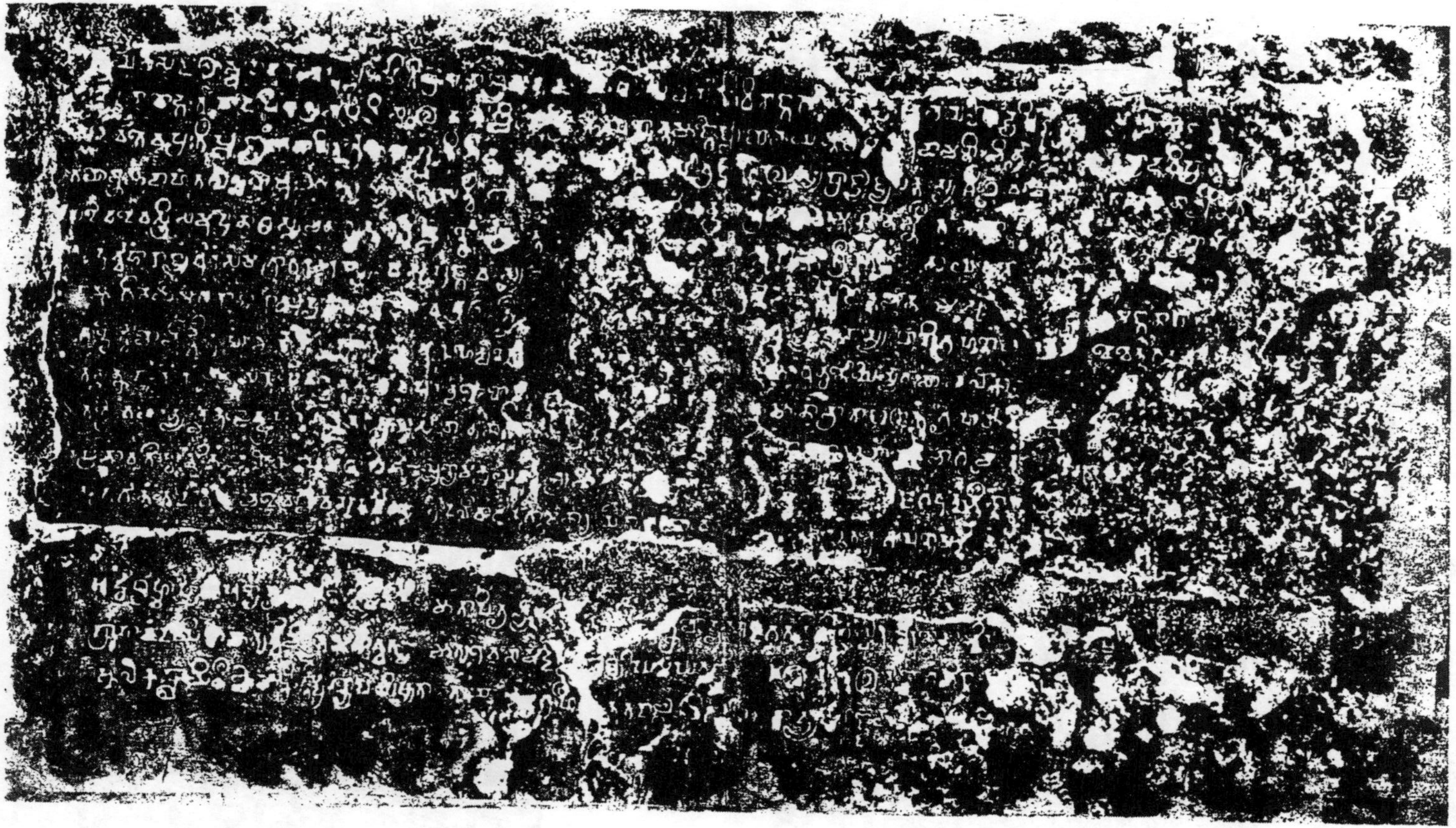

Pl. LXVIII. Rāmṭek Inscription Commemorating Prabhāvatī Guptā

Pls. LXIX-LXXII. Māṇḍhaḷ Plates of Pṛithivī Sheṇa II, Year 2

i

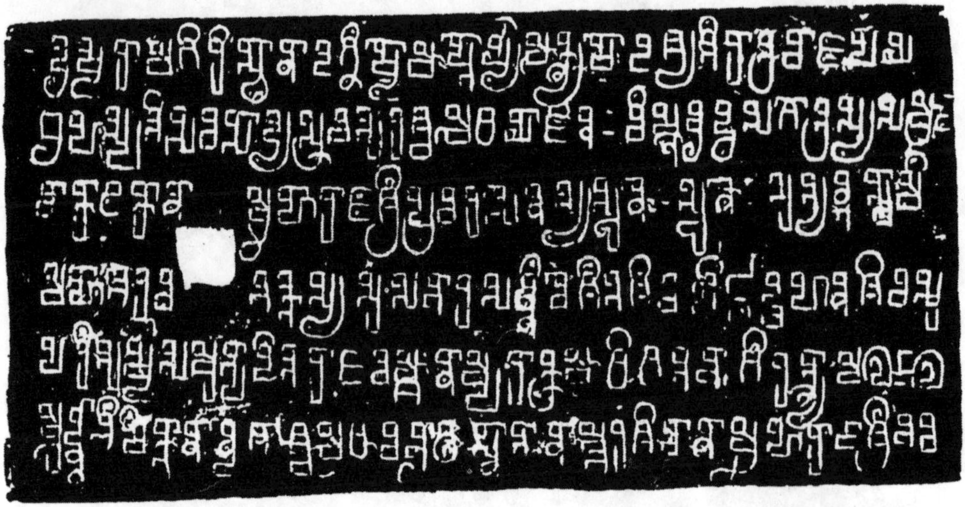

ii,a

ii,b

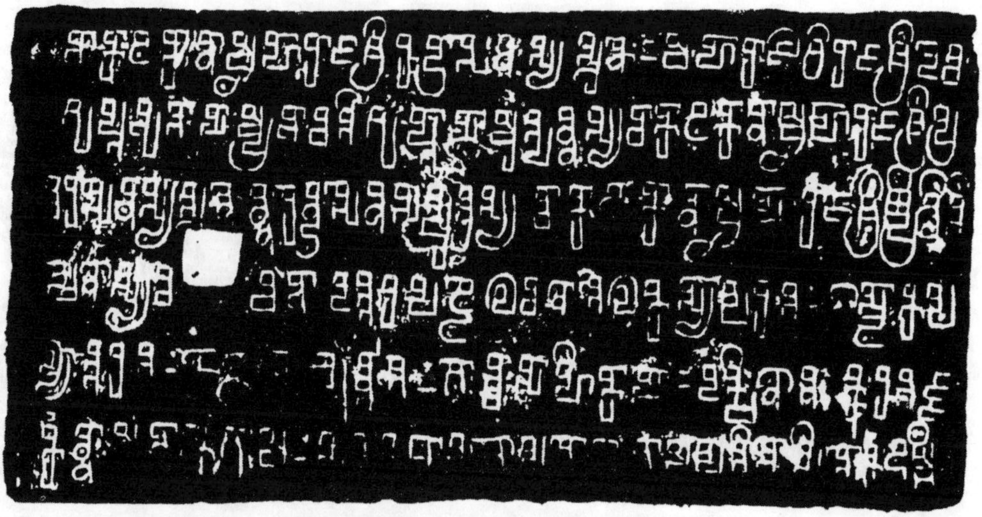

14

16

18

iii,a

20

2

4

iii,b

iv,a

iv,b

38

40

SEAL

2

4

LXXII

Pls. LXXIII-LXXVI. Māṇḍhaḷ Plates of Pṛithivī Sheṇa II, Year 10

i

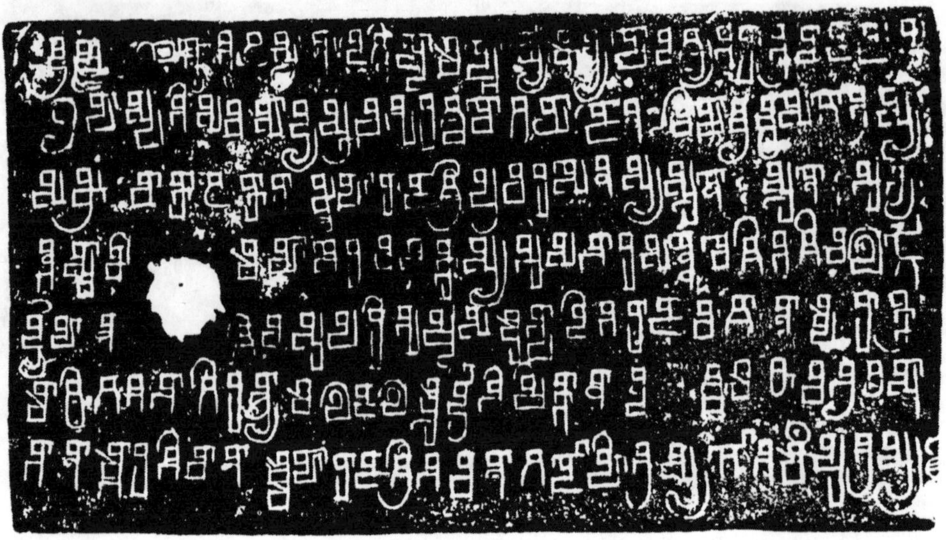

ii,a

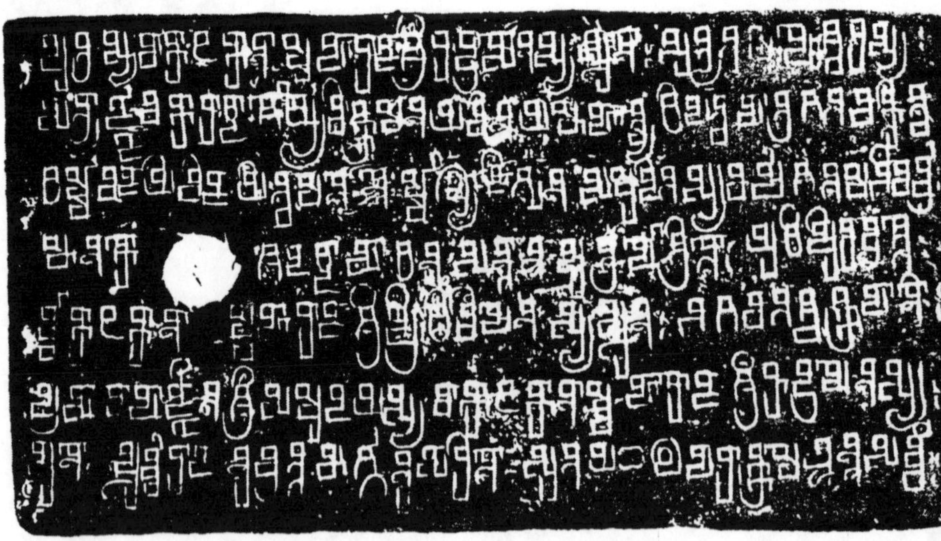

ii,b

iii,a

iii,b

iv,a

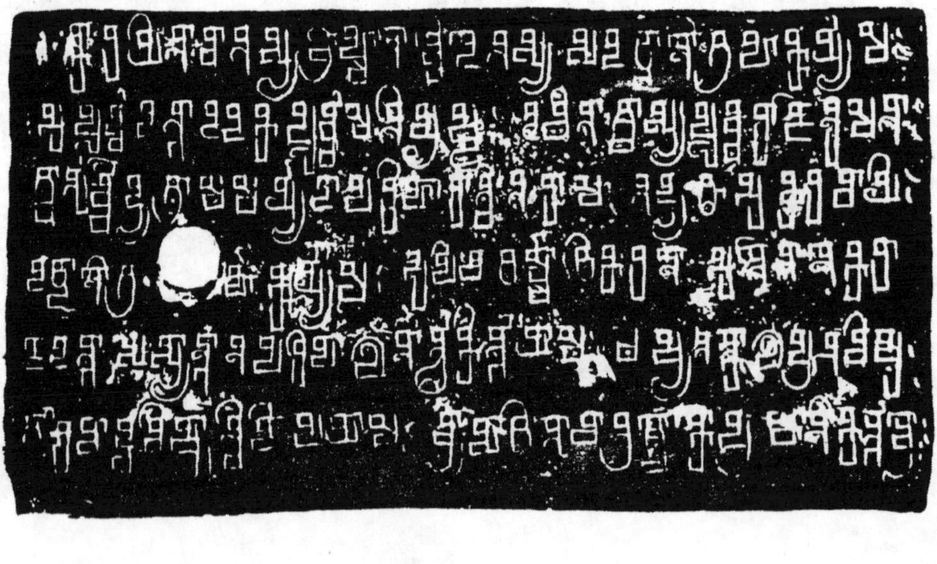

iv,b

42

44

46

SEAL

2

4

LXXVI

Pls. LXXVII-LXXX. Māhurjharī Plates of Pṛithivī Sheṇa II, Year 17

i

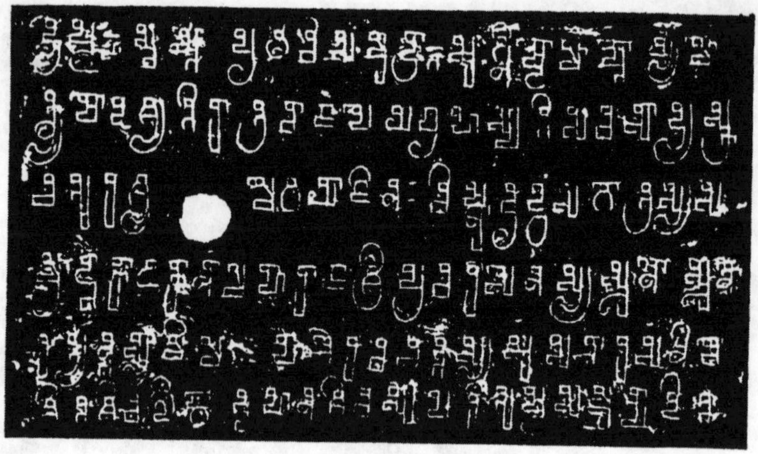

ii,a

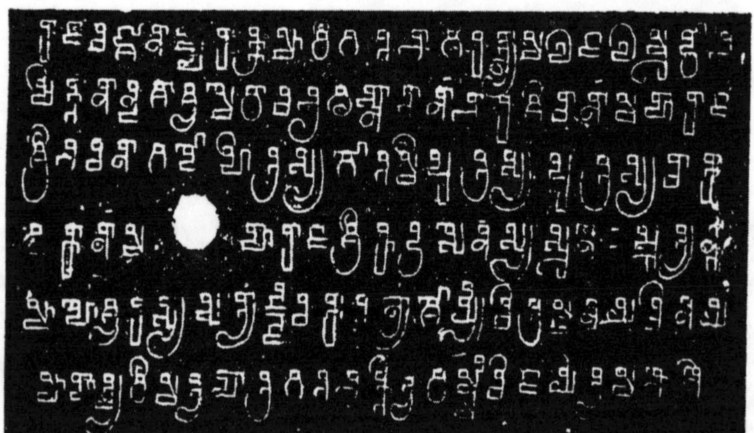

LXXVII

ii,b

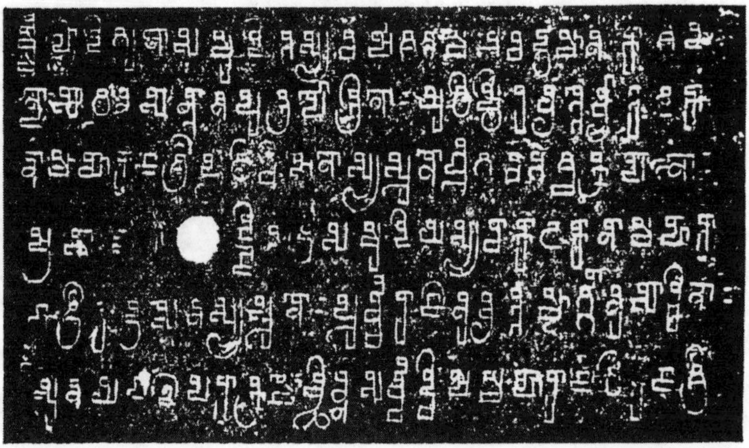

iii,a

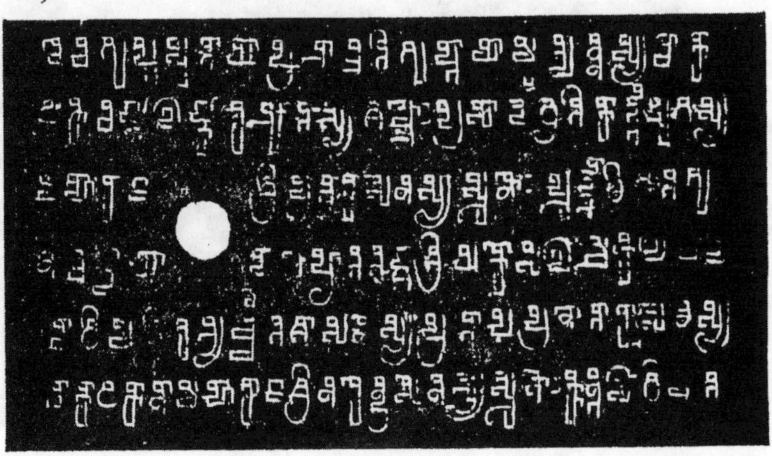

iii,b

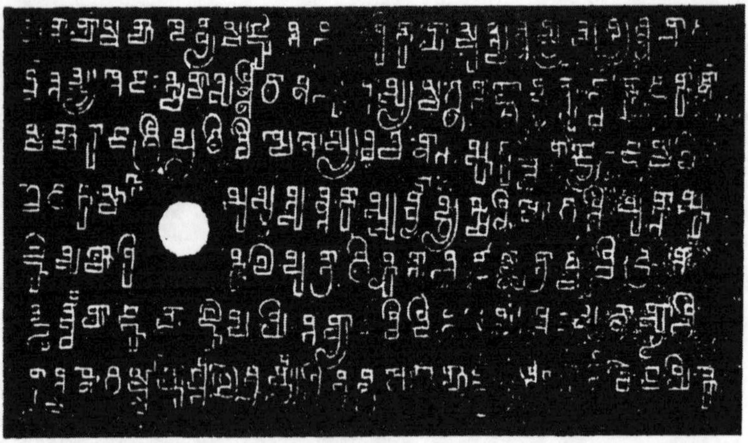

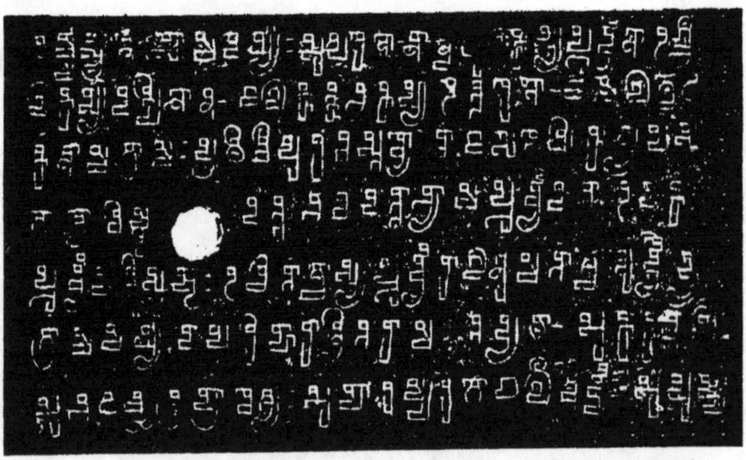

iv,b

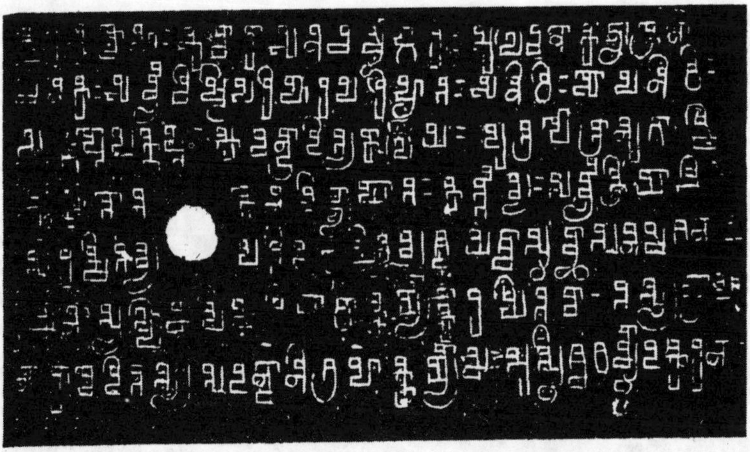

v

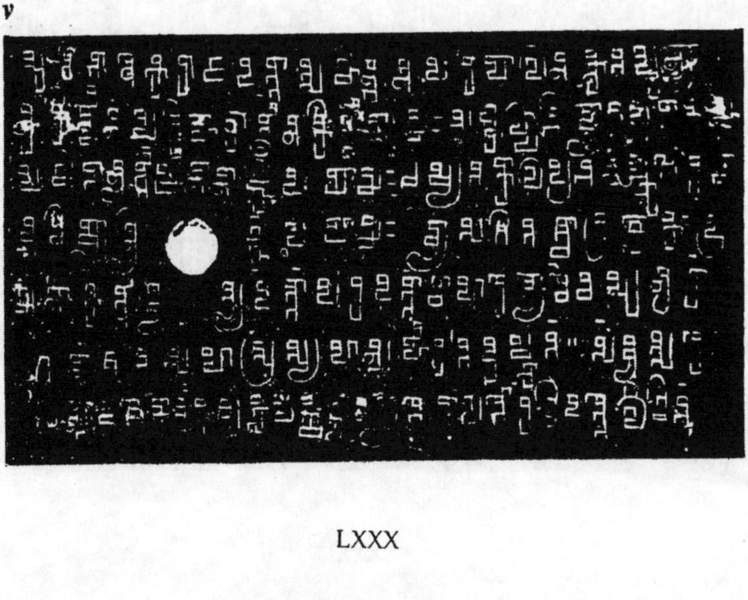

Pls. LXXXI-LXXXII. Unfinished Bālāghāṭ Plates of Pṛithivī Sheṇa II

i

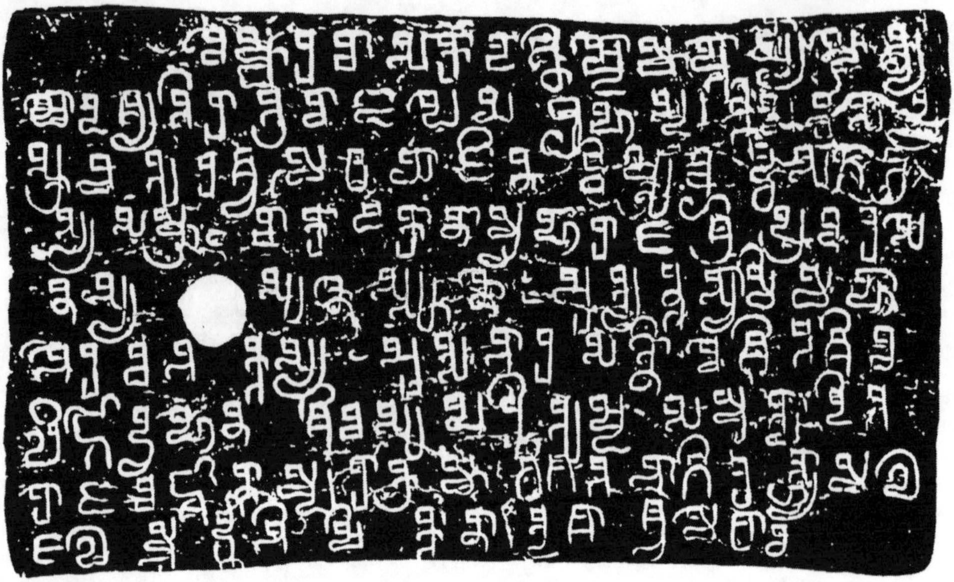

ii,a

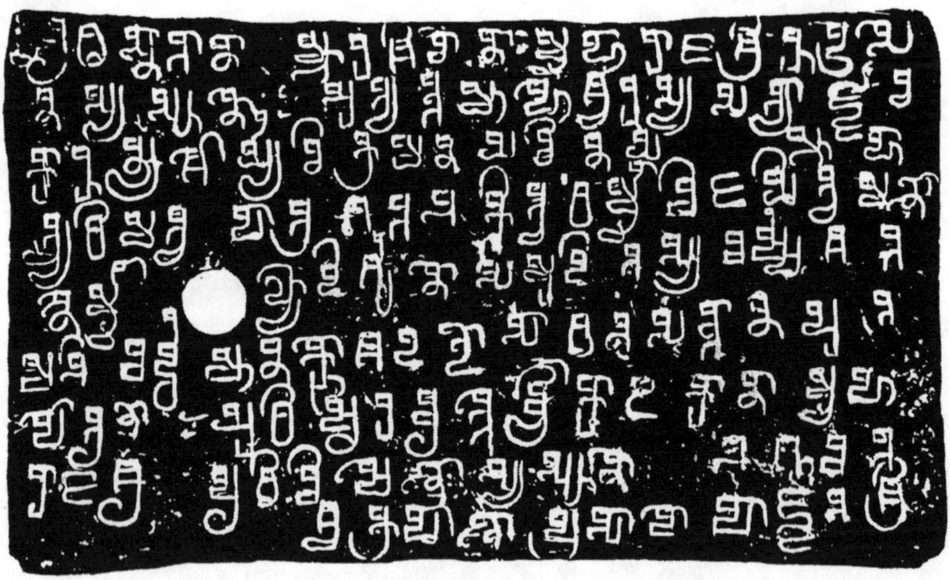

ii,b

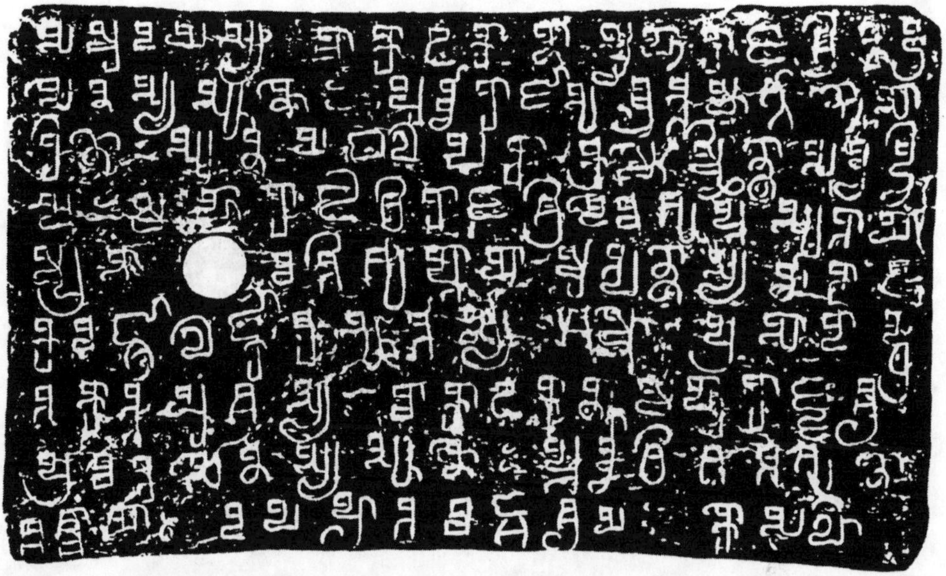

iii

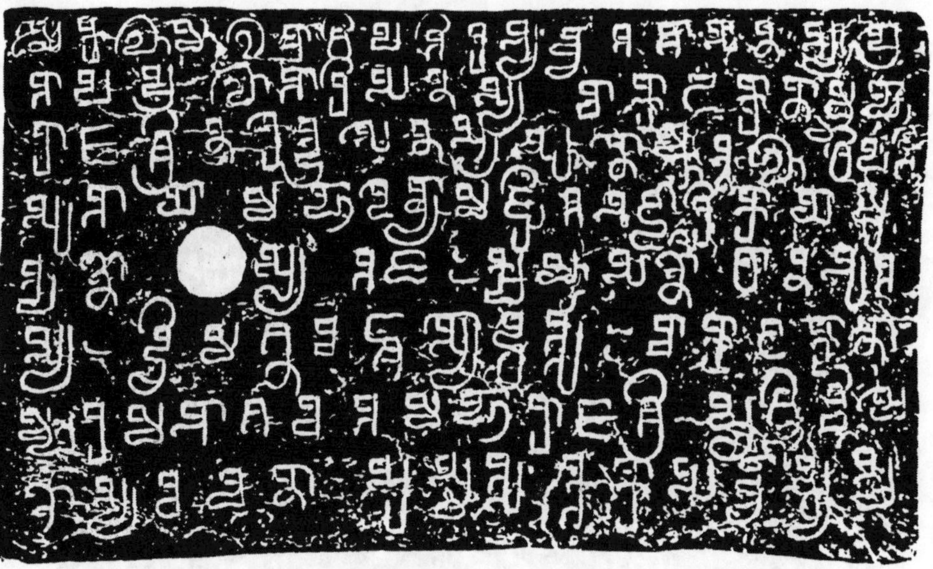

Pls. LXXXIII-LXXXV. Wāshim Plates of Vindhyaśakti II, Year 37

i

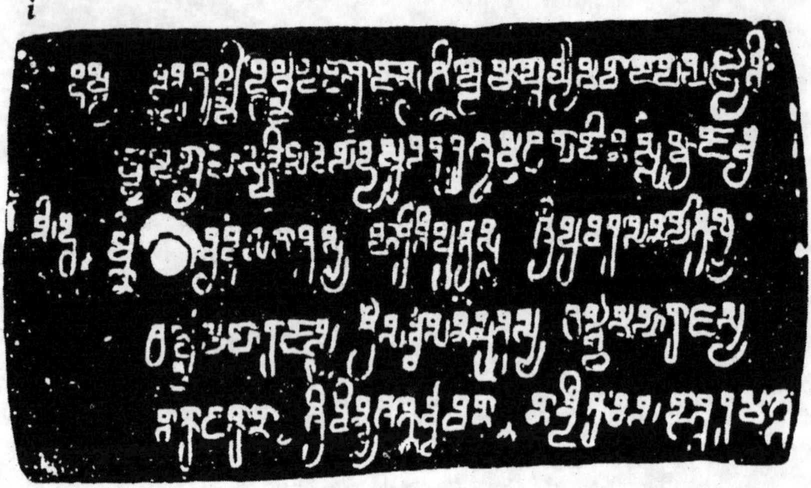

ii,a

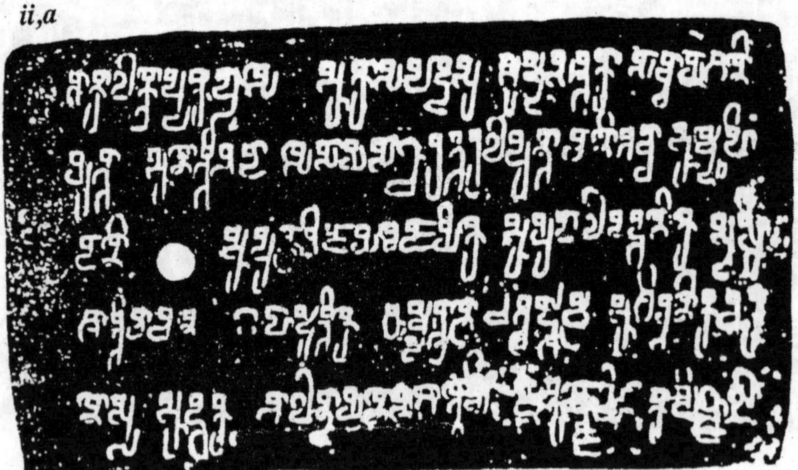

ii,b

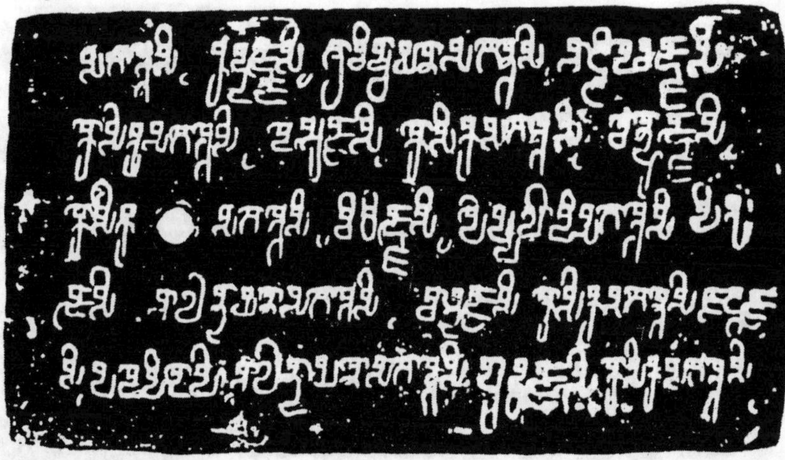

iii,a

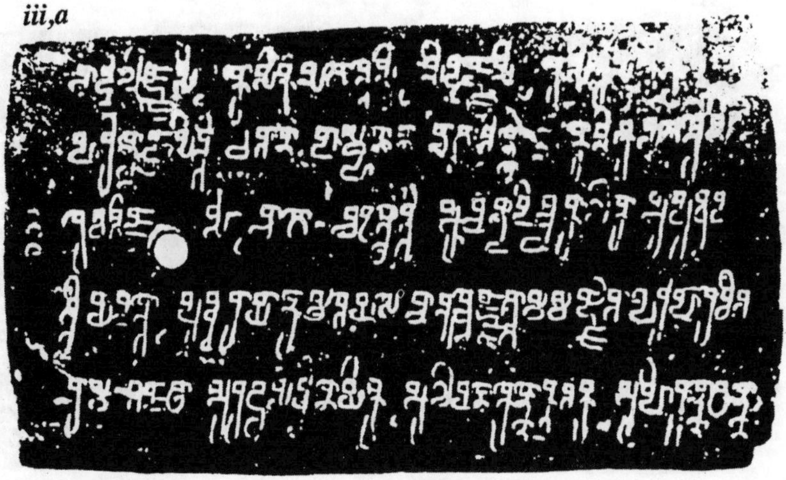

LXXXIV

iii,b

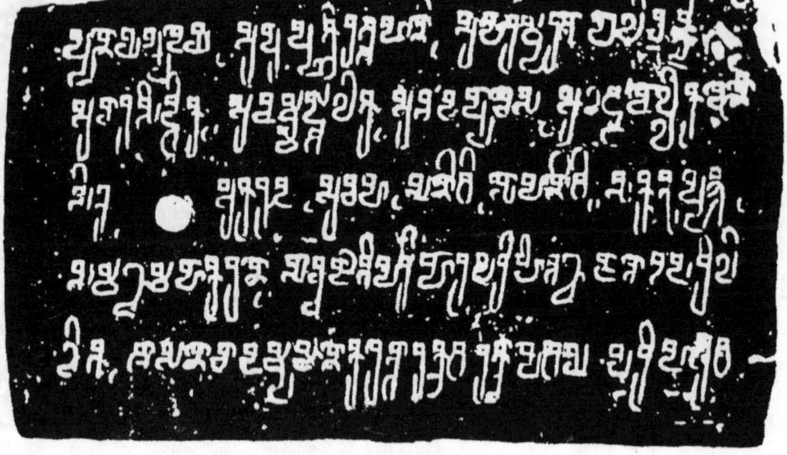

iv

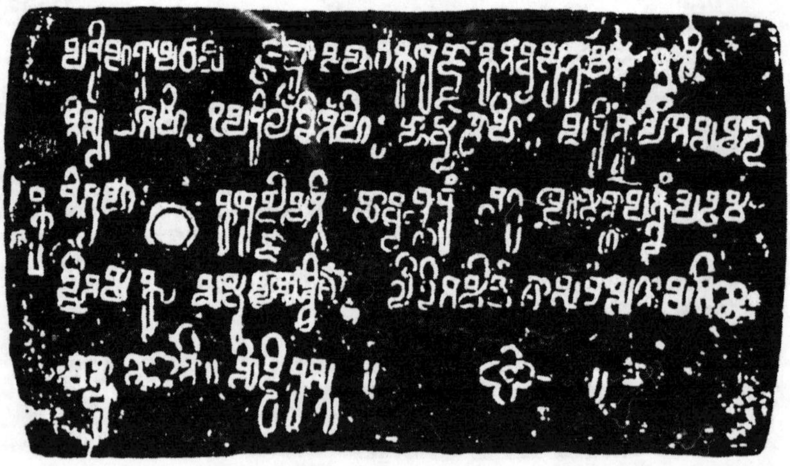

Pls. LXXXVI-LXXXVIII. Bīdar Plates of Deva Sena, Year 5

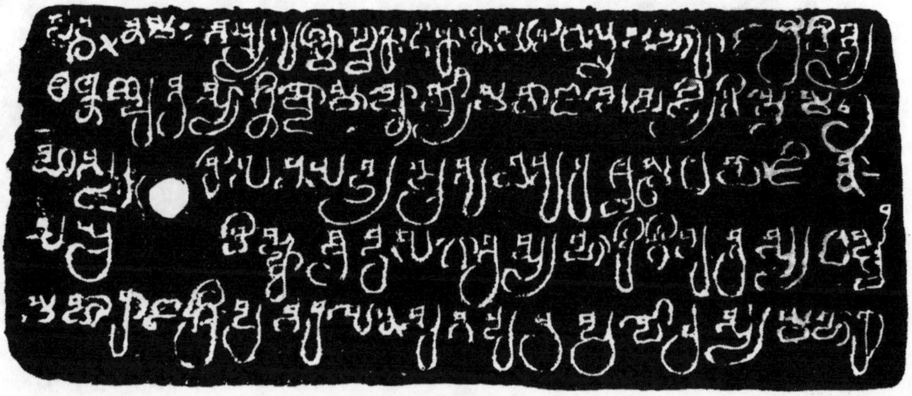

LXXXVI

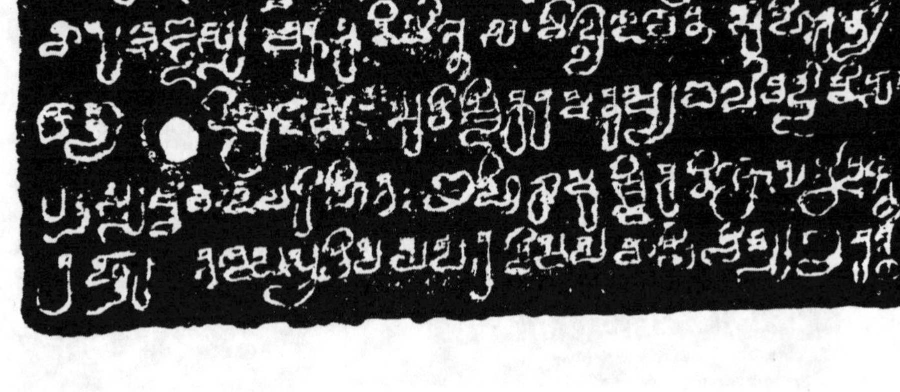

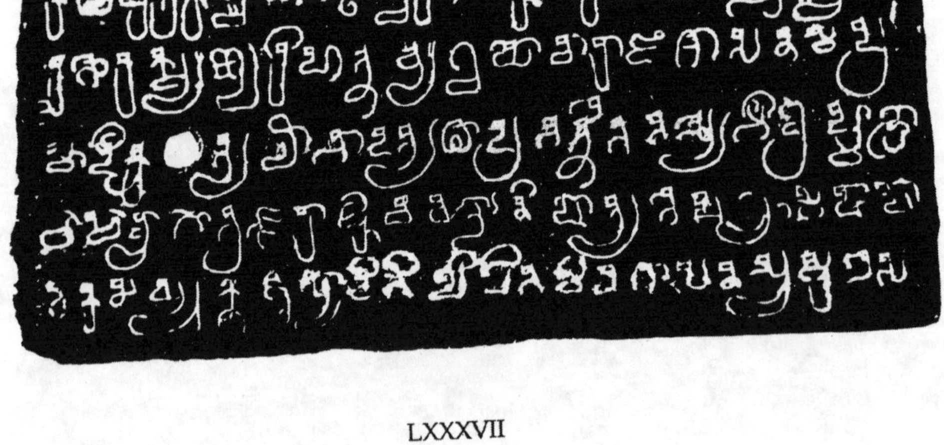

22

LXXXVIII

2

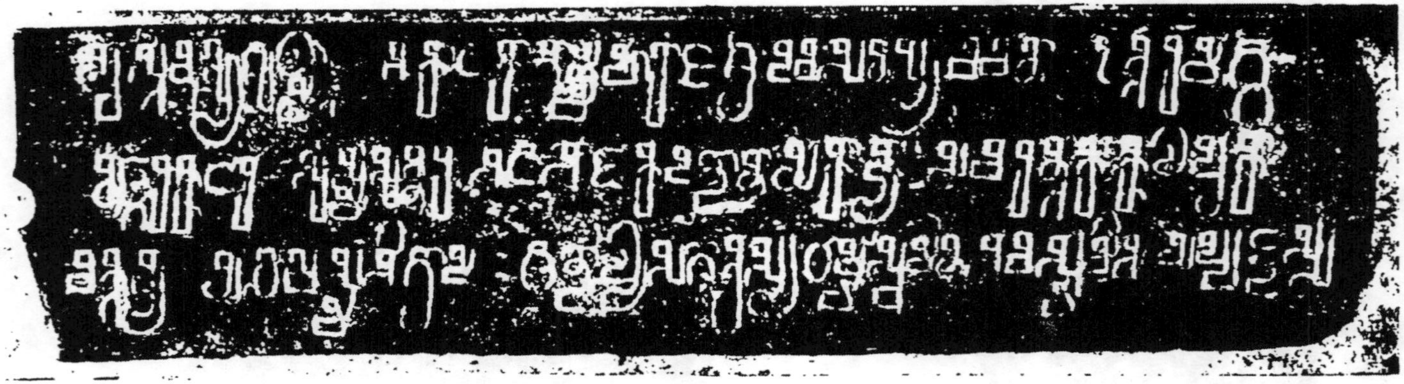

Pl. LXXXIX. India Office Plate of Deva Sena

2

4

Pl. XC. Hisse-Bōrālā Inscription of Deva Sena, Śaka 380

Pls. XCI-XCII. Thālner Plates of Hari Sheṇa, Year 3

i

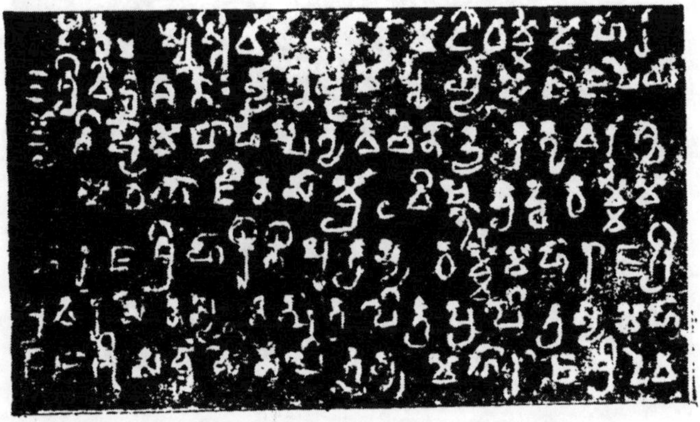

ii,a

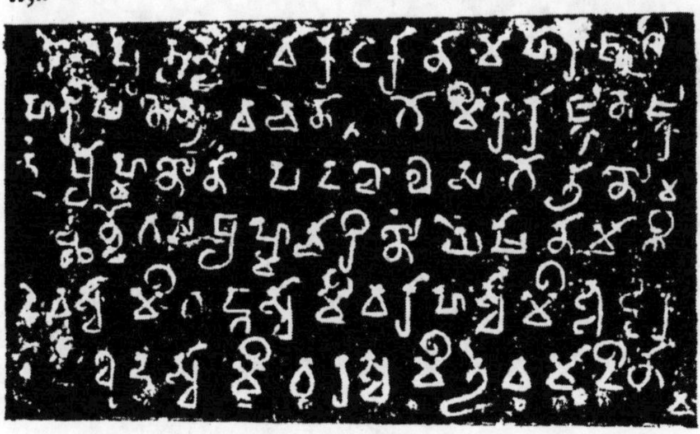

ii,b

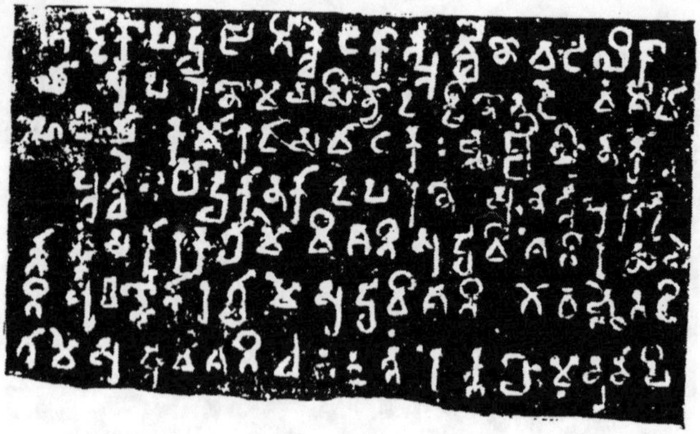

iii

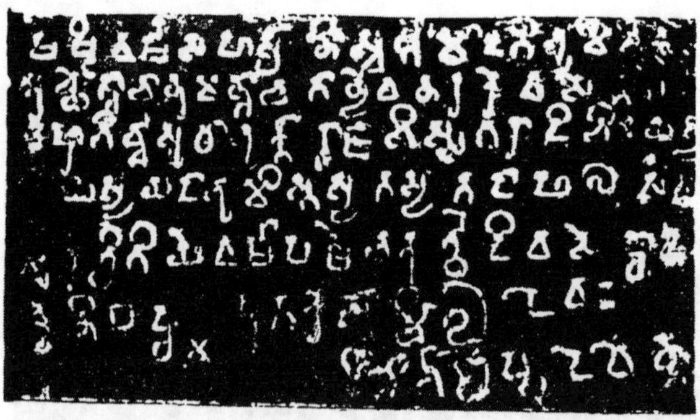

Pl. XCIII. Ajantā Cave 16 Inscription of Varāhadeva, Minister of Hari Sheṇa

Pls. XCIV-XCV. Ghaṭotkacha Cave Inscription of Varāhadeva, Minister of Hari Sheṇa

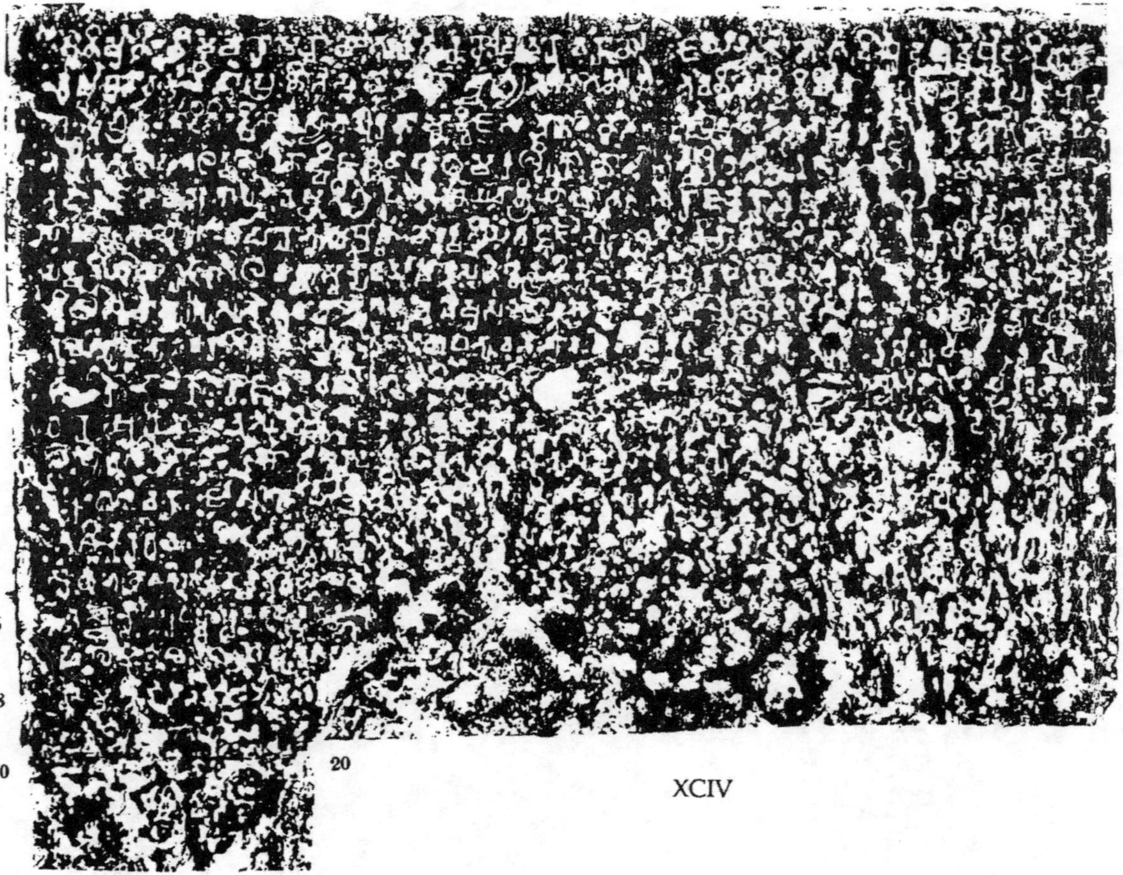

XCIV

2
4
6
8
10
12
14

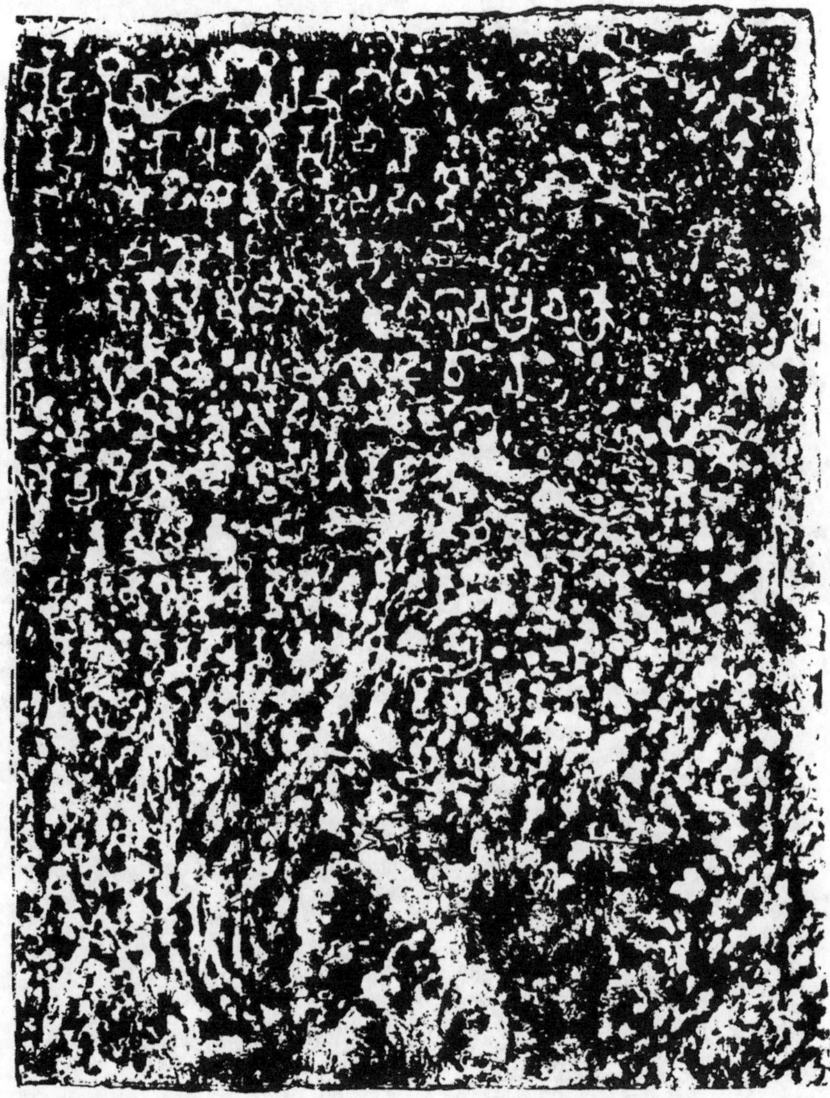

XCV

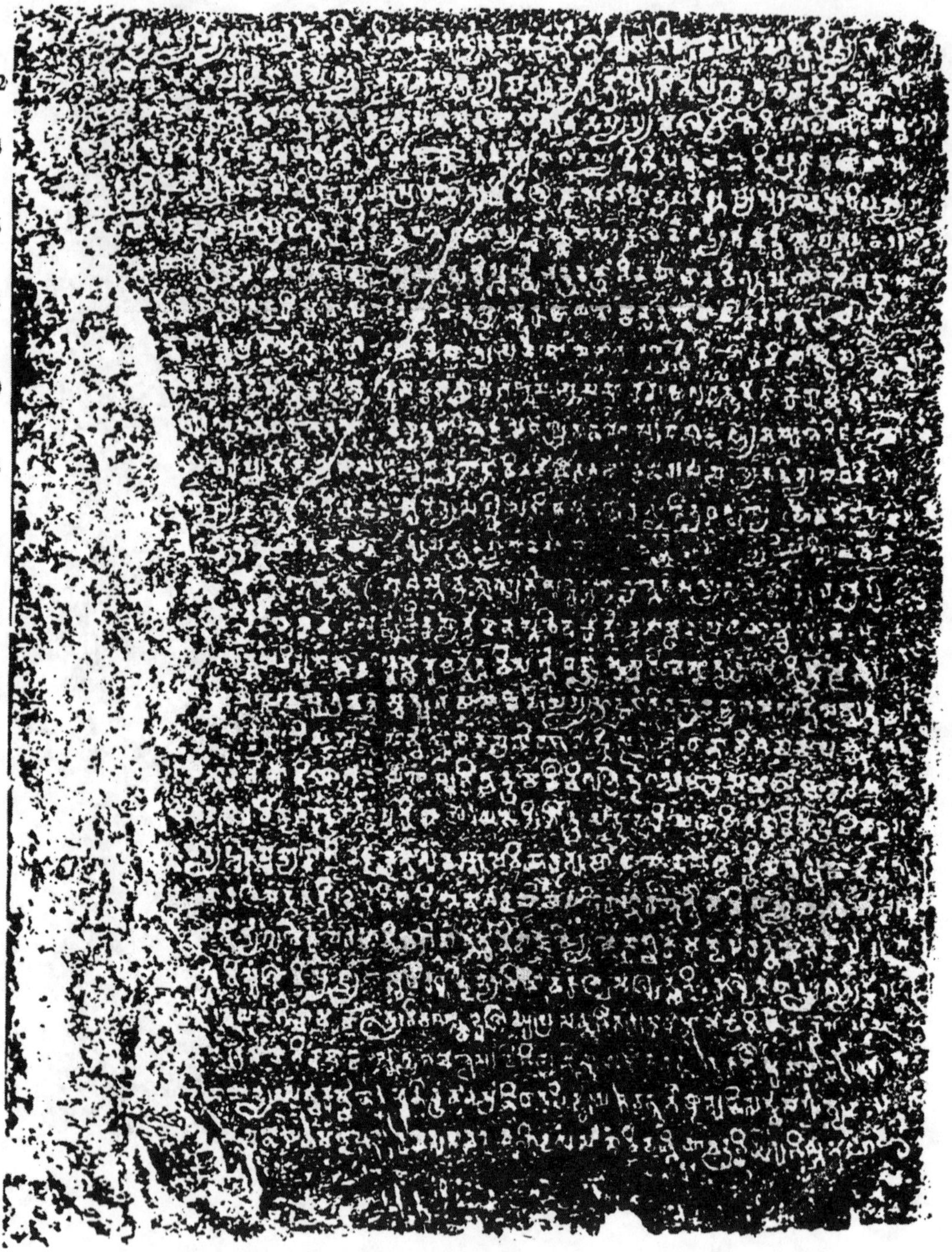

Pl. XCVI. Ajantā Cave 17 Inscription of the Time of Hari Sheṇa

Pls. XCVII-XCIX. Mūḍigere Plates of Kadamba Simhavarman, Year 5

i

ii,a

ii b

8

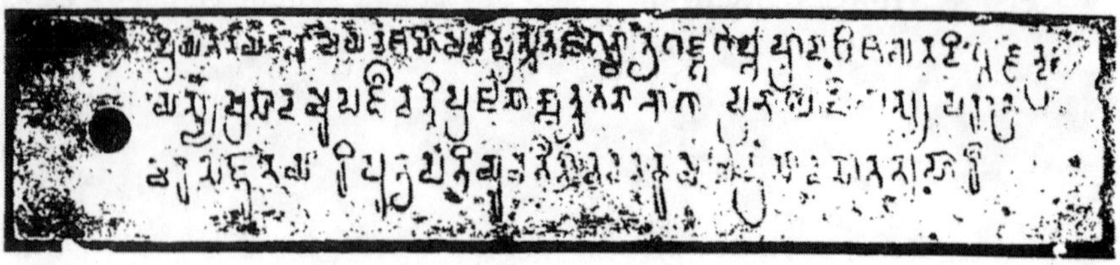

iii a

10

12

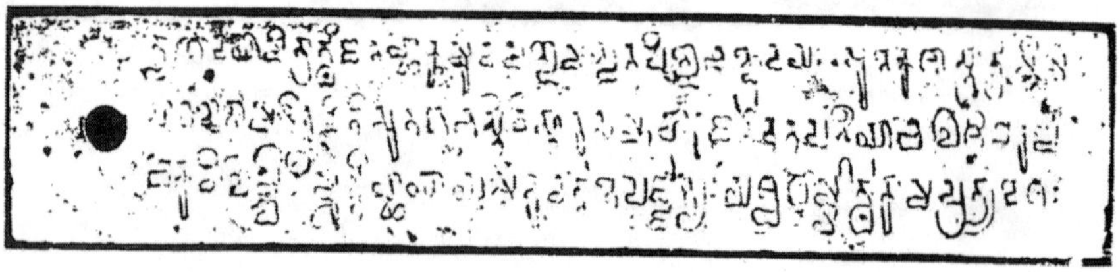

iii b

14

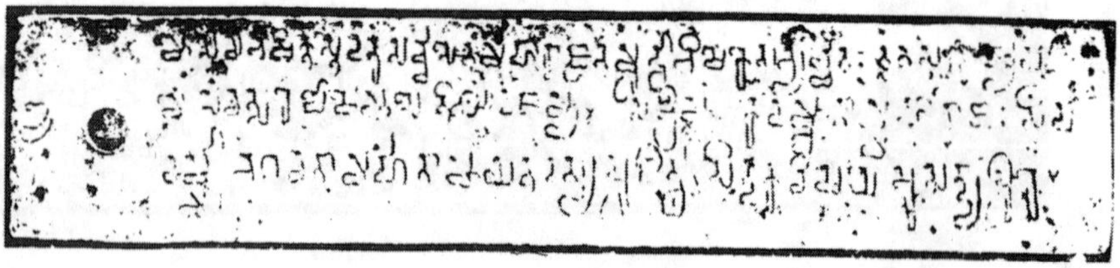

iv

16

18

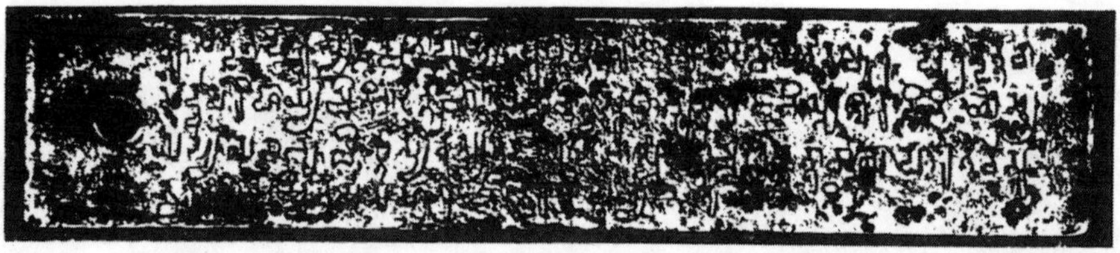

SEAL

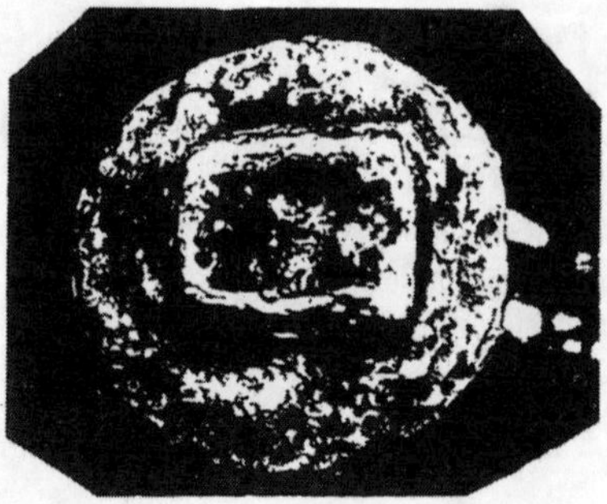

XCIX

Pls. C-CII. Vākāṭaka Coins

I

II A

II B

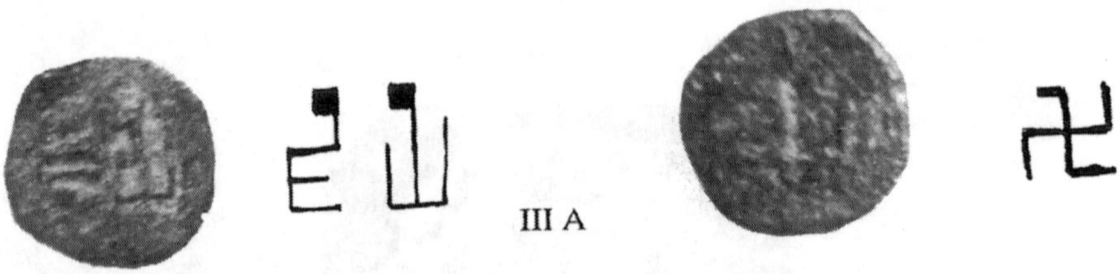

III A

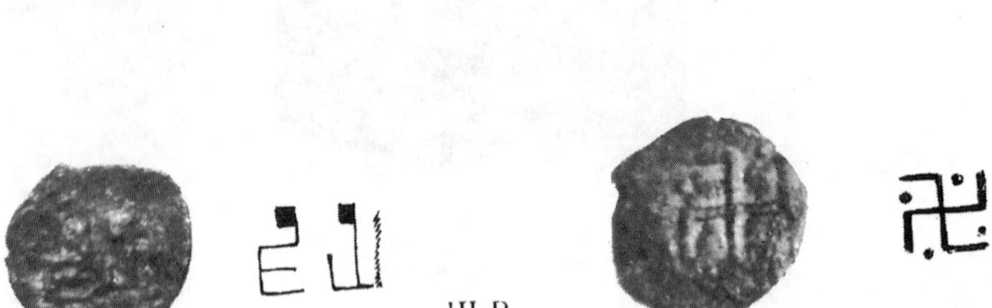

III B

IV A

IV B

IV C

CI

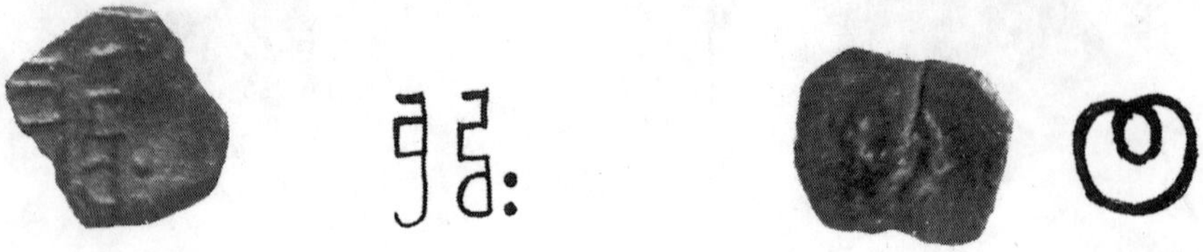

V

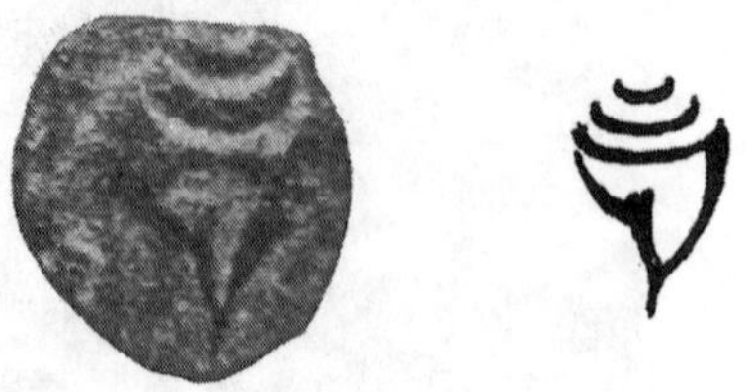

VI

VII

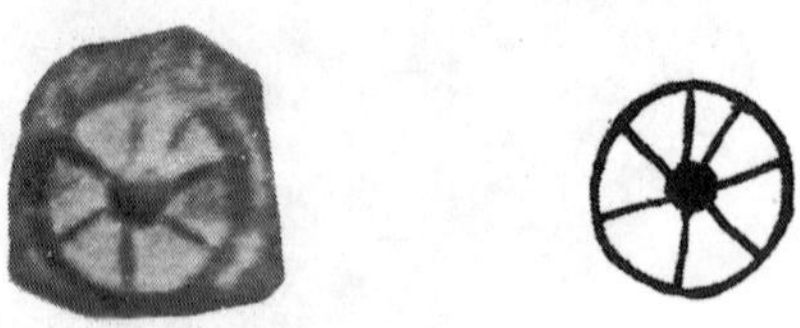

VIII

CII